Advanced Microprocessor Interfacing and the 68000
Peripherals and Systems

Microprocessor Interfacing and the 68000 Peripherals and Systems

Alan Clements
Teesside Polytechnic,
Middlesbrough, UK

John Wiley & Sons
Chichester · New York · Brisbane · Toronto · Singapore

Library of Congress Cataloging-in-Publication Data:

Clements, Alan, 1948–
    Microprocessor interfacing and the 68000 : peripherals and systems
    / Alan Clements.
        p.   cm.
    Bibliography: p.
    ISBN 0 471 91575 0
    1. Motorola 68000 (Microprocessor)   2. Computer interfaces.
    I. Title.
    QA76.8.M6895C53   1989
    621.398'1—dc19   88-14202
                                                                CIP

British Library Cataloguing in Publication Data:

Clements, Alan, 1948–
    Microprocessor interfacing and the 68000: peripherals and systems.
    1. Motorola 68000 microprocessor systems
    I. Title
    004.165

ISBN 0 471 91575 0

Typeset by Wyvern Typesetting Ltd, Bristol
Printed and bound in Great Britain by the Anchor Press Ltd, Tiptree, Essex

For
J. K. Darby

Contents

3   Serial Input/Output   113

4   The Real-Time Clock   167

5   Analog Input/Output   204

6   The CRT Controller   253

7   The Disk Drive and its Interface   315

8   Multiprocessor Systems   366

Preface

A future historian might view the growth of microcomputer technology since the mid 1970s as a series of waves of progress. The first four-bit microprocessors, the Intel 4004 and 4040, were rapidly followed by the first eight-bit microprocessors. A single microprocessor was able to replace tens of SSI and MSI TTL packages in an intelligent controller. These microprocessors also made possible the low-cost, single-board, general-purpose microcomputers.

The second wave of innovation brought special-purpose peripherals (strictly speaking we should use the term *interfaces* rather than *peripherals*), allowing these microprocessors to communicate with the outside world. Included here are the 6850 serial interface and the 6820 parallel interface. Just as the microprocessor made it possible to design low-cost microcomputers, the peripheral made it possible to connect the microcomputers to external systems cheaply and efficiently. Clearly, it does not make economic sense to build low-cost microcomputers with a handful of chips if microcomputers require large numbers of devices to interface with, say, CRT displays and printers.

In the late 1970s, microcomputers had tiny memories and 1024-bit memory chips were the state of the art. With the third wave came the high-density, low-cost memory component, and just after the mid 1980s 1 Mbyte memory chips had become commonplace. These 1 Mbyte chips represented a 1024-fold increase in density in half a decade. The availability of low-cost memory made the personal computer (as opposed to the single-board computer) really possible.

The fourth wave of progress has seen the introduction of more sophisticated microprocessor architectures, from the 8086 to the 68030, the 32000 and the RISC machines. Modern microprocessors are distinguished by their powerful instruction sets, their wealth of addressing modes and their ability to access very large memory spaces. Taken together, the developments in microprocessor and memory technology have led to powerful minicomputers that can be bought with large random access memories, a disk drive, CRT display and a printer for less than the cost of a two-week holiday in the sun or a translatlantic return flight.

Advances in microprocessor architecture and memory technology have not, of course, taken place strictly one after another – there has been a considerable degree of overlap with each advance forcing new developments in related areas. Increasing processor power leads to demands for larger memories to exploit this new power. In turn, larger memories call for yet more processing power to take advantage of the new generation of large programs.

Changes in microcomputer technology have initiated a corresponding development in the books written about microprocessor systems. Early books described basic microprocessor technology and were written for a relatively naïve audience. Later books were able to start from a higher level of assumed knowledge, as computer science gradually filtered down through the education system.

Microprocessor Interfacing and the 68000 has been written to fill a gap in the spectrum of books currently available. It does not attempt to teach microprocessor technology or programming and assumes that the reader is already well versed in these topics, or at least has access to information about them. This book is about the components that are needed to interface a microprocessor system to the outside world. These components range from parallel and serial interfaces to disk controllers and real-time clocks. Many books on microprocessors have devoted so much space to the microprocessor itself that they have had relatively little to say about interface chips. Some of the peripheral chips now available are very complex and a few are considerably more complex than the microprocessor itself. Consequently, there is a danger that students may leave university with a thorough grounding in certain aspects of microcomputer design while having little more than a vague and unsatisfactory knowledge of, for example, microprocessor support chips.

One of the most difficult tasks facing the newly qualified electronic engineer or computer technologist is bridging the gap between the theory learned in university and the practical experience required by an employer. Nowhere is this more evident than in interfacing. Students are taught the basic principles of microprocessor systems in their digital design courses, but are later confronted by highly complex data sheets written by manufacturers using their own in-house jargon. *Microprocessor Interfacing and the 68000* provides designers with a stepping stone between the general course on microprocessor systems design and the requirements of the real world.

The treatment of microprocessor interfacing

The author of a book on microprocessor interfacing must steer a course between the extremes of a vague and 'woolly' text that glosses over all the practical details of peripheral chips and a book which merely repeats the manufacturer's data sheet in all its gory detail. I have selected a middle course and have attempted to show how peripherals are employed and the difficulties encountered in using them. Once readers understand how a generic interface works, they are then in a position to deal with the data sheets of the new generation of interface chips.

In choosing suitable interfaces to describe, I have avoided compiling a list of available chips and have not attempted to compare and contrast one manufacturer's device with another's. *Microprocessor Interfacing and the 68000* introduces a range of interface chips varying from the mundane parallel port to the more esoteric multiprocessor interface.

I have written this book for students taking second-level courses in computer technology or electronic engineering with a computer science bias, and for engineers in industry who have to design microcomputers using these new components.

Contents

Chapter 1 describes the design of a simple microcomputer based on the 68000. Although I do not wish to write yet another microprocessor textbook, it is important to consider the operation of a microprocessor from the point of view of the peripherals that are connected to it. The first part of this chapter concentrates on the 68000's buses and shows how they are used to transfer information between the microprocessor and a peripheral. The second part of Chapter 1 presents the design of a typical 68000 system which can be used in conjunction with the interface components described in this book.

Chapter 2 introduces the peripheral interface chip that allows a microprocessor to be connected to an external system with a minimum of hardware overhead. The chapter begins with an overview of *the generic interface* and discusses some of the ways in which they are connected to a host microprocessor. Topics introduced in Chapter 2 include the way in which registers in a memory-mapped peripheral are accessed by the CPU and the timing requirements of peripherals.

Chapter 3 is devoted to the DUART, dual universal asynchronous receiver/transmitter. The DUART, or a similar peripheral interface component, is found in almost every general-purpose digital computer with some form of external interface and permits a microprocessor to be interfaced easily, flexibly and efficiently to an asynchronous serial data link.

Chapter 4 looks at the real-time clock (RTC). A real-time clock performs two functions: it generates the stream of interrupt requests required by a multitasking processor and maintains a copy of the time of day. The RTC is an unusual peripheral, because it does not link a microprocessor to an external device. In at least one sense, the RTC is *an end in itself.*

Chapter 5 shows how a microcomputer communicates with the analog world. Techniques of converting a voltage into a digital value are described. The inverse process of converting the digital output of a computer into a voltage whose value is a function of the binary value is also considered. Practical examples of analog to digital and digital to analog converters are given.

Chapter 6 looks at one of the most important interfaces found in the general-purpose digital computer, the CRT controller that performs almost all the functions required to map digitally encoded data stored in memory onto the screen of a CRT terminal (i.e. a television). Before the advent of the CRT controller, between 20 and 100 MSI and SSI chips were required to perform this function. An example of a display system suitable for use in a microcomputer is described.

Chapter 7 is concerned with the interface between a microprocessor system and a floppy disk drive. The principles of the operation of a floppy disk drive, together with the way in which data is encoded before recording, are discussed, and an example of a typical floppy disk controller (FDC) chip is given. This section is completed by showing how an FDC is interfaced to a 68000, and a brief introduction to the software needed to drive the FDC is provided.

Chapter 8 applies the maxim 'You can't have too much of a good thing' to microprocessor systems and shows how several microprocessors can be coupled to increase the power or computational throughput of a system. We examine two aspects of multiprocessor systems here: their topology and the way in which they communicate with each other. Chapter 8 provides us with an opportunity to examine the interface between a 68000 system and the VMEbus which is used in many 68000-based multiprocessors.

Acknowledgements

I would like to thank all those who helped me to write this book. In particular, I would like to thank the semiconductor manufacturers who provided me with the source information that enabled me to write about the peripherals I have described. My special thanks goes to Motorola, Philips/Signetics, GE Solid State, Analog Devices, Hitachi, and Western Digital.

In attempting to interpret manufacturers' data sheets and application reports, it is inevitable that I have made both errors of comprehension and mechanical errors. All such errors are my own responsibility.

I would also like to thank those at John Wiley engaged in the commissioning and production of my book.

Finally I would like to thank Paul Lambert in the Computer Centre at Teesside Polytechnic who checked the pseudocode programs in Chapters 6 and 7.

Any readers who wish to 'close the loop' and comment on my book or who find errors that should be removed in later editions can contact me via my publisher, or direct (School of Information Engineering, Teesside Polytechnic, Middlesbrough TS1 3BA, UK), or via E-mail (JANET address ACT012@UK.AC.TP.PA).

Chapter 1

The

Microcomputer

Before we can even begin to look at the characteristics of microprocessor peripherals and their interface to microprocessors, it is necessary to examine the nature of the microprocessor to which they are interfaced. In this book we are going to concentrate on the interface between peripherals and the popular 16/32-bit 68000 microprocessor. Chapter 1 introduces the 68000 microprocessor from the point of view of its external interface through its 64 pins. We show how the 68000 is connected to memory components and to peripherals, and provide an example of a microcomputer built around a 68000.

The old Roman god Janus is always depicted as facing in two opposite directions at the same time. Interfaces share the same ability to look in two directions at once. An interface looks one way to the computer that it is interfacing and it looks in the opposite direction to the external system that it is controlling. Microcomputer designers must consider both these *directions* separately. Engineers generally refer to the *computer side* and the *peripheral side* of an interface.

As most interfaces are connected to a computer, often called *the host computer*, it is important to examine the relationship between the interface and the computer. A practical difficulty arises here because not all computers have the same characteristics or behave in the same way as far as the interface is concerned. We are therefore forced to adopt either a general approach to interfacing or a more specific approach centred on one particular computer. I have followed the latter path and have decided to adopt the 68000 microprocessor as a vehicle to teach microcomputer interfacing. Fortunately, once the way in which an interface is connected to a 68000 is understood, it is easy to design a connection between the interface and almost any other microprocessor.

1.1 The 68000

If asked why I chose the 68000 to illustrate microcomputer interfacing, I could give the mountaineer's answer – 'Because it's there'. Such an answer would be a reaction to the spate of articles I have seen in the technical press in recent years. Each article is written by a 'high priest' of one of the major faiths: the 68000, the 8086 and the 32000.

Such articles really do belong to the realms of theology. They take a minor attribute of one microprocessor and show that the microprocessor is much better than its rivals. In this way, any microprocessor can always be proven better than any other. Articles like these are most unhelpful to students or to newly qualified engineers who have not built up a personal fund of knowledge and expertise to see through the articles and to realize that one microprocessor may represent an optimum choice for a word processor, while an entirely different device may be optimum for a number cruncher.

I have chosen the 68000 for this book because it is an excellent device for teaching purposes. The reasons for selecting a 68000 can be summarized as follows:

1. The 68000 has a powerful instruction set which is relatively easy to learn. Students new to the 68000 are able to absorb its mnemonics quickly, while more advanced students can make good use of its variable-size operations and powerful addressing modes.
2. The 68000 has much to offer from an interfacing point of view. The three most important features of the 68000's interface are its non-multiplexed asynchronous address and data buses, its prioritized vectored interrupt structure and its support for multiprocessing and DMA through its bus arbitration control pins.
3. The 68000 supports real-time programming and multiprocessing environments. At any instant, the 68000 is in one of two states: user mode or supervisor (or system) mode. As far as the execution of the majority of instructions is concerned, there is no difference between these modes. However, certain instructions can be executed only when the 68000 is in the supervisor mode. By dedicating the system mode to the operating system, it is possible to preserve system integrity and prevent user tasks from playing havoc with the system. For example, one user can be prevented from accessing the memory space assigned to another user. Similarly, it is possible to deny user programs direct access to I/O devices (i.e. the interfaces). Consequently, a user program must perform I/O operations by means of requests to the operating system which runs under the supervisor mode. Note that external logic to the 68000 is necessary to implement these functions.

The 68000's sophisticated interrupt handling (exception processing) facilities also contribute to this end, because they can be used to take all input/output transactions out of the hands of user tasks and make certain that only the operating system can control input/output operations.

As I indicated in the introduction, this book is not primarily about microprocessors themselves. Therefore, fine details concerning the 68000 are omitted here. Readers not already familiar with the 68000 will find suitable reading matter listed in the Bibliography. What does interest us is the way in which 68000 communicates with peripherals.

1.2 The 68000 data and address bus

Broadly speaking, the physical interface of any microprocessor (i.e. its pins) can be divided into two parts: a communication path between the microprocessor and its external memory, and a control structure that determines the sequence of operations carried out by the microprocessor. The *communication path* is composed of the microprocessor's address bus, data bus and data-flow control bus. Similarly, the *control structure* includes the microprocessor's reset, interrupt and bus arbitration control facilities. We discuss first the 68000's data and address bus which we call the DAT (data and address transfer).

The structure of the 68000's address and data bus is illustrated in Figure 1.1, and Figure 1.2 shows how it is used to effect two-way communication between the microprocessor and its memory or peripherals.

The 68000 DAT is almost entirely conventional and presents only two tiny surprises to the system designer. First, unlike some other 16-bit microprocessors, the DAT is non-multiplexed and therefore has entirely separate address and data paths. Separate address and data buses simplifies microprocessor to memory interfacing and, some would say, enhances processor throughput while increasing system cost due to the large number of signal-carrying paths. The DAT is made up of three elements: a 23-bit address bus, A_{01}–A_{23}, which allows $2^{23} = 8$ Mwords to be uniquely addressed, a 16-bit data bus, D_{00}–D_{15}, and five data-flow control lines: R/W*, AS*, UDS*, LDS* and DTACK*. R/W* (read/write*) is high during a read cycle or when the 68000 is inactive, and is low during a write cycle. AS*, LDS*, UDS* are the address, lower data and upper data strobes respectively. It is often convenient to write DS* rather than UDS* or LDS* when we wish to describe one or both the 68000's data strobes and are not particularly interested in whether the strobe is UDS* or LDS*.

Although the 68000 has 32-bit address registers and a 32-bit program counter, only 24 bits of an address are available off-chip (i.e. A_{01}–A_{23} and UDS*/LDS* which serves as A_{00} for byte accesses). Consequently, it is common practice to express 68000 addresses by *six* hexadecimal characters rather than

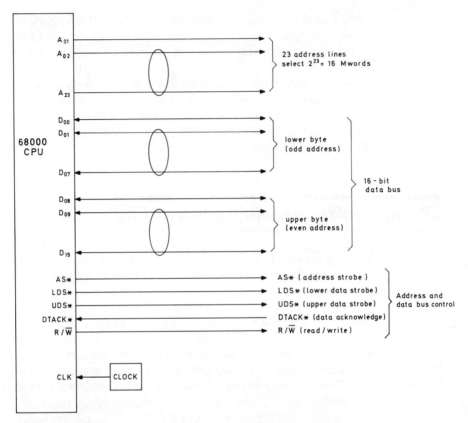

FIGURE 1.1   The data and address buses (DAT) of the 68000

eight. For example, we will write an address as \$001234 rather than \$00001234.

During a read cycle, an address is placed on A_{01}–A_{23} and AS* is asserted to indicate a valid memory access. At this time, memory components know that the 68000 is about to execute either a read or a write cycle by detecting AS* asserted. Here we meet one of the 68000's little complexities. As the 68000 can access word quantities (D_{00}–D_{15}) or byte quantities (D_{00}–D_{07} or D_{08}–D_{15}), two data access signals, LDS* and UDS*, are provided. When LDS* (lower data strobe) is asserted, the 68000 is accessing the *odd* byte on D_{00}–D_{07}. When UDS* (upper data strobe) is asserted, the 68000 is accessing the *even* byte on D_{08}–D_{15}. Of course, when *both* LDS* and UDS* are simultaneously asserted, the 68000 is accessing a word on D_{00}–D_{15}. Thirty-two bit longword values must be accessed by two consecutive 16-bit operations (the 68020 has a 32-bit data bus and can therefore read a longword in a single bus cycle).

Figure 1.2 demonstrates how two OR gates (AND gates in negative logic) combine the active-low select signal from an address decoder with UDS* and LDS* to select the two byte-wide memory arrays. Note that UDS* and LDS*

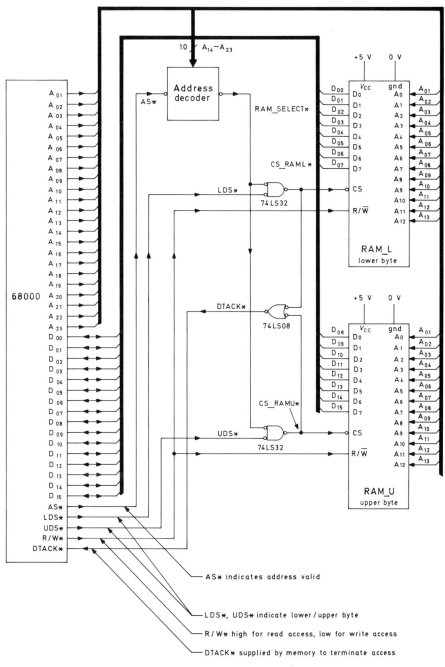

FIGURE 1.2 Communication paths between the 68000 and memory

perform *two* functions. In addition to distinguishing between the upper and lower bytes of a word, they act as data strobes and indicate the validity of a memory access only when they are asserted. The function of LDS* and UDS* is similar to (but not the same as) the address strobe, AS*. The greatest difference between the strobe functions of AS* and UDS*/LDS* appears only in write cycles; in a read cycle AS* and UDS*/LDS* are asserted simultaneously and, as we shall see, in a write cycle UDS*/LDS* is asserted one clock cycle after AS* in order to cater for the data setup time.

The 68000 differs from many other microprocessors by having an asynchronous DAT. A memory access is not completed until the addressed device asserts the DTACK* (data acknowledge) strobe input to the 68000. By providing a delay between the time at which a device asserts DTACK* and the

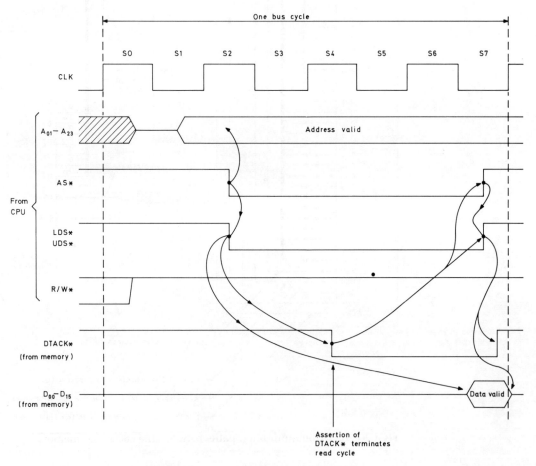

FIGURE 1.3 The 68000 read cycle. (a) Without wait states

time at which the 68000 receives DTACK* asserted, it is possible to cater for memory components with relatively long access times.

1.2.1 The 68000 read cycle

Figure 1.3(a) gives the timing diagram of a 68000 read cycle. Each memory access is composed of a minimum of eight clock states, labelled S0–S7. The *standard* 68000 runs at 8 MHz, requiring four cycles per access with each state 62.5 ns long. Faster 68000s operate at up to 12.5 MHz.

During state zero (S0), address lines are tri-stated from the value they had in the previous cycle and R/W* is set high. In S1, the address on A_{01}–A_{23} becomes valid for the duration of the current memory access.

In state S2, the address strobe, AS*, is asserted to indicate that the current contents of the address bus are valid. During a read cycle, UDS* and/or LDS* is asserted concurrently with AS*. Devices connected to the address bus may now respond to the read cycle.

Assuming that the memory and microprocessor combination is able to operate without the insertion of wait states, the addressed device must assert DTACK* before the falling edge of the S4 state. If this does not happen, wait states are introduced between states S4 and S5 until DTACK* is asserted as shown in Figure 1.3(b). At the end of a read cycle, the microprocessor latches the data on its data bus and negates AS*, UDS*/LDS* to complete the cycle.

A more detailed timing diagram of a 68000 read cycle is given in Figure 1.4. To keep things simple, not all the parameters from the 68000 data sheet have been included here. The points of interest are noted below.

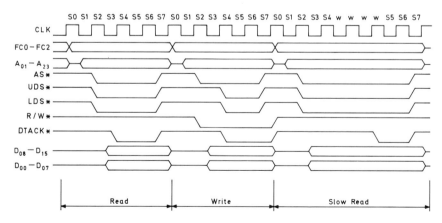

FIGURE 1.3 The 68000 read cycle. (b) With wait states

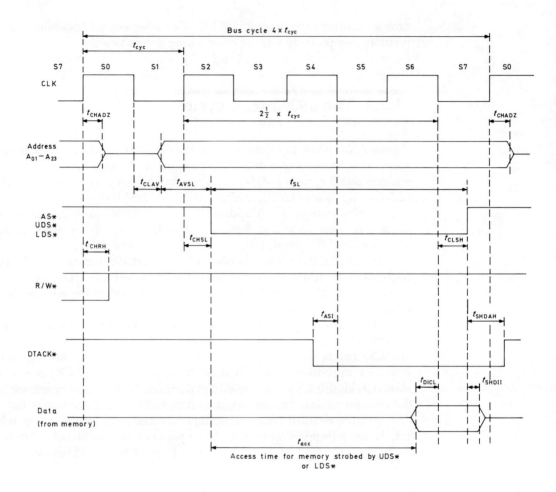

Read cycle parameters		8 Mhz		12.5 MHz	
		Min.	Max.	Min.	Max.
t_{CHADZ}	Clock high to address float	0 ns	80 ns	0 ns	60 ns
t_{CLAV}	Clock low to address valid		70 ns		55 ns
t_{AVSL}	Address valid to AS*, DS* asserted	30 ns		0 ns	
t_{SL}	AS*, DS* asserted	240 ns		160 ns	
t_{CHSL}	Clock high to AS*, DS* asserted	0 ns	60 ns	0 ns	55 ns
t_{CLSH}	Clock low to AS*,DS* negated		70 ns		50 ns
t_{SHDAH}	AS*, DS* negated to DTACK* negated	0 ns	245 ns	0 ns	150 ns
t_{CHRH}	Clock high to R/W* high	0 ns	70 ns	0 ns	60 ns
t_{DICL}	Data in to clock low (data setup)	15 ns		10 ns	
t_{SHDII}	DS* negated to data invalid (data hold)	0 ns		0 ns	
t_{ASI}	DTACK* low to clock low setup time	20 ns		20 ns	

FIGURE 1.4   Details of the 68000 read cycle

1. The address strobe is asserted t_{AVSL} seconds after the address has become valid. The delay between address valid and AS* valid provides a setup time for an address decoder or latch strobed by AS*. For an 8 MHz 68000, t_{AVSL} is no less than 30 ns. However, for the 12.5 MHz version, t_{AVSL} is 0 ns, and the user must supply an appropriate delay if the memory system calls for it. The data strobe, LDS* and/or UDS*, is asserted for t_{SL} seconds during a read cycle (t_{SL} = 240 ns min. at 8 MHz and 160 ns min. at 12.5 MHz).
2. The setup time for DTACK*, t_{ASI}, is 20 ns prior to the falling edge of state S4. If DTACK* violates this condition, wait states are introduced until DTACK* is recognized at least t_{ASI} seconds before the falling edge of the clock.
3. The data from the memory is latched by the falling edge of S6 and must be valid at least t_{DICL} seconds before this. The data setup time is 15 ns for an 8 MHz 68000 and 10 ns for a 12.5 MHz version. The data bus must be stable for at least t_{SHDII} seconds (0 ns min.) after the rising edge of UDS*/LDS*.

When evaluating a memory–microprocessor combination, the first step is to calculate the access time required by the microprocessor. From Figure 1.4, the maximum access time for a memory component strobed by AS* is from the falling edge of AS* to t_{DICL} seconds before the rising edge of S6.

Therefore, $t_{SL} = t_{acc} + t_{DICL} + t_{CLSH}$

$$\text{or} \quad t_{acc} = t_{SL} - t_{DICL} - t_{CLSH}$$

$$= 240 - 15 - 70 = 155 \, \text{ns} \, (8 \, \text{MHz})$$

$$= 160 - 10 - 50 = 100 \, \text{ns} \, (12.5 \, \text{MHz})$$

The values quoted above are calculated from the worst-case parameters and do not include any circuit losses such as delays through address and data buffers or signal propagation delays. It is rather difficult to perform *accurate* worst-case calculations from a manufacturer's data sheet without additional information (e.g. from an application report or a technical note). For example, we can recalculate the worst-case access time by noting that there are $2\frac{1}{2}$ clock cycles (i.e. 5 clock states) between the start of state S2 and the start of state S6. This time is made up of t_{CHSL} (S2 clock high to DS* low) plus t_{acc} plus t_{DICL}. That is:

$$2\frac{1}{2}t_{cyc} = t_{CHSL} + t_{acc} + t_{DICL}$$

$$\text{or} \quad t_{acc} = 2\frac{1}{2}t_{cyc} - t_{CHSL} - t_{DICL}$$

$$= 2\frac{1}{2} \times 125 - 70 - 15 \, (8 \, \text{MHz})$$

$$= 225 \, \text{ns} \, (\text{at} \, 8 \, \text{MHz})$$

$$= 2\frac{1}{2} \times 80 - 55 - 10 \, (12.5 \, \text{MHz})$$

$$= 135 \, \text{ns} \, (\text{at} \, 12.5 \, \text{MHz})$$

In practice, the designer should be reasonably safe using the maximum calculated value of any particular worst-case parameter.

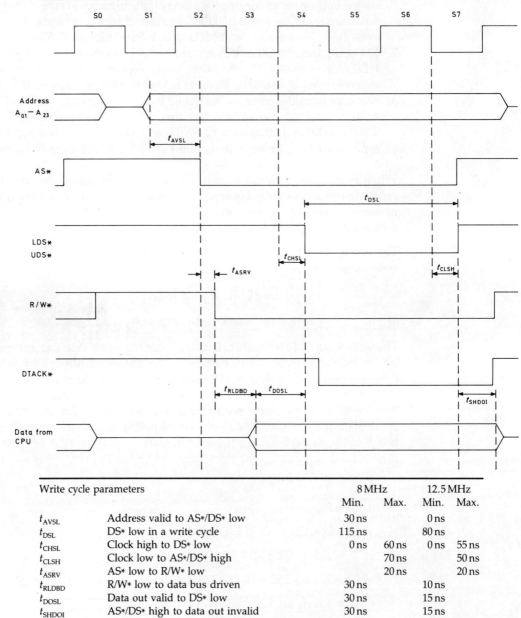

1.2.2 The 68000 write cycle

The 68000 write cycle is similar to the corresponding read cycle except that R/W*
goes low in state S2 and the 68000 places data on the data bus rather than
reading from it. Figure 1.5 gives a simplified timing diagram of a write cycle
without wait states.

Write cycle parameters		8 MHz		12.5 MHz	
		Min.	Max.	Min.	Max.
t_{AVSL}	Address valid to AS*/DS* low	30 ns		0 ns	
t_{DSL}	DS* low in a write cycle	115 ns		80 ns	
t_{CHSL}	Clock high to DS* low	0 ns	60 ns	0 ns	55 ns
t_{CLSH}	Clock low to AS*/DS* high		70 ns		50 ns
t_{ASRV}	AS* low to R/W* low		20 ns		20 ns
t_{RLDBD}	R/W* low to data bus driven	30 ns		10 ns	
t_{DOSL}	Data out valid to DS* low	30 ns		15 ns	
t_{SHDOI}	AS*/DS* high to data out invalid	30 ns		15 ns	

FIGURE 1.5 The 68000 write cycle

The principal points of interest in Figure 1.5 are the sequence of events at the beginning and end of a write cycle.

1. The address is placed on A_{01}–A_{23}.
2. The address strobe is asserted t_{AVSL} seconds later, exactly as in a read cycle.
3. R/W* is forced low no later than t_{ASRV} seconds (20 ns) after AS* has been asserted.
4. The 68000 places data on the data bus no more than t_{RLDBD} seconds (30 ns at 8 MHz, 10 ns at 12.5 MHz) after the R/W* signal is low. Data is valid t_{DOSL} seconds before the falling edge of LDS*/UDS* (30 ns min. at 8 MHz and 15 ns min. at 12.5 MHz). The data from the CPU is held for a minimum of t_{SHDOI} seconds after the rising edge of AS*/LDS*/UDS* (30 ns at 8 MHz and 15 ns at 12.5 MHz).
5. Unlike the corresponding read cycle, the data strobe (UDS*/LDS*) is not asserted concurrently with AS*. It is asserted in S4 after the data from the 68000 has become valid. The data strobe is asserted for a minimum of t_{DSL} seconds during a write cycle (115 ns at 8 MHz and 80 ns at 12.5 MHz).
6. A write cycle ends in state S7 with the negation of both AS* and LDS*/UDS*. If DTACK* is not asserted before the end of S4, wait states are introduced.

1.2.3 The 68000 memory interface

Interfacing a 68000 to static RAM requires very little in the way of additional circuit complexity. Figure 1.6 shows how a 68000 is connected to two 3264, 8K × 8, static RAMs. As the address space of the 68000 is 2^{24} bytes, the 16 Kbytes of memory space occupied by the RAMs must be decoded. Address decoding is carried out by means of a five-input 74LS260 NOR gate and a demultiplexer (74LS138). These two logic elements locate the memory in the range $004000–$007FFF by decoding address lines A_{14}–A_{23}. Note that AS* does not take part in the selection of these memory components, as it is not necessary to latch the address bus or to strobe the address decoder. UDS*/LDS* is used to strobe the address decoder or to select a memory component.

The active-low output of the decoder is combined with LDS* to select the lower byte of a word or with UDS* to select the upper byte. The chip-selects of the RAMs are each connected to one of the inputs of an AND (OR in negative logic) gate to generate an active-low memory access signal. If either UDS* or LDS* is asserted during an access to the memory components, the output of the AND gate (OR in negative logic) goes low, enabling the shift register (74LS164). The shift register is used to generate the appropriate number of wait states (should they be needed) by delaying the assertion of DTACK*.

Some of the 68000's pins shown at the bottom of Figure 1.6 are control signals which must be pulled up into their inactive-high state when they are not actually being used for a control function.

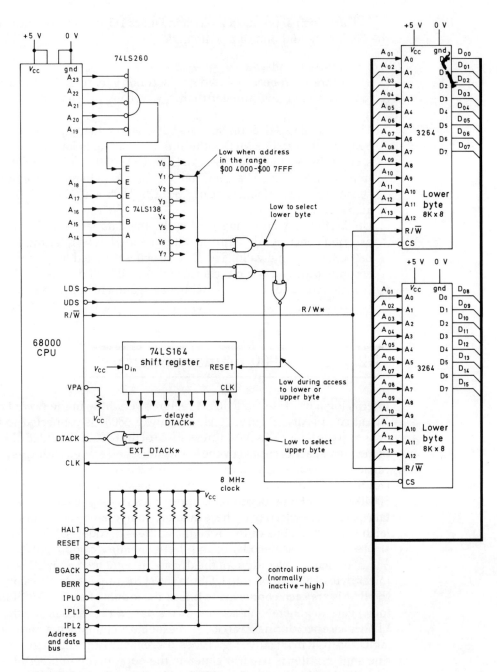

FIGURE 1.6   Connecting the 68000 to memory components

1.2.4 The interrupt interface

If ever the 68000 were to be granted the power to speak to its 8-bit predecessors, it would probably say, 'Anything you can do I can do better.' In fact, 'Anything you can do, I can do in a thousand different ways.' This statement is particularly true with reference to the 68000's interrupt interface.

An interrupt is a request to the microprocessor and is made by a peripheral that requires servicing. The interrupt request originates in hardware because the peripheral sends a message to the microprocessor by means of one or more dedicated interrupt request lines. However, the request is dealt with in software when the microprocessor executes the interrupt handling routine appropriate to the device that initiated the interrupt.

Children are taught from an early age, that it is wrong for them to interrupt adults when they are speaking. Why then, should peripherals display this apparent rudeness to the processors by interrupting them when they are busy executing a program? It is, in fact, possible to design 'polite' systems in which the microprocessor polls each peripheral in turn and checks to see if it requires attention. The polling procedure involves little more than testing the status of a bit in one of the peripheral's registers.

Modern microprocessor systems frequently operate in a multitasking mode. They execute two or more programs or tasks concurrently by switching between the tasks. I do not wish to write about multitasking here, as that is the province of the operating system text or the real-time system text. All I want to indicate is that a microprocessor can be operated very efficiently by letting it execute a *background task* while it is waiting for a peripheral to request service. When the peripheral is ready, it interrupts the CPU, the CPU deals with the peripheral and then returns to the background task. In this way, no time is wasted while the CPU is polling the peripheral to determine whether it requires service.

The minimum requirement to implement an interrupt system is a single line between an interrupt request output from the peripheral and an interrupt request input to the processor. Eight-bit microprocessors like the 6800 have a single IRQ* input. When the interrupt request input is asserted, the microprocessor finishes its current instruction, saves its return address (and certain other information) on the stack and then executes a jump to the interrupt handling routine. After this routine has been executed, an RTI (return from interrupt) is executed and a return made to the point immediately after the last instruction executed before the interrupt. Some microprocessors (including the 68000) have a non-maskable interrupt request input that cannot be suspended and must always be serviced.

The 68000 has a seven-level, prioritized vectored interrupt structure. *Seven-level* means that there are seven interrupt request lines and a peripheral can be connected to any one of these lines. *Prioritized* means that a priority is associated with each of these seven lines or levels and that, in the event of simultaneous interrupts on two or more levels, only the level with the highest priority may be serviced. *Vectored* means that the peripheral that originated the interrupt is able to identify itself to the processor and to force a jump to its own interrupt handling routine. The 68000's seven levels of interrupt request are normally written IRQ1*–IRQ7*. IRQ1* has the lowest priority and IRQ7* the highest. However, IRQ7* is also a non-maskable interrupt because a level-7 interrupt request on IRQ7* can *always* be interrupted by another level-7 interrupt.

Figure 1.7 provides an illustration of how the 68000's interrupt system is arranged. Interrupt requests on levels IRQ1*–IRQ7* are applied to an eight-input priority encoder, which transmits the binary code for the highest level of interrupt to the 68000's interrupt request input pins IPL0*–IPL2*. Note that IPL0* to IPL2* are active-low, so that no interrupt request is indicated by 1,1,1 and a level–7 interrupt is indicated by 0,0,0.

The 68000 compares the current level of interrupt request with its internal interrupt mask status bits (I0–I2) which form part of the 68000's status byte. If the interrupt level is greater than the current level indicated by I0–I2, then interrupt is serviced. Otherwise, the interrupt remains pending until the value of I0–I2 is modified.

When an interrupt is accepted, the current bus cycle is completed and the 68000's status register and program counter are saved on the stack. Note that the 68000 goes into its *supervisor* mode after it accepts an interrupt or other exception and also selects the supervisor stack (see later). The interrupt priority level reflected by I0–I2 in the status byte is set to the same value as the current interrupt which means that the 68000 can now be interrupted again only by a higher level of priority. The 68000 determines the address of its interrupt handling routine by executing an IACK cycle. The interrupt acknowledge function code of 1,1,1 is put out on FC0,FC1,FC2. An external decoder detects this and enables a three-line to eight-line decoder. The 68000 indicates the level of interrupt being serviced by placing the appropriate code on A_{01}–A_{03}. The decoder decodes this code to produce seven levels of interrupt acknowledge IACK1*–IACK7*.

The peripheral that requested the interrupt recognizes the IACK*i** and then places an 8-bit interrupt vector number on D_{00}–D_{07}. The peripheral must assert DTACK* to complete the IACK cycle.

The 68000 multiplies the vector by 4 and uses the result as an index to the interrupt vector table in the range $000000–$0003FF. The longword contents of this addresses the starting point of the interrupt handling routine. For example, if the peripheral supplies the vector number $42, the 68000 multiplies it by 4 to get $108 and then loads the longword at address $108 into the program counter.

At the end of the interrupt handling routine, an RTE (return from exception) instruction is executed which restores the value of the micro-processor status byte and CCR before the interrupt was serviced. Program execution continues with the instruction following the interrupted instruction.

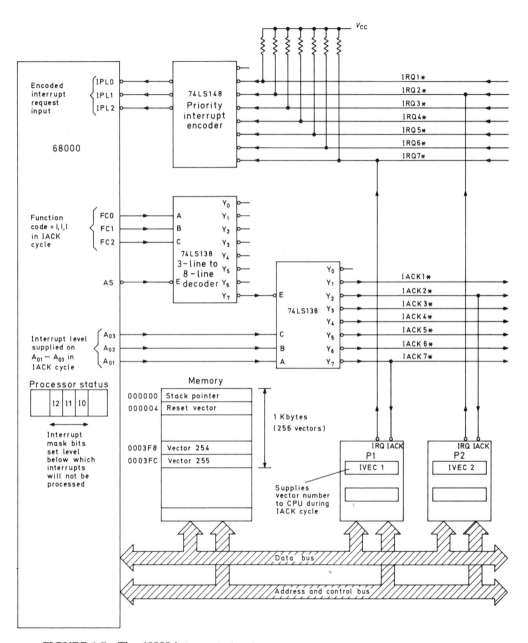

FIGURE 1.7   The 68000 interrupt structure

The above description is intended to provide only an overview of the 68000's interrupt handling procedure. The following notes should clear up a few points:

1. Assuming that the peripherals have an (open-collector/drain) IRQ* output and an IACK* input, the only interrupt control hardware required by the 68000 is three MSI integrated circuits.
2. The peripheral has its IRQ* output connected to IRQi* and its IACK* input to IACKi*. That is, IRQ* and IACK* must share the same level.
3. The arrangement of Figure 1.7 caters for up to seven peripherals. If two or more peripherals share the same level, they must be daisy-chained to allow only one of them to respond to an IACK cycle. Figure 1.8 shows how they are daisy-chained. Each peripheral has two IACK* lines; IACK_IN* and IACK_OUT*. When an IACK* is transmitted from the microprocessor, the first peripheral receives it. If that peripheral generated the interrupt, it supplies the IACK vector. If the peripheral did not generate the request it asserts an internal signal BYPASS* and passes on the IACK* on its IACK_OUT* to the next peripheral in the chain. Note that the peripherals are automatically prioritized by their position in the daisy-chain.
4. If a device does not respond to an IACK* cycle, a timer should assert BERR* after a suitable delay and thereby force a *spurious interrupt* response. The

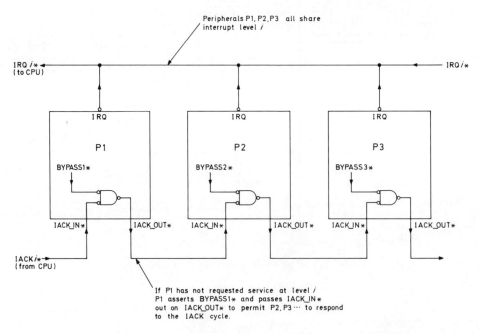

FIGURE 1.8 Daisy-chaining peripherals at the same interrupt level

68000 generates vector number 24 ($18) internally in response to a spurious interrupt.

5. If a peripheral asserts VPA* rather than DTACK* during an IACK cycle, the 68000 generates vector numbers 25–31 ($19–$1F), corresponding to interrupt levels 1 to 7 respectively. The 68000's ability to generate vector numbers when VPA* is asserted is called *autovectoring* and is suitable for peripherals that cannot supply their own vector.

6. The interrupt vector table in the range $000000–$0003FF may be in read/write memory or ROM. If it is in read/write memory, the vectors are loaded by the operating system.

7. The 68000 operates in one of two modes: user and supervisor. An S-bit in the microprocessor status byte is set up when the 68000 is operating in the supervisor mode. An interrupt forces the S-bit to be set which means that the interrupt handling routine runs in the supervisor mode. The RTE restores the old value of the microprocessor status at the end of the interrupt and the microprocessor returns to the state it was in before the interrupt. Because the function code outputs on FC0–FC2 reflect the state of the 68000, external hardware can be used to protect supervisor memory (or peripherals) from access when the 68000 is in the user mode. In practice, this means that interrupt handling software is part of the operating system and the user accesses these facilities only through the appropriate operating system utilities. The 68000 has two stack pointers (i.e. A7s). In the user mode, the user stack pointer is active and in the supervisor mode the supervisor stack pointer is active. By providing two stack pointers for the storage of subroutine return addresses, etc., the operating system stack is protected from abuse by user tasks.

In Chapter 8 we show how the 68000 is interfaced to the VMEbus and how interrupt generator and interrupt handler chips are interfaced both to the 68000 and to the VMEbus.

1.3 An example of a 68000-based microcomputer

Now that we have briefly examined the 68000's pins and its read and write cycles, the next step is to design a basic 68000-based microcomputer which can be connected to the interfaces described in later chapters. This microcomputer is called, somewhat unimaginatively, Microprocessor Interface Controller One (MICI).

1.3.1 Specifying a microcomputer

I find it difficult to specify the design of a microcomputer, as I always succumb to a temptation to include more and more in the basic design. My temptation is understandable, because a major facility such as a real-time clock can easily be added to the circuit for the cost of five or six components. However, I do not wish to introduce too much complexity at this point and will design a minimal-component, single-board 68000 microcomputer subject to the following constraints.

1. The single-board computer, MICI, should be able to operate in a stand-alone mode, making it possible to test the module independently of any other subsystem (other than a power supply).
2. A consequence of item 1 above is that the 68000 on the module should have all the necessary control signals, read/write memory and read-only memory.
3. In order to make testing easy, MICI has a serial interface with signals conforming to RS232C levels. Although we do not deal with serial interfaces until Chapter 3, it would be wrong to omit such an interface from MICI. Similarly, a 68230 parallel interface and a 68901 multifunction peripheral are also provided on this module.
4. The component count should be reduced as far as is conveniently possible. The term *conveniently* implies that no unusual or custom components can be used.
5. MICI must have buffered data and address buses to allow it to be connected to other modules.
6. Although MICI is to be as simple as realistically possible, its features should not compromise any future additions or interfaces. That is, no feature should be included which severely limits the 68000's performance. For example, full address decoding should be employed to avoid dedicating large blocks of memory space to, say, an interface component.

Figure 1.9 provides the block diagram of MICI. There are three control blocks associated with the 68000. A clock/reset block supplies an 8 MHz clock to the 68000 and the RESET* and HALT* signals required during the power-up sequence when the system is first switched on. An interrupt control block decodes the 68000's three interrupt request inputs into one of seven levels of interrupt request (the eighth level corresponds to no interrupt request) and also provides an interrupt acknowledge signal (IACK*) for each of seven levels of interrupt request.

An address decoder and DAT (data and address transfer) control block maps the address space of the on-board RAM and ROM onto the 68000's memory space and controls the system buffers. The control block is also responsible for generating a DTACK* handshake during an access to on-board

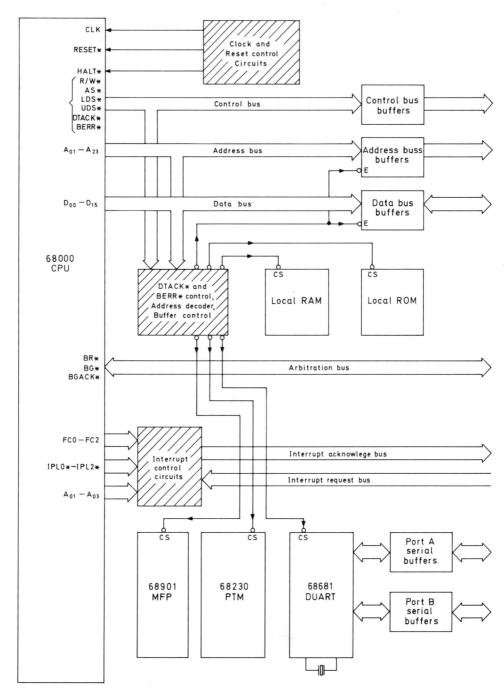

FIGURE 1.9 The block diagram of MICI – a basic microcomputer

memory and for generating a BERR* signal if the system hangs up. The memory block consists of two components: ROM which holds the system monitor and read/write memory which acts as scratchpad memory.

The serial peripheral provided on MICI is a 68681 DUART (dual universal asynchronous receiver transmitter) which interfaces the 68000 to any of the widely used CRT terminals. As the 68681 is a dual UART, two terminals can be handled simultaneously. Later we will see that the provision of two serial interfaces can be used to connect MICI to other computers as well as to a CRT terminal. Because the signals required by CRT terminals are non-TTL compatible, interfaces (level converters) must be placed between the DUART and the external equipment to which it is interfaced. A second interface is a 68230 PI/T (parallel interface and timer) which provides two 8-bit bidirectional parallel interfaces. We do not deal with the 68230 further in this text – references to the 68230 and its applications are provided in the Bibliography. A third interface provided by MICI is a 68901 multifunction peripheral, MFP, which is described in Chapter 2.

1.3.2 Designing a microcomputer

It is not very difficult to design a modest microcomputer, largely because the microprocessor manufacturers invariably make their chips easy to use. Figure 1.10 presents a block diagram of MICI's control system and Figure 1.11 a detailed circuit diagram. The address decoders are shown separately in Figure 1.12. A monolithic 8 MHz clock supplies the 68000's clock signal. Although a monolithic circuit is often more expensive than a discrete-component oscillator, it takes up less board space and is usually more reliable.

The reset circuit contains two parts: a power-on-reset generator built around a 555 monostable and a manual reset based on cross-coupled NAND gates. The monostable generates a single pulse which forces both HALT* and RESET* active-low immediately after the initial application of power to the module. The manual reset circuit permits the operator to force a full system reset in the event of a crash from which automatic recovery is not possible.

Interrupt control

The interrupt control circuitry uses three components. A 74LS148 eight-line to three-line priority encoder, IC 7, transforms any active-low interrupt request input into a 3-bit code on IPL0*–IPL2*. During an interrupt acknowledge cycle, the 68000 puts out 1,1,1 on FC0,FC1,FC2 which is detected by the 74SL10 three-input NAND gate IC 8a. The output of the NAND gate enables the three-line to eight-line decoder IC 6, which decodes the value on A_{01}–A_{03} into

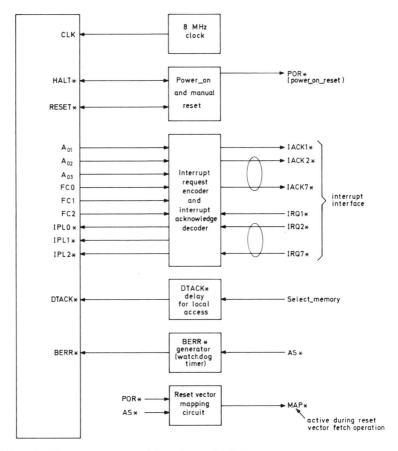

FIGURE 1.10 The system control functions of MICI

seven levels of interrupt acknowledge. Unless interrupts are implemented, these three ICs play no role in the operation of the microprocessor module.

Address decoding

One important circuit required by all microcomputers is an address decoder. The address space of memory components on the microprocessor module must be located somewhere within the 68000's 16 Mbyte memory space. As the 68000's reset (and other) exception vectors are located in the region $000000–$0003FF, it is necessary to assign some memory to this region. Figure 1.12 shows the address decoder that selects the memory components in the 128 Kbyte region $000000–$01FFFF and up to eight peripherals in the 1024 byte region $020000–$0203FF.

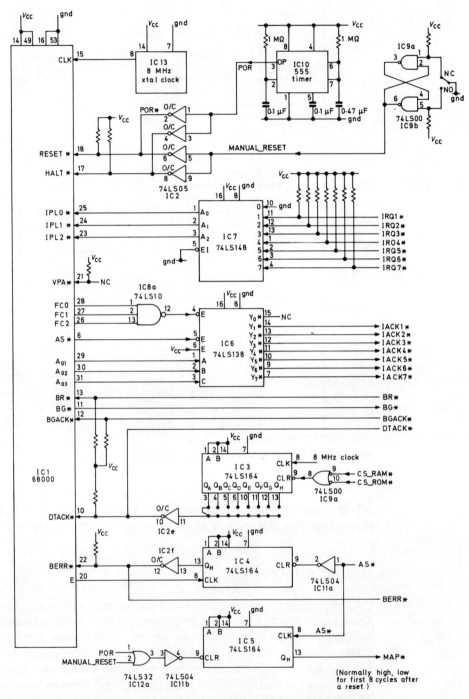

FIGURE 1.11   The circuit diagram of MICI's system control functions

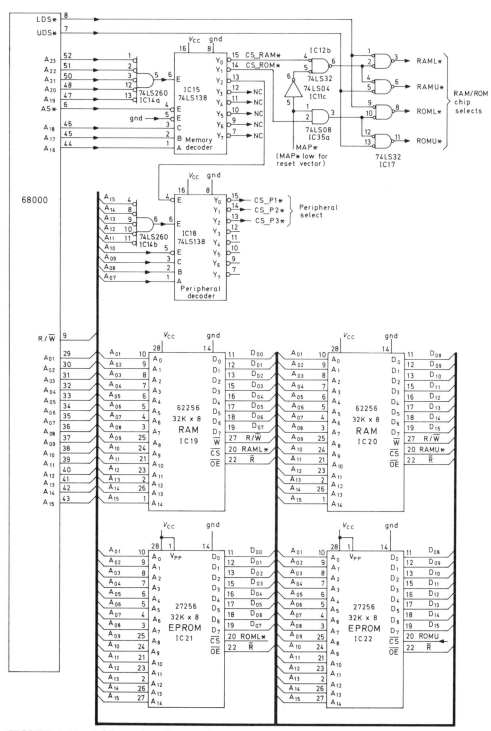

FIGURE 1.12 Address decoding and memory components on the microprocessor module

Memory address decoding is carried out by a 74LS260 five-input NOR gate, IC 14a, and a 74LS138 three-line to eight-line decoder, IC 15. The 64 Kbytes of memory from $000000 to $00FFFF are assigned to read/write components and the next 64 Kbytes from $010000 to $01FFFF are assigned to read-only memory.

Peripheral address decoding is performed by two chips, the other half of the 74LS260 NOR gate, IC 14b, and a second 74LS138, IC 18. These two devices decode address lines A_{07}–A_{15}, leaving 128 bytes of address space for each of the eight possible peripherals.

It is sensible to locate the exception vector table, which occupies 256 longwords from $000000 to $0003FF, in read/write memory. By putting the table in read/write memory, rather than ROM, it is easy to modify exception vectors dynamically under software control. Consequently, MICI has its 64 Kbyte read/write memory space mapped between $000000 and $00FFFF. In order to keep the design of MICI simple, $32K \times 8$ static RAMs are used.

Read-only memory, implemented as $32K \times 8$ 27256 EPROMs, occupies the memory space in the region $010000–$01FFFF. Such a memory map leaves us with a headache! Whenever the 68000 is reset by asserting HALT* and RESET* simultaneously, it loads longwords from $000000 and $000004 into its supervisor stack pointer and its program counter respectively. Clearly, we need some way of presetting the read/write memory at these locations with the appropriate longwords.

An elegant way out of this dilemma is to note that a reset exception lasts eight machine cycles after the RESET* line makes its inactive-high transition. During this time, we force the read-only memory at $010000 to respond to the reset-vector fetch operation. That is, although the 68000 reads longwords at $000000 and $000004, the actual memory locations accessed are at $010000 and $010004.

Figure 1.11 shows how a 74LS164 shift register, IC 5, is held in a clear state when POR or MANUAL RESET are low. When the 68000 comes out of reset (i.e. RESET* goes high), the shift register is enabled and is clocked by each transition of the address strobe, AS*. As the serial inputs of the shift register are strapped to Vcc, it takes eight cycles for the Q_H output, MAP*, to go high.

Now consider the memory select logic shown in Figure 1.12 (i.e. ICs 14a, and 15 that perform the address decoding, ICs 11c, 12b, 35a and 17 that select the ROM or RAM chips plus ICs 12a, 11b and 5 in Figure 1.15 that generate MAP*). Whenever MAP* is active-low, the read/write memory is disabled by OR gate (AND gate in negative logic) IC 12b, and the read-only memory is enabled by AND gate IC 35a.

DTACK* generation

An access to memory (RAM or ROM) results in the Y0* or the Y1* output of the main address decoder, IC 15, going active-low, forcing the clear input of shift register, IC 3, high. At the start of a memory access AS* (and therefore CS_RAM* or CS_ROM*) is asserted, releasing the shift register from it reset (clear) state. A logical one is propagated through the register at each clock pulse. By connecting one of the register's parallel outputs (Q_A to Q_H) to DTACK* via the open-collector inverter IC 2e, a delayed DTACK* is produced.

Bus error control

At the start of each memory access, another 74LS164 shift register, IC 4, is enabled by AS* asserted low and is clocked by the E clock from the 68000. The E clock runs at CLK/10. After 16 E clocks (i.e. 160 cycles), the Q_H output goes high, which, in turn, asserts the BERR* line through the open-collector inverter IC 2f. Thus, if no device terminates a memory access by asserting DTACK* within 160 clock cycles, BERR* is asserted to force an exception state and thereby terminate the current memory access.

Bus interface

As MICI must be able to communicate with external subsystems on other modules, a bus interface is provided on MICI. Figure 1.13 illustrates the address, control and data bus buffers. During normal operation, the address from the 68000 (and associated DAT control signals) are buffered by four 74LS244 octal tri-state buffers.

However, there are occasions (e.g. DMA operations) when another device wishes to control the DAT. Therefore, whenever the BGACK* (bus grant acknowledge) input to the 68000 is asserted, all address and control buffers are disabled, leaving the address bus free for use by another device.

The control of the data bus buffers, implemented by two 74LS245 tri-state transceivers is rather more complex. During a read cycle, they buffer from system to microprocessor and in a write cycle from microprocessor to system. The direction of data flow is determined by the state of their DIR input, which is connected to the 68000's R/W* pin. During a read cycle to local memory (i.e. on-board memory in the range $000000–$01FFFF) or to peripherals it is necessary to disable the data bus buffers. Otherwise, data bus contention would occur with both local memory and the data bus buffers trying to drive the 68000 data bus simultaneously. To avoid this, IC 29, a 74LS30 eight-input NAND gate, disables the data bus buffers if a local memory component or a peripheral is selected. The data bus buffers are also disabled whenever BGACK* is asserted.

The only peripherals currently implemented on MICI are a 68681 DUART that provides two serial data links, a 68230 PI/T that provides a parallel interface and a 68901 multifunction peripheral (MFP) that is described in Chapter 2. Figure 1.14 shows how these devices are interfaced to the 68000.

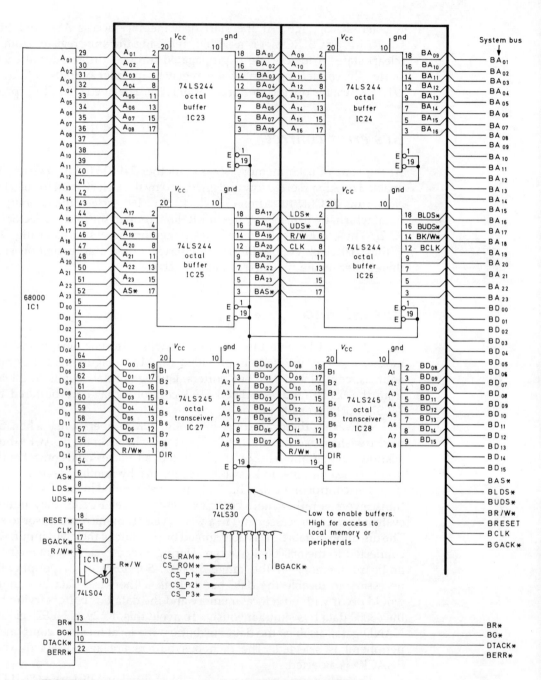

FIGURE 1.13   MICI's data, address and control bus buffers

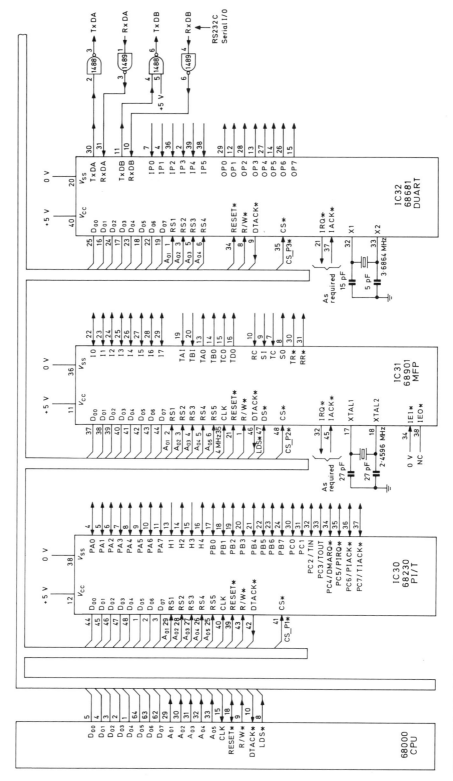

FIGURE 1.14 Interface components on the microprocessor module

Summary

In this chapter we have introduced the 68000 microprocessor and its interface to memory components. We have examined the 68000's read and write cycles and briefly looked at some of its control pins. The 68000's control pins provide a very comprehensive interrupt-handling facility, a mechanism whereby the 68000 is able to give up the data and address bus in an orderly fashion and a mechanism for dealing with faulty bus cycles (i.e. memory accesses). We have concluded the chapter by designing a simple 68000-based single-board microcomputer that can be used to drive many of the interface chips introduced in later chapters. Later in this text, as we describe a range of peripherals, we will spend some time designing suitable interfaces between the 68000 and these peripherals.

Chapter 2

Input/Output

Devices

Now that we have taken a brief look at the microprocessor, the next step is to consider some of the many factors involved in designing the input/output interfaces. In principle, data can be moved out of a computer by clocking it into latches connected to the data bus or it can be read from latches connected to the data bus. And that is all there is to input/output devices. In practice, the situation is rather different because many real interfaces carry out highly sophisticated operations at very great speeds and must co-ordinate their activity closely with that of the host processor. In this chapter we examine some of the issues raised by today's interface chips and then describe one of the simpler general-purpose chips currently available.

Before we continue, it is necessary to make a comment on terminology. There are three entities to be considered when dealing with input/output techniques. One is termed variously the *processor*, the *CPU* or the *microprocessor* and performs the computational and control functions in the system. The second is the *interface chip* that is connected to the processor and which executes the actual input or output operation (i.e. the chip moves data into or out of the CPU or its memory system). Interface chips range from parallel ports to floppy-disk controllers and IEEE 488 bus controllers. The third is the external system to be controlled (e.g. disk drive, printer, display) and is called the *peripheral*. Unfortunately, the term peripheral is often used to describe both the interface chip and the peripheral proper. I would prefer to employ the term *interface* to refer to the interface chips described throughout this text. However, the strict adherence to this rule would lead to phrases like 'an interface to the interface chip' and, therefore, I sometimes use the term 'peripheral'. The reader should have no difficulty in distinguishing between 'peripheral' meaning 'interface chip' (or interface subsystem) and 'peripheral' meaning 'external system controlled by the interface chip'.

2.1 Input/output fundamentals

It would be very nice to connect an interface chip to a microprocessor's data and address buses, switch the system on and watch it work. Unfortunately, life is a little more complex. It is often possible to wire a Motorola-made interface to a Motorola-made computer with minimal problems, because the computer and interface are tailor-made for each other. It may not be such an easy task to connect, say, an interface manufactured by AMD to a 68000, because the AMD part may be designed to interface directly with a microprocessor manufactured by AMD. In this section we look at the way in which interface chips are connected to the 68000 microprocessor and introduce some of the concepts fundamental to the design of interfaces based on these components.

2.1.1 Memory-mapped input/output

In the best of all possible worlds, microprocessors would have a dedicated input/output data bus. Such a bus separates input/output transactions and normal memory accesses and permits the use of special-purpose I/O operations. Indeed, there is no reason why both I/O operations and memory accesses should not take place concurrently. Unfortunately, the vast majority of real microprocessors do not have dedicated I/O data buses. The only reason for this omission is that an I/O bus would take up quite a number of precious pins and add relatively little in the way of performance.

Some microprocessors have special input/output instructions that rely on the existing address and data buses to move information between the microprocessor and an interface chip. These microprocessors normally have one or more special-purpose control signals, such as IOR* and IOW* (input/output read and write), that indicate to the interface that an I/O transaction is taking place.

The 68000 has neither special-purpose I/O instructions nor special-purpose I/O hardware. Consequently, the 68000 must rely on its existing memory interface to carry out all I/O transactions. Such an organization is known as memory-mapped I/O; Figure 2.1 shows how this is arranged in a typical microcomputer and it is immediately apparent that the I/O device is treated *exactly* like any other read/write memory component. A possible memory map for this system is presented in Figure 2.2. Note that the memory space devoted to an interface is very much less than that allocated to the memory devices proper (i.e. the RAM and ROM chips). Note also that the allocation of memory space to I/O devices is, essentially, arbitrary and is normally left up to the system designer. Generally speaking, engineers do not place I/O space within a block of memory used to store programs or data and

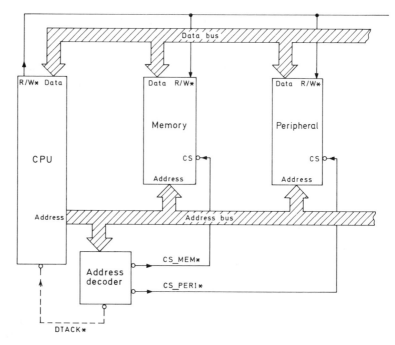

FIGURE 2.1 Memory mapped I/O

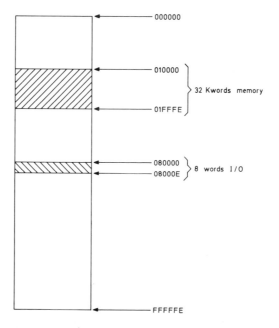

FIGURE 2.2 An example of memory mapped I/O

prefer to keep blocks of read/write memory, read-only memory and I/O space separate from each other. There is no strong reason for this, other than habit.

There are no great, or at least insurmountable, penalties to be paid for implementing memory-mapped input/output. In the days of the 8-bit microprocessor, the loss of some of its 64 Kbyte memory space to interfaces was occasionally inconvenient. The 68000 with its 16 Mbytes of memory space can allocate a few bytes to I/O with good grace.

A more serious objection to memory-mapped I/O has always been that the interfaces are particularly prone to program errors or even to programmer abuse. For example, in Figure 2.1, the operation MOVE.B #$F0,$010000 stores the byte $F0 in the memory location $010000. Executing a MOVE.B #$F0,$080000 stores the same byte at address $080000 which corresponds to a memory-mapped interface. In reasonably sophisticated systems, it is not desirable to permit a user to directly access an interface – all accesses should be made by appropriate calls to the operating system.

The 68000 provides a simple solution to the problem of protecting interface memory space. If we assume that the operating system runs in the 68000's supervisor mode, the 68000 puts out the function code 1,0,1 on its FC0,FC1,FC2 pins whenever it accesses supervisor data space. If we make this code a necessary condition to select the interface, it becomes impossible to access the device when the 68000 is running in the user mode. Figure 2.3 demonstrates how this is achieved. The interface can be accessed only when it is correctly addressed and when the 68000 is executing a memory data reference while in the supervisor mode.

There are other techniques for protecting memory-mapped I/O space from illegal accesses, the most popular of which involves memory management and is illustrated in Figure 2.4. The address generated by a microprocessor, called a logical address, is applied to a memory management unit, MMU, which translates it into a physical address. The physical address is the address of the operand in physical (i.e. real) memory.

Inside the MMU are a number of mapping registers that translate logical addresses into physical addresses. Most MMUs do not translate all the bits of a logical address into the corresponding physical address. They divide the logical address space into pages (or segments) so that an address in a logical page is translated into the corresponding address in the appropriate physical page.

There are two immediate advantages of memory management. The first is that the programmer does not need to know the actual address of memory-mapping I/O devices. The operating system is responsible for maintaining the mapping tables in the MMU and therefore the programmer may use any address he or she wishes for the I/O device. The MMU automatically translates the user address (i.e. virtual address) into its actual address (i.e. real address).

A second advantage of memory management comes from its ability to check each memory access against a number of privileges. Whenever the microprocessor generates a logical address, the logical page address is used to interrogate a register in the MMU which defines the privileges of that address.

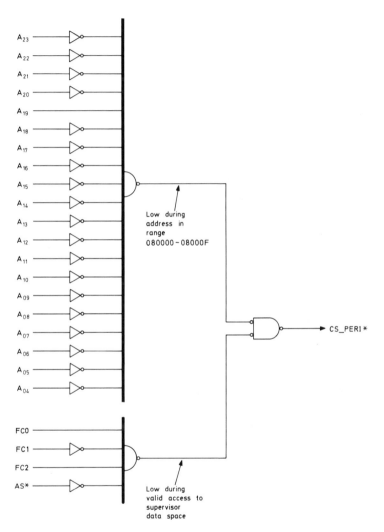

FIGURE 2.3 Locating memory mapped I/O devices in supervisor memory space

The 68000 supplies status information to the MMU by means of its function code outputs. Therefore, if the current logical address is not associated the appropriate function code, a physical address translation is not possible and the MMU forces a bus error by asserting BERR* to terminate the memory access.

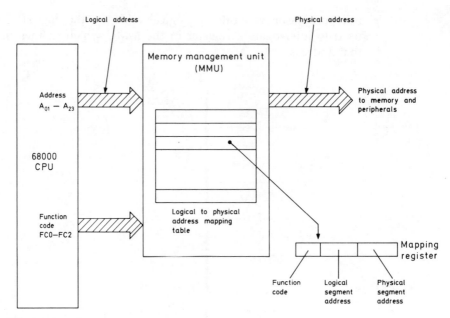

FIGURE 2.4   Memory management

2.1.2 The basic interface

Let us start interfacing at the easy end. The 68901 multi-function peripheral, MFP, is a relatively simple device that performs three functions: an 8-bit parallel I/O port, a single-channel serial interface and a two-channel timer. Although the MFP contains three interfaces on a single chip, each of these interfaces is very much less sophisticated than those found in other dedicated interfaces. The MFP has been designed for use in very low cost 68000 systems. However, at the moment we are interested only in its interface to a 68000.

The interface between an MFP and a 68000 is simplicity itself as Figure 2.5 demonstrates. Almost no special logic is required for this interface other than an address decoder to map the MFP's address space onto the 68000's. Most real systems combine the interface address decoder with the memory address decoder as we did in Figure 1.15. The active-low output from the address decoder is connected to the MFP's CS* input and the 5-bit code applied to RS1–RS5 selects one of the MFP's 32 internal registers. Invariably, RS1–RS5 are connected to A_{01}–A_{05} respectively from the 68000's address bus.

It is possible to connect the MFP's eight data lines, D_0–D_7, to either the 68000 lower byte data bus, D_{00}–D_{07}, or to its upper byte data bus, D_{08}–D_{15}. In the former case the data strobe of the MFP is connected to LDS* and in the latter case it is connected to UDS*. Unfortunately, the MFP cannot be connected to

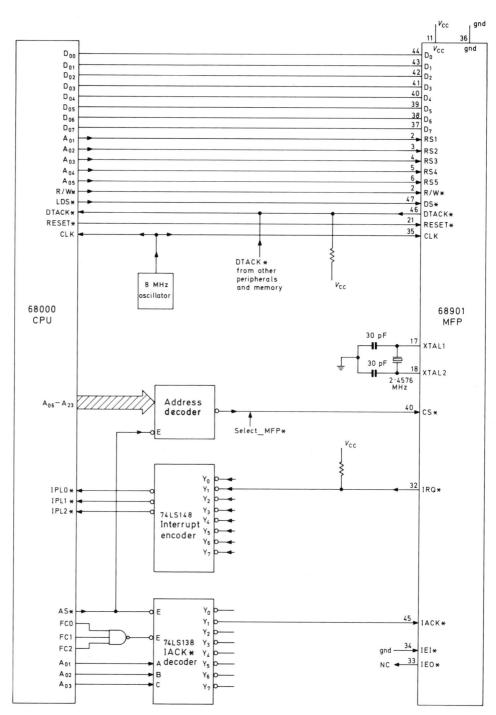

FIGURE 2.5 The interface between an MFP and a 68000 microprocessor

$D_{08}-D_{15}$ if it is to take part in vectored interrupts. Why? Because the 68000 responds to an interrupt request by executing an IACK* cycle and then reading the vector number on $D_{00}-D_{07}$.

In Figure 2.5, the MFP has been connected to the lower byte of the address bus in order to permit correct operation of the MFP's vectored interrupt mechanism. The single composite interrupt request output, IRQ*, from the MFP is wired to the appropriate input of the 74LS148 priority interrupt encoder. It is up to the user to select a suitable interrupt level for the MFP. The corresponding IACK* level from the 74LS138 decider is connected to the MFP's IACK* input. Note that, in this application, the MFP's interrupt acknowledge daisy-chain input, IEI*, is not needed and must be grounded. We will return to the subject of daisy-chaining later. The 68000's R/W*, RESET*, CLK and DTACK* pins are all connected to the corresponding pins of the 68000.

Now that we have sorted out the connections of the microprocessor-side interface, the next step is to make sure that it will work with the 68000. We must check whether any of the 68000's timing requirements are violated by the MFP in a read cycle or in a write cycle.

Figures 2.6 and 2.7 illustrate the 68000's and the MFP's read cycle timing diagrams respectively, and the parameters appropriate to these diagrams are given in Tables 2.1 and 2.2 respectively.

The best way to approach timing diagrams is to consider the devices (i.e. microprocessors and interfaces) as *producers* and *consumers* of parameters. For example, the 68000 is a producer of parameter t_{AVSL} (the address valid to AS* low time). Table 2.1 tells us that the 8 MHz 68000 produces a minimum value of t_{AVSL} of 30 ns. Parameter t_{AVCS}, the register select valid to CS* low setup time, of the MFP is a consumer parameter, because the MFP requires that this parameter be no less than 30 ns. Note that, in this case, the 68000 supplies a 30 ns address valid to AS*/LDS* low and the MFP requires a minimum 30 ns register select setup time to DS* low. Therefore, the *consumer* parameter of the MFP is just satisfied by a zero margin.

We could go through all parameters in turn, but I will consider only those of particular importance. The 68000 requires that its DTACK* input goes low at least t_{ASI} (20 ns min.) before the falling edge of the clock at the end of state S4. It is clear from Figure 2.7 that the MFP does not assert its DTACK* output until *its* state S5. I have assumed that CS* goes low in 68000 state S2 and have counted from that reference point. Consequently, DTACK* will not be recognized by the 68000 before the end of state S4 and therefore two wait states will be introduced while the 68000 waits for DTACK* from the MFP.

The next parameter to consider is the access time of the interface. The 68000 requires that data be valid in a read cycle t_{DICL} seconds (15 ns min.) before the falling edge of S6. It is perfectly possible to calculate whether t_{DICL} is satisfied by noting that the MFP provides data t_{DVCS} seconds (250 ns max.) after the falling edge of CS* and then working out when the data is valid in the 68000 cycle. But I am not going to do this. The reason for my apparent laziness should be evident from Figure 2.7. Note that DTACK* is not asserted until at least t_{DVDL}

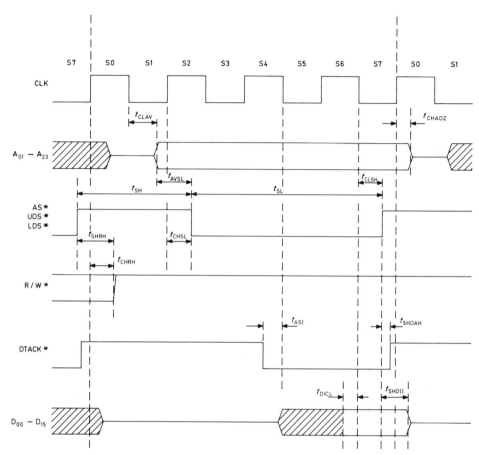

FIGURE 2.6 The 68000 read cycle timing diagram

TABLE 2.1 The 68000's read cycle timing parameters

t_{CLAV}	Clock low to address valid	70 ns min.
t_{CHADZ}	Clock high to address/data bus floating	80 ns max.
t_{AVSL}	Address valid to AS*/DS* asserted low	30 ns min.
t_{SH}	AS*/DS* high (negated)	150 ns min.
t_{SL}	AS*/DS* asserted low	240 ns min.
t_{CLSH}	Clock low to AS*/DS* negated	70 ns max.
t_{SHRH}	AS*/DS* negated to R/W* high	40 ns min.
t_{CHRH}	Clock high to R/W* high	0–70 ns
t_{CHSL}	Clock high to AS*/DS* asserted low	0–60 ns
t_{ASI}	Asynchronous setup time	20 ns min.
t_{SHDAH}	AS*/DS* negated high to DTACK* rescinded high	0–245 ns
t_{DICL}	Data in to clock low (data setup time)	15 ns min.
t_{SHDII}	AS*/DS* high to data in invalid (data hold time)	0 ns min.

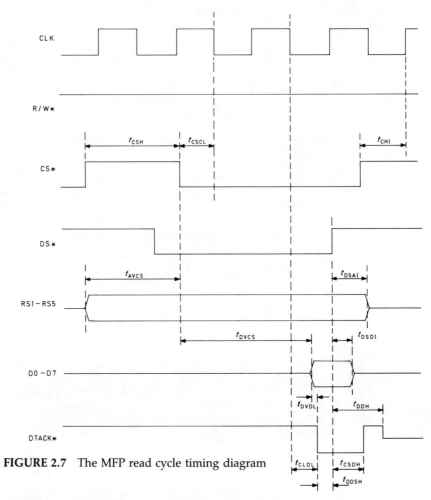

FIGURE 2.7 The MFP read cycle timing diagram

TABLE 2.2 The MFP's read cycle timing parameters

t_{CSH}	CS*/IACK*/DS* width negated high	50 ns min.
t_{CSCL}	CS*/IACK* valid (asserted low) to falling clock	50 ns min.
t_{CHI}	CS*/IACK* inactive high to rising clock setup time	100 ns min.
t_{AVCS}	Address valid to falling edge of CS* setup time	30 ns min.
t_{DSAI}	CS*/DS* negated high to address invalid hold time	0 ns min.
t_{DVCS}	Data valid from CS* asserted low (access time)	250 ns max.
t_{DSDI}	CS*/DS* negated high to data invalid/floating	0–50 ns
t_{DVDL}	Read data valid to DTACK* low setup time	50 ns min.
t_{CLDL}	Clock low to DTACK* asserted low	220 ns max.
t_{DDH}	CS*/DS* to DTACK* floating	100 ns max.
t_{CSDH}	CS*/DS* high to DTACK* high	60 ns max.
t_{DDSH}	DTACK* asserted low to DS*/CS* negated high hold	0 ns min.

Note: CS* is normally strobed by AS* from the 68000 and therefore CS* goes low approximately 10 ns after AS*.

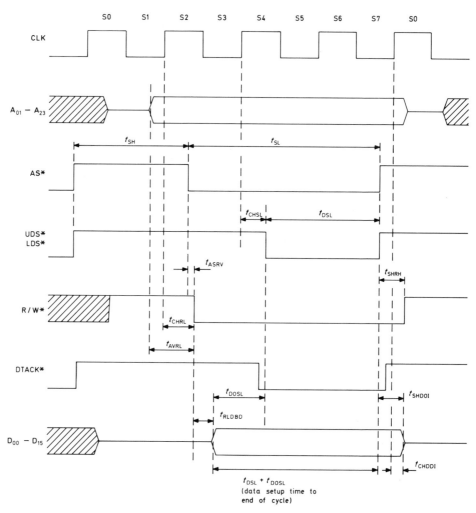

FIGURE 2.8   The 68000 write cycle timing diagram

TABLE 2.3   The 68000's write cycle timing parameters

t_{SH}	AS*/DS* width high	150 ns min.
t_{SL}	AS* asserted low	240 ns min.
t_{DSL}	DS* asserted low during write	115 ns min.
t_{CHSL}	Clock high to AS*/DS* low	0–60 ns
t_{ASRV}	AS* asserted low to R/W* low for write	20 ns max.
t_{SHRH}	AS*/DS* negated high to R/W* high	40 ns min.
t_{CHRL}	Clock high to R/W* low	70 ns max.
t_{AVRL}	Address valid to R/W* low for write	20 ns min.
t_{DOSL}	Data out valid to DS* asserted low	30 ns min.
t_{SHDOI}	AS*/DS* negated high to data out invalid	30 ns min.
t_{RLDBD}	R/W* low to data bus driven	30 ns min.
t_{CHDOI}	Clock high to data out invalid	0 ns min.

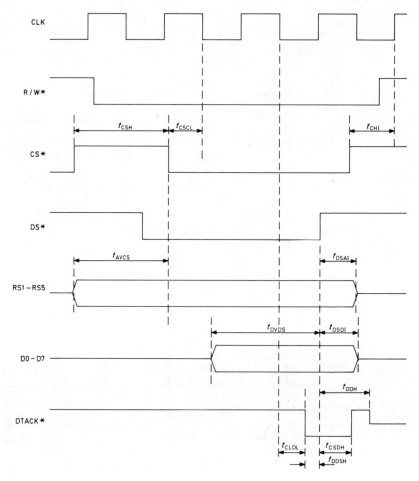

FIGURE 2.9 The MFP write cycle timing diagram

TABLE 2.4 The MFP's write cycle timing parameters

t_{CSH}	CS*/IACK*/DS* width high	50 ns min.
t_{CLSL}	CS*/IACK* valid to falling clock setup time	50 ns min.
t_{CHI}	CS*/IACK* inactive to rising edge clock setup	100 ns min.
t_{AVCS}	Address valid to falling edge CS* setup time	30 ns min.
t_{DSAI}	CS*/DS* high to address invalid hold time	0 ns min.
t_{DVDS}	Data valid prior to rising DS* setup time	280 ns min.
t_{DSDI}	CS*/DS* high to data invalid hold time	0 ns min.
t_{DDH}	CS*/DS* high to DTACK* high impedance	100 ns max.
t_{CLDL}	Clock low to DTACK* low	220 ns max.
t_{CSDH}	CS*/DS* high to DTACK* high	60 ns max.
t_{DDSH}	DTACK* low to DS*/CS* high hold time	0 ns min.

seconds (50 ns min.) *after* the data is valid. Consequently, data from the MFP will be valid before the 68000's state S5 (because of the wait states introduced due to the delayed DTACK*).

Another parameter of interest in a read cycle is the data hold time of the interface. That is, at the end of the cycle, the interface must maintain its data output until the 68000 has latched it. Figure 2.6 indicates that the 68000 requires a data hold time, DS* negated to data in invalid (t_{SHDII}), of no less than 0 ns and Figure 2.7 shows that the MFP has a minimum data hold time, t_{DSDI}, of 0 ns. Therefore, the 68000's data hold time criterion is satisfied.

The MFP write cycle

The write cycle timing diagram of the 68000 and the MFP are provided in Figures 2.8 and 2.9, respectively. The corresponding timing parameters are defined in Tables 2.3 and 2.4.

The fundamental producer/consumer relationships in a write cycle can be expressed in the following way:

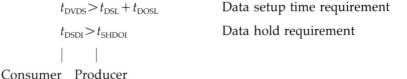

$$t_{DVDS} > t_{DSL} + t_{DOSL} \qquad \text{Data setup time requirement}$$

$$t_{DSDI} > t_{SHDOI} \qquad \text{Data hold requirement}$$

Consumer   Producer

Note that, as in the case of the read cycle, DTACK* from the MFP is not asserted until its state S5 which forces two wait states. This has the effect of increasing t_{DSL} in the above equations by one clock cycle, 125 ns at 8 MHz.

2.1.3 Dealing with timing problems

We now look at the problem of interfacing a non-68000-series memory-mapped interface to a 68000. We will call this interface HIC which stands for 'hypothetical interface component', although this device is based on a real chip. The interface between an HIC and a 68000 can be treated almost exactly like any other processor to memory interface. The processor interface of the HIC is similar to that of a block of static read/write memory, except that it has separate read and write strobes (RE* and WE*), rather than a single R/W* input. The HIC's interface is typical of many interfaces intended primarily for interfacing to 8080A and Z80 microprocessors. RE* and WE* can readily be synthesized from, say, the 68000's R/W*, data and address strobes. Figure 2.10 gives the HIC's read cycle timing diagram and Figure 2.11 its write cycle timing diagram.

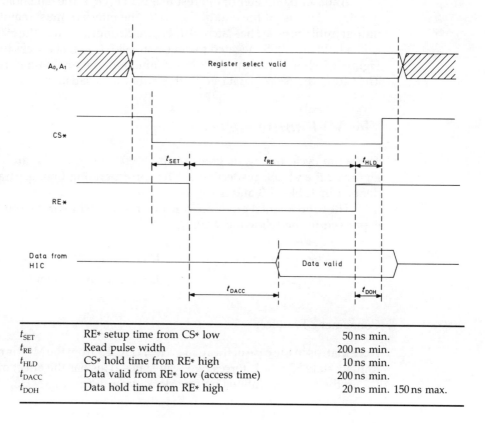

t_{SET}	RE* setup time from CS* low	50 ns min.
t_{RE}	Read pulse width	200 ns min.
t_{HLD}	CS* hold time from RE* high	10 ns min.
t_{DACC}	Data valid from RE* low (access time)	200 ns min.
t_{DOH}	Data hold time from RE* high	20 ns min. 150 ns max.

FIGURE 2.10   The HIC read cycle timing diagram

The read cycle timing diagram presents no insurmountable problems for the systems designer. The access time is just about low enough to require no wait states with the 8 MHz version of the 68000. Only one parameter causes eyebrows to be raised. This parameter is t_{SET}, the setup time between address valid and CS* asserted, and the falling edge of the read strobe, RE*. The minimum value of t_{SET} is quoted as 50 ns. If RE* is derived from AS*, RE* is asserted t_{AVSL} seconds after the address from the 68000 is valid. The value of t_{AVSL} is 30 ns for a 68000L8 and higher-speed versions of the 68000 have values of t_{AVSL} considerably less than the 50 ns required by t_{SET}. Therefore, if the HIC is to be used with the 68000, the falling edge of RE* must be delayed by user-supplied logic.

The situation in a write cycle is slightly more complex. WE* must be asserted no sooner than t_{SET} seconds after the address is valid and held low

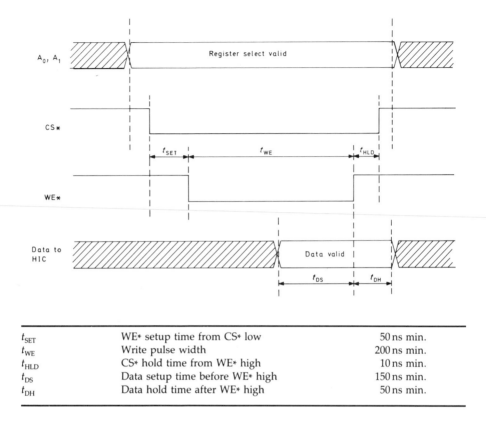

t_{SET}	WE* setup time from CS* low	50 ns min.
t_{WE}	Write pulse width	200 ns min.
t_{HLD}	CS* hold time from WE* high	10 ns min.
t_{DS}	Data setup time before WE* high	150 ns min.
t_{DH}	Data hold time after WE* high	50 ns min.

FIGURE 2.11 The HIC write cycle timing diagram

for at least t_{WE} seconds (i.e. 200 ns). The HIC's data setup and hold times ($t_{DS} = 150$ ns min. and $t_{DH} = 50$ ns min.) must also be complied with.

Figure 2.12 provides the circuit diagram of a suitable interface between the HIC and a 68000 capable of operating at 8 MHz. The corresponding read and write cycle timing diagrams are given in Figures 2.13 and 2.14 respectively.

The basic source of incompatibility between the 68000 and the HIC is the relatively high value for the HIC's minimum data hold time, t_{DH}. The solution adopted in Figure 2.12 is to latch data from the 68000 in an octal latch during a write cycle. In this way, the data is held stable for the HIC long after the 68000 has completed its write cycle.

D flip-flop IC1 generates delayed RE* and WE* strobes, ensuring that the minimum value of t_{SET} is exceeded. Similarly, D flip-flop IC2 delays the CS* input to the HIC with respect to its RE* and WR* strobes.

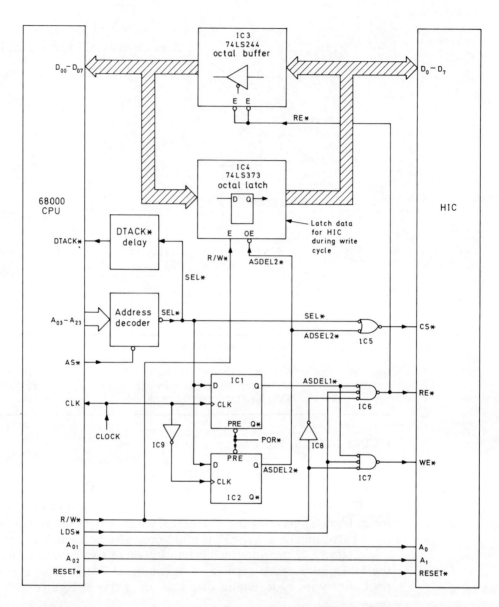

FIGURE 2.12 The circuit diagram of a possible interface between the HIC and a 68000 microprocessor

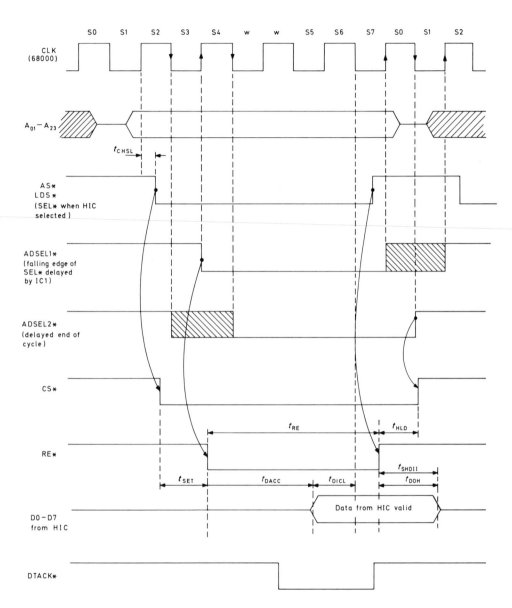

FIGURE 2.13 The read cycle timing diagram for a HIC-68000 combination

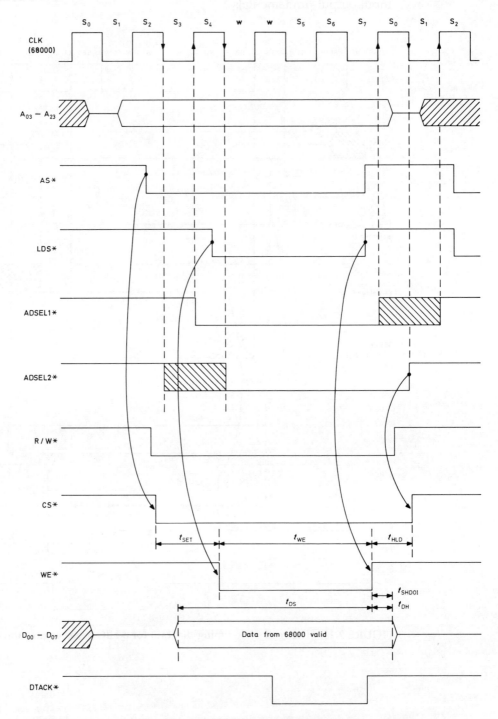

FIGURE 2.14 The write cycle timing diagram for a HIC-68000 combination
Note: Data from the 68000 is latched by IC4 and held until R/W* returns high. This holds the data constant until S2 in the following cycle.

2.1.4 Interfacing the 68661 to a 68000

As a last example of microprocessor-side interfacing, we look at the 68661 enhanced programmable communications interface (EPCI). The '68' in the 68661 implies that the EPCI is a 68000-series device, rather like the MFP, and that it can be connected directly to the 68000 without any special difficulties. However, the 68661 is a component originally designed by Signetics and was not intended, primarily, to interface directly with the 68000.

Figure 2.15 illustrates the structure of the EPCI. At first sight, it appears very much like a memory component with an address input, a data bus, a chip select or enable and a R*/W input. Note that the R*/W input operates in the opposite sense to the R/W* input of most peripherals!

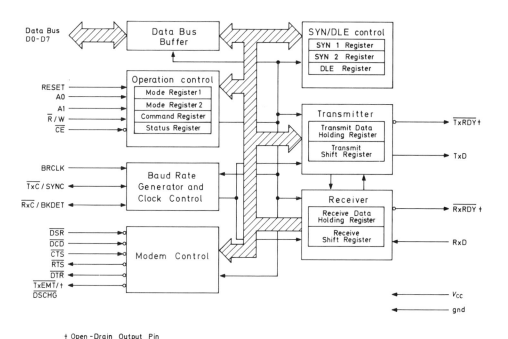

† Open-Drain Output Pin

FIGURE 2.15   The structure of the EPCI

The read access time of the EPCI is 200 ns which means that it can operate with the 68000 at 8 MHz without wait states. Unfortunately, the duration of t_{CE} (chip select down time) is quoted as 250 ns which means that two wait states must be inserted for correct operation at 8 MHz. If CE* is derived from AS* from the 68000, the down time for AS* is $t_{SL} = 240$ ns minimum. Adding two wait states gives an AS∗ down time of 240 ns + 125 ns = 365 ns which exceeds the minimum down time of 250 ns for CE∗. The wait states are introduced by delaying the assertion of DTACK∗. If you look at the other parameters of the EPCI in Figure 2.16, you will see that they are all well-behaved.

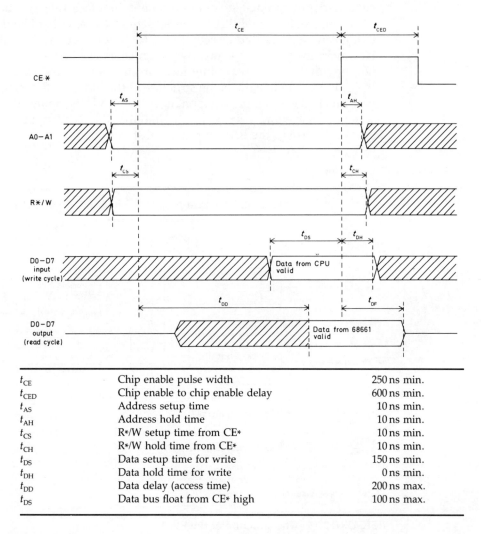

t_{CE}	Chip enable pulse width	250 ns min.
t_{CED}	Chip enable to chip enable delay	600 ns min.
t_{AS}	Address setup time	10 ns min.
t_{AH}	Address hold time	10 ns min.
t_{CS}	R∗/W setup time from CE∗	10 ns min.
t_{CH}	R∗/W hold time from CE∗	10 ns min.
t_{DS}	Data setup time for write	150 ns min.
t_{DH}	Data hold time for write	0 ns min.
t_{DD}	Data delay (access time)	200 ns max.
t_{DS}	Data bus float from CE∗ high	100 ns max.

FIGURE 2.16 The timing diagram of the 68661 EPCI

Now look again. The value for t_{CED}, the chip-enable to chip-enable delay, is a rather large 600 ns minimum. What this means is that the EPCI cannot be accessed more than once within a 600 ns period. Any instruction that causes the 68000 to perform two or more successive accesses to the EPCI (e.g. a MOVEP) will violate the minimum value for EPCI. The data sheet of the EPCI presents a possible interface between the EPCI and a 68000 which solves the problem, together with a timing diagram. These illustrations are reproduced in Figures 2.17 and 2.18 respectively.

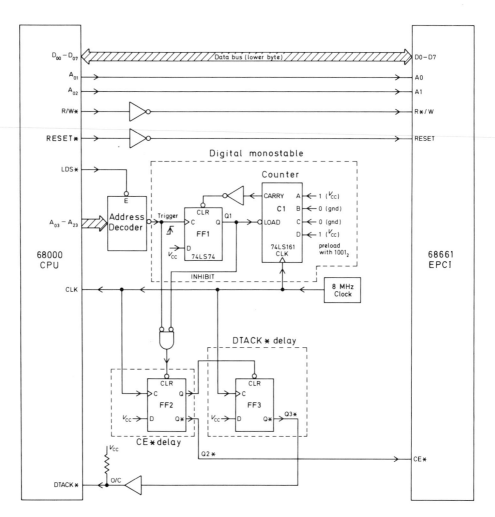

FIGURE 2.17   The recommended interface between a 68000 and an EPCI

A state machine consisting of a 74LS161 binary counter and a 74LS74 D flip-flop is configured as a digital monostable that produces a single pulse each time it is triggered by a signal from the address decoder. The rising edge from the address decoder clocks the D flip–flop (FF1) which, in turn, enables the counter. After five cycles have been counted, the CARRY output from the

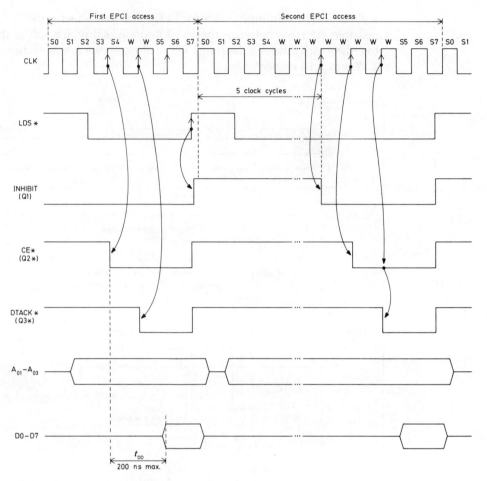

FIGURE 2.18   The timing diagram for Figure 2.17

counter resets the flip-flop. Five cycles are chosen to yield a 625 ns delay at 8 MHz, which exceeds the value of t_{CED} by 25 ns.

Figure 2.18 illustrates the timing diagram for two consecutive read bus cycles. The INHIBIT signal prevents CE* from being asserted, and causes the processor to insert wait states until INHIBIT is negated.

2.1.5 Peripheral access principles

In the previous section, we indicated that a memory-mapped interface looks exactly like a block of random access memory, as far as the 68000 is concerned.

This block of memory is normally very tiny and ranges from, typically, 1 to 128 bytes. Most interfaces have byte-wide data buses, although there is a trend towards 16-bit data buses with the latest generation of highly sophisticated interfaces. We are now going to look at how the registers of an interface are actually addressed.

The memory space taken by an interface consists of three classes of storage: control, status and data. Control locations are used by the programmer to define the operational characteristics of the interface. Status locations contain information about the current status of the interface and its activity. Data locations are used by the microprocessor to pass user or device-dependent data to the interface or to receive data from the interface.

Memory-mapped registers with unique addresses

Consider the simple interface of Figure 2.19 which has four memory locations. In this case the device is mapped at an address, say, BASE and the address of each register is given as BASE + OFFSET, where the offset is 0 for the command register, 2 for the status register, and so on. Each internal register is uniquely addressable and such an interface may be accessed in a read cycle in the following way.

Access_peripheral
        Write setup data to peripheral control register at base address
        REPEAT
                Read status byte at base address + 2
        UNTIL device NOT busy
        Read data from interface at base address + 6
End access_peripheral

Possibly the greatest limitations on the designer of peripherals is the number of pins available. Larger packages are more expensive to produce than smaller

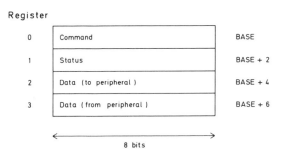

FIGURE 2.19 A memory-mapped peripheral with four addressable locations

ones and they are less attractive to users because they take up more board area. Consequently, there is tremendous pressure on the designer to reduce the number of microprocessor-side pins in order to leave more room for peripheral-side pins. After all, the chip is sold for its peripheral-side functions – the microprocessor-side interface is just a necessary evil.

Register addressing by means of read-only and write-only register pairs

Designers have reduced the number of pins by getting rid of some of the register select inputs. Consider the previous example of a peripheral which has four internal registers. It requires two address lines to uniquely select one of these registers, doesn't it?

If we look at the *type* of registers in this interface, we find that two are read-only and two write-only. The command and data to peripheral registers are write-only and the status and data from peripheral registers are read-only. There is no need for the microprocessor to read a command from the interface any more than there is to write to the status register. It is therefore possible to employ a *single* address line to distinguish between two *pairs* of registers (i.e. command/status and data in/data out) and then use the R/W* signal to distinguish between the registers of a pair. The memory map of such an interface appears in Figure 2.20.

Address	Register	Type	A_{01} (RS)	R/W*
BASE	Command	Write – only	0	0
BASE	Status	Read – only	0	1
BASE + 2	Data (to peripheral)	Write – only	1	0
BASE + 2	Data (from peripheral)	Read – only	1	1

FIGURE 2.20   Using the R/W* signal to distinguish between registers

One of the first interfaces to adopt this strategy was the 6850 ACIA (asynchronous communications interface adaptor). A single register select, RS, line distinguishes between the 6850's control/transmit-data registers and its status/receive-data registers.

Register addressing by means of pointer bits

Another technique used to reduce the number of register select lines involves a pointer bit in one of the registers. Two (or more) registers share a common address and are both read/write registers. Therefore R/W* cannot be used to distinguish between them. By defining a bit in another register as a pointer, it is possible to distinguish between two registers at the same address by associating one of them with the pointer bit set to zero and the other with the pointer bit set to one. For example, bit zero of register A can be used to select *either* register B or register C which share the same address. When bit zero of register A is zero, register B is selected at address X and when bit zero of register A is one, register C is selected at address X. The same technique is found in the 6821 PIA (peripheral interface adapter). Figure 2.21 provides an address map of the PIA and shows how its registers are selected by two register select lines (RS0 and RS1) and two *internal* bits (CRA_2 and CRB_2). Note that CRA_2 is read as bit 2 of register CRA. We will use the convention that R_i denotes bit i of register R.

Address	Register		A_{02} RS1	A_{01} RS0	CRA_2	CRB_2
BASE	Peripheral register A	PDRA	0	0	1	X
BASE	Data direction register A	DDRA	0	0	0	X
BASE + 2	Control register A	CRA	0	1	X	X
BASE + 4	Peripheral register B	PDRB	1	0	X	0
BASE + 4	Data direction register B	DDRB	1	0	X	0
BASE + 6	Control register B	CRB	1	1	X	X

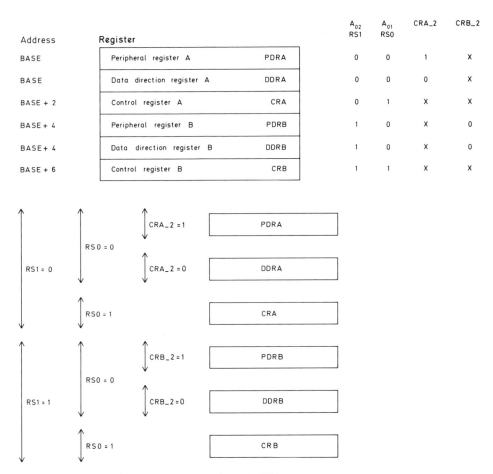

FIGURE 2.21. The memory map of a 6821 PIA

The PIA has two independent 8-bit ports, A and B. Port A registers are selected when RS1 = 0 and port B registers when RS1 = 1. RS0 selects either a control register when RS0 = 1, or one of a *pair* of registers (peripheral data or data direction) when RS0 = 0. A peripheral data register (PDR) or a data direction register (DDR) is selected by setting or clearing, respectively, bit 2 of the appropriate control register. The control register itself is, of course, uniquely addressable.

A PIA is set up or configured by the following sequence of actions:

1. Load the control register with the appropriate parameters for the specified application and set bit 2 of the control register, CR_2, to zero to select the data direction register, DDR.
2. Load the data direction register, DDR, to define individual bits of the parallel port as inputs or outputs.
3. Set bit 2 of the control register to one to select the peripheral data register.
4. Access the peripheral data register.

Steps 1, 2 and 3 are performed during the PIA's initialization phase. Therefore, once the PIA has been set up, the peripheral data register is always selected rather than the DDR at the same address. In general, the DDR is not modified once it has been set up.

We perform a read access to the A-side of a PIA in the following way. Note that registers are suffixed by *A* to denote *A-side*.

PIA_access
                  Access control register A, CRA, at base address + 2
                  Set bit 2 of CRA to zero to select the side-A DDR
                  Load the DDR with zero to define side-A as an input
                  Set bit 2 of CRA to one to select the side-A data register
                  REPEAT
                                    Read from the PIA side A data port at base address
                                    Move the data to its destination
              UNTIL   ⟨end of application⟩
End PIA_access

Register addressing by means of pointer registers

Some interfaces have such a large number of internal registers that it is impractical to provide sufficient register select lines to address each register uniquely. In such cases, two addressable registers are defined: one is a pointer register and the other a data register. The programmer accesses an internal data register by loading the pointer register with the offset of the required data register and then accessing the data register of the interface. This technique requires only one register select pin but suffers a penalty in the form of a reduced access rate. Internal pointer-based addressing is cost effective for peripherals such as cathode ray tube controllers CRTCs, which are infrequently accessed once they have been initialized.

A variation on the pointer-based addressing mode involves the use of an automatically incrementing internal pointer. After the interface has been reset, the internal pointer is loaded with zero. Each successive access to the interface increments the pointer and therefore selects the next register in sequence. Peripherals with auto-incrementing pointers are useful mainly when the registers will always be accessed in sequence.

Peripherals with off-chip registers

The final example of interface register addressing is found in some of the new generation of powerful interfaces such as the IMDC to be described in Chapter 7. What do we do when very large numbers of registers are required by the interface? The solution adopted by some disk controllers or communication controllers is to locate the registers in the microprocessor's own random access, read/write memory space! The interface now requires little more than a pointer to its own register set in read/write memory. These interfaces have to resort to DMA (direct-memory access) in order to access their own registers in memory. That is, the interface must use the 68000's bus arbitration control lines in order to get access to the address and data bus before it can access its own registers. Equally, these interfaces can operate at high speed and maintain large data buffers. For example, an intelligent multiple disk controller can read an entire sector into a memory buffer without any direct action by the microprocessor.

2.1.6 Handshaking

The function of all interfaces, apart from some timers, is to move data into or out of the microprocessor system. There are two approaches to this activity; one called *open-loop data transfer* and the other *closed-loop data transfer*. In an open-loop data transfer, the computer throws data at the interface or it grabs data from the interface. The open-loop data transfer is rather like religion – it is all a matter of faith. You hope that the interface caught the data or that the data you grabbed was actually valid, but you have no way of knowing it.

A closed-loop data transfer does not rely on faith. When data is transferred to an interface, the interface signifies that it has received the data. Similarly, when the microprocessor reads data from the interface, the interface and the peripheral is informed that the reading has taken place. Under these circumstances, there is never any confusion or ambiguity about a data transfer. The mechanism used to do this is called a handshake.

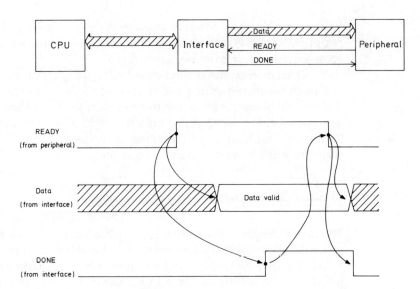

FIGURE 2.22   The closed-loop output data transfer

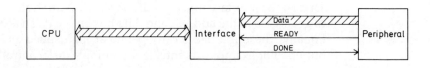

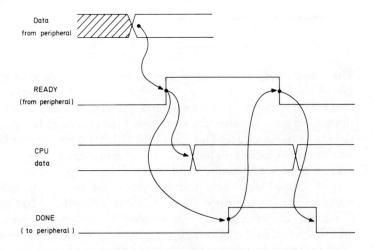

FIGURE 2.23   The closed-loop input data transfer

Figure 2.22 illustrates a closed-loop output handshake procedure. Two control lines are required between the interface and the peripheral. I have called one line READY and the other DONE. The peripheral asserts READY to indicate that it is ready to receive data from the interface. The microprocessor detects that READY has been asserted by reading a READY status bit within the interface. Assuming that the microprocessor has some data to send, it transmits the data to the interface which transfers it to the peripheral.

The interface asserts DONE to indicate to the peripheral that it has transferred data to it. Once DONE has been asserted, the peripheral negates READY and the interface negates DONE to complete the handshake.

Figure 2.23 illustrates the opposite process, the fully interlocked closed-loop input handshake.

Handshaking is associated with parallel interfaces and buses. For example, the 6821 PIA and the more sophisticated 68230 parallel interface/timer (PI/T) both implement fully interlocked I/O handshaking procedures.

2.2 The 68901 multi-function peripheral (MFP)

One of the most clearly defined trends in the manufacture of interfaces for microprocessors is the movement towards very complex peripherals that carry out complete system functions. That is, these new peripherals are able to perform some of the tasks formerly undertaken by a processor plus a first-generation unintelligent interface chip. However, in many systems the new interface chips represent a great degree of overkill and there are many occasions when a less complex interface is perfectly adequate. The 68901 multi-function peripheral (MFP) is such a device.

The MFP replaces three simple interface chips: the parallel interface, the serial interface and the timer. It is possible to design a complete single-board 68000 system around an MFP with remarkably few components. Indeed, if the 68008 with its 8-bit data bus is used instead of the 68000, the component count is even lower. Later, we reproduce a Motorola application note that demonstrates how an MFP is interfaced to a 68008 microprocessor. In this section, an overview of the 68901 is provided, together with its data manual. We have chosen to describe the MFP here because it lacks the complexity of many of today's interface chips. Equally, it demonstrates many of the features associated with its more sophisticated brothers.

There is little point in describing the MFP in great detail here, as extracts from its data manual is included at the end of this section. At the moment we are more interested in looking at the MFP as a *generic interface chip*. We begin by describing the MFP's interrupt structure which is exceptionally versatile and provides a common backbone to the MFP's three functional blocks. We must note here that the interrupt structure can be used even when the MFP is not being operated in an interrupt-driven mode! The MFP's interrupt structure allows us to decide what events may generate an interrupt. However, we can define a set of activities that cause interrupt request bits to be set by particular events but ensure that the host processor is not interrupted. In this mode we can make use of the MFP's interrupt structure while operating it in a polled mode.

2.2.1 Interrupts and the MFP

Although the MFP performs three separate functions, it has an interrupt structure common to all three functions. The MFP has an interrupt request output, IRQ*, and an IACK* input which enables it to take part in vectored interrupts. We are now going to describe how interrupts are generated by the MFP.

The registers of the MFP dedicated to interrupt control are illustrated in Table 2.5. Interestingly enough, the MFP has more registers devoted to interrupt handling than many ultra-complex interface chips. The MFP has a single composite interrupt request output and it is up to the designer or user to assign a suitable priority level to this interrupt and to connect it to the appropriate IRQ$i*$ input of a priority encoder.

TABLE 2.5   Registers of the MFP dedicated to interrupt control

ADDRESS OFFSET	RS5–RS1	MNEMONIC	NAME	RESET VALUE
07	00011	IERA	Interrupt enable register A	$00
09	00100	IERB	Interrupt enable register B	$00
0B	00101	IPRA	Interrupt pending register A	$00
0D	00110	IPRB	Interrupt pending register B	$00
0F	00111	ISRA	Interrupt in-service register A	$00
11	01000	ISRB	Interrupt in-service register B	$00
13	01001	IMRA	Interrupt mask register A	$00
15	01010	IMRB	Interrupt mask register B	$00
17	01011	VR	Interrupt vector register	$2F

The MFP is said to have 16 *interrupt channels* because there are 16 possible sources of interrupt and any one of them can assert the MFP's IRQ* output. These channels are listed in Table 2.6.

Note that the 16 interrupt channels of the MFP are prioritized from 1 (highest) to 16 (lowest), and that this order of priority is *fixed* and cannot be modified by the programmer. For example, if the MFP generates internal interrupts on its receiver error and its timer C channels simultaneously, the receiver error channel has the highest priority.

TABLE 2.6 The MFP's 16 interrupt channels and their prioritization

PRIORITY	CHANNEL NUMBER	CHANNEL NAME
1 (highest)	1111 (15)	General purpose interrupt 7
2	1110 (14)	General purpose interrupt 6
3	1101 (13)	Timer A
4	1100 (12)	Receiver buffer full
5	1011 (11)	Receiver error
6	1010 (10)	Transmitter buffer empty
7	1001 (9)	Transmit error
8	1000 (8)	Timer B
9	0111 (7)	General purpose interrupt 5
10	0110 (6)	General purpose interrupt 4
11	0101 (5)	Timer C
12	0100 (4)	Timer D
13	0011 (3)	General purpose interrupt 3
14	0010 (2)	General purpose interrupt 2
15	0001 (1)	General purpose interrupt 1
16 (lowest)	0000 (0)	General purpose interrupt 0

In many applications of the MFP, all 16 interrupt channels will not be needed, or some of the channels may have to be temporarily disabled to make way for more important activities. Of course, the 68000 can turn off or mask all interrupts from the MFP by setting its interrupt mask bits to the same level (or a higher level) as the composite interrupt request from the MFP. Fortunately, the MFP has a better method of fine tuning interrupt requests.

Interrupt channels are enabled or disabled by setting or clearing, respectively, the appropriate bits of the MFP's two *interrupt enable registers*, IERA and IERB.

The MFP has two *interrupt mask registers*, IMRA and IMRB, which, taken together, provide 16 independent mask bits. One mask bit is associated with each interrupt channel. If a bit in the interrupt mask register is set, the corresponding channel is enabled. That is, an interrupt on that channel will assert the IRQ* output (if no other higher-level channel is active). If the mask bit is clear and the interrupt channel *masked*, the IRQ* output will not be asserted. An interrupt request will set the appropriate interrupt pending bit of the *interrupt pending registers* (see later) even if that channel is masked. The difference between IERA/B and IMRA/B (i.e. interrupt *enable* and interrupt *mask* registers) is that the enable registers permit the source of an interrupt to be masked or turned-off, while the mask registers allow the interrupt to be passed on to the host CPU via the MFP's IRQ* output.

Table 2.7 relates the interrupt mask bits of IMRA and IMRB to the 16 interrupt channels. Note that the order of the bits is the *same* for the interrupt mask, the interrupt pending and the interrupt in-service registers. Suppose a programmer wishes to permit interrupts only from the timer D and general-purpose inputs 6 and 7. The interrupt enable and mask registers should be initialized as follows:

TABLE 2.7 Decoding the bits of the MFP's interrupt mask and enable registers

REGISTER	BIT	FUNCTION
IMRA	0	Timer B
IMRA	1	Transmit error
IMRA	2	Transmit buffer empty
IMRA	3	Receive error
IMRA	4	Receiver buffer full
IMRA	5	Timer A
IMRA	6	GPIP6
IMRA	7	GPIP7
IMRB	0	GPIP0
IMRB	1	GPIP1
IMRB	2	GPIP2
IMRB	3	GPIP3
IMRB	4	Timer D
IMRB	5	Timer C
IMRB	6	GPIP4
IMRB	7	GPIP5

Note: The bits of the interrupt mask and interrupt enable registers are in the same order. For example, bit 5 of IMRA masks timer A while bit 5 of IERA enables timer A.

```
MFP     EQU     ⟨MFP base address⟩
IERA    EQU     MFP + 6              Interrupt enable register A
IERB    EQU     MFP + 8              Interrupt enable register B
IMRA    EQU     MFP + $12            Interrupt mask register A
IMRB    EQU     MFP + $14            Interrupt mask register B
        MOVE.B  #%11000000,IERA     Enable channels GPIP6 and GPIP7
        MOVE.B  #%00010000,IERB     Enable timer D channel
        MOVE.B  #%11000000,IMRA     Enable GPIP6 and GPIP7 interrupts
        MOVE.B  #%00010000,IMRB     Enable timer D interrupts
```

The interrupt pending registers, IPRA and IPRB, provide the programmer with a means of identifying the source of an interrupt. When a channel generates an interrupt and the channel is enabled, the appropriate bit of the interrupt pending register is set. The bit is cleared *automatically* during an IACK cycle. It is also cleared if the interrupt channel is disabled, the processor writes a zero into it or the MFP is reset. If the MFP is designed to respond to vectored interrupts (i.e. by asserting its IACK* input) it returns the contents of its 8-bit *vector register* on D_{00}–D_{07} during the IACK cycle. The vector from the peripheral is, as we have already said, multiplied by 4 by the 68000 and the resulting value used as a pointer to the address of the actual interrupt handling routine in the interrupt vector table.

As the MFP has 16 interrupt channels, it is not entirely unreasonable that it should have 16 vector registers, one for each channel. Such a luxury is not provided by the MFP, so a compromise has to be found. Figure 2.24 illustrates the structure of the MFP's interrupt vector and its interrupt vector register, VR. The four most-significant bits of the interrupt vector, V4–V7, are supplied by the programmer by loading the vector register. The least-significant four bits, IV0–IV3, are supplied by the MFP itself and correspond to the highest priority channel generating the interrupt. For example, if the VR is loaded with the value %10100000, the GPIP0 channel generates an interrupt vector number %10100000 (lowest priority) and the GPIP7 channel generates an interrupt vector number %10101111. The MFP takes a block of 16 longwords in the 68000's exception vector table, and the 4-bit value loaded into V4–V7 provides the index into this table (when multiplied by 4).

| V7 | V6 | V5 | V4 | IV3 | IV2 | IV1 | IV0 | Interrupt vector supplied to 68000 during IACK cycle |

| V7 | V6 | V5 | V4 | S | 0 | 0 | 0 | Interrupt vector register format (loaded by programmer) |

FIGURE 2.24 The MFP vector register

Note that the interrupt vector supplied by the MPF during an IACK cycle consists of V4 to V7, previously loaded into the MFP by the host processor, plus IV0 to IV3 determined by the MFP. IV0 to IV3 reflect the value of the highest priority interrupt requesting service. When the interrupt vector is loaded by the host processor, bits 4–7 contain V4–V7, bit 3 is the S bit and bits 0–2 are unused bits. The S-bit determines whether the MFP operates in its automatic end-of-interrupt mode (S = 0), or in its software end-of-interrupt mode (S = 1).

The MFP's *interrupt in-service registers* are used to mark an interrupt channel as being serviced. A bit in one of the in-service registers is set when the associated interrupt channel passes a vector number during an IACK cycle and the S-bit of the vector register is zero. The S-bit, bit 3 of the interrupt vector register, is an in-service register enable bit. When S = 0, the MFP is in the automatic end-of-interrupt mode and the in-service register bits are forced low. When S = 1, the MFP is in the software end-of-interrupt mode and the in-service register bits are enabled. The difference between these modes is that the automatic end-of-interrupt mode forces the bits of the interrupt in-service registers, ISRA and ISRB, low after an IACK cycle, while the software end-of-interrupt mode sets the corresponding bit of ISRA or ISRB after the IACK cycle. Setting a bit in ISRA or ISRB stops interrupt sources with a lower priority requesting an interrupt. Note that the interrupt pending register tells us that a channel is waiting to be serviced and the in-service register tells us that the interrupt is currently being serviced. These two registers are not vital to the operation of either the MFP or the 68000. They provide the programmer (or operating system) with a convenient way of keeping track of interrupt activity. An interrupt in-service bit is cleared when the interrupt service has been completed for the associated interrupt channel, when the S-bit of the vector register is set, when the microprocessor writes a zero or when the MFP is reset.

Interrupt prioritization by daisy-chaining

The 68901 MFP has two special-purpose interrupt control pins, IEI* (interrupt enable in) and IEO* (interrupt enable out), that permit two or more MFPs to be connected together and to share the same level of interrupt priority as far as the 68000 is concerned.

Figure 2.25 shows how three MFPs are connected to the same interrupt level, IRQ2*, and to the same IACK* level, IACK2*. The problem posed by this circuit is what happens if two or more MFPs assert their IRQ* outputs at the same time? As all three peripherals are connected to the same IACK* line, which MFP supplies the vector during the IACK cycle?

The MFP solves this problem with the two control signals mentioned above. Whenever an MFP has asserted IRQ* and receives IACK* asserted from

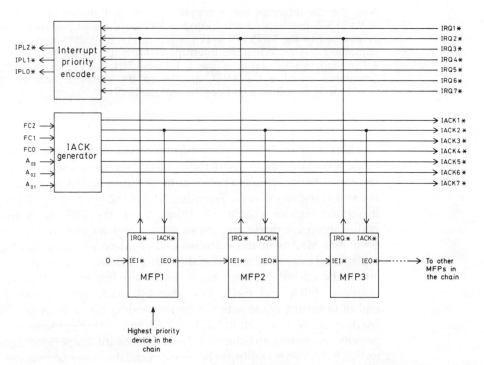

FIGURE 2.25 Connecting more than one MFP to the same interrupt level

the 68000, it checks its IEI* pin. If IEI* is low, it responds to the IACK cycle. If IEI* is high, it ignores the IACK cycle. If the MFP has *not* generated an interrupt, it passes the level at its IEI* input pin to its IEO* output pin.

Consider Figure 2.25. Suppose that MFP2 and MFP3 both assert their IRQ* outputs. When the 68000 executes an IACK cycle, all three MFPs detect it. MFP1 did not originate the interrupt request *and* its IEI* input is low. Therefore, MFP1 passes the low level on to its IEO* pin. MFP2 detects the low level at its IEI* pin and responds to the IACK cycle by providing a vector number. It does not pass a low level on to its IEO* pin which stops MFP3 from responding to the IACK cycle.

We can now see how daisy-chaining automatically prioritizes the 16 interrupt channels of each MFP. The MFP at the end of the chain with its IEI* strapped to ground has the highest priority and the MFP at the other end of the chain has the lowest priority. In the example of Figure 2.25, the 68000's level 2 IRQ* is shared by 48 interrupt channels.

The interrupt structure of the MFP demonstrates both the strength and the weakness of 'engineering on silicon'. As an MFP has 16 prioritized interrupt channels with interrupt enable, mask, pending and in-service registers, it is possible to design a relatively complex interrupt structure with no additional hardware. The sheer volume of facilities is the strength of the approach that puts everything on the chip.

However, the MFP assigns fixed priorities to its 16 interrupt channels and assigns a block of 16 contiguous vector numbers to these channels. It is not possible to, say, have a rotating priority in which the most recently served interrupt becomes the lowest priority interrupt. In this way, all channels are treated fairly. Similarly, it is not possible to assign a variable interrupt vector to each of the 16 channels. The weakness of the engineering on silicon approach is that the system may not do something that the user requires or the system may implement a facility in a suboptimal fashion.

2.2.2 The MFP's parallel port

The MFP has a simple 8-bit parallel input/output port called the GPIP (general-purpose I/O port). Here, the word *simple* means that the port is without handshaking facilities and can implement only open-loop I/O data transfers.

Three registers are associated with the GPIP: a data register, a data direction register and an active-edge register. The data direction register, DDR, determines whether the bits of the GPIP are inputs or outputs. Writing a zero to bit *i* of the DDR, makes bit *i* of the GPIP an input. Writing a one to bit *i* of the DDR makes bit *i* of the GPIP an output. After a reset, the DDR is cleared and the GPIP is configured as an input port. Note that we can define any bits of the

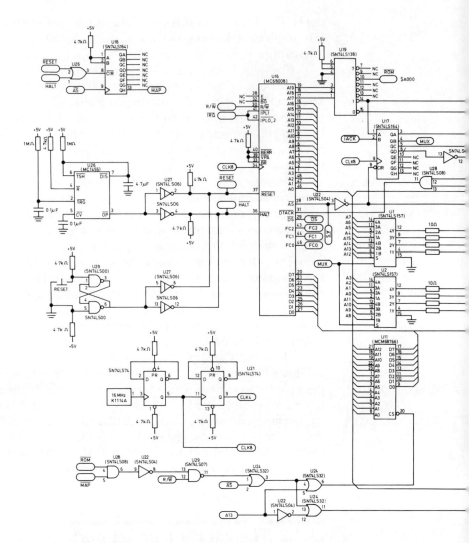

FIGURE 2.26 Using the 68901 MFP with a 68008 CPU

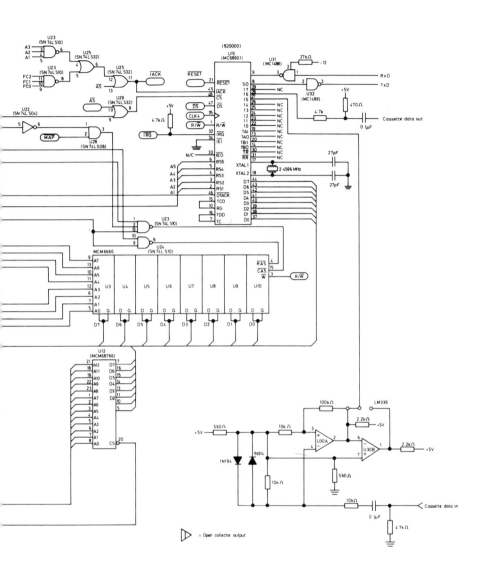

GPIP as inputs or outputs under software control and, if we wish, change them dynamically.

When data is written to the GPIP data register, only those pins defined as outputs will be affected. When the GPIP is read by the host microprocessor, data comes from the output latches of pins defined as outputs or from the pins themselves of pins defined as inputs.

The *active edge register* (AER) is used in conjunction with input bits of the GPIP. Sometimes it is important to know the point at which a signal changes level. By suitably programming the AER, we can force inputs to generate an interrupt when they change state. When bit i of the AER is zero, input i generates an interrupt on the falling edge of the input signal. When bit i of the AER is one, an interrupt is generated when input i makes a positive transition. Of course, the interrupt is detected only if the appropriate channel is enabled.

The MFP also contains four timers that can be programmed to generate periodic signals and clocks for various parts of a microprocessor system. These timers can also be used to measure elapsed time. We will not deal with them here, as Chapter 4 is devoted to real-time clocks. Similarly, the MFP contains a very basic serial interface which is not described further because Chapter 3 looks at asynchronous serial interfaces. It is suggested that readers omit the timer and serial interface parts of the MFP's data sheet until they have read Chapters 3 and 4.

2.2.3 Using the 68901 MFP – an application note

The following example of a 68901 MFP application is taken from Motorola's Application Note AN896A in which a 68901 is interfaced to a 68008 CPU. The 68008 is essentially identical to a 68000 but has an 8-bit data bus and uses A_{00} to distinguish between the upper and lower byte of a word. The only other significant difference between the 68008 and the 68000 (for our present purposes) is that the 68008 has only two interrupt request inputs (IPL1* and IPL2*). The 68008's IPL0* is connected to IPL2* *internally* to save a pin. Only A_{00} to A_{19} are available from the 68008 which therefore supports a 1 Mbyte physical address space.

The circuit diagram of Figure 2.26 provides a single-board microcomputer with a 68008 CPU, EPROM and 64 Kbytes of dynamic RAM. A simple interface to an audio cassette is included which uses the MFP's parallel interface to store and to retrieve data from a domestic cassette recorder.

Address decoding

As the addressing range of the 68008 exceeds the needs of this application, it is possible to implement a simple address decoding scheme. A 74LS138 3-to-8 demultiplexer (IC 19) divides the 68008's 1 Mbyte address map into eight 128 Kbyte segments. Three of these eight segments are assigned to RAM, the MFP and ROM respectively. RAM begins at $00000, MFP at $20000 and ROM (EPROM) at $A0000. The other five segment select control lines are available for expansion.

One problem associated with placing system ROM at any segment other than the bottom of memory is that the 68008 looks at location $00000 for its reset vector. It is, however, impractical to place ROM at the bottom of the memory map because this would prohibit dynamic interrupt vector programming. This can be resolved by mapping the ROM to the lower portion of memory at reset. In this application, a 74LS164 shift register (IC 18) is used to force selection of ROM for the first eight memory cycles after reset to allow the processor to fetch the reset vector and supervisor stack pointer from ROM. When Q_H of the 74LS164 shift register is low, selection of ROM is automatic and selection of RAM is inhibited. Once Q_H goes high, selection proceeds in a normal fashion. IC18 is reset whenever HALT* and RESET* are both active (the system reset condition). Once RESET* or HALT* become inactive, a logic one is shifted into IC 18 by the rising edge of AS*. After eight memory cycles, Q_H goes high and ROM returns to its normal location in the memory map.

RAM control

A second 74LS164 (IC 17) generates the RAS*, CAS*, MUX and DTACK* signals. The RAS*, CAS* and MUX signals control the dynamic RAM, and DTACK* is applied to the CPU to complete memory accesses to the RAM and ROM. Shift register IC 17 is inhibited from shifting by IACK cycles and by memory cycles to the 68901. For all other memory cycles, the shift register is allowed to shift and generate DTACK*. Note that DTACK* is automatically generated for all areas of memory other than that assigned to the 68901 and that only one DTACK* time is generated (500 ns after AS*). System performance could be improved by optimizing dynamic RAM sequencing and DTACK* generation. RAS* is generated for all memory cycles but CAS* is enabled by selection of RAM. By generating RAS* for all memory cycles, it is possible to refresh RAM by executing instructions out of ROM (software refresh). Address multiplexing for the dynamic RAM is accomplished with two 74LS157 two-input multiplexers (IC 1 and IC 2).

The 68008 to 68901 interface

Interfacing the 68901 is fairly simple. RESET*, DS*, R/W* and D_{00}–D_{07} on the 68901 connect directly to the corresponding pins on the 68008. RS1–RS5 on the 68901 connect to the A_{01}–A_{05} pins on the 68008. Chip_select (CS*) is generated by qualifying the memory segment signal from IC 19 with AS*. DTACK* is gated with the Q_D output from IC 17 and passed to the 68008. The preceding signals are the only ones that are required for interfacing the CPU with the MFP.

This application uses the interrupt capability of the 68901. The IRQ* line of the 68901 is connected directly to both of the 68008 IPL* pins, which corresponds to a level 7 interrupt (a non-maskable interrupt, NMI). It is imperative that the IRQ* interrupt be of the highest priority because this application uses the 68901 to time dynamic refresh intervals. If the interrupt capabilities of the 68901 are to be more fully exploited, it is important that no interrupt level be implemented that is higher than one used for software refresh. The user must never disable or mask the refresh interrupt as this will result in the loss of data. IACK* for the 68901 is generated when the three function codes (FC0–FC2) and A_{03}, A_{02} and A_{01} are all high.

For the purpose of baud-rate generation, a 2.4576 MHz crystal is connected to the 68901. Timer C (TCO) is externally connected to the receiver clock (RC) and timer D (TDO) is externally connected to the transmitter clock (TC). Although the software included with this application assumes that the receiver and transmitter clocks operate at the same frequency, the MFP allows for separate clocks.

Reset and timing

The 68008 requires that an external reset must be applied for at least 100 ms to allow stabilization of the on-chip circuitry and system clock. In this application, system reset is caused at power-up by a 1455 timer circuit output or it can be generated via a debounced switch. The outputs of the timer and the switch are buffered by open-collector drivers (IC 27) the outputs of which are connected to HALT* and RESET*.

System timing is provided by a 16 MHz oscillator (IC 20) which is divided by the two flip-flops of IC 21 to provide 8 MHz (CLK8) and 4 MHz (CLK4) on-chip clocks. The 4 MHz clock is used only by the 68901 which does not require that its clock be of the same frequency or phase as the system clock.

Cassette interface

Two general-purpose I/O lines of the 68901 (I5 and I6) are used for the cassette interface. Data is transmitted and received as square waves and the length of a single cycle of the square wave determines whether a '1' or a '0' is being transferred.

Data for the cassette interface is output at pin I6 of the MFP. This output drives a resistor network that divides the voltage by approximately 10. The cassette data output line is then connected to the microphone input of a cassette recorder.

Data to be received from the cassette tape player is shaped in a comparator, IC 30A. Two IN914 diodes limit the voltage swing to the input of the comparator. The second comparator (IC 30B) is used to invert the output of IC 30A. Inversion may or may not be needed depending on whether or not the cassette plays back an inverted signal. The software in this application note assumes that the signal is not inverted. Comparator IC 30A provides one level of inversion so if the cassette tape player does not provide a level of inversion then a second one must be provided by IC 30B. The output of comparator IC 30A is connected to I5 of the MFP (unless IC 30B is needed).

Software

There are six basic software routines listed in Listing 2.1: 68901 initialization; software dynamic RAM refresh; transmit character to and receive character from the serial port; transmit character to and receive character from cassette tape. This software represents the basic core of hardware dependent routines necessary for this system.

68901 initialization

Initialization of the 68901 consists of starting the serial communication clocks, loading the USART control register and enabling the refresh clock interrupt. Timers C and D are used for serial receiver and transmitter clocks. In this application both timers are programmed for 9600 bits/s operation. The 2.4576 MHz reference clock is divided by 16 by loading $02 into both data registers C and D and by starting timers C and D in the divide-by-4 mode. The USART control register is initialized to operate in the divide-by-16 mode $(2.4576 \text{ MHz}/(16 \times 16) = 9600 \text{ bits/s})$. In addition, the proper serial communications protocol must be loaded into the USART control register. In this case the USART is programmed for asynchronous communication with one start bit, 1.5 stop bits and odd parity.

To facilitate software refresh of dynamic RAM, the 68901 interrupt vector is initialized and the timer B interrupt enable and mask bits are set. The timer B output serves as the refresh clock.

Software refresh

Software refresh consists of accessing 128 consecutive memory locations at regularly timed intervals, and is accomplished by executing 64 no-operation (NOP) instructions of which each requires two memory fetches. The software refresh program is written as a subroutine that may be called at any time to force a refresh. The refresh subroutine resets timer B (the refresh clock) and executes 64 NOP instructions. Timer B is programmed to generate interrupts every 2 ms. The interrupt routine consists simply of a call to the refresh subroutine. One of the main concerns with software refresh is that programs that have critical timing loops (for example the cassette tape interface routines) could be interrupted for refresh if care were not taken. To avoid problems, the refresh routine is written so that an interrupt may be forced before a critical timing loop. The user may then be certain that an interrupt will not occur for at least 1.8 ms. A call to the refresh subroutine should be included in any reset routine in order to preclude loss of data.

Serial I/O

Both the receive and transmit routines check for a break by reading a bit in the receiver status register. If a break is received at any time during serial communications then a jump to a break character handler routine is made. The exact nature of this subroutine is undefined in this note but it could consist of transmitting a message and then returning to the user's monitor. The transmit routine also checks for a control-W character and halts if one is received. Transmission is then resumed if any character is received. For serial communications, the divide-by-16 mode (a USART control bit) should be used since it results in increased noise rejection. To operate the USART in the divide-by-1 mode the receiver clock must be synchronized externally to the received data.

Cassette tape interface software

Data is transmitted to the cassette through GPIP6 (bit 6 of the general-purpose I/O control register) and received through GPIP5 (bit 5 of the general-purpose I/O port control register). Data is recorded as a sequence of single-cycle square waves with a $500 \mu s$ period representing a logic 1 and a 1 ms period representing a logic 0. Before any critical timing loop is executed, in either the transmit or receive routine, a branch to the refresh software is made in order to guarantee that the timing loop will not be interrupted. Timer A of the 68901 is used for period measurement in both routines. The transmit routine transmits a single byte with the most significant bit first. It is assumed that the first byte of any data stream to be transmitted will be a synchronizing character. The receive routine measures the period length of all incoming square waves in order to generate a bit stream. A simple synchronization routine is included in the program which scans the bit stream for an S. After synchronization data, bytes are assembled from each successive 8-bit block.

Summary

In this chapter we have introduced some of the fundamental concepts related to typical interface chips for microprocessors. In particular we have looked at some of the schemes for accessing the internal registers of an interface chip, and the timing problems likely to arise when interfacing a brand X peripheral to a brand Y microprocessor. We have described the 68901 multifunction peripheral that performs three important interface functions in a simple microcomputer. In later chapters we will be looking at some rather more complex components that carry out a wide range of interface duties. We have concluded our introduction to peripherals with an example of the hardware and software required to implement a single-board microcomputer of the type widely used to teach the basic principles of microprocessors and their interfaces.

LISTING 2.1 Software to control the 68008–68901 SBC

```
MOTOROLA M68000 ASM VERSION 1.30MFPS     .SA 08/23/84 09:25:40     PAGE   1

  3
  4           *
  5           *  68901 I/O ROUTINES INCLUDING:
  6           *  TRANSMIT CHARACTER THROUGH SERIAL PORT,
  7           *  RECEIVE CHARACTER FROM SERIAL PORT,
  8           *  TRANSMIT CHARACTER TO TAPE,
  9           *  RECEIVE CHARACTER FROM TAPE,
 10           *  AND SOFTWARE REFRESH FOR RAM.
 11           *
 12
 13 00001000          ORG    $1000
 14 00020000   BASE   EQU    $20000      MFP BASE ADDRESS
 15 00020001   GPIP   EQU    BASE+$01    GENERAL PURPOSE I/O
 16 00020003   AFR    EQU    BASE+$03    ACTIVE EDGE
 17 00020005   DDR    EQU    BASE+$05    DATA DIRECTION
 18 00020007   IERA   EQU    BASE+$07    INTERRUPT ENABLE A
 19 0002000B   IPRA   EQU    BASE+$0B    INTERRUPT PENDING A
 20 00020013   IMRA   EQU    BASE+$13    INTERRUPT MASK A
 21 00020017   VR     EQU    BASE+$17    VECTOR
 22 00020019   TACR   EQU    BASE+$19    TIMER A CONTROL
 23 0002001B   TBCR   EQU    BASE+$1B    TIMER B CONTROL
 24 0002001D   TCDCR  EQU    BASE+$1D    TIMER C/D CONTROL
 25 0002001F   TADR   EQU    BASE+$1F    TIMER A DATA
 26 00020021   TBDR   EQU    BASE+$21    TIMER B DATA
 27 00020023   TCDR   EQU    BASE+$23    TIMER C DATA
 28 00020025   TDDR   EQU    BASE+$25    TIMER D DATA
 29 00020029   UCR    EQU    BASE+$29    USART CONTROL
 30 0002002B   RSR    EQU    BASE+$2B    RECEIVER STATUS
 31 0002002D   TSR    EQU    BASE+$2D    TRANSMITTER STATUS
 32 0002002F   UDR    EQU    BASE+$2F    USART DATA
 33 00000017   CTLW   EQU    $17
 34
 35           *  INITIALIZE 68901
 36           *  START TRANSMITTER AND RECEIVER CLOCKS
 37           *  FOR 9600 BAUD COMMUNICATION
 38           *  LOAD USART CONTROL REGISTER
 39           *  INITIALIZE REFRESH INTERRUPT VECTOR
 40           *
 41
 42 00001000 13FC00020002  INIT  MOVE.B  #$02,TCDR   1/4 TRANSMITTER CLOCK
           0023
 43 00001008 13FC00020002        MOVE.B  #$02,TDDR   1/4 RECEIVER CLOCK
           0025
 44 00001010 13FC00110002        MOVE.B  #$11,TCDCR  DIVIDE BY 4
           001D
 45 00001018 13FC00940002        MOVE.B  #$94,UCR    ODD PARITY,1 1/2 STOP,
           0029                                      1 START, ASYNC, 8 BITS
 46
 47           *                                      1/16 FOR 9600 BAUD
 48 00001020 13FC00010002        MOVE.B  #$01,RSR    START RECEIVER CLOCK
           002B
 49 00001028 13FC00050002        MOVE.B  #$05,TSR    START TRANSMITTER CLOCK
           002D
```

```
MOTOROLA M68000 ASM VERSION 1.30MFPS     .SA 08/23/84 09:25:40     PAGE   2

 51
 52           *    INITIALIZE REFRESH INTERRUPT
 53           *
 54 00001030 13FC0C000002      MOVE.B  #$C0,VR     LOAD MFP VECTOR REG
           0017
 55 00001038 21FC000010E8      MOVE.L  #RFR2,$320  LOAD INT VECTOR
           0320
 56 00001040 08F900000002      BSET.B  #0,IERA     ENABLE TIMER B INT
           0007
 57 00001048 08F900000002      BSET.B  #0,IMRA     SET MASK BIT
           0013
 58           *
 59           *    REFRESH SUBROUTINE TO ALLOW SOFTWARE
 60           *    TO FORCE AN EARLY REFRESH
 61           *
 62 00001050 42390002001B  REFRESH  CLR.B  TBCR      STOP TIMER B
 63 00001056 13FC00310002           MOVE.B  #$49,TBDR  LOAD TIMER B DATA REG
           0021
 64 0000105E 13FC00060002           MOVE.B  #$6,TBCR   START TIMER B 1/100
           001B
 65 00001066 00004671      NOP  EQU  $4671
 66 0000106A 0000E671      RF1  DCB.W  64,NOP     64 NOPs
 67 0000106E 4E75          RF2  RTS
 68 000010E6 6100FF7C           BSR  RF1
 69 000010EC 4E73               RTE        INTERRUPT HANDLER
 70                                         FOR REFRESH
```

LISTING 2.1 *(continued)*

```
MOTOROLA M68000 ASM VERSION 1.30MFPS     .SA 08/23/84 09:25:40     PAGE 3

 72            *
 73            *          INPUT CHARACTER FROM SERIAL PORT INTO D0
 74            *
 75 000010E6 0839000030002 INCHNE BTST.B #3,RSR       (INCH NO ECHO)
        0028
 76 000010F6 6654            BNE.S  BREAK             CHECK FOR BREAK
 77 000010F8 0839000070002   BTST.B #7,RSR            GO PROCESS IT
 78                                                   CHECK FOR CHARACTER
 79 00001102 67EC            BEQ.S  INCHNE            IF NOT READY
 80 00001102 103900002002F   MOVE.B UDR,D0            READ DATA SIDE
 81 00001108 4E75            RTS
 82            *
 83            *          SEND CHARACTER IN D0.8 TO SERIAL PORT
 84            *
 84 0000110A 6134     OUTCH  BSR.S  CHKBRK            CHECK FOR BREAK
 85 0000110C 0839000070002   BTST.B #7,TSR            BUFFER EMPTY?
        002D
 86 00001114 67F4            BEQ.S  OUTCH             STILL NOT READY
 88 00001116 13C000002002F   MOVE.B D0,UDR            SEND CHARACTER
 89            *
 90            *          CHECK FOR CONTROL W
 91            *
 92 0000111C 0839000070002 CTLWH  BTST.B #7,RSR       READ STATUS
 93 00001124 6718            BEQ.S  CTLW9             CHAR NOT READY
 94 00001126 123900002002F   MOVE.B UDR,D1            READ CHARACTER
 95 0000112C 0C010017        CMP.B  #CTLW,D1          NOT CNTL/W
 96 00001130 660C            BNE.S  CTLW9             CHECK FOR BREAK
 97 00001132 610C            BSR.S  CHKBRK            READ STATUS
 98 00001134 0839000070002   BTST.B #7,RSR
        002D
 99 0000113C 6774     CTLWH  BEQ    CTLWH             WAIT FOR ANY CHAR
100                                                   TO CONTINUE
101 0000113E 4E75     CTLW9  RTS
102            *
103            *          CHECK FOR BREAK ON SERIAL PORT
104            *
105 00001140 0839000030002 CHKBRK BTST.B #3,RSR       READ STATUS
        0028
106 00001148 6692            BNE.S  BREAK
107 0000114A 4E75            RTS
108            *
109            *          WHAT TO DO WHEN THE BREAK IS PRESSED
110            *
111            *
112 0000114C 0839000070002 BREAK  BTST.B #7,TSR       CHECK "TRANSMIT READY"
        002D
113 00001154 6776            BEQ.S  BREAK             WAIT FOR READY
114 00001156 103900002002F   MOVE.B UDR,D0            READ CHARACTER
115 0000115C 0839000030002   BTST.B #3,RSR            BREAK BUTTON RELEASED?
        0028
116 00001164 66E6            BNE    BREAK             NO... KEEP LOOPING
117            *
118            *          USER SHOULD INSERT BREAK HANDLER HERE
119            *
120 00001166 4E75            RTS
```

```
MOTOROLA M68000 ASM VERSION 1.30MFPS     .SA 08/23/84 09:25:40     PAGE 4

122            *
123            *          TRANSMIT CHARACTER IN D2 TO TAPE
124            *
125            *          A LOGIC '0' IS RECORDED AS ONE SQUARE WAVE
126            *          PERIOD OF 1 MILLISECOND DURATION. A LOGIC
127            *          '1' IS RECORDED AS ONE SQUARE WAVE PERIOD
128            *          OF 500 MICROSECOND DURATION
129            *
130 00001168 08F900060002 TAPE0  BSET.B #6,DDR        SET GPIP6 AS OUTPUT
        0005
131 00001170 08F900050002        BSET.B #5,IERA       ENABLE TIMER A INTERRUPT
        0007
132 00001178 103C0001        MOVE.L #1,D0             STOP BIT INTO D0
134 0000117E 6100FE00 TAPE01 BOL.B  #1,D2             DATA BIT INTO D2
135 00001182 61C             BSR.S  TTST              FORCE REFRESH
136 00001184 13FC00000002    MOVE.B #$00,TACR         HALT TIMER A
        0019
137 0000118C 123C000A        MOVE.B #10,D1            TIMER COUNT FOR 1
138            *
139            *
140 00001190 08020000        BTST.L #0,D2             SENDING 1?
141 00001196 6606            BNE.S  TAPE02            YES
142 00001196 0681000000A     ADDI.L #10,D1            NO. TIMER COUNT FOR 0
143 0000119C 13FC0002001F    MOVE.B D1,TACR           SET TIMER PRELOAD
        0001                                          SEND 1 TO TAPE
144 000011AA 13FC00060002 TAPE02 BSET.B #6,GPIP       START TIMER A 1/64
        0001
145 000011B2 611C            BSR.S  TTST              WAIT UNTIL PULSE DONE
146 000011B4 42390020019     CLR.B  TACR              HALT TIMER
147 000011BA 08990060002     BCLR.B #6,GPIP           SEND 0 TO TAPE
        0001
148 000011C2 13FC00050002    MOVE.B #$05,TACR         START TIMER A 1/64
        0019
149 000011CA E300            ASL.B  #1,D0             SENT 8 BITS?
150 000011CC 64AE            BNE    TAPE01            NO. CONTINUE
151 000011CE 4E75            RTS
152            *
153            *
154            *          TIMER TEST
155 000011D0 0C3900020002 TTST   CMP.B  #$0,TACR      TIMER RUNNING?
        0019
156 000011D8 6712            BEQ.S  TTST1             NO. RETURN
157 000011DA 08390005002     BTST.B #5,IPRA           TIME DELAY ELAPSED?
        000B
158 000011E2 67EC            BEQ.S  TTST              NO. WAIT
159 000011E4 08B90005002     BCLR.B #5,IPRA           CLEAR INTERRUPT
        000B
160 000011EC 4E75     TTST1  RTS
```

LISTING 2.1 (*continued*)

```
MOTOROLA M68000 ASM VERSION 1.30MFPS      .SA 08/23/84 09:25:40      PAGE 5

162
163
164                           *          RECEIVE CHARACTER FROM TAPE INTO D0-B
165                           *
166  000011EE 423900020019 TAPEIN CLR.B  TACR       STOP TIMER A
167  000011F4 4201                CLR.B  D1         CLEAR D1 FOR DATA
168  000011F6 083900050002 T10    BTST.B #5,GPIP    WAIT FOR LOW
         0006
169  000011FE 66F6                BNE.S  T10
170  00001200 083900050002 T20    BTST.B #5,GPIP    WAIT FOR HIGH
         0001
     00001208 67F6                BEQ    T20
171                           *
172                           *    SYNCHRONIZE ON S CHARACTER
173                           *
174                           *    THIS ROUTINE LOOKS FOR AN ASCII 'S'
175                           *    TO SYNCHRONIZE THE TAPE DATA
176                           *
177  0000120A E301         TS     ASL.B  #1,D1      GET BIT FROM TAPE
178  0000120C 6114                BSR.S  T30
179  0000120E 0C010053            CMP.B  #'S',D1    S?
180  00001212 66F6                BNE.S  TS         NO, CONTINUE
181  00001214 1CC1                MOVE.B D1,(A6)+
182                           *
183                           *    GET CHARACTER FROM TAPE
184                           *
185  00001216 7202         GC     MOVEQ  #2,D1      SET STOP BIT
186  00001218 6108                BSR.S  T30        GET BIT FROM TAPE
187  0000121A E308         GC10   ASL.B  #1,D1      STOP IN CARRY?
188  0000121C 64FA                BCC.S  GC10       NO
189  0000121E 6102                BSR.S  T30        GET LAST BIT
190  00001220 4E75                RTS
191
192  00001222 13FC003B0002 T30    MOVE.B #3B,TADR   LOAD TIMER PRELOAD
         001F
193  0000122A 13FC00050002        MOVE.B #5,TACR    START TIMER IN
         0019
194                           *
195  00001232 6100FE1C            BSR    REFRESH    DIVIDE BY 64 MODE
                                                    FORCE REFRESH
196  00001236 083900050002 T40    BTST.B #5,GPIP    WAIT FOR LOW
         0001
197  0000123E 66F6                BNE.S  T40
198  00001240 083900050002 T50    BTST.B #5,GPIP    WAIT FOR HIGH
         0001
199  00001248 67F6                BEQ.S  T50
200  0000124A 423900020019        CLR.B  TACR       STOP TIMER
201
202  00001250 16390002001F        MOVE.B TADR,D3    STORE MEASUREMENT
203  00001256 0C03001F            CMPI.B #1F,D3     LOGIC 17
204  0000125A 4902                BLT.S  T60        NO
205  0000125C 5201                ADDQ.B #1,D1      STORE 1
206  0000125E 4E75         T60    RTS
```

```
MOTOROLA M68000 ASM VERSION 1.30MFPS      .SA 08/23/84 09:25:40      PAGE 6

SYMBOL TABLE LISTING
```

SYMBOL NAME	SECT	VALUE	SYMBOL NAME	SECT	VALUE
AER		00020003	T20		00001200
BASE		00020000	T30		00001222
BREAK		0001114C	T40		00001236
CHKBRK		00001140	T50		00001240
CTLW		00000017	T60		0000125E
CTLW9		0001113E	TACR		00020019
CTLWH		00011132	TADR		0002001F
DDR		00011205	TAPEO		0001117C
GC10		00011216	TAPEO1		000111C8
GPIP		00011218	TAPEO2		000111EE
IERA		00020001	TAPEIN		000111EE
IMRA		00020013	TBCR		0002001B
INCHNE		0001100E	TBDR		00020021
INIT		00001000	TCDCR		0002001D
IPRA		0002000B	TCDR		00020023
NOP		00004E71	TDDR		00020025
OUTCH		0001105D	TS		0000120A
REFRESH		00011066	TSR		0002002D
RF1		00011050	TTST		000111DD
RFR2		0001106A	TTST1		000111EC
RSR		00011028	UCR		0002002F
T10		000111F6	UDR		00020017
			VR		00020017

Appendix: The 68901 MFP Data Sheet

SECTION 1
INTRODUCTION

The MC68901 multi-function peripheral (MFP) is a member of the M68000 Family of peripherals. The MFP directly interfaces to the MC68000 processor via an asynchronous bus structure. Both vectored and polled interrupt schemes are supported, with the MFP providing unique vector number generation for each of its 16 interrupt sources. Additionally, handshake lines are provided to facilitate DMAC interfacing. Refer to Figure 1-1 for a block diagram of the MC68901.

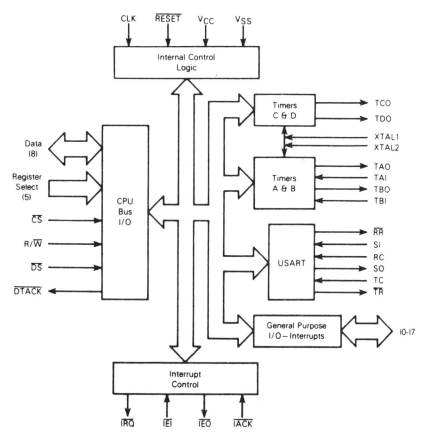

Figure 1-1. MFP Block Diagram

The MC68901 performs many of the functions common to most microprocessor-based systems. The resources available to the user include:

- Eight Individually Programmable I/O Pins with Interrupt Capability
- 16-Source Interrupt Controller with Individual Source Enabling and Masking
- Four Timers, Two of which are Multi-Mode Timers
- Timers May Be Used as Baud Rate Generators for the Serial Channel
- Single-Channel Full-Duplex Universal Synchronous/Asynchronous Receiver-Transmitter (USART) that Supports Asynchronous and with the Addition of a Polynomial Generator Checker Supports Byte Synchronous Formats

By incorporating multiple functions within the MFP, the system designer retains flexibility while minimizing device count.

From a programmer's point of view, the versatility of the MFP may be attributed to its register set. The registers are well organized and allow the MFP to be easily tailored to a variety of applications. All of the 24 registers are also directly addressable which simplifies programming. The register map is shown in Table 1-1.

Table 1-1. MFP Register Map

Address						Abbreviation	Register Name
	Binary						
Hex	RS5	RS4	RS3	RS2	RS1		
01	0	0	0	0	0	GPIP	General Purpose I/O Register
03	0	0	0	0	1	AER	Active Edge Register
05	0	0	0	1	0	DDR	Data Direction Register
07	0	0	0	1	1	IERA	Interrupt Enable Register A
09	0	0	1	0	0	IERB	Interrupt Enable Register B
0B	0	0	1	0	1	IPRA	Interrupt Pending Register A
0D	0	0	1	1	0	IPRB	Interrupt Pending Register B
0F	0	0	1	1	1	ISRA	Interrupt In-Service Register A
11	0	1	0	0	0	ISRB	Interrupt In-Service Register B
13	0	1	0	0	1	IMRA	Interrupt Mask Register A
15	0	1	0	1	0	IMRB	Interrupt Mask Register B
17	0	1	0	1	1	VR	Vector Register
19	0	1	1	0	0	TACR	Timer A Control Register
1B	0	1	1	0	1	TBCR	Timer B Control Register
1D	0	1	1	1	0	TCDCR	Timers C and D Control Register
1F	0	1	1	1	1	TADR	Timer A Data Register
21	1	0	0	0	0	TBDR	Timer B Data Register
23	1	0	0	0	1	TCDR	Timer C Data Register
25	1	0	0	1	0	TDDR	Timer D Data Register
27	1	0	0	1	1	SCR	Synchronous Character Register
29	1	0	1	0	0	UCR	USART Control Register
2B	1	0	1	0	1	RSR	Receiver Status Register
2D	1	0	1	1	0	TSR	Transmitter Status Register
2F	1	0	1	1	1	UDR	USART Data Register

NOTE: Hex addresses assume that RS1 connects with A1, RS2 connects with A2, etc. and that DS is connected to LDS on the MC68000 or DS is connected to DS on the MC68008.

SECTION 2
SIGNAL AND BUS OPERATION DESCRIPTION

This section contains a brief description of the input and output signals. A discussion of bus operation during the various operations is also presented.

NOTE

The terms **assertion** and **negation** will be used extensively. This is done to avoid confusion when dealing with a mixture of "active low" and "active high" signals. The term assert or assertion is used to indicate that a signal is active or true, independent of whether that level is represented by a high or low voltage. The term negate or negation is used to indicate that a signal is inactive or false.

2.1 SIGNAL DESCRIPTION

The input and output signals can be functionally organized into the groups shown in Figure 2-1. The following paragraphs provide a brief description of the signal and a reference (if applicable) to other sections that contain more detail about its function.

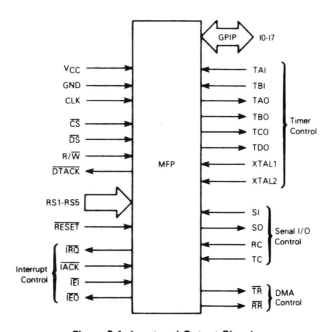

Figure 2-1. Input and Output Signals

2.1.1 V$_{CC}$ and GND

These inputs supply power to the MFP. The V$_{CC}$ is power at +5 volts and GND is the ground connection.

2.1.2 Clock (CLK)

The clock input is a single–phase TTL-compatible signal used for internal timing. This input should not be gated off at any time and must conform to minimum and maximum pulse width times. The clock is not necessarily the system clock in frequency nor phase.

2.1.3 Asynchronous Bus Control

Asynchronous data transfers are controlled by chip select, data strobe, read/write, and data transfer acknowledge. The low order register select lines, RS1-RS5, select an internal MFP register for a read or write operation. The reset line initializes the MFP registers and the internal control signals.

2.1.3.1 CHIP SELECT ($\overline{\text{CS}}$). This input activates the MFP for internal register access.

2.1.3.2 DATA STROBE ($\overline{\text{DS}}$). This input is part of the internal chip select and interrupt acknowledge functions. The MFP must be located on the lower portion of the 16-bit data bus so that the vector number passed to the processor during an interrupt acknowledge cycle will be located in the low byte of the data word. As a result, $\overline{\text{DS}}$ must be connected to the processor's lower data strobe if vectored interrupts are to be used. Note that this forces all registers to be located at odd addresses and latches data on the rising edge for writes.

2.1.3.3 READ/WRITE (R/$\overline{\text{W}}$). This input defines a data transfer as a read (high) or a write (low) cycle.

2.1.3.4 DATA TRANSFER ACKNOWLEDGE ($\overline{\text{DTACK}}$). This output signals the completion of the operation phase of a bus cycle to the processor. If the bus cycle is a processor read, the MFP asserts $\overline{\text{DTACK}}$ to indicate that the information on the data bus is valid. If the bus cycle is a processor to the MFP, $\overline{\text{DTACK}}$ acknowledges the acceptance of the data by the MFP. $\overline{\text{DTACK}}$ will be asserted only by an MFP that has $\overline{\text{CS}}$ or $\overline{\text{IACK}}$ (and $\overline{\text{IEI}}$) asserted.

2.1.3.5 REGISTER SELECT BUS (RS1 THROUGH RS5). The lower five bits of the register select bus select an internal MFP register during a read or write operation.

2.1.3.6 DATA BUS (D0 THROUGH D7). This bidirectional bus is used to receive data from or transmit data to the MFP's internal registers during a processor read or write cycle. During an interrupt acknowledge cycle, the data bus is used to pass a vector number to the processor. Since the MFP is an 8-bit peripheral, the MFP could be located on either the upper or lower portion of the 16-bit data bus (even or odd address). However, during an interrupt acknowledge cycle, the vector number passed to the processor must be located in the low byte of the data word. As a result, D0-D7 of the MFP must be connected to the low order eight bits of the processor data bus, placing MFP registers at odd addresses if vectored interrupts are to be used.

2.1.3.7 RESET ($\overline{\text{RESET}}$). This input will initialize the MFP during power up or in response to a total system reset. Refer to **2.2.3 Reset Operation** for further information.

2.1.4 Interrupt Control

The interrupt request and interrupt acknowledge signals are handshake lines for a vectored interrupt scheme. Interrupt enable in and the interrupt enable out implement a daisy-chained interrupt structure.

2.1.4.1 INTERRUPT REQUEST ($\overline{\text{IRQ}}$). This output signals the processor that an interrupt is pending from the MFP. There are 16 interrupt channels that can generate an interrupt request. Clearing the interrupt pending registers (IPRA and IPRB) or clearing the interrupt mask registers (IMRA and IMRB) will cause $\overline{\text{IRQ}}$ to be negated. $\overline{\text{IRQ}}$ will also be negated as the result of an interrupt acknowledge cycle, unless additional interrupts are pending in the MFP. Refer to **SECTION 3 INTERRUPT STRUCTURE** for further information.

2.1.4.2 INTERRUPT ACKNOWLEDGE ($\overline{\text{IACK}}$). If both $\overline{\text{IRQ}}$ and $\overline{\text{IEI}}$ are active, the MFP will begin an interrupt acknowledge cycle when $\overline{\text{IACK}}$ and $\overline{\text{DS}}$ are asserted. The MFP will supply a unique vector number to the processor which corresponds to the interrupt handler for the particular channel requiring interrupt service. In a daisy-chained interrupt structure, all devices in the chain must have a common $\overline{\text{IACK}}$. Refer to **2.2.2 Interrupt Acknowledge Operation** and **3.1.2 Interrupt Vector Number Format** for additional information.

2.1.4.3 INTERRUPT ENABLE IN ($\overline{\text{IEI}}$). This input, together with the $\overline{\text{IEO}}$ signal, provides a daisy-chained interrupt structure for a vectored interrupt scheme. $\overline{\text{IEI}}$ indicates that no higher priority device is requesting interrupt service. So, the highest priority device in the chain should have its $\overline{\text{IEI}}$ pin tied low. During an interrupt acknowledge cycle, an MFP with a pending interrupt is not allowed to pass a vector number to the processor until its $\overline{\text{IEI}}$ pin is asserted. When the daisy-chain option is not implemented, all MFPs should have their $\overline{\text{IEI}}$ pin tied low. Refer to **3.2 DAISY-CHAINING MFPs** for additional information.

2.1.4.4 INTERRUPT ENABLE OUT ($\overline{\text{IEO}}$). This output, together with the $\overline{\text{IEI}}$ signal, provides a daisy-chained interrupt structure for a vectored interrupt scheme. The $\overline{\text{IEO}}$ of a particular MFP signals lower priority devices that neither the MFP nor any other higher-priority device is requesting interrupt service. When a daisy-chain is implemented, $\overline{\text{IEO}}$ is tied to the next lower priority device's $\overline{\text{IEI}}$ input. The lowest priority device's $\overline{\text{IEO}}$ is not connected. When the daisy-chain option is not implemented, $\overline{\text{IEO}}$ is not connected. Refer to **3.2 DAISY-CHAINING MFPs** for additional information.

2.1.5 General Purpose I/O Interrupt Lines (I0 Through I7)

This is an 8-bit pin-programmable I/O port with interrupt capability. The data direction register (DDR) individually defines each line as either a high-impedance input or a TTL-compatible output. As an input, each line can generate an interrupt on the user selected transition of the input signal. Refer to **SECTION 4 GENERAL PURPOSE I/O INTERRUPT PORT** for further information.

2.1.6 Timer Control

These lines provide internal timing and auxiliary timer control inputs required for certain operating modes. Additionally, the timer outputs are included in this group.

2.1.6.1 TIMER CLOCK (XTAL1 AND XTAL2). This input provides the timing signal for the four timers. A crystal can be connected between the timer clock inputs, XTAL1 and XTAL2, or XTAL1 can be driven with a TTL-level clock while XTAL2 is not connected. The following crystal parameters are suggested:

a) Parallel resonance, fundamental mode AT-cut, ·HC6 or HC33 holder
b) Frequency tolerance measured with 18 picofarads load (0.1% accuracy) — drive level 10 microwatts
c) Shunt capacitance equals 7 picofarads maximum
d) Series resistance:
$2.0 < f < 2.7$ MHz; $R_S \leq 300\ \Omega$
$2.8 < f < 4.0$ MHz; $R_S \leq 150\ \Omega$

2.1.6.2 TIMER INPUTS (TAI AND TBI). These inputs are control signals for timers A and B in the pulse width measurement mode and event count mode. These signals generate interrupts at the same priority level as the general purpose I/O interrupt lines I4 and I3, respectively. While I4 and I3 do not have interrupt capability when the timers are operated in the pulse width measurement mode or the event count mode, I4 and I3 may still be used for I/O. Refer to **5.1.2 Pulse Width Mode Operation** and **5.1.3 Event Count Mode Operation** for further information.

2.1.6.3 TIMER OUTPUTS (TAO, TBO, TCO, AND TDO). Each timer has an associated output which toggles when its main counter counts through 01 (hexadecimal), regardless of which operational mode is selected. When in the delay mode, the timer output will be a square wave with a period equal to two timer cycles. This output signal may be used to supply the universal synchronous/asynchronous receiver-transmitter (USART) baud rate clocks. Timer outputs TAO and TBO may be cleared at any time by writing a one to the reset location in timer control registers A and B. Also, a device reset forces all timer outputs low. Refer to **5.2.2 Timer Control Registers** for additional information.

2.1.7 Serial I/O Control

The full duplex serial channel is implemented by a serial input and output line. The independent receive and transmit sections may be clocked by separate timing signals on the receiver clock input and the transmitter clock input.

2.1.7.1 SERIAL INPUT (SI). This input line is the USART receiver data input. This input is not used in the USART loopback mode. Refer to **6.3.2 Transmitter Status Register** for additional information.

2.1.7.2 SERIAL OUTPUT (SO). This output line is the USART transmitter data output. This output is driven high during a device reset.

2.1.7.3 RECEIVER CLOCK (RC). This input controls the serial bit rate of the receiver. This signal may be supplied by the timer output lines or by any external TTL-level clock which meets the minimum and maximum cycle times. This clock is not used in the USART loopback mode. Refer to **6.3.2 Transmitter Status Register** for additional information.

2.1.7.4 TRANSMITTER CLOCK (TC). This input controls the serial bit rate of the transmitter. This signal may be supplied by the timer output lines or by an external TTL-level clock which meets the minimum and maximum cycle times.

2.1.8 DMA Control

The USART supports DMA transfers through its receiver ready and transmitter ready status lines.

2.1.8.1 RECEIVER READY ($\overline{RR}$). This output reflects the receiver buffer full status for DMA operations.

2.1.8.2 TRANSMITTER READY ($\overline{TR}$). This output reflects the transmitter buffer empty status for DMA operations.

2.1.9 Signal Summary

Table 2-1 is a summary of all the signals discussed in the previous paragraphs.

Table 2-1. Signal Summary

Signal Name	Mnemonic	I/O	Active
Power Input	V_{CC}	Input	High
Ground	GND	Input	Low
Clock	CLK	Input	N/A
Chip Select	$\overline{CS}$	Input	Low
Data Srobe	$\overline{DS}$	Input	Low
Read/Write	$R/\overline{W}$	Input	Read — High, Write — Low
Data Transfer Acknowledge	$\overline{DTACK}$	Output	Low
Register Select Bus	RS1-RS5	Input	N/A
Data Bus	D0-D7	I/O	N/A
Reset	$\overline{RESET}$	Input	Low
Interrupt Request	$\overline{IRQ}$	Output	Low
Interrupt Acknowledge	$\overline{IACK}$	Input	Low
Interrupt Enable In	$\overline{IEI}$	Input	Low
Interrupt Enable Out	$\overline{IEO}$	Output	Low
General Purpose I/O — Interrupt Lines	I0-I7	I/O	N/A
Timer Clock	XTAL1, XTAL2	Input	High
Timer Inputs	TAI, TBI	Input	N/A
Timer Outputs	TAO, TBO, TCO, TDO	Output	N/A
Serial Input	SI	Input	N/A
Serial Output	SO	Output	N/A
Receiver Clock	RC	Input	N/A
Transmitter Clock	TC	Input	N/A
Receiver Ready	$\overline{RR}$	Output	Low
Transmitter Ready	$\overline{TR}$	Output	Low

2.2 BUS OPERATION

The following paragraphs explain the control signals and bus operation during data transfer operations and reset.

2.2.1 Data Transfer Operations

Transfer of data between devices involves the following pins:

Register Select Bus — RS1 through RS5
Data Bus — D0 through D7
Control Signals

The address and data buses are separate parallel buses used to transfer data using an asynchronous bus structure. In all cycles, the bus master assumes responsibility for deskewing all signals it issues at both the start and end of a cycle. Additionally, the bus master is responsible for deskewing the acknowledge and data signals from the peripheral devices.

2.2.1.1 READ CYCLE. To read an MFP register, $\overline{CS}$ and $\overline{DS}$ must be asserted, and R/$\overline{W}$ must be high. The MFP will place the contents of the register which is selected by the register select bus (RS1 through RS5) on the data bus (D0 through D7) and then assert $\overline{DTACK}$. The register addresses are shown in Table 1-1.

After the processor has latched the data, $\overline{DS}$ is negated. The negation of either $\overline{CS}$ or $\overline{DS}$ will terminate the read operation. The MFP will drive $\overline{DTACK}$ high and place it in the high-impedance state. Also, the data bus will be in the high-impedance state. The timing for a read cycle is shown in Figure 2-2. Refer to **7.7 AC ELECTRICAL CHARACTERISTICS** for actual timing numbers.

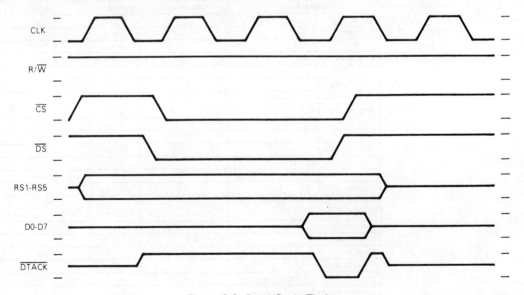

Figure 2-2. Read Cycle Timing

2.2.1.2 WRITE CYCLE. To write a register, $\overline{CS}$ and $\overline{DS}$ must be asserted, and R/$\overline{W}$ must be low. The MFP will decode the address bus to determine which register is selected (the register map is shown in Table 1-1). Then the register will be loaded with the contents of the data bus and $\overline{DTACK}$ will be asserted.

When the processor recognizes $\overline{DTACK}$, $\overline{DS}$ will be negated. The write cycle is terminated when either $\overline{CS}$ or $\overline{DS}$ is negated. The MFP will drive $\overline{DTACK}$ high and place it in the high-impedance state. The timing for a write cycle is shown in Figure 2-3. Refer to **7.7 AC ELECTRICAL CHARACTERISTICS** for actual numbers.

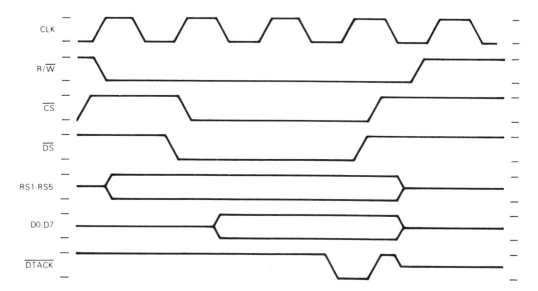

Figure 2-3. Write Cycle Timing

2.2.2 Interrupt Acknowledge Operation

The MFP has 16 interrupt sources, eight internal sources, and eight external sources. When an interrupt request is pending, the MFP will assert $\overline{IRQ}$. In a vectored interrupt scheme, the processor will acknowledge the interrupt request by performing an interrupt acknowledge cycle. $\overline{IACK}$ and $\overline{DS}$ will be asserted. The MFP responds to the $\overline{IACK}$ signal by placing a vector number on the lower eight bits of the data bus. This vector number corresponds to the $\overline{IRQ}$ handler for the particular interrupt requesting service. The format of this vector number is given in Figure 3-1.

When the MFP asserts $\overline{DTACK}$ to indicate that valid data is on the bus, the processor will latch the data and terminate the bus cycle by negating $\overline{DS}$. When either $\overline{DS}$ or $\overline{IACK}$ are negated, the MFP will terminate the interrupt acknowledge operation by driving $\overline{DTACK}$ high and placing it in the high-impedance state. Also, the data bus will be placed in the high-impedance state. $\overline{IRQ}$ will be negated as a result of the $\overline{IACK}$ cycle unless additional interrupts are pending.

The MFP can be part of a daisy-chain interrupt structure which allows multiple MFPs to be placed at the same interrupt level by sharing a common $\overline{IACK}$ signal. A daisy-chain priority scheme is implemented with signals $\overline{IEI}$ and $\overline{IEO}$. $\overline{IEI}$ indicates that no higher priority device is requesting interrupt service. $\overline{\text{IEO}}$ signals lower priority devices that neither this device nor any higher priority device is requesting service. To daisy-chain MFPs, the highest priority MFP has its $\overline{\text{IEI}}$ tied low and successive MFPs have their $\overline{\text{IEI}}$ connected to the next higher priority device's $\overline{\text{IEO}}$. Note that when the daisy-chain interrupt structure is not implemented, the $\overline{\text{IEI}}$ of all MFPs must be tied low. Refer to **3.2 DAISY-CHAINING MFPs** for additional information.

When the processor initiates an interrupt acknowledge cycle by driving $\overline{\text{IACK}}$ and $\overline{\text{DS}}$, the MFP whose $\overline{\text{IEI}}$ is low may respond with a vector number if an interrupt is pending. If this device does not have a pending interrupt, $\overline{\text{IEO}}$ is asserted which allows the next lower priority device to respond to the interrupt acknowledge. When an MFP propagates $\overline{\text{IEO}}$, it will not drive the data bus nor $\overline{\text{DTACK}}$ during the interrupt acknowledge cycle. The timing for an $\overline{\text{IACK}}$ cycle is shown in Figure 2-4. Refer to **7.6 CLOCK TIMING** for further information.

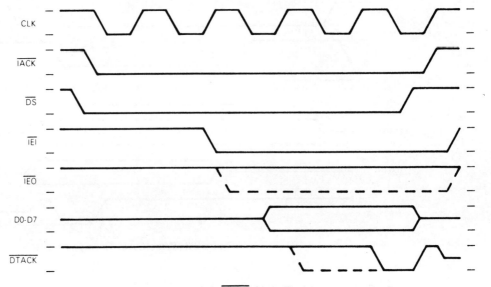

Figure 2-4. $\overline{\text{IACK}}$ Cycle Timing

2.2.3 Reset Operation

The reset operation will initialize the MFP to a known state. The reset operation requires that the $\overline{\text{RESET}}$ input be asserted for a minimum of two microseconds. During a device reset condition, all internal MFP registers are cleared except for the timer data registers (TADR, TBDR, TCDR, and TDDR), the USART data register (UDR), the transmitter status register (TSR) and the interrupt vector register. All timers are stopped and the USART receiver and transmitter are disabled. The interrupt channels are also disabled and any pending interrupts are cleared. In addition, the general purpose interrupt I/O lines are placed in the high-impedance input mode and the timer outputs are driven low. External MFP signals are negated. The interrupt vector register is initialized to a $0F.

SECTION 3
INTERRUPT STRUCTURE

In an MC68000 system, the MFP will be assigned to one of the seven possible interrupt levels. All interrupt service requests from the MFP's 16 interrupt channels will be presented at this level. Although, as an interrupt controller, the MFP will internally prioritize its 16 interrupt sources. Additional interrupt sources may be placed at the same interrupt level by daisy-chaining multiple MFPs. The MFPs will be prioritized by their position in the chain.

3.1 INTERRUPT PROCESSING

Each MFP provides individual interrupt capability for its various functions. When an interrupt is received on one of the external interrupt channels or from one of the eight internal sources, the MFP will request interrupt service. The 16 interrupt channels are assigned a fixed priority so that multiple pending interrupts are serviced according to their relative importance. Since the MFP can internally generate 16 vector numbers, the unique vector number which corresponds to the highest priority channel that has a pending interrupt is presented to the processor during an interrupt acknowledge cycle. This unique vector number allows the processor to immediately begin execution of the interrupt handler for the interrupting source, decreasing interrupt latency time.

3.1.1 Interrupt Channel Prioritization

The 16 interrupt channels are prioritized as shown in Table 3-1. General purpose interrupt 7 (I7) is the highest priority interrupt channel and I0 is the lowest priority channel. Pending interrupts are presented to the CPU in order of priority unless they have been masked off. By selectively masking interrupts, the channels are in effect re-prioritized.

Table 3-1. Interrupt Channel Prioritization

Priority	Channel	Description
Highest	1111	General Purpose Interrupt 7 (I7)
	1110	General Purpose Interrupt 6 (I6)
	1101	Timer A
	1100	Receiver Buffer Full
	1011	Receive Error
	1010	Transmit Buffer Empty
	1001	Transmit Error
	1000	Timer B
	0111	General Purpose Interrupt 5 (I5)
	0110	General Purpose Interrupt 4 (I4)
	0101	Timer C
	0100	Timer D
	0011	General Purpose Interrupt 3 (I3)
	0010	General Purpose Interrupt 2 (I2)
	0001	General Purpose Interrupt 1 (I1)
Lowest	0000	General Purpose Interrupt 0 (I0)

3.1.2 Interrupt Vector Number Format

During an interrupt acknowledge cycle, a unique 8-bit vector number is presented to the system which corresponds to the specific interrupt source which is requesting service. The format of the vector is shown in Figure 3-1. The most significant four bits of the interrupt vector number are user programmable. These bits are set by writing the upper four bits of the vector register which is shown in Figure 3-2. The low order bits are generated internally by the MC68901. Note that the binary channel number shown in Table 3-1 corresponds to the low order bits of the vector number associated with each channel.

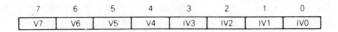

7	6	5	4	3	2	1	0
V7	V6	V5	V4	IV3	IV2	IV1	IV0

V7-V4   The four most significant bits are copied from the vector register.

IV3-IV0   These bits are supplied by the MFP. They are the binary channel number of the highest priority channel that is requesting interrupt service.

Figure 3-1. Interrupt Vector Format

Address 17 (Hex)

7	6	5	4	3	2	1	0
V7	V6	V5	V4	S	*	*	*

*Unused bits are read as zero.

V7-V4   The upper four bits of the vector register are written by the user. These bits become the most significant four bits of the interrupt vector number.
        SET   a) MPU writes a one
        CLEARED   a) MPU writes a zero
                   b) Reset

S   In-Service Register Enable. When the S bit is zero, the MFP is in the automatic end-of-interrupt mode and the in-service register bits are forced low. When the S bit is a one, the MFP is in the software end-of-interrupt mode and the in-service register bits are enabled. Refer to **3.4.2 Automatic End-of-Interrupt** and **3.4.3 Software End-of-Interrupt** for additional information.
        SET   a) MPU writes a one
        CLEARED   a) MPU writes a zero
                   b) Reset

Figure 3-2 Vector Register Format (VR)

3.2 DAISY-CHAINING MFPs

As an interrupt controller, the MC68901 MFP will support eight external interrupt sources in addition to its eight internal interrupt sources. When a system requires more than eight external interrupt sources to be placed at the same interrupt level, sources may be added to the prioritized structure by daisy-chaining MFPs. Interrupt sources are prioritized internally within each MFP and the MFPs are prioritized by their position in the chain. Unique vector numbers are provided for each interrupt source.

The $\overline{IEI}$ and $\overline{IEO}$ signals implement the daisy-chained interrupt structure. The $\overline{IEI}$ of the highest priority MFP is tied low and the $\overline{IEO}$ output of this device is tied to the next highest priority MFP's $\overline{IEI}$. The $\overline{IEI}$ and $\overline{IEO}$ signals are daisy-chained in this manner for all MFPs in the chain, with the lowest priority MFP's $\overline{IEO}$ left unconnected. A diagram of an interrupt daisy-chain is shown in Figure 3-3.

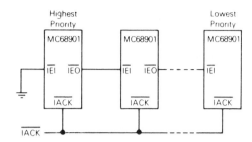

Figure 3-3. Daisy-Chained Interrupt Structure

Daisy-chaining requires that all parts in the chain have a common $\overline{\text{IACK}}$. When the common $\overline{\text{IACK}}$ is asserted during an interrupt acknowledge cycle, all parts will prioritize interrupts in parallel. When the $\overline{\text{IEI}}$ signal to an MFP is asserted, the part may respond to the $\overline{\text{IACK}}$ cycle if it requires interrupt service. Otherwise, the part will assert $\overline{\text{IEO}}$ to the next lower priority device. Thus, priority is passed down the chain via $\overline{\text{IEI}}$ and $\overline{\text{IEO}}$ until a part which has a pending interrupt is reached. The part with the pending interrupt passes a vector number to the processor and does not propagate $\overline{\text{IEO}}$.

3.3 INTERRUPT CONTROL REGISTERS

MFP interrupt processing is managed by the interrupt enable registers A and B, interrupt pending registers A and B, and interrupt mask registers A and B. These registers allow the programmer to enable or disable individual interrupt channels, mask individual interrupt channels, and access pending interrupt status information. In-service registers A and B allow interrupts to be nested as described in **3.4 NESTING MFP INTERRUPTS.** The interrupt control registers are shown in Figure 3-4.

3.3.1 Interrupt Enable Registers

The interrupt channels are individually enabled or disabled by writing a one or zero, respectively, to the appropriate bit of interrupt enable register A (IERA) or interrupt enable register B (IERB). The processor may read these registers at any time.

When a channel is enabled, interrupts received on the channel will be recognized by the MFP and $\overline{\text{IRQ}}$ will be asserted to the processor, indicating that interrupt service is required. On the other hand, a disabled channel is completely inactive; interrupts received on the channel are ignored by the MFP.

Writing a zero to a bit of interrupt enable register A or B will cause the corresponding bit of interrupt pending register A or B to be cleared. This will terminate all interrupt service requests for the channel and also negate $\overline{\text{IRQ}}$, unless interrupts are pending from other sources. Disabling a channel, however, does not affect the corresponding bit in interrupt in-service registers A or B. So, if the MFP is in the software end-of-interrupt mode (see **3.4.3 Software End-Of-Interrupt)** and an interrupt is in service when a channel is disabled, the in-service status bit for that channel will remain set until cleared by software.

(a) Interrupt Enable Registers (IERA and IERB)

	7	6	5	4	3	2	1	0
Address 07 (Hex)	GPIP7	GPIP6	Timer A	RCV Buffer Full	RCV Error	XMIT Buffer Empty	XMIT Error	Timer B

	7	6	5	4	3	2	1	0
Address 09 (Hex)	GPIP5	GPIP4	Timer C	Timer D	GPIP3	GPIP2	GPIP1	GPIP0

When a bit is a zero, the associated interrupt channel is disabled. When a bit is a one, the associated interrupt channel is enabled.

SET   a) MPU writes a one
CLEARED   a) MPU writes a zero
            b) Reset

(b) Interrupt Pending Registers (IPRA and IPRB)

	7	6	5	4	3	2	1	0
Address 0B (Hex)	GPIP7	GPIP6	Timer A	RCV Buffer Full	RCV Error	XMIT Buffer Empty	XMIT Error	Timer B

	7	6	5	4	3	2	1	0
Address 0D (Hex)	GPIP5	GPIP4	Timer C	Timer D	GPIP3	GPIP2	GPIP1	GPIP0

When a bit is a zero, no interrupt is pending on the associated interrupt channel. When a bit is a one, an interrupt is pending on the associated interrupt channel.

SET   a) Interrupt is received on an enabled interrupt channel
CLEARED   a) Interrupt vector for the associated interrupt channel is passed during an $\overline{\text{IACK}}$ cycle
            b) Associated interrupt channel is disabled
            c) MPU writes a zero
            d) Reset

(c) Interrupt In-Service Registers (ISRA and ISRB)

	7	6	5	4	3	2	1	0
Address 0F (Hex)	GPIP7	GPIP6	Timer A	RCV Buffer Full	RCV Error	XMIT Buffer Empty	XMIT Error	Timer B

	7	6	5	4	3	2	1	0
Address 11 (Hex)	GPIP5	GPIP4	Timer C	Timer D	GPIP3	GPIP2	GPIP1	GPIP0

When a bit is a zero, no interrupt processing is in progress for the associated interrupt channel. When a bit is a one, interrupt processing is in progress for the associated interrupt channel.

SET   a) Interrupt vector number for the associated interrupt channel is passed during an $\overline{\text{IACK}}$ cycle and the S bit of the vector register is a zero
CLEARED   a) Interrupt service is completed for the associated interrupt channel
            b) The S bit of the vector register is set
            c) MPU writes a zero
            d) Reset

Figure 3-4. Interrupt Control Registers (Sheet 1 of 2)

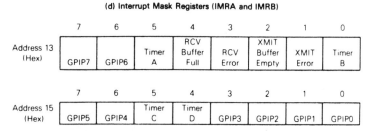

(d) Interrupt Mask Registers (IMRA and IMRB)

	7	6	5	4	3	2	1	0
Address 13 (Hex)	GPIP7	GPIP6	Timer A	RCV Buffer Full	RCV Error	XMIT Buffer Empty	XMIT Error	Timer B

	7	6	5	4	3	2	1	0
Address 15 (Hex)	GPIP5	GPIP4	Timer C	Timer D	GPIP3	GPIP2	GPIP1	GPIP0

When a bit is zero, interrupts are masked for the associated interrupt channel. When a bit is a one, interrupts are not masked for the associated interrupt channel.
SET   a) MPU writes a one
CLEARED   a) MPU writes a zero
                b) Reset

Figure 3-4. Interrupt Control Registers (Sheet 2 of 2)

3.3.2 Interrupt Pending Registers

When an interrupt is received on an enabled channel, the corresponding interrupt pending bit is set in interrupt pending register A or B (IPRA or IPRB). In a vectored interrupt scheme, this bit will be cleared when the processor acknowledges the interrupting channel and the MFP responds with a vector number. In a polled interrupt system, the interrupt pending registers must be read to determine the interrupting channel and then the interrupt pending bit is cleared by the interrupt handling routine without performing an interrupt acknowledge sequence.

A single bit of the interrupt pending registers is cleared in software by writing ones to all bit positions except the bit to be cleared. Note that writing ones to IPRA and IPRB has no effect on the contents of the register. A single bit of the interrupt pending registers is also cleared when the corresponding channel is disabled by writing a zero to the appropriate bit of IERA or IERB.

3.3.3 Interrupt Mask Registers

Interrupts are masked for a channel by clearing the appropriate bit in interrupt mask register A or B (IMRA or IMRB). Even though an enabled channel is masked, the channel will recognize subsequent interrupts and set its interrupt pending bit. However, the channel is prevented from requesting interrupt service ($\overline{\text{IRQ}}$ to the processor) as long as the mask bit for that channel is cleared.

If a channel is requesting interrupt service at the time that its corresponding bit in IMRA or IMRB is cleared, the request will cease and $\overline{\text{IRQ}}$ will be negated, unless another channel is requesting interrupt service. Later, when the mask bit is set, any pending interrupt on the channel will be processed according to the channel's assigned priority. IMRA and IMRB may be read at any time.

3.4 NESTING MFP INTERRUPTS

In an MC68000 vectored interrupt system, the MFP is assigned to one of seven possible interrupt levels. When an interrupt is received from the MFP, an interrupt acknowledge for that level is initiated. Once an interrupt is recognized at a particular level, interrupts at that same level or below are masked by the MC68000. As long as the processor's interrupt mask is unchanged, the MC68000 interrupt structure will prohibit the nesting of interrupts at the same interrupt level. However, additional interrupt requests from the MFP can be recognized before a previous channel's interrupt service routine is completed by lowering the processor's interrupt mask to the next lower interrupt level within the interrupt handler.

When nesting MFP interrupts, it may be desirable to permit interrupts on any MFP channel, regardless of its priority, to preempt or delay interrupt processing of an earlier channel's interrupt service request. Or, it may be desirable to only allow subsequent higher priority channel interrupt requests to supercede previously recognized lower priority interrupt requests. The MFP interrupt structure provides this flexibility by offering two end-of-interrupt options for vectored interrupt schemes. Note that the end-of-interrupt modes are not active in a polled interrupt scheme.

3.4.1 Selecting The End-Of-Interrupt Mode

In a vectored interrupt scheme, the MFP may be programmed to operate in either the automatic end-of-interrupt mode or the software end-of-interrupt mode. The mode is selected by writing the S bit of the vector register (see Figure 3-2). When the S bit is programmed to a one, the MFP is placed in the software end-of-interrupt mode and when the S bit is a zero, all channels operate in the automatic end-of-interrupt mode.

3.4.2 Automatic End-Of-Interrupt

When an interrupt vector number is passed to the processor during an interrupt acknowledge cycle, the corresponding channel's interrupt pending bit is cleared. In the automatic end-of-interrupt mode, no further history of the interrupt remains in the MFP. The in-service bits of the interrupt in-service registers (ISRA and ISRB) are forced low. Subsequent interrupts which are received on any MFP channel will generate an interrupt request to the processor, even if the current interrupt's service routine has not been completed.

3.4.3 Software End-Of-Interrupt

In the software end-of-interrupt mode, the channel's associated interrupt pending bit is cleared and in addition, the channel's in-service bit of in-service register A or B is set when its vector number is passed to the processor during an $\overline{IACK}$ cycle. A higher priority channel may subsequently request interrupt service and be acknowledged, but as long as the channel's in-service bit is set, no lower priority channel may request interrupt service nor pass its vector during an interrupt acknowledge sequence.

While only higher priority channels may request interrupt service, any channel can receive an interrupt and set its interrupt pending bit. Even the channel whose in-service bit is set can receive a second interrupt. However, no interrupt service request is made until its in-service bit is cleared.

The in-service bit for a particular channel can be cleared by writing a zero to its corresponding bit in ISRA or ISRB and ones to all other bit positions. Since bits in the in-service registers can only be cleared in software and not set, writing ones to the registers does not alter their contents. ISRA and ISRB may be read at any time.

SECTION 4
GENERAL PURPOSE INPUT/OUTPUT INTERRUPT PORT

The general purpose interrupt input/output (I/O) port (GPIP) provides eight I/O lines (I0 through I7) that may be operated as either inputs or outputs under software control. In addition, these lines may optionally generate an interrupt on either a positive transition or a negative transition of the input signal. The flexibility of the GPIP allows it to be configured as an 8-bit I/O port or for bit I/O. Since interrupts are enabled on a bit-by-bit basis, a subset of the GPIP could be programmed as handshake lines or the port could be connected to as many as eight external interrupt sources, which would be prioritized by the MFP interrupt controller for interrupt service.

4.1 M6800 INTERRUPT CONTROLLER

The MFP interrupt controller is particularly useful in a system which has many M6800-type devices. Typically, in a vectored MC68000 system, M6800-type peripherals use the autovector which corresponds to their assigned interrupt level since they do not provide a vector number in response to an $\overline{IACK}$ cycle. The autovector interrupt handler must then poll all M6800-type devices at that interrupt level to determine which device is requesting service. However, by tying the $\overline{IRQ}$ output from an M6800-type device to the general purpose I/O interrupt port (GPIP) of an MFP, a unique vector number will be provided to the processor during an interrupt acknowledge cycle. This interrupt structure will significantly reduce interrupt latency for M6800-type devices and other peripheral devices which do not support vector-by-device.

4.2 GPIP CONTROL REGISTERS

The GPIP is programmed via three control registers shown in Figure 4-1. These registers control the data direction, provide user access to the port, and specify the active edge for each bit of the GPIP which will produce an interrupt. These registers are described in detail in the following paragraphs.

4.2.1 GPIP Data Register

The general purpose I/O data register is used to input or output data to the port. When data is written to the GPIP data register, those pins which are defined as inputs will remain in the high-impedance state. Pins which are defined as outputs will assume the state (high or low) of their corresponding bit in the data register. When the GPIP is read, data will be passed directly from the bits of the data register for pins which are defined as outputs. Data from pins defined as inputs will come from the input buffers.

4.2.2 Active Edge Register

The active edge register (AER) allows each of the GPIP lines to produce an interrupt on either a one-to-zero or a zero-to-one transition. Writing a zero to the appropriate edge bit of the active edge

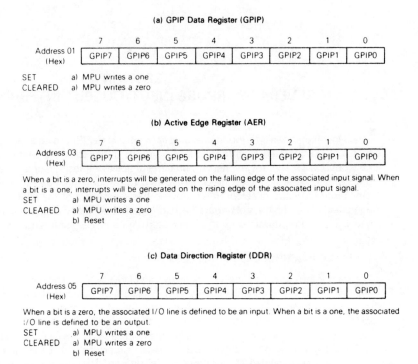

Figure 4-1. GPIP Control Registers

register causes the associated input to generate an interrupt on the one-to-zero transition. Writing a one to the edge bit will produce an interrupt on the zero-to-one transition of the corresponding GPIP line.

NOTE

The transition detector is an exclusive-OR gate whose inputs are the edge bit and the input buffer. As a result, writing the AER may cause an interrupt-producing transition, depending upon the state of the input. So, the AER should be configured before enabling interrupts via the interrupt enable registers (IERA and IERB). Also, changing the edge bit while interrupts are enabled may cause an interrupt on the corresponding channel.

4.2.3 Data Direction Register

The data direction register (DDR) allows the programmer to define I0 through I7 as inputs or outputs by writing the corresponding bit. When a bit of the data direction register is written as a zero, the corresponding interrupt I/O pin will be a high-impedance input. Writing a one to any bit of the data direction register will cause the corresponding pin to be configured as a push-pull output.

SECTION 5
TIMERS

The MFP contains four 8-bit timers which provide many functions typically required in microprocessor systems. The timers can supply the baud rate clocks for the on-chip serial I/O channel, generate periodic interrupts, measure elapsed time, and count signal transitions. In addition, two timers have waveform generation capability.

All timers are prescaler/counter timers with a common independent clock input (XTAL1 or XTAL2) and are not required to be operated from the system clock. Each timer's output signal toggles when the timer's main counter times out. Additionally, timers A and B have auxiliary control signals which are used in two of the operation modes. An interrupt channel is assigned to each timer and when the auxiliary control signals are used, a separate interrupt channel will respond to transitions on these inputs.

5.1 OPERATION MODES

Timers A and B are full function timers which, in addition to the delay mode, operate in the pulse width measurement mode and the event count mode. Timers C and D are delay timers only. A brief discussion of each of the timer modes follows.

5.1.1 Delay Mode Operation

All timers may operate in the delay mode. In this mode, the prescaler is always active. The prescaler specifies the number of timer clock cycles which must elapse before a count pulse is applied to the main counter. A count pulse causes the main counter to decrement by one. When the timer has decremented down to 01 (hexadecimal), the next count pulse will cause the main counter to be reloaded from the timer data register and a time out pulse will be produced. This time out pulse is coupled to the timer's interrupt channel and, if the channel is enabled, an interrupt will occur. The time out pulse also causes the timer output pin to toggle. The output will remain in this new state until the next time out pulse occurs.

For example, if delay mode with a divide-by-10 prescaler is selected and the timer data register is loaded with 100 (decimal), the main counter will decrement once every 10 timer clock cycles. After 1,000 timer clocks, a time out pulse will be produced. This time out pulse will generate an interrupt if the channel is enabled (IERA, IERB) and in addition, the timer's output line will toggle. The output line will complete one full period every 2,000 cycles of the timer clock.

If the prescaler value is changed while the timer is enabled, the first time out pulse will occur at an indeterminate time no less than one nor more than 200 timer clock cycles. Subsequent time out pulses will then occur at the correct interval.

If the main counter is loaded with 01 (hexadecimal), a time out pulse will occur every time the prescaler presents a count pulse to the main counter. If the main counter is loaded with 00, a time out pulse will occur every 256 count pulses.

5.1.2 Pulse Width Measurement Operation

Besides the delay mode, timers A and B may be programmed to operate in the pulse width measurement mode. In this mode an auxiliary control input is required; timers A and B auxiliary input lines are TAI and TBI. Also, in the pulse width measurement mode, interrupt channels normally associated with I4 and I3 will respond to transitions on TAI and TBI, respectively. General purpose lines I3 and I4 may still be used for I/O. A conceptual circuit of the timers in the pulse width measurement mode is shown in Figure 5-1.

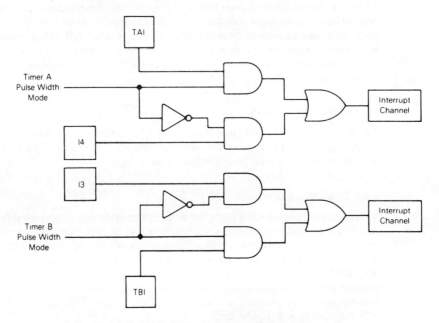

Figure 5-1. Conceptual Circuit of Timers A and B
in Pulse Width Measurement Mode

The pulse width measurement mode functions similarly to the delay mode, with the auxiliary control signal acting as an enable to the timer. When the control signal is active, the prescaler and main counter are allowed to operate. When the control signal is negated, the timer is stopped. So, the width of the active pulse on TAI or TBI is measured by the number of timer counts which occur while the timer is allowed to operate.

The active state of the auxiliary input line is defined by the associated interrupt channel's edge bit in the active edge register (AER). GPIP4 of the AER is the edge bit associated with TAI and GPIP3 is associated with TBI. When the edge bit is a one, the auxiliary input will be active high, enabling the timer while the input signal is at a high level. If the edge bit is low, the auxiliary input will be active low and the timer will operate while the input signal is at a low level.

The state of the active edge bit also specifies whether a zero-to-one transition or a one-to-zero transition of the auxiliary input pin will produce an interrupt when the interrupt channel is enabled. In normal operation, programming the active edge bit to a one will produce an interrupt on the zero-to-one transition of the associated input signal. Alternately, programming the edge bit to a zero will produce an interrupt on the one-to-zero transition of the input signal. However, in the pulse width measurement mode, the interrupt generated by a transition on TAI or TBI will occur on the opposite transition as that normally defined by the edge bit.

For example, in the pulse width measurement mode, if the edge bit is a one, the timer will be allowed to run while the auxiliary input TAI is high. When TAI transitions from high to low, the timer will stop and, if the interrupt channel is enabled, an interrupt will occur. By having the interrupt occur on the one-to-zero transition instead of the zero-to-one transition, the processor will be interrupted when the pulse being measured has terminated and the width of the pulse is available from the timer. Therefore, the timers act like a divide-by-prescaler that can be programmed by the timer data register and the timers' C and D control register.

After reading the contents of the timer, the main counter must be reinitialized by writing to the timer data register to allow consecutive pulses to be measured. If the timer is written after the auxiliary input signal is active, the timer will count from the previous contents of the timer data register until it counts through 01 (hexadecimal). At that time, the main counter is loaded with the new value from the timer data register, a time out pulse is generated which will toggle the timer output, and an interrupt may be optionally generated on the timer interrupt channel. Note that the pulse width measured will include counts from before the main counter was reloaded. If the timer data register is written while the pulse is transitioning to the active state, an indeterminate value may be written into the main counter.

Once the timer is reprogrammed for another mode, interrupts will again occur as normally defined by the edge bit. Note that an interrupt may be generated as the result of placing the timer into the pulse width measurement mode or by reprogramming the timer for another mode. Also, an interrupt may be generated by changing the state of the edge bit while in the pulse width measurement mode.

5.1.3 Event Count Mode Operation

In addition to the delay mode and the pulse width measurement mode, timers A and B may be programmed to operate in the event count mode. Like the pulse width measurement mode, the event count mode also requires an auxiliary input signal, TAI or TBI, and the interrupt channels normally associated with I4 and I3 will respond to transitions on TAI and TBI, respectively. General purpose lines I3 and I4 still function normally.

In the event count mode the prescaler is disabled, allowing each active transition on TAI and TBI to produce a count pulse. The count pulse causes the main counter to decrement by one. When the timer counts through 01 (hexadecimal), a time out pulse is generated which will cause the output signal to toggle and may optionally produce an interrupt via the associated timer interrupt channel. The timer's main counter is also reloaded from the timer data register. To count transitions reliably, the input signal may only transition once every four timer clock periods. For this reason, the input signal must have a maximum frequency equal to one-fourth that of the timer clock.

The active edge of the auxiliary input signal is defined by the associated interrupt channel's edge bit. GPIP4 of the AER specifies the active edge for TAI and GPIP3 defines the active edge for TBI. When the edge bit is programmed to a one, a count pulse will be generated on the zero-to-one transition of the auxiliary input signal. When the edge bit is programmed to a zero, a count pulse will be generated on the one-to-zero transition. Also, note that changing the state of the edge bit while the timer is in the event count mode may produce a count pulse.

Besides generating a count pulse, the active transition of the auxiliary input signal will also produce an interrupt on the I3 or I4 interrupt channel, if the interrupt channel is enabled. Typically, in the event count mode, these channels are not enabled since the timer is automatically counting transitions on the input signal. If the interrupt channel were enabled, the number of transitions could be counted in the interrupt routine without requiring the use of the timer.

5.2 TIMER REGISTERS

The four timers are programmed via three control registers and four timer data registers. Control registers TACR and TBCR and timer data registers TADR and TBDR (refer to Figure 5-1) are associated with timers A and B respectively. Timers C and D are controlled by the control register TCDCR and the data registers TCDR and TDDR (refer to Figure 5-2).

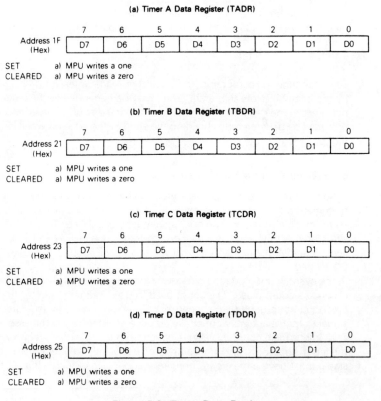

Figure 5-2. Timer Data Registers

5.2.1 Timer Data Registers

Each timer's main counter is an 8-bit binary down counter. The value of the main counter may be read at any time by reading the timer's data register. The information read is the value of the counter which was captured on the last low-to-high transition of the $\overline{DS}$ pin.

The main counter is initialized by writing to the timer's data register. If the timer is stopped, data is loaded simultaneously into both the timer data register and the main counter. If the timer data register is written while the timer is enabled, the value is not loaded into the timer until the timer counts through 01 (hexadecimal). Writing the timer data register while the timer is counting through 01 (hexadecimal) will cause an indeterminate value to be loaded into the timer's main counter. The four data registers are shown in Figure 5-2.

5.2.2 Timer Control Registers

Bits in the timer control registers select the operation mode, select the prescale value, and disable the timers. Timer control registers TACR and TBCR also have bits which allow the programmer to reset output lines TAO and TBO. These control registers are shown in Figure 5-3.

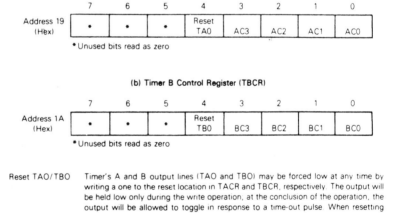

(a) Timer A Control Register (TACR)

	7	6	5	4	3	2	1	0
Address 19 (Hex)	*	*	*	Reset TAO	AC3	AC2	AC1	AC0

*Unused bits read as zero

(b) Timer B Control Register (TBCR)

	7	6	5	4	3	2	1	0
Address 1A (Hex)	*	*	*	Reset TBO	BC3	BC2	BC1	BC0

*Unused bits read as zero

Reset TAO/TBO   Timer's A and B output lines (TAO and TBO) may be forced low at any time by writing a one to the reset location in TACR and TBCR, respectively. The output will be held low only during the write operation; at the conclusion of the operation, the output will be allowed to toggle in response to a time-out pulse. When resetting TAO and TBO, the remaining bits in the control register must be written with their previous value to avoid altering the operating mode.

SET   a) End of write cycle which clears the bit
CLEARED   a) MPU writes a zero
              b) Reset

AC3-AC0, BC3-BC0 These bits are decoded to determine the timer operation mode.

Figure 5-3. Timer Control Registers (Sheet 1 of 2)

AC3 BC3	AC2 BC2	AC1 BC1	AC0 BC0	Operation Mode
0	0	0	0	Timer Stopped*
0	0	0	1	Delay Mode, ÷ 4 Prescaler
0	0	1	0	Delay Mode, ÷ 10 Prescaler
0	0	1	1	Delay Mode, ÷ 16 Prescaler
0	1	0	0	Delay Mode, ÷ 50 Prescaler
0	1	0	1	Delay Mode, ÷ 64 Prescaler
0	1	1	0	Delay Mode, ÷ 100 Prescaler
0	1	1	1	Delay Mode, ÷ 200 Prescaler
1	0	0	0	Event Count Mode
1	0	0	1	Pulse Width Mode, ÷ 4 Prescaler
1	0	1	0	Pulse Width Mode, ÷ 10 Prescaler
1	0	1	1	Pulse Width Mode, ÷ 16 Prescaler
1	1	0	0	Pulse Width Mode, ÷ 50 Prescaler
1	1	0	1	Pulse Width Mode, ÷ 64 Prescaler
1	1	1	0	Pulse Width Mode, ÷ 100 Prescaler
1	1	1	1	Pulse Width Mode, ÷ 200 Prescaler

*Regardless of the operation mode, counting is inhibited when the timer is stopped. The contents of the timer's main counter is not affected, although any residual count in the prescaler is lost.

SET   a) MPU writes a one
CLEARED   a) MPU writes a zero
            b) Reset

(c) Timers C and D Control Register (TCDCR)

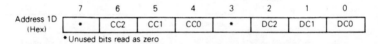

Address 1D
(Hex)

7	6	5	4	3	2	1	0
*	CC2	CC1	CC0	*	DC2	DC1	DC0

*Unused bits read as zero

CC2-CC0, DC2-DC0 The bits are decoded to determine the timer operation mode.

CC2 DC2	CC1 DC1	CC0 DC0	Operation Mode
0	0	0	Timer Stopped*
0	0	1	Delay Mode, ÷ 4 Prescaler
0	1	0	Delay Mode, ÷ 10 Prescaler
0	1	1	Delay Mode, ÷ 16 Prescaler
1	0	0	Delay Mode, ÷ 50 Prescaler
1	0	1	Delay Mode, ÷ 64 Prescaler
1	1	0	Delay Mode, ÷ 100 Prescaler
1	1	1	Delay Mode, ÷ 200 Prescaler

*When the timer is stopped, counting is inhibited. The contents of the timer's main counter is not affected, although any residual count in the prescaler is lost.

SET   a) MPU writes a one
CLEARED   a) MPU writes a zero
            b) Reset

Figure 5-3. Timer Control Registers (Sheet 2 of 2)

SECTION 6
UNIVERSAL SYNCHRONOUS/ASYNCHRONOUS
RECEIVER-TRANSMITTER

The universal synchronous/asynchronous receiver-transmitter (USART) is a single full-duplex serial channel with a double-buffered receiver and transmitter. There are separate receive and transmit clocks and separate receive and transmit status and data bytes. The receive and transmit sections are also assigned separate interrupt channels. Each section has both a normal condition interrupt channel and an error condition interrupt channel. These channels can be optionally disabled from interrupting the processor and instead, DMA transfers can be performed using the receiver ready and transmitter ready external MFP signals.

6.1 CHARACTER PROTOCOLS

The MFP USART supports asynchronous and with the aid of a polynomial generator checker (PGC) supports byte synchronous character formats. These formats are selected independently of the divide-by-one and divide-by-16 clock modes.

When the divide-by-one clock mode is selected, synchronization must be accomplished externally. The receiver will sample the serial data on the rising edge of the receiver clock. In the divide-by-16 clock mode, the data is sampled at mid-bit time to increase transient noise rejection.

Also, when the divide-by-16 clock mode is selected, the USART resynchronization logic is enabled. This logic increases the channel's clock skew tolerance. When a valid transition is detected, an internal counter is reset to state zero. Transition checking is then inhibited until state four. Then at state eight, the previous state of the transition checking logic is clocked into the receive shift register.

6.1.1 Asynchronous Format

Variable word length and start/stop bit configurations are available under software control for asynchronous operation. The word length can be five to eight bits and one, one and one-half, or two stop bits can be selected. The user can also select odd, even, or no parity. For character lengths of less than eight bits, the assembled character will consist of the required number of data bits followed by zeros in the unused bit positions and a parity bit, if parity is enabled.

In the asynchronous format, start bit detection is always enabled. New data is not shifted into the receive shift register until a zero bit is received. When the divide-by-16 clock mode is selected, the false start bit logic is also active. Any transition must be stable for three positive receive clock edges to be considered valid. Then a valid zero-to-one transition must not occur for at least eight additional positive clock edges.

6.1.2 Synchronous Format

When the synchronous character format is selected, the 8-bit synchronous character loaded into the synchronous character register is compared to received serial data until a match is found. Once synchronization is established, incoming data is clocked into the receiver. The synchronous word will be continuously transmitted during an underrun condition. All synchronous characters can be optionally stripped from the receive buffer. Figure 6-1 shows the synchronous character register.

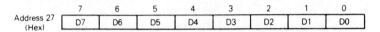

Figure 6-1. Synchronous Character Register (SCR)

The synchronous character is typically written after the data word length is selected, since unused bits in the synchronous character register are zeroed out. When parity is enabled, synchronous word length is the data word length plus one. The MFP will compute and append the parity bit for the synchronous word when a word length of eight is selected. However, if the word length is less than eight, the user must determine the synchronous word parity and write it into the synchronous character register along with the synchronous character. The MFP will then transmit the extra bit in the synchronous word as a parity bit.

6.1.3 USART Control Register

The USART control register (UCR) selects the clock mode and the character format for the receive and transmit sections. This register is shown in Figure 6-2.

6.2 RECEIVER

As data is received on the serial input line (SI), it is clocked into an internal 8-bit shift register until the specified number of data bits have been assembled. This character will then be transferred to the receive buffer, assuming that the last word in the receiver buffer has been read. This transfer produces a buffer full interrupt to the processor.

Reading the receive buffer satisfies the buffer full condition and allows a new data word to be transferred to the receive buffer when it is assembled. The receive buffer is accessed by reading the USART data register (UDR). The UDR is simply an 8-bit data register used when transferring data from the MFP and the CPU.

Each time a word is transferred to the receive buffer, its status information is latched into the receiver status register (RSR). The RSR is not updated again until the data word in the receive buffer has been read. When a buffer full condition exists, the RSR should always be read before the receive buffer (UDR) to maintain the correct correspondance between data and flags. Otherwise, it is possible that after reading the UDR and prior to reading the RSR, a new word could be received and transferred to the receive buffer. Its associated flags would be latched into the RSR, overwriting the flags for the previous data word. Then when the RSR were read to access the status information for the first data word, the flags for the new word would be retrieved.

	7	6	5	4	3	2	1	0
Address 29 (Hex)	CLK	WL1	WL0	ST1	ST0	PE	E/O	*

*Unused bit read as zero

CLK — Clock Mode. When this bit is zero, data will be clocked into and out of the receiver and transmitter at the frequency of their respective clocks. When this bit is a one, data will be clocked into and out of the receiver and transmitter at one sixteenth the frequency of their respective clocks. Also, the receiver data transition resynchronization logic will be enabled.

SET   a) MPU writes a one
CLEARED   a) MPU writes a zero
           b) Reset

WL0, WL1 — Word Length. These two bits specify the length of the data word exclusive of start bits, stop bits, and parity.

WL1	WL0	Word Length
0	0	8 Bits
0	1	7 Bits
1	0	6 Bits
1	1	5 Bits

SET   a) MPU writes a one
CLEARED   a) MPU writes a zero
           b) Reset

ST0, ST1 — Start/Stop Bit and Format Control. These two bits select the number of start and stop bits and also specify the character format.

ST1	ST0	Start Bits	Stop Bits	Format
0	0	0	0	Synchronous
0	1	1	1	Asynchronous
1	0	1	1½	Asynchronous*
1	1	1	2	Asynchronous

*Only used with divide-by-16 clock mode

SET   a) MPU writes a one
CLEARED   a) MPU writes a zero
           b) Reset

PE — Parity Enable. When this bit is zero, no parity check will be made and no parity bit will be computed for transmission. When this bit is a one, parity will be checked by the receiver and parity will be calculated and inserted during data transmission. Note that parity is not automatically appended to the synchronous character for word lengths of less than eight bits. In this case, the parity should be written into the synchronous character register along with the synchronous word.

SET   a) MPU writes a one
CLEARED   a) MPU writes a zero
           b) Reset

E/O — Even/Odd Parity. When this bit is zero, odd parity is selected. When this bit is a one, even parity is selected.

SET   a) MPU writes a one
CLEARED   a) MPU writes a zero
           b) Reset

Figure 6-2. USART Control Register (UCR)

6.2.1 Receiver Interrupt Channels

The USART receive section is assigned two interrupt channels. One indicates the buffer full condition, while the other channel indicates an error condition. Error conditions include overrun, parity error, synchronous found, and break. These interrupting conditions correspond to the BF, OE, PE, and F/S or B bits of the receiver status register. These flags will function as described in **6.2.2 Receiver Status Register** whether the receiver interrupt channels are enabled or disabled.

While only one interrupt is generated per character received, two dedicated interrupt channels allow separate vector numbers to be assigned for normal and abnormal receiver conditions. When a received word has an error associated with it and the error interrupt channel is enabled, an interrupt will be generated on the error channel only. However, if the error channel is disabled, an interrupt for an error condition will be generated on the buffer full interrupt channel along with interrupts produced by the buffer full condition. The receiver status register must always be read to determine which error condition produced the interrupt.

6.2.2 Receiver Status Register

The receiver status register contains the receive buffer full flag, the synchronous strip enable, the receiver enable, and various status information associated with the data word in the receive buffer. The RSR is latched each time a data word is transferred to the receive buffer. RSR flags cannot change again until the data word has been read. The exception is the character in progress flag which monitors when a new word is being assembled in the asynchronous character format. The receiver status register is shown in Figure 6-3.

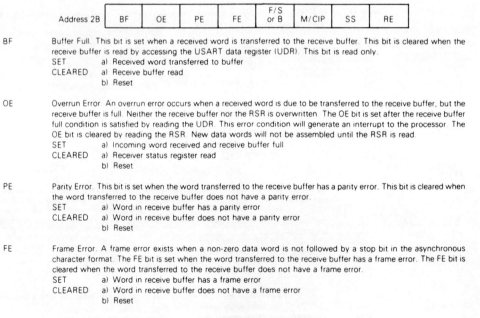

Address 2B	BF	OE	PE	FE	F/S or B	M/CIP	SS	RE

BF   Buffer Full. This bit is set when a received word is transferred to the receive buffer. This bit is cleared when the receive buffer is read by accessing the USART data register (UDR). This bit is read only.
    SET   a) Received word transferred to buffer
    CLEARED a) Receive buffer read
               b) Reset

OE   Overrun Error. An overrun error occurs when a received word is due to be transferred to the receive buffer, but the receive buffer is full. Neither the receive buffer nor the RSR is overwritten. The OE bit is set after the receive buffer full condition is satisfied by reading the UDR. This error condition will generate an interrupt to the processor. The OE bit is cleared by reading the RSR. New data words will not be assembled until the RSR is read.
    SET   a) Incoming word received and receive buffer full
    CLEARED a) Receiver status register read
               b) Reset

PE   Parity Error. This bit is set when the word transferred to the receive buffer has a parity error. This bit is cleared when the word transferred to the receive buffer does not have a parity error.
    SET   a) Word in receive buffer has a parity error
    CLEARED a) Word in receive buffer does not have a parity error
               b) Reset

FE   Frame Error. A frame error exists when a non-zero data word is not followed by a stop bit in the asynchronous character format. The FE bit is set when the word transferred to the receive buffer has a frame error. The FE bit is cleared when the word transferred to the receive buffer does not have a frame error.
    SET   a) Word in receive buffer has a frame error
    CLEARED a) Word in receive buffer does not have a frame error
               b) Reset

Figure 6-3. Receiver Status Register (RSR) (Sheet 1 of 2)

F/S or B   Found/Search or Break Detect. In the synchronous character format this bit can be set or cleared in software. When the bit is a zero, the USART receiver is placed in the search mode. The incoming data is compared to the synchronous character register (SCR) and the word length counter is disabled. The F/S bit will automatically be set when a match is found and the word length counter will be enabled. An interrupt will also be produced on the receive error channel.

                 SET   a) Incoming word matches synchronous character
                 CLEARED   a) MPU writes a zero
                                     b) Incoming word does not match synchronous character
                                     c) Reset

                 In the asynchronous character format, this flag indicates a break condition. A break is detected when an all zero data word with no stop bit is received. The break condition continues until a non-zero data bit is received. The B bit is set when the word transferred to the receive buffer is a break indication. A break condition generates an interrupt to the processor. This bit is cleared when a non-zero data bit is received and the break condition has been acknowledged by reading the RSR at least once. An end of break interrupt will be generated when the bit is cleared.

                 SET   a) Word in receive buffer is a break
                 CLEARED   a) Break terminates and receiver status register read since beginning of break condition
                                     b) Reset

M or CIP   Match/Character in Progress. In the synchronous character format, this flag indicates that a synchronous character has been received. The M bit is set when the word transferred to the receive buffer matches the synchronous character register. The M bit is cleared when the word transferred to the receive buffer does not match the synchronous character register.

                 SET   a) Word transferred to receive buffer matches the synchronous character
                 CLEARED   a) Word transferred to receive buffer does not match synchronous character
                                   b) Reset

                 In the asynchronous character format, this flag indicates that a word is being assembled. The CIP bit is set when a start bit is detected. The CIP bit is cleared when the final stop bit has been received.

                 SET   a) Start bit is detected
                 CLEARED   a) End of word detected
                                   b) Reset

SS   Synchronous Strip Enable. When this bit is a zero, data words that match the synchronous character register will not be loaded into the receive buffer and no buffer full condition will be produced. When this bit is a one, data words that match the synchronous character register will be transferred to the receive buffer and a buffer full condition will be produced.

                 SET   a) MPU writes a one
                 CLEARED   a) MPU writes a zero
                                   b) Reset

RE   Receiver Enable. When this bit is a zero, the receiver will be immediately disabled. All flags will be cleared. When this bit is a one, normal receiver operation is enabled. This bit should not be set to a one until the receiver clock is active.

                 SET   a) MPU writes a one
                                   b) Transmitter is disabled in auto-turnaround mode
                 CLEARED   a) MPU writes a zero
                                 b) Reset

Figure 6-3. Receiver Status Register (RSR) (Sheet 2 of 2)

6.2.3 Special Receive Considerations

Certain receive conditions relating to the overrun error flag and the break detect flag require further explanation. Consider the following examples:

   1) A break is received while the receive buffer is full.

      This does not produce an overrun condition. Only the B flag will be set after the receiver buffer is read.

   2) A new word is received and the receive buffer is full. A break is received before the receive buffer is read.

      Both the B and OE flags will be set when the buffer full condition is satisfied.

6.3 TRANSMITTER

The transmit buffer is loaded by writing to the USART data register (UDR). The data word will be transferred to an internal 8-bit shift register when the last word in the shift register has been transmitted. This will produce a buffer empty condition. If the transmitter completes the transmission of the word in the shift register before a new word is written to the transmit buffer, an underrun error will occur. In the asynchronous character format, the transmitter will send a mark until the transmit buffer is written. In the synchronous character format, the transmitter will continuously send the synchronous character.

The transmit buffer can be loaded prior to enabling the transmitter. After the transmitter is enabled, there is a delay before the first bit is output. The serial output line (SO) should be programmed to be high, low, or high impedance when the transmitter is enabled to force the output line to the desired state until the first bit is shifted out. Note that a one bit will always be transmitted prior to the word in the transmit shift register when the transmitter is first enabled.

When the transmitter is disabled, any word currently being transmitted will continue to completion. However, any word in the transmit buffer will not be transmitted and will remain in the buffer. So, no buffer empty condition will occur. If the buffer is empty when the transmitter is disabled, the buffer empty condition will remain, but no underrun condition will be generated when the word in transmission is completed. If no word is being transmitted when the transmitter is disabled, the transmitter will stop at the next rising edge of the internal shift clock.

In the asynchronous character format, the transmitter can be programmed to send a break. The break will be transmitted once the word currently in the shift register has been sent. If the shift register is empty, the break command will be effective immediately. An END interrupt will be generated at every normal character boundary to aid in timing the break transmission. The break will continue until the break command is cleared.

Any character in the transmit buffer at the start of a break will be transmitted when the break is terminated. If the transmit buffer is empty at the start of a break, it may be written at any time during the break. If the buffer is still empty at the end of the break, an underrun condition will exist.

Disabling the transmitter during a break condition causes the transmitter to cease transmission of the break character at the end of the current character. No end of break stop bit will be transmitted. Even if the transmit buffer is empty, no buffer empty condition will occur nor will an underrun condition occur. Also, any word in the transmit buffer will remain.

6.3.1 Transmitter Interrupt Channels

The USART transmit section is assigned two interrupt channels. One channel indicates a buffer empty condition and the other channel indicates an underrun or end condition. These interrupting conditions correspond to the BE, UE, and END flag bits of the transmitter status register (TSR). The flag bits will function as described in **6.3.2 Transmitter Status Register** whether their associated interrupt channel is enabled or disabled.

6.3.2 Transmitter Status Register

The transmitter status register contains various transmitter error flags and transmitter control bits for selecting auto-turnaround and loopback mode. The TSR is shown in Figure 6-4.

	7	6	5	4	3	2	1	0
Address 2D (Hex)	BE	UE	AT	END	B	H	L	TE

BE
Buffer Empty. This bit is set when the word in the transmit buffer is transferred to the transmit shift register. This bit is cleared when the transmit buffer is reloaded by writing to the USART data register (UDR).
SET   a) Transmit buffer contents transferred to transmit shift register
CLEARED   a) Transmit buffer written

UE
Underrun Error. This bit is set when the word in the transmit shift register has been transmitted before a new word is loaded into the transmit buffer. This bit is cleared by reading the TSR or by disabling the transmitter. This bit does not need to be cleared before writing to the UDR.
SET   a) Transmit shift register contents transmitted before transmit buffer written
CLEARED   a) Transmitter status register read
                 b) Transmitter disabled

AT
Auto-Turnaround. When this bit is set, the receiver will be enabled automatically after the transmitter has been disabled and the last character being transmitted is completed. This bit is cleared at the end of the transmission.
SET   a) MPU writes a one
CLEARED   a) Transmitter disabled

END
End of Transmission. When the transmitter is disabled while a character is being transmitted, the END will be set after the character transmission is complete. If no word is being transmitted when the transmitter is disabled, the END bit will be set immediately. The END bit is cleared by reenabling the transmitter.
SET   a) Transmitter disabled
CLEARED   a) Transmitter enabled

B
Break. This bit has no function in the synchronous character format. In the asynchronous character format, when this bit is set to a one, a break will be transmitted upon the completion of the transmission of any word in the transmit shift register. A break consists of an all zero data word with no stop bit. When this bit is cleared by software, the break indication will cease and normal transmission will resume. Note that when B is set, BE cannot be set.
SET   a) MPU writes a one
CLEARED   a) MPU writes a zero

H, L
High and Low. These control bits configure the transmitter output (SO) when the transmitter is disabled. These bits also force the transmitter output after the transmitter is enabled until END is cleared.

H	L	Output State
0	0	High Impedance
0	1	Low
1	0	High
1	1	Loopback Mode

Loopback mode internally connects the transmitter output to the receiver input and the transmitter clock to the receiver clock internally. The receiver clock (RC) and the serial input (SI) are not used. When the transmitter is disabled, SO is forced high.
SET   a) MPU writes a one
CLEARED   a) MPU writes a zero

TE
Transmitter Enable. When this bit is cleared, the transmitter is disabled. The UE bit will be cleared and the END bit will be set. When this bit is set, the transmitter is enabled. The transmitter output will be driven according to the H and L bits until transmission begins. A one bit will be transmitted before the transmission of the word in the transmit shift register is begun.
SET   a) MPU writes a one
CLEARED   a) MPU writes a zero
                 b) Reset

Figure 6-4. Transmitter Status Register (TSR)

6.4 DMA OPERATION

USART error conditions are only valid for each character boundary. When the USART performs block data transfers by using the DMA handshake lines $\overline{RR}$ (receiver ready) and $\overline{TR}$ (transmitter ready), errors must be saved and checked at the end of a block. This is accomplished by enabling the error channel for the receiver or transmitter and by masking interrupts for this channel. Once the transfer is complete, interrupt pending register A is read. Any pending receiver or transmitter error indicates an error in the data transfer.

7.4 DC ELECTRICAL CHARACTERISTICS ($T_A = 0°C$ to $70°C$, $V_{CC} = -5$ V $\pm 5\%$, unless otherwise noted)

Characteristic	Symbol	Min	Max	Unit
Input High Voltage	V_{IH}	2.0	$V_{CC} + 0.3$	V
Input Low Voltage	V_{IL}	-0.3	0.8	V
Output High Voltage, Except $\overline{DTACK}$ ($I_{OH} = -120$ μA)	V_{OH}	2.4	—	V
Output Low Voltage, Except $\overline{DTACK}$ ($I_{OL} = 2.0$ mA)	V_{OL}	—	0.5	V
Power Supply Current (Outputs Open)	I_{LL}	—	180	mA
Input Leakage Current ($V_{in} = 0$ to V_{CC})	I_{LI}	—	10	μA
Hi-Z Output Leakage Current in Float ($V_{out} = 2.4$ to V_{CC})	I_{LOH}	—	10	μA
Hi-Z Output Leakage Current in Float ($V_{out} = 0.5$ V)	I_{LOL}	—	-10	μA
$\overline{DTACK}$ Output Source Current ($V_{out} = 2.4$ V)	I_{OH}	—	-400	μA
$\overline{DTACK}$ Output Sink Current ($V_{out} = 0.5$ V)	I_{OL}	—	5.3	mA

7.5 CAPACITANCE ($T_A = 25°C$, f = 1 MHz, unmeasured pins returned to ground)

Characteristic	Symbol	Min	Max	Unit
Input Capacitance	C_{in}	—	10	pF
Hi-Z Output Capacitance	C_{out}	—	10	pF

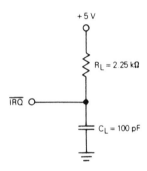

Figure 7-1. $\overline{IRQ}$ Test Load

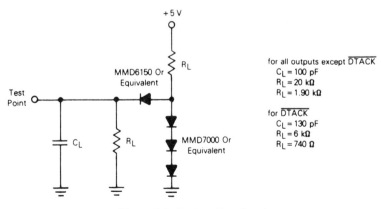

Figure 7-2. Typical Test Load

7.6 CLOCK TIMING

Characteristic	Symbol	Min	Max	Unit
Frequency of Operation	f	1.0	4.0	MHz
Cycle Time	t_{cyc}	250	1000	ns
Clock Pulse Width	t_{CL}, t_{CH}	110	250	ns
Rise and Fall Times	t_{Cr}, t_{Cf}	–	15	ns

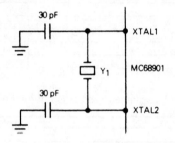

Crystal Parameters
 Parallel resonance fundamental mode AT cut
 $R_S \leq 150\ \Omega$ (f = 2.8 – 4.0 MHz)
 $R_S \leq 300\ \Omega$ (f = 2.0 – 2.7 MHz)
 $C_L = 18$ pF, $C_M = 0.02$ pF, $C_R = 5$ pF, $L_M = 96$ MHz
 f (typical) = 2.4576 MHz

Figure 7-3. MFP External Oscillator Components

7.7 AC ELECTRICAL CHARACTERISTICS ($V_{CC} = 5.0$ Vdc $\pm 5\%$, $V_{SS} = 0$ Vdc, $T_A = 0°C$ to $70°C$ unless otherwise noted; See Figures 7-4 through 7-7)

Num	Characteristic	Min	Max	Unit
1	$\overline{CS}$, $\overline{IACK}$, $\overline{DS}$ Width High	50	–	ns
2	Address Valid to Falling $\overline{CS}$ Setup Time	30	–	ns
3	Data Valid Prior to Rising $\overline{DS}$ Setup Time	280	–	ns
4(1)	$\overline{CS}$, $\overline{IACK}$ Valid to Falling Clock Setup Time	50	–	ns
5	Clock Low to $\overline{DTACK}$ Low	–	220	ns
6	$\overline{CS}$ or $\overline{DS}$ High to $\overline{DTACK}$ High	–	60	ns
7	$\overline{CS}$ or $\overline{DS}$ High to $\overline{DTACK}$ High Impedance	–	100	ns
8	$\overline{CS}$ or $\overline{DS}$ High to Data Invalid Hold Time	0	–	ns
9	$\overline{CS}$ or $\overline{DS}$ High to Data High Impedance	–	50	ns
10	$\overline{CS}$ or $\overline{DS}$ High to Address Invalid Hold Time	0	–	ns
11	Data Valid from $\overline{CS}$ Low	–	250	ns
12	Read Data Valid to $\overline{DTACK}$ Low Setup Time	50	–	ns
13	$\overline{DTACK}$ Low to $\overline{DS}$ or $\overline{CS}$ High Hold Time	0	–	ns
14	$\overline{IEI}$ Low to Clock Falling Setup Time	50	–	ns
15	$\overline{IEO}$ Valid from Clock Low Delay Time	–	220	ns
16	Data Valid from Clock Low Delay Time	–	300	ns
17	$\overline{IEO}$ Invalid from $\overline{IACK}$ High Delay Time	–	100	ns
18	$\overline{DTACK}$ Low from Clock High Delay Time	–	220	ns
19	$\overline{IEO}$ Valid from $\overline{IEI}$ Low Delay Time	–	140	ns
20	Data Valid from $\overline{IEI}$ Low Delay Time	–	200	ns
21	Clock Cycle Time	250	1000	ns
22	Clock Width Low	110		ns
23	Clock Width High	110		ns
24(2)	$\overline{CS}$, $\overline{IACK}$ Inactive to Rising Clock Setup Time	100	–	ns
25	I/O Minimum Active Pulse Width	100	–	ns
26	I/O Minimum Time Between Active Edges	100	–	ns
27	I/O Data Valid from Rising $\overline{CS}$ or $\overline{DS}$	–	500	ns
28	Receiver Ready Delay from Rising RC	–	240	ns
29	Transmitter Ready Delay from Rising TC	–	295	ns
30	Timer Output Low from Rising Edge of $\overline{CS}$ or $\overline{DS}$ (A and B) (Reset Output Time)	–	500	ns
31	Output Time Valid from Internal Timeout	–	$2 t_{CLK}$ + 300	ns
32	Timer Clock Low Time	110	–	ns
33	Timer Clock High Time	110	–	ns
34	Timer Clock Cycle Time	250	1000	ns
35	$\overline{RESET}$ Low Time	2	–	μs
36	Delay to Falling $\overline{INTR}$ from External Interrupt Active Transition	–	380	ns
37	Transmitter Internal Delay from Rising or Falling Edge of TC	550	–	ns
38	Receiver Buffer Full Interrupt Transition Delay Time from Rising Edge of RC	750	–	ns
39	Receiver Error Interrupt Transition Delay Time from Falling Edge of RC	750	–	ns
40	Serial Input Setup Time from Rising Edge of RC (Divide-by-One Only)	80	–	ns
41	Data Hold Time from Rising Edge of RC (Divide-by-One Only)	350	–	ns
42	Serial Output Data Valid from Falling Edge of TC	–	390	ns
43	Transmitter Clock Low Time	500	–	ns

NOTES:

1. If the setup time is not met, $\overline{CS}$ will not be recognized until the next falling clock.

2. If this setup time is met (for consecutive cycles), the minimum hold-off time of one clock cycle will be obtained. If not met, the hold-off time will be two clock cycles.

7.7 AC ELECTRICAL CHARACTERISTICS (Continued)

($V_{CC} = 5.0$ Vdc $\pm 5\%$, $V_{SS} = 0$ Vdc, $T_A = 0°C$ to $70°C$, unless otherwise noted; See Figures 7-4 through 7-7)

Num	Characteristic	Min	Max	Unit
44	Transmitter Clock High Time	500	—	ns
45	Transmitter Clock Cycle Time	1.05	—	ns
46	Receiver Clock Low Time	500	—	ns
47	Receiver Clock High Time	500	—	ns
48	Receiver Clock Cycle Time	1.05	—	ns
49	$\overline{CS}$, $\overline{IACK}$, $\overline{DS}$ Width Low	—	80	t_{CLK}
50	Serial Output Data Valid from Falling Edge of TC (Divided-by 16)	—	490	ns

> Timing diagrams (Figures 7-4, 7-5, 7-6, and 7-7) are located on foldout pages 1 through 4 at the end of this document.

7.8 TIMER AC CHARACTERISTICS

Definitions:
Error = Indicated time value − actual time value
$t_{psc} = t_{CLK} \times$ Prescale Value

Internal Timer Mode:
Single Interval Error (Free Running) (See Note 2) .... ± 100 ns
Cumulative Internal Error 0
Error Between Two Timer Reads .... $\pm (t_{psc} - 4 t_{CLK})$
Start Timer to Stop Timer Error .... $2 t_{CLK} + 100$ ns to $- (t_{psc} + 6 t_{CLK} + 100$ ns)
Start Timer to Read Timer Error .... 0 to $- (t_{psc} + 6 t_{CLK} + 400$ ns)
Start Timer to Interrupt Request Error (See Note 3) .... $-2 t_{CLK}$ to $- (4 t_{CLK} + 800$ ns)

Pulse Width Measurement Mode:
Measurement Accuracy (See Note 1) .... $2 t_{CLK}$ to $- (t_{psc} + 4 t_{CLK})$
Minimum Pulse Width .... $4 t_{CLK}$

Event Counter Mode:
Minimum Active Time of TAI and TBI .... $4 t_{CLK}$
Minimum Inactive Time of TAI and TBI .... $4 t_{CLK}$

NOTES:
1. Error may be cumulative if repetitively performed.
2. Error with respect to t_{out} or $\overline{IRQ}$ if note 3 is true.
3. Assuming it is possible for the timer to make an interrupt request immediately.

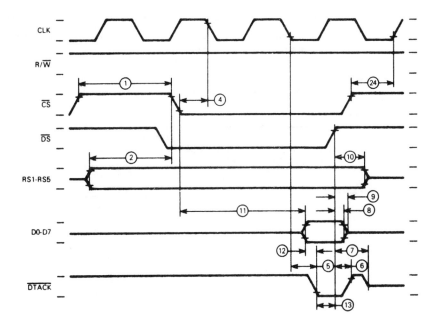

Figure 7-4. Read Cycle Timing

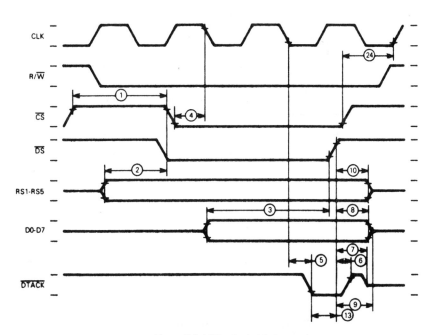

Figure 7-5. Write Cycle Timing

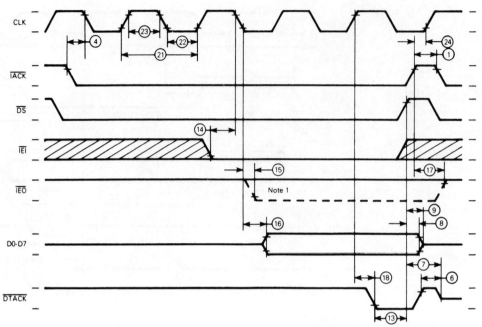

NOTE 1. IEO only goes low if no acknowledgeable interrupt is pending. If IEO goes low, DTACK and the data bus remain in the high-impedance state.

Figure 7-6. Interrupt Acknowledge Cycle (IEI Low)

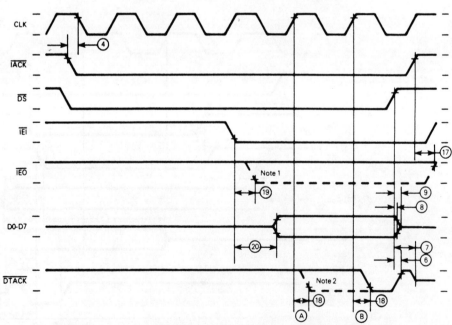

NOTES: 1. IEO only goes low if no acknowledgeable interrupt is pending. If IEO goes low, DTACK and the data bus remain in the high-impedance state.
2. DTACK will go low at Ⓐ if specification number 14 is met. Otherwise, DTACK will go low at Ⓑ.

Figure 7-7. Interrupt Acknowledge Cycle (IEI High)

Chapter 3

Serial

Input/Output

In this section we examine the serial interface between computers and VDTs, modems and printers. A description of a powerful and versatile single-chip serial interface controller, the 68681 DUART, is included.

Serial input/output data links transmit information across a channel one bit at a time. Serial data transmission is clearly inefficient as, at a bit rate of m bits/second, an n-bit message takes n/m seconds to transmit. If the n bits of the message were transmitted in parallel on n lines, the effective transmission rate would be n times greater. The appeal of the serial data link is not its efficiency but its simplicity, or to be more precise, its low cost.

A short serial data link requires, typically, a two-wire connection between a transmitter and a receiver. Such a link is not expensive to implement as it uses a low-cost transmission path (coaxial cable or a twisted pair) and relatively cheap connectors. The hidden cost of a serial data link lies in its inefficient operation in comparison with the parallel data link.

If information is transmitted serially, one bit at a time, the receiver has the problem of dividing the incoming data stream into separate bits and then grouping these bits into separate *characters*, *words* or *messages*. Any of today's engineers could readily design an appropriate scheme for the division of a data stream into bits and words. In order to make serial data transmission systems compatible, two arrangements for the transmission of digital data between computers and their peripherals have been adopted and standardized. These are asynchronous serial systems and synchronous serial systems.

3.1 The serial interface

Asynchronous serial transmission systems have been around for a very long time and provide a crude but effective approach to the division of a data stream into distinct bits and characters. Information is transmitted in the form of individual characters, each encoded as 7 or 8 bits (plus a 2- to 4-bit overhead). The majority of modern systems employ the ISO 7-bit code to encode data (formerly called the American Standard Code for Information Interchange, ASCII) which provides $2^7 = 128$ unique characters. The alphanumeric symbols (upper and lower case letters, numbers and symbols such as *, +, −, ., :, etc.) are represented by 96 characters. Another 32 characters are non-printing characters such as back-space, carriage return, and data link control characters. The ISO 7-bit code is well suited to the transmission of text but is not optimum for the transmission of pure binary data.

If the receiver end of a data link had access to the clock at the transmitter end, there would be little problem in separating the individual bits. The incoming data stream is divided into bits by sampling the state of the received data on each, say, positive transition of the clock. Synchronous serial transmission systems provide the receiver with a clock by *combining* the clock and data signals into a composite signal. An asynchronous system prefixes each character with a start bit which resynchronizes a free-running clock at the receiver for the duration of the character. Figure 3.1 illustrates asynchronous serial transmission.

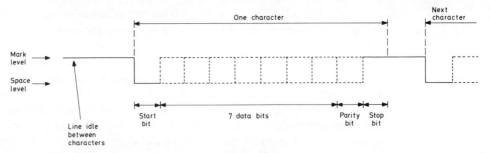

FIGURE 3.1 Asynchronous serial transmission

Between characters, the line lies in its idle or mark state. When the transmitter wishes to send a character, it puts a space state on the line for one bit period. The 7-bit character is then transmitted following this so-called start bit. After the character has been transmitted, a parity bit is sent to provide a limited measure of error protection. Finally, the line returns to its idle state for one (or optionally two) bit periods to provide a stop bit between successive characters. Because this arrangement permits 7- or 8-bit characters, odd, even or no parity options, and one or two stop bits, there are 12 options for asynchronous serial transmission systems!

As the line is *never* at a space level for more than about ten bit periods (i.e. one character), the transmission of a continuous space level can be used to signify a fault or an interrupt condition. Some asynchronous transmitters are able to force the line into a constant space level, called a *break*, under program control. Equally, some asynchronous receivers are able to detect a break and to interrupt the host microprocessor.

To be honest, it would not be difficult to construct an asynchronous receiver (or a transmitter) from SSI and MSI TTL logic. But it would be cumbersome – especially if the system is to deal with the various options available. Fortunately, one of the first peripherals to appear after the introduction of the microprocessor was the ACIA – the asynchronous communications interface adaptor. The ACIA combines both the receiver and transmitter functions in a single package, is programmable and interfaces readily with microprocessors.

3.1.1 The RS232C physical layer protocol

The first really universal standard for the physical layer was published in 1969 by the Electronic Industry Association (EIA) in the USA and is known as RS232C (Recommended Standard 232 version C). Because 1969 is a long time ago in the world of electronics and predates the microprocessor revolution, RS232C could not have been developed for today's world. It was intended for a specialized purpose but has now been adapted by many manufacturers to suit modern data links. The development of such an early standard is good because RSC232C was there ready to be used when today's new microcomputer equipment first appeared. Unfortunately, it was not optimized for such a role.

The Electronics Industry Association revised the RS232C specification in 1987 and produced a new specification EIA 232D. Recommended specification 232C has been updated to 232D and the *RS* replaced by the more logical *EIA*. Differences between versions C and D are quite small and, for the remainder of this chapter, we will continue to use the term RS232C, as it will be some time before most engineers change their terminology.

The 1960s saw a rapid expansion in the popularity of the general-purpose digital computer. As computers were then large and expensive, it was often necessary to link them to remote terminals or to the source of data (e.g. a scientific experiment) by means of a data link. In those days, the idea of dedicating a computer to a single experiment or to one user was almost unheard of. Wherever the transmission path between the terminal and the computer was greater than some hundreds of metres, it was necessary to use the only existing communication network to carry the digital data. The *existing communication network* was, and still is, the telephone system or, to give it its more formal title, *the public switched telephone network* (PSTN). The word *switched* is used because the act of dialling a telephone number causes links to be connected (i.e. switched) between telephone exchanges to build up an end-to-end path.

It is impossible to connect computers directly to the telephone network, as the former uses two-state binary signals to represent data and the latter transmits only time-varying analog signals. The PSTN can transmit only signals whose amplitudes are not constant (i.e. a steady logical zero or logical one cannot be transmitted). Moreover, the PSTN cannot faithfully transmit signals whose levels change rapidly (for example a zero-to-one transition). Basically, the PSTN transmits signals whose rate of change falls in the range 300–3000 Hz.

Data signals can be sent over the PSTN by first encoding them into analog form at the transmitter and then decoding them back into digital form at the receiver. The encoder is called a modulator and the decoder a demodulator. Equipment performing both functions (needed for two-way transmission) is known as a modem (*mod*ulator *dem*odulator). Figure 3.2 illustrates a data link employing three stages: a transmission path between a terminal and a modem, a path between the modem at one point in the PSTN and a modem at another point in the PSTN, and a path between the second modem and a computer. Incidentally, the transmission path linking modems is called a bandpass channel, and that linking a modem with digital equipment is called a baseband channel. A bandpass channel transmits signals only between two frequencies, while a baseband channel transmits signals with frequency components from zero up to some maximum value.

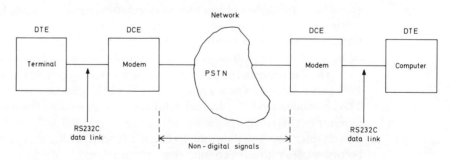

FIGURE 3.2   The role of RS232C in computer communications

There are three types of transmission path between stations. The most basic transmission path is called *simplex* and permits the transmission of information in one direction only. That is, there is a single transmitter at one end of the transmission path and a single receiver at the other end. There is no reverse flow of information. The other two arrangements are more interesting and are called half-duplex and full–duplex. These are illustrated by Figures 3.3(a) and (b). In a half-duplex data link, information is transmitted in only one direction at a time (e.g. from A to B or from B to A). Two-way transmission is achieved by *turning round* the channel. For example, the radio found in a taxi represents a half-duplex system. Either the driver speaks to the base station or the base station speaks to the driver. They cannot have a simultaneous two-way conversation. When the driver has finished speaking, he or she says 'over' and switches the radio from transmit mode to receive mode. On hearing 'over', the base station is switched from receive mode to transmit mode. In a full-duplex system, simultaneous transmission in both directions is possible. The telephone channel is an example of a full-duplex system, because it is possible to both speak and listen at the same time. However, some data transmission systems use the telephone network in a half-duplex mode.

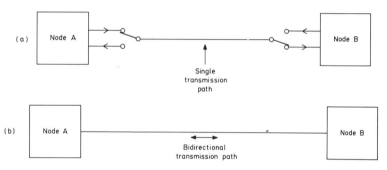

FIGURE 3.3 (a) The half-duplex channel. (b) The full-duplex channel

Early in the development of data transmission systems, RS232C was created as a standard for the connection between computer equipment and modems so that any manufacturer's computer equipment can be simply plugged into another manufacturer's modem, as long as both systems conform to RS232C. Such a standard allows one manufacturer to produce equipment for a different manufacturer's computers. Although it is sometimes said that standards limit progress, the converse is true. Without agreed standards, a manufacturer is very wary of entering a market. Who would produce LP phonogram records if there were, say, 20 different speeds instead of the standard speed of $33\frac{1}{3}$ r.p.m.? RS232C specifies the plug and socket at the modem and the digital equipment (i.e. their mechanics), the nature of the transmission path and the signals required to control the operation of the modem (i.e. the functionality of the data link).

From the point of view of the standard, the modem is known as *data communications equipment* (DCE) and the digital equipment to be connected to the modem is known as *data terminal equipment* (DTE). A corollary is that RS232C specifies a link between a DTE and a DCE rather than a link between two similar devices. This is important, because the RS232C standard is now largely used to link together two similar pieces of equipment (i.e. both ends are DTEs). We will soon see the significance of this.

Because RS232C was intended for DTE–DCE links, its functions are very largely those needed to control a modem. Unfortunately, the control functions provided by RS232C data links are not always suited to, or needed by, links between two DTEs. In practice, this means that a computer manufacturer and a printer manufacturer may both supply equipment sold as *conforming to RS232C*. Yet each may choose to implement a subset of the many functions provided by RS232C, as not all the functions are required by this application. Unfortunately, they may choose slightly different subsets, making it impossible to plug the printer into the computer with a cable and connector conforming to RS232C.

The mechanical part of the RS232C standard

We deal with the mechanical part of the RS232C standard first because it is the easiest part of the standard to understand and because it is the most widely accepted aspect of the standard. That is, although many manufacturers implement DTEs or DCEs which conform only to subsets of RS232C, or which violate some aspect of RS232C, few manufacturers violate the mechanical part of RS232C. Curiously enough, the mechanical aspect of the RS232C standard is relegated to an appendix and is a non-mandatory part of the standard. However, the newer EIA232D does include the mechanical details of the connectors in the body of the standard.

The mechanical connectors conforming to RS232C and illustrated in Figure 3.4 are called DB–25 (or 25–pin D-type) connectors. They are also

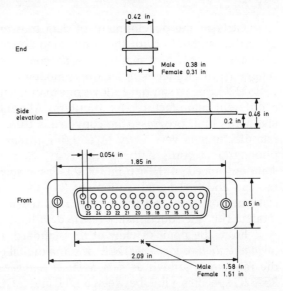

FIGURE 3.4　The mechanics of connectors conforming to RS232C

defined by BS 4505 part 5 and by ISO standard 2110-1972. There are two types of DB-25 connector, male and female. The male connector (DB-25-P) is associated with DTEs and the female connector (DB-25-S) is associated with DCEs.

As we pointed out above, most equipment said to have an *RS232C interface* employs the correct type of mechanical connector. Unfortunately, some equipment uses a plug (male) when it should use a socket (female). Therefore, the equipment user must invariably check the RS232C interface of new equpment before connecting it to existing apparatus. It is very rare that an RS232C lead, made to connect equipment A to equipment B, can be used without modification to connect X to Y; this is usually because the functions performed by the wires and their connectors vary, rather than because of the use of non-standard connectors.

The electrical part of the RS232C standard

The electrical aspects of RS232C define the nature of the signals using the data link. Ultimately, the electrical nature of RS232C determines how long the data link can be and how fast data can be transmitted over it. As in the case of the mechanical interface, the electrical characteristics of RS232C links are normally complied with by most manufacturers and gross violations of RS232C signal levels are rare.

Information within digital systems is represented by two *ranges* of voltages, one range representing a logical one and the other a logical zero. Figure 3.5(a) illustrates the situation for the TTL logic found in the majority of

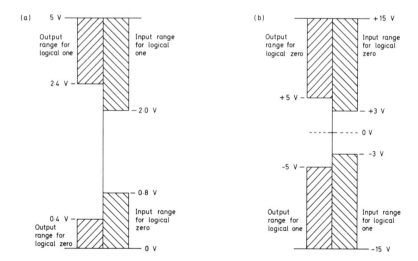

FIGURE 3.5 Signal levels in TTL and RS232C circuits'. (a) Signals in a TTL circuit, (b) Signals in an RS232C circuit

digital systems. Note that there are different voltage ranges for outputs and for inputs. For example, a TTL output in a logical one state is guaranteed (by the manufacturer) to fall within the range 2.4–5 V. A logical input in the range 2.0–5.0 V is guaranteed to be interpreted as a logical one. Consequently, the worst-case output (2.4 V) exceeds the lower level at which a logical one will reliably be detected (i.e. 2.0 V) by 0.4 V. This figure is known as the d.c. noise immunity of the system for a logical one state. It is a measure of the tolerance of the system to noise signals. A worst-case logical one output at 2.4 V can have a noise spike of up to −0.4 V added to it and still be reliably interpreted as a logical one. TTL signals in a logical zero state have a 0.4 V noise immunity. Within digital systems, noise pulses of 0.4 V or more are rare and this level of guaranteed noise immunity is adequate. However, it is not suitable for signals which travel outside the equipment and which have path lengths greater than a few centimetres.

Figure 3.5(b) shows the signal levels specified for RS232C circuits. The guaranteed output range for logical zero signals is +5 to +15 V and for logical one signals it is −5 to −15 V. Similarly, input signals are guaranteed to be reliably detected if they fall within the range +3 to +15 V (logical zero) and −3 to −15 V (logical one).

Three things can be observed from Figure 3.5(b). Logical one signals are more negative (electrically) than logical zero signals. The way in which signal levels are named is purely arbitrary. In the world of data transmission, a logical zero is also called a *space* and a logical one a *mark* for reasons which go back to the days of the telegraph. Second, the signal levels are symmetric about zero volts (ground level). Finally, the d.c. noise immunity of RS232C signals is 2.0 V for both logical zero and one states, which is five times that of TTL signals.

The voltage levels chosen for the RS232C interface permit reliable communication over a maximum specified distance of 15 metres (50 ft) at rates of up to 20 000 bits/second. Consequently, an RS232C data link can operate over a distance of no more than 15 metres. The maximum path length was determined by testing ordinary cable with RS232C signals using worst-case signal values.

In practice, an RS232C system will almost certainly operate over very much greater distances of hundreds or even thousands of metres, because the transmitter will invariably put out a signal of approximately +10 V or −10 V and the typical receiver will normally detect a signal of greater than about +1.8 V as a logical zero and a signal of less than +0.8 V as a logical one. Here we have an interesting situation. Commercially available components sold as conforming to RS232C exceed the minima defined by the standard. Therefore, it is possible to exceed the maximum length of the data link operationally. Equally, such a link can no longer be said to conform to the RS232C standard. A wise (cautious?) manufacturer should not sell equipment as being RS232C compatible if the data link exceeds 15 metres (50 feet), even if the manufacturer *knows* that the system will operate over 100 feet. If you are confused, consider the following. The manufacturer of an aircraft states that the airframe should be checked by X-raying it after 10 000 flying hours. An airframe has flown for 9 995 hours and has a trip of 10 hours ahead of it. Can the owner leave the test until the end of the trip? After all, 10 000 is an approximate value and what's 10 hours in 10 000? But, we all know the answer to the above question. A standard should be observed. It was not created as a guideline.

One of the reasons that the electrical characteristics of the RS232C standard are complied with by most systems is that they are very conservative in terms of today's available technology. Integrated circuits that convert TTL signals into RS232C format (line drivers) and circuits which convert RS232C signals into TTL format (line receivers) are widely available at very low cost. Figure 3.6 shows how such circuits are used. Due to modern component packaging, there are usually four line drivers or receivers per 14-pin package.

Because of the limitations on RS232C signals in terms of signalling speed and distance, new standards have been defined to permit operation over much greater distances and at much higher data rates. These will be dealt with later.

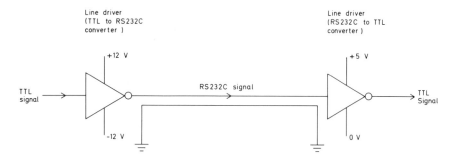

FIGURE 3.6 The RS232C circuit

3.1.2 The functionality of RS232C signals

The next step in our examination of the RS232C standard is to describe the *functions* carried out by the RS232C signals flowing between the DTE and the DCE. It is this aspect of RS232C that causes all the trouble when printer X is connected to microcomputer Y. Table 3.1 provides a list of the pins specified by the RS232C standard and the names of the associated circuits. RS232C circuits are classified as ground or common circuits (prefix A), data circuits (prefix B), control circuits (prefix C) or timing circuits (prefix D). RS232C also makes provision for a secondary channel with limited facilities. Secondary circuits are prefixed by SB (data) or by SC (control). In practice, many applications of RS232C use a subset of the lines defined in the standard. Here we consider only the most widely used functions provided by RS232C.

TABLE 3.1   RS232 connections for DTE

PIN NUMBER	CIRCUIT	DESCRIPTION
1	AA	Protective Ground
2	BA	Transmitted Data
3	BB	Received Data
4	CA	Request to Send
5	CB	Clear to Send
6	CC	Data Set Ready
7	AB	Signal Ground (Common Return)
8	CF	Received Line Signal Detector
9	—	(Reserved for Data Set Testing)
10	—	(Reserved for Data Set Testing)
11		Unassigned
12	SCF	Secondary received Line signal Detector
13	SCB	Secondary Clear to Send
14	SBA	Secondary Transmitted Data
15	DB	Transmission Signal Element Timing (DCE Source)
16	SBB	Secondary Received Data
17	DD	Receiver Signal Element Timing (DCE Source)
18		Unassigned
19	SCA	Secondary Request to Send
20	CD	Data Terminal Ready
21	CG	Signal Quality Detector
22	CE	Ring Indicator
23	CH/CI	Data Signal Rate Selector (DTE/DCE Source)
24	DA	Transmit Signal Element Timing (DTE Source)
25		Unassigned

The minimal RS232C function

The absolute minimum service provided by an RS232C data link is the point-to-point transmission of data without any associated control or timing functions. Figure 3.7 illustrates such a subset. Information is transmitted between DTE and DCE (or DTE and DTE) in a single direction (called simplex) or in two directions (called full-duplex), providing the four variations in Figure 3.7.

Note that when DTE is connected to DCE (Figure 3.7(a)), the corresponding pins of the DTE and DCE are connected together (i.e. 2 to 2, 3 to 3), because the data-out pin of the DTE is the corresponding data-in pin of the DCE. When DTE is connected to DTE (Figures 3.7(b) and 3.7(d)), it is necessary to *cross over* pins 2 and 3 as shown.

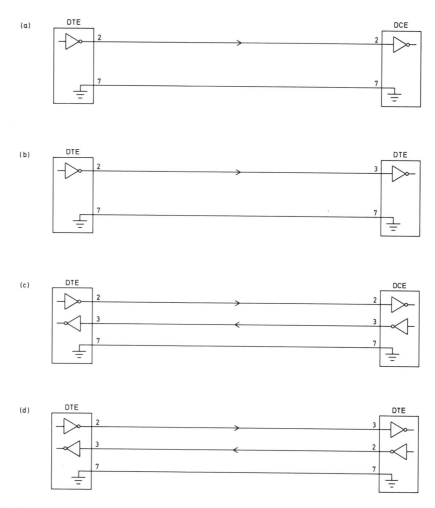

FIGURE 3.7 A minimal subset of RS232C signals. (a) DTE connected to DCE simplex, (b) DTE connected to DTE simplex, (c) DTE connected to DCE full-duplex, (d) DTE connected to DTE full-duplex

Basic RS232C control lines

Relatively few data links use the absolute minimum subset of functions described in Figure 3.7. Even modest peripherals such as printers require some form of control. Figure 3.8 illustrates the most widely used control lines. The arrows at the end of signal lines show the direction of data transmission with respect to the DTE. The function of these control lines is described below.

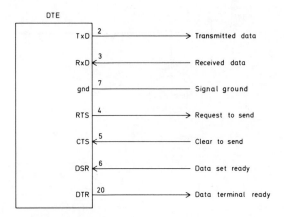

FIGURE 3.8   Some RS232C control functions

Request to send (RTS)

This is a signal from the DTE to the DCE. When asserted, RTS indicates to the DCE that the DTE wishes to transmit data to it.

Clear to send (CTS)

CTS is a signal from the DCE to the DTE and, when asserted, indicates that the DCE is ready to receive data from the DTE.

Data set ready (DSR)

This is a signal from the DCE to the DTE which indicates the readiness of the DCE. When this signal is asserted, the DCE is able to receive from the DTE. DSR indicates that the DCE (usually a modem) is switched on and is in its normal functioning mode (as opposed to its self-test mode).

Data terminal ready (DTR)

DTR is a signal from the DTE to the DCE. When asserted, DTR indicates that the DTE is ready to accept data from the DCE. In systems with a modem, it maintains the connection and keeps the channel open. If DTR is negated, the communication is broken, causing the removal of the DCE from the communications channel. Negating DTR is the same as hanging up a phone.

The way in which the RTS and CTS pair of control signal is applied is illustrated by Figure 3.9. In Figure 3.9(a), DTE is connected to DCE without any lines being crossed over. In Figure 3.9(b), DTE is connected to DTE and pins 4 (RTS) and 5 (CTS) are crossed over. We must do this because the RTS output of one side of the data link serves as the CTS input at the other side.

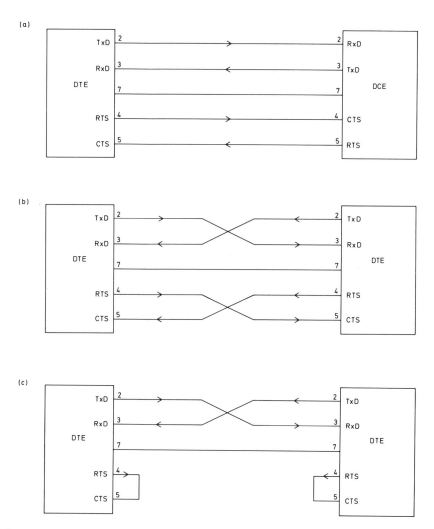

FIGURE 3.9 A basic subset of RS232C control functions. (a) DTE to DCE with remote control, (b) DTE to DTE with remote control, (c) DTE to DTE with local control.

Figure 3.10 gives a timing diagram for the *RTS–CTS* handshaking procedure. At point A, RTS is asserted by the DTE which wishes to send data. At B, the remote DCE (or DTE) asserts CTS, in turn, to indicate that it is ready to receive data. The DTE then begins transmitting data at C. When the DTE has finished transmitting data, it negates RTS (at E) and the DCE responds by negating CTS at F. The delay between A and B is an operational parameter of the DTE–DCE (or DTE–DTE) pair and does not form part of the RS232C standard.

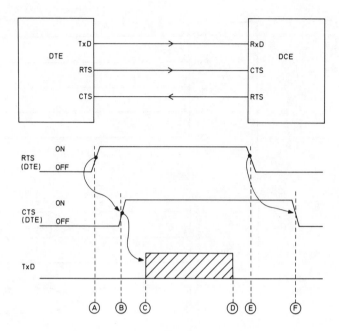

FIGURE 3.10   Handshaking between RTS and CTS

Sometimes, DTE is connected to a DCE (or a DTE) and the RTS–CTS handshaking procedure between the pair is not required (or is not implemented), *but* the DTE requires a response to the assertion of its RTS output. Figure 3.9(c) shows how this situation can be handled. The RTS output is connected *directly* to the CTS input at the connector. In this way, the DTE automatically receives a handshake whenever it asserts its RTS output. Of course, in this mode the DTE may *think* that the remote DCE–DTE is ready to receive data when it is not.

The null modem

Because there are so many computer peripherals conforming (wholly or partially) to RS232C, it is highly likely that most applications of RS232C circuits will involve the connection of a computer (DTE) to a peripheral (DTE), rather than a computer to a mode (DCE).

The difficulties in connecting DTE to DTE (i.e. the crossed connections) are often overcome by means of the *null modem*, which is a specially wired cable with DTE connectors at both ends. The appropriate wires are crossed over at one of the connectors, permitting the one DTE to be connected to another. The null modem simulates a DTE–DCE–DCE–DTE circuit. Figure 3.11 illustrates such a null modem.

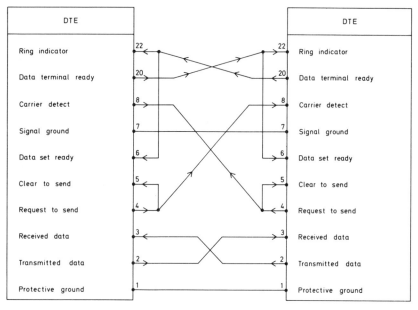

FIGURE 3.11 The null modem

RS232C becomes EIA232D

As we said earlier in this chapter, RS232C has now been replaced by EIA232D. The new standard is, as we might expect, compatible with the old standard and only slight modifications have been made in order to match RS232C more closely to its European equivalents CCITT V24 and V28 and to take account of actual current practice in linking DCEs and DTEs. Some of the changes are as follows:

1. The RS232C pin 1, protective ground, has been replaced by a shield. Pin 1 may be used to connect the screen of an interface cable to the frame of the DTE. That is, pin 1 is connected to the screen at only one end of the data link (this avoids ground-loop problems).
2. EIA232D now specifies the mechanical characteristics of the 25-pin interfaces. The old RS232C specification only *recommended* the use of 25-pin D connectors in an appendix.
3. Provision for local and remote loopback testing has been made by defining three new signals (on pins 21, 18 and 25). Pin 21 is RL (remote loopback) and is asserted by the DTE to tell the local DCE to instruct the remote DCE to go into its loopback mode, allowing the local DTE to test both DCEs and the channel linking them. The remote DCE will return signals received from the local DCE via the communication channel. In the old RS232C standard, pin

21 was a *signal quality detector* used by the modem to indicate when a signal was of such a poor quality that it was no longer reliable. Pin 18 is LL (local loopback) and acts like pin 21 except that it establishes a loopback path through the local DCE only. Local loopback permits the system to be tested from the local CPU to the local DCE and back. Pin 25 is TM (test mode) and is asserted by the DCE to inform the DTE that the DCE is in a test mode because it has received either RL or LL from the local DTE or a message from the remote DCE requesting a test mode.

4. The recommendation that the RS232C cable length be restricted to no more than 15 m (50 ft) has been removed and EIA232D permits longer transmission paths whose length is determined by the electrical loading on the cable. Not least one of the reasons for including this modification is that many users of the RS232C standard have been tolerating longer transmission paths than the legal maximum of 15 m.

3.1.3 Replacements for RS232C

We have already hinted that, from an electrical standpoint, the RS232C standard lags behind the available technology. Modern equipment needs to transmit data further and faster than that envisaged by RS232C. Consequently, two new standards have been devised to overcome some of RS232C's limitations. These are RS422 and RS423 which have also been devised by the EIA. RS422 is fully compatible with CCITT recommendations V11 and X27, and RS423 is fully compatible with V10 and X26.

Unlike RS232C, these newer standards specify only the electrical aspects of a data link and do not specify its functional characteristics. In other words, they allow signals to be transmitted from point-to-point but do not specify how the signals are to be used.

RS422 and RS423 are designed to suit two types of transmission path. The RS422 standard relates to a balanced transmission path and RS423 relates to an unbalanced transmission path. In this context, the term *balanced* refers to a type of data transmission circuit in which signals are not referenced to the electrical potential of the ground.

As we have already seen, information is normally transmitted as a voltage. The term *voltage* on its own has little meaning. What is important is the *potential difference* between two points. In an unbalanced data link (Figure 3.12(a)) the transmitter produces a potential difference between its output terminal and ground. This potential difference is transmitted to a remote receiver at the other end of the transmission path and the receiver determines whether it corresponds to a logical one or to a logical zero state. For example, an RS232C transmitter puts out a signal which is, typically, +12 V with respect to the ground or −12 V with respect to the ground.

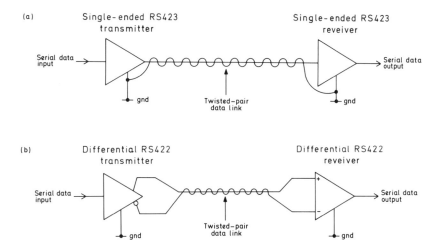

FIGURE 3.12 Unbalanced and balanced data links. (a) The unbalanced interfaces, (b) the balanced interface

A problem inherent in unbalanced data transmission results from the so-called *earth loop* or *ground loop*. Although there is only one data-carrying path between the transmitter and receiver in Figure 3.12(a), there are two ground paths. One is the ground lead between transmitter and receiver and the other is the ground itself, formed by the transmission path between the earth separating the transmitter and receiver. In an ideal world, this would not be a cause for concern if the earth potential was everywhere the same.

Unfortunately, there are many different sources of man-made electric current that induce disturbance in the ground potential. The switching of heavy currents is one of the worst sources of electrical noise (e.g. lifts and other motors). Natural electrical activity such as lightning also causes considerable (short-term) variations in the ground potential. Clearly, if the ground potential at the transmitter differs from that at the receiver, a current flows around the loop made up of the common lead between transmitter and receiver and the ground path itself. Current flowing in the ground loop generates a potential difference between the transmitter and receiver which appears as an error component in the received signal. If this signal is sufficiently large, the received signal is incorrectly interpreted and an error made. The longer the transmission path, the greater the effect of the current loop.

Figure 3.12(b) illustrates the balanced transmission path adopted by RS442. The output of the transmitter appears as a potential difference between two terminals. The potential difference generated by the transmitter is transmitted to the receiver by means of two signal-carrying wires. This output is balanced with respect to the local ground and the information content of the signal is not dependent on the potential difference between the transmission path and the ground. Note that a balanced link usually requires three wires: the two signal-carrying wires and a ground line which shields the other wires from electromagnetic pick-up.

At the receiver, the potential difference between the two transmission paths is measured and used to determine whether the signal represents a logical one or a logical zero. It is the potential difference between the lines that matters, and not their potential with respect to ground. Suppose, for example, that one signal line is at $+1$ V with respect to ground and the other is at -1 V. The potential difference between the lines is 2 V. Imagine now that an electrical disturbance affects the ground path between the transmitter and the receiver. The signals may be received as, say, $+5$ V and $+3$ V respectively with respect to ground because *both* their levels have been increased by $+4$ V. However, the difference between the signals is still $+2$ V and therefore no error is made. The ability of a balanced transmission path to discriminate against noise voltages induced equally in both lines is called its *common mode rejection*.

RS423: a standard for unbalanced data links

The unbalanced RS423 interface is very similar to the older RS232C interface and has been introduced to provide manufacturers with a step between RS232C and RS422.

RS423 is broadly similar to RS232C but has a much tighter specification and can therefore be used under circumstances that would violate the RS232C specification. Table 3.2 compares the characteristics of RS423 and RS232C.

TABLE 3.2   The electrical details of RS232C and RS423 data links

CHARACTERISTIC	EIA RS232C	EIA RS423
Form of operation (transmission path)	Single ended	Single ended
Maximum signalling rate	20 Kbaud	300 Kbaud
Maximum transmission path	15 m	700 m
Transmitter output voltage V_0	$-25\,\text{V} < V_0 < 25\,\text{V}$	$-6\,\text{V} < V_0 < +6\,\text{V}$
Transmitter output voltage V_0 (open circuit)	$-15\,\text{V} < V_0 < +15\,\text{V}$	$-3.6\,\text{V} < V_0 < +3.6\,\text{V}$
Transmitter output impedance	50 ohms max.	Not specified
Transmitter output resistance (power off)	300 ohms min.	
Transmitter output short circuit current I_0	$-150\,\text{mA} < I_0 < 150\,\text{mA}$	$-150\,\text{mA} < I_0 < 150\,\text{mA}$
Transmitter output slew rate	30 V/μs max.	Slew rate controlled by cable length and modulation rate
Receiver input resistance	3–7 komh	>4 kohm
Receiver input threshold	-3 V and $+3$ V	-0.2 V and $+0.2$ V
Receiver input voltage range	$-25\,\text{V} < V_i < +25\,\text{V}$	$-12\,\text{V} < V_i < +12\,\text{V}$

The most important observation from Table 3.2 is that the input thresholds for RS423 signals are −0.2 V and +0.2 V and the corresponding worst-case outputs are −3 V and +3 V. These signal levels provide a reasonable noise immunity of 2.8 V for both high-level and low-level signals and yet do not have the massive undefined signal range between −3 V and +3 V that RS232C signals have.

RS423 is compatible with RS232C because its output levels ($-3.6 < V_0 < 3.6$) will drive RS232C inputs. Similarly, RS232C outputs will drive RS423 inputs.

RS422: a standard for balanced data links

Table 3.3 gives the characteristics of the RS422 balanced interface, which are broadly the same as RS423 except that transmission paths of up to 1200 m (4000 ft) and signalling rates of up to 10 Mbaud are supported. The greater transmission path and signalling rate are due to the balanced nature of the network and its greater immunity to common mode noise because of the absence of earth loop currents.

TABLE 3.3   Electrical characteristics of RS422 and RS485 data links

CHARACTERISTIC	EIA RS422	EIA RS485
Form of operation (transmission path)	Balanced (differential)	Balanced (differential)
Maximum signalling rate	10 Mbaud	10 Mbaud
Maximum transmission path	1300 m	1300 m
Transmitter output voltage (open circuit)	≤6 V between output terminals	−7 V to +12 V
Transmitter output voltage (loaded)	≥2 V between output terminals	≥1.5 V between output terminals
Transmitter output impedance	<100 ohms	<54 ohms
Transmitter output (power off)	$I_{\text{leakage}} \leqslant 100\,\mu A$	$I_{\text{leakage}} \leqslant 100\,\mu A$
Transmitter output short circuit current	$-150\,\text{mA} < I_0 < 150\,\text{mA}$	150 mA to ground, 250 mA to −8 V or +12 V
Transmitter output slew rate	No control required	No control required
Receiver input resistance	>4 kohms	>12 kohms
Receiver input threshold	−0.2 V and +0.2 V	−0.2 V and +0.2 V
Receiver input voltage range	$-12\,V < V_i < +12\,V$	$-7\,V < V_i < +12\,V$

It should be noted that RS422 does not support its maximum data rate and maximum transmission path length simultaneously. Figure 3.13 provides a graph of the transmission path length against signalling rate for RS422. Increasing the length of the data link reduces the maximum rate at which the data can be transmitted.

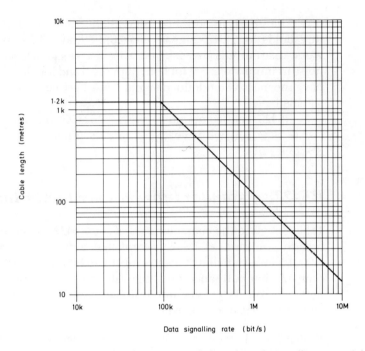

FIGURE 3.13   The relationship between path length and signalling speed for RS422 data link

RS449: a modern replacment for RS232C (EIA232D)

The RS449 standard was adopted by the Electronic Industries Association in 1977 as an upgrade from the older and more conservative RS232C while still permitting compatibility with RS232C. In short, RS449 provides all the facilities of RS232C but permits a maximum data rate of 2 Mbps and transmission paths of up to 1200 m (4000 ft). Unlike RS232C, RS449 defines only the mechanical, functional and procedural elements of the interface. Electrical characteristics are excluded because RS449 is built on the electrical characteristics of RS423A and RS422A. Interestingly enough, the RS449 standard specifies *two* mechanical connectors. One is a 9-pin D connector and the other a 37-pin D connector. By specifying two possible connectors, it is possible to use either a maximum set of RS449 functions or a minimum subset. The standard specifies the 37-pin connector for a primary channel and the 9-pin connector for a secondary channel. Table 3.4 lists the circuits provided by the RS449 interface. Note that RS449 includes the LL, RL and TM pins that have now been added to RS232C by its upgrade to EIA232D.

TABLE 3.4 The RS449 interface

EIA RS-449		EIA RS-232C		CCITT RECOMMENDATION	
SG	Signal ground	AB	Signal ground	102	Signal ground
SC	Send common			102a	DTE common
RC	Receive common			102b	DCE common
IS	Terminal in service				
IC	Incoming call	CE	Ring indicator	125	Calling indicator
TR	Terminal ready	CD	Data terminal ready	108/2	Data terminal ready
DM	Data mode	CC	Data set ready	107	Data set ready
SD	Send data	BA	Transmitted data	103	Transmitted data
RD	Received data	BB	Received data	104	Received data
TT	Terminal timing	DA	Transmitter signal element timing (DTE source)	113	Transmitter signal element timing (DTE source)
ST	Send timing	DB	Transmitter signal element timing (DCE source)	114	Transmitter signal element timing (DCE source)
RT	Receive timing	DD	Receiver signal element timing	115	Receiver signal element timing (DCE source)
RS	Request to send	CA	Request to send	105	Request to send
CS	Clear to send	CB	Clear to send	106	Ready for sending
RR	Receiver ready	CF	Received line signal detector	109	Data channel received line signal detector
SQ	Signal quality	CG	Signal quality detector	110	Data signal quality detector
NS	New signal				
SF	Select frequency			126	Select transmit frequency
SR	Signalling rate selector	CH	Data signal rate selector (DTE source)	111	Data signalling rate selector (DTE source)
SI	Signalling rate indicator	CI	Data signal rate selector (DCE source)	112	Data signalling rate selector (DCE source)
SSD	Secondary send data	SBA	Secondary transmitted data	118	Transmitted backward channel data
SRD	Secondary receive data	SBB	Secondary received data	119	Received backward channel data
SRS	Secondary request to send	SCA	Secondary request to send	120	Transmit backward channel line signal
SCS	Secondary clear to send	SCB	Secondary clear to send	121	Backward channel ready
SRR	Secondary receiver ready	SCF	Secondary received line signal detector	122	Backward channel received line signal detector
LL	Local loopback			141	Local loopback
RL	Remote loopback			140	Remote loopback
TM	Test mode			142	Test indicator
SS	Select standby			116	Select standby
SB	Standby indicator			117	Standby indicator

RS485: a standard for party-lines

RS422 is an excellent choice for anyone implementing a reasonably long transmission path between a transmitter and a number of receivers at data rates well above those supported by RS232C. Unfortunately, RS422 does not permit *party-line* operation in which a number of potential transmitters may be connected to the channel as well as the receivers.

In 1983 the Electronics Industries Association approved a new standard for balanced data transmission which was based on RS422 but which would allow multipoint operation (i.e. more than one transmitter may be connected to the transmission path). Figure 3.14 illustrates the arrangement of a possible RS485 party-line circuit. Note that the standard specifies only the electrical properties of the circuit and leaves all protocols to the user. In effect, the RS485 standard provides the user with a tool for implementing simple bus-based LANs.

The RS485 standard specifies the electrical characteristics of drivers and receivers to be connected to the party-line of Figure 3.14. These drivers and receivers must be able to operate reliably in the presence of common-mode signal errors and permit up to 32 drivers or receivers to be connected to the party-line. RS485 is intended to be used with a twisted-pair transmission medium with a characteristic impedance of 120 ohms. Moreover, RS485 specifies that drivers and receivers must not be harmed in the event of a short circuit or bus contention in which two transmitters attempt to drive the bus in opposite directions at the same time.

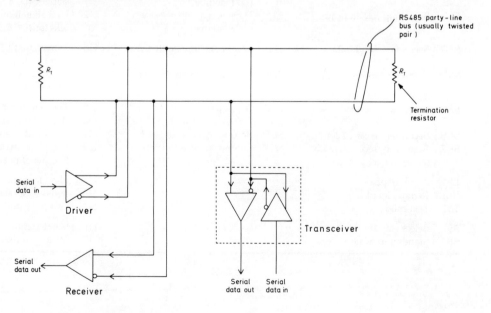

FIGURE 3.14 The RS485 circuit

The major characteristics of RS485 drivers are as follows:

1. A driver's off-state output leakage current must be less than $100\,\mu$A.
2. A driver must be able to source a differential output voltage of 1.5–5 V under common-mode voltage conditions of -7 to $+12$ V.
3. As a measure of protection from bus contention, a driver must not suffer damage if its outputs are connected to a voltage source between -7 V and $+12$ V when its output state is logical zero, logical one or floating. Table 3.3 provides some of the characteristics of RS485 alongside its predecessor RS422.

3.2 The 68681 DUART

An early, and still very popular, ACIA is the 6850 which was designed for the 6800 microprocessor. The 6850 acts as a receiver and a transmitter and also carries out some functions associated with modems. The 16-bit 68000 brought with it a new generation of more sophisticated peripherals. One of which is the 68681 DUART (dual asynchronous receiver/transmitter) which interfaces with the 68000, performs the functions of two 6850-type ACIAs, and has an on-board baud-rate generator. The latter facility removes the need for a separate transmitter/receiver clock circuit.

Like many of today's interface chips, the 68681 is a powerful and versatile device but it is also rather complex. Adding more facilities to a chip increases the number of options available to the programmer, which, in turn, increases the number of registers within the chip that must be set up by the programmer before it can be used.

3.2.1 The 68681 microprocessor-side

The pin-out of the 68681 and its microprocessor-side interface is illustrated in Figure 3.15 and, as might be expected, the DUART can be connected to a 68000 with minimal hardware. Because it is an 8-bit peripheral and the 68000 has a 16-bit data bus, the DUART's data bus (D_0–D_7) must be connected to D_{00}–D_{07} or to D_{08}–D_{15} from the 68000. If D_{00}–D_{07} is used, the DUART is strobed by LDS$*$ and if D_{08}–D_{15} is used it must be strobed by UDS$*$. In Figure 3.15, the DUART is connected to D_{00}–D_{07} because we wish to make use of its vectored interrupt facility.

Address lines A_{01}–A_{04} from the 68000 are connected to the DUART's four register select inputs, RS1–RS4, allowing the programmer to select one of the

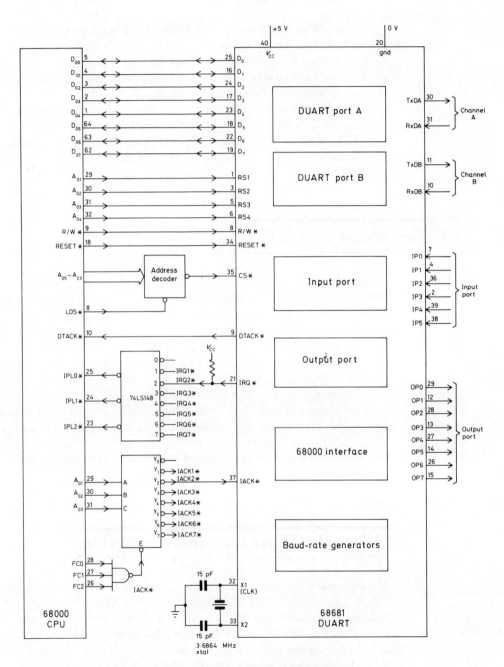

FIGURE 3.15   The microprocessor-side interface of the 68681 DUART

DUART's 16 uniquely addressable internal registers. Note that there are, in fact, more than 16 internal registers. The DUART can be accessed only when its CS* input is asserted. CS* is connected to an address decoder strobed by LDS* so that the DUART is selected only by a valid access to D_{00}–D_{07} which falls within its memory space.

The DUART's RESET* input is connected to the 68000's RESET* line, resetting the DUART whenever the microprocessor is reset or whenever the 68000 pulses RESET* active-low under software control. Resetting the DUART forces its internal registers into their default states, as we shall soon see.

If the DUART is to operate in conjunction with interrupt-driven I/O, its single interrupt request output (IRQ*) must be connected to one of the seven inputs of a 74LS148 priority encoder as shown in Figure 3.15. Whenever the 68000 responds to an interrupt request at this level, it executes an interrupt acknowledge cycle to read the interrupt vector number from the DUART. An IACK cycle is detected by the NAND gate and used to strobe the 74LS138 IACK decoder. A level 2 IACK* from the decoder is connected to the DUART's IACK* input.

The only other hardware support required by the DUART is a clock for its baud-rate generators and internal timing. Either a 3.6864 MHz quartz crystal is connected across the X1, X2 pins or X1 is wired to an external 3.6864 MHz oscillator.

The peripheral side of the DUART has four groups of pins. Channel A and channel B are both independent, asynchronous, serial receiver/transmitters and each has a data-in pin (RxDA, RxDB) and a data-out pin (TxDA, TxDB). Two special-purpose parallel ports are also provided. The input port, IP_0 to IP_5, and the output port, OP_0 to OP_7, provide simple input or output ports or they can be dedicated to port A or port B modem control functions. In other words, the DUART furnishes the user with two basic ACIAs and two basic parallel ports, *or* two ACIAs with modem control functions.

3.2.2 Facilities provided by the DUART

Whenever a salesman knocks at the door and tries to sell you a new super interface chip, the obvious question to ask is, 'Well, what does it do?' Here we describe some of the more interesting features of the 68681.

In principle, all asynchronous receivers/transmitters carry out the same function – they convert data between serial and parallel forms and vice versa. In practice, some manufacturers have endowed their chips with many very helpful attributes.

One such feature is the extensive buffering of both transmitter and receiver ports. The former is doubly buffered and the latter quadruply buffered. Most receivers in other ACIAs or UARTs have only double buffering, which means that one character is held in a register while the next character is being received. If a character is received when both buffers are full, the oldest character is lost. By means of quadruple buffering, the 68681 can receive up to four characters before the microprocessor *must* read the input. Quadruple buffering stops characters being lost whenever the microprocessor is *busy* for up to four character durations. Received characters are held in the DUART's first-in first-out (FIFO) buffer which is arranged as a queue.

Basic DUART operating modes

Apart from providing all the commonly used character formats, the DUART can be programmed to operate in one of five modes (the 6850 operates only in a normal (full-duplex) mode). The modes offered by the DUART are

Normal (i.e. full duplex)
Automatic echo
Local loopback
Remote loopback
Multidrop

Figure 3.16 illustrates the first four operating modes of the DUART. In Figure 3.16(a), the DUART operates in a full-duplex mode with totally independent receiver and transmitter channels. This is the DUART's normal mode and is the same as the operating mode of most other ACIAs.

Automatic-echo mode

Figure 3.16(b) illustrates the automatic-echo mode. Each character received at the RxD terminal from the remote peripheral is *automatically* retransmitted on the TxD terminal back to the peripheral. Automatic echo is necessary when the remote peripheral requires each character to be echoed and it is wished to avoid software echo by the host microprocessor (or software echo is not available). The microprocessor-to-receiver communications path is unaffected by this mode. Note that the remote loopback can be provided for any receiver/transmitter by a few TTL gates. The whole point about the 68681 is that it saves these components. When the DUART is in the automatic-echo mode, data cannot be sent from the host (i.e. local) microprocessor to the 68681 and transmitted via TxD, as this would conflict with its automatic-echo operation.

Other features of the automatic-echo mode are

1. The received data is reclocked before being transmitted on the TxD output by the DUART's *receiver clock*.

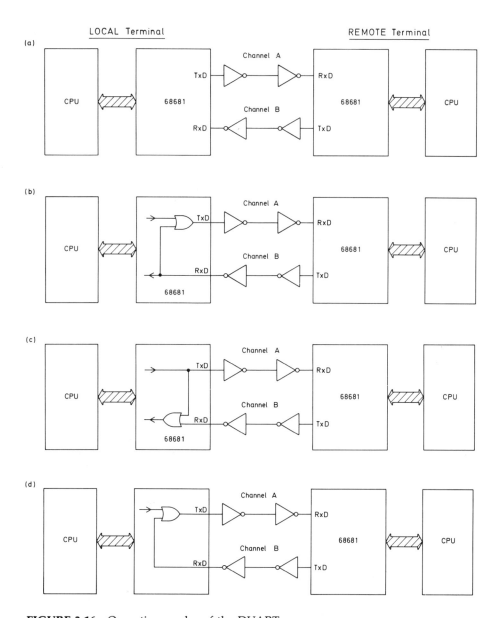

FIGURE 3.16 Operating modes of the DUART
(a) Full-duplex (normal mode): Channel A sends data from the local to the remote terminal and channel B sends data from the remote terminal to the local terminal
(b) Automatic echo: Data transmitted from the remote terminal on channel B is automatically echoed back to the remote terminal on channel A.
(c) Local loop-back: Data sent by the local terminal on channel A is echoed back to the remote terminal on channel B
(d) Remote loop-back: Data from the remote terminal transmitted on channel B is automatically transmitted back to the remote terminal on channel A.

2. The receiver must be enabled, but the transmitter may be inactive. The transmitter's TxRDY and TxEMT status bit are inactive in this mode.
3. The received parity bit is checked by the receiver, but it is not regenerated by the transmitter before retransmission. That is, it is transmitted as received.
4. A received break is echoed by the transmitter.

Local-loopback mode

In the local-loopback mode (Figure 3.16(c)), the output of the transmitter is internally connected to the input of the receiver so that RxD = TxD. In other words, the DUART talks to itself. This mode is, of course, a test mode and is used to verify the operation of the system, as it tests both transmitter and receiver hardware and software. While the DUART is in the local-loopback mode, it is still possible to transmit data to, and to receive data from, the remote peripheral. A simple transmitter/receiver test routine is implemented by means of the following procedure.

```
Self_test_DUART
      Select local-loopback mode
      Error:= false
      FOR I = 0 TO 255
      Transmit Test_data[I]
      Receive data
      IF Received-data ≠ Test_data[I] THEN Error:= true ENDIF
      ENDFOR
      Clear local-loopback mode
End Self_test_DUART
```

Remote-loopback mode

The remote-loopback mode (Figure 3.16(d)) causes incoming data on RxD from the remote peripheral to be automatically echoed back to the remote peripheral on TxD, bit by bit. The remote-loopback mode is very similar to the automatic-echo mode described above and differs only in fine detail. Remote loopback is a diagnostic mode that allows the remote peripheral to test the transmission path. The host microprocessor cannot receive data from the DUART while it is in this mode, but it can transmit data. The features of this mode are identical to the automatic-echo mode with the following exceptions.

1. The received data is not sent to the host microprocessor and error status conditions are inactive. That is, the data is echoed blindly, as if the local DUART's receiver and transmitter terminals were shorted and the DUART disconnected from these terminals.
2. The character framing is not checked.

The multidrop mode

In the multidrop mode the DUART is able to operate in a master–slave arrangement in which one DUART (the master station) is able to communicate with up to 256 other DUARTs (the slave stations). The master is able to communicate with a particular slave by uniquely addressing that slave.

In order to provide an address and a data transmission facility, the DUART does not use the standard asynchronous character format. Each character transmitted by the master (when the DUART is in its multidrop mode) consists of a start bit, the programmed number of data bits, an address/data tag bit and the programmed number of stop bits. That is the address/data bit replaces the normal parity bit. If the tag is *one*, the received character is interpreted as *data*, if it is *zero*, the received character is interpreted as an *address*. Because the parity error detecting bit is lost in this mode, it is up to the users to incorporate their own error detecting code in software (e.g. by transmitting a check-sum character after each block of data).

In the multidrop mode the slaves may have their receivers disabled – they do not interrupt their host microprocessor when data is received. Whenever they receive an address character they *wake up* and interrupt their host microprocessor (if so programmed). The microprocessor reads the address and, if it is valid for that slave, the receiver is enabled and the following data characters are read. If the address is not valid, the microprocessor does not enable the slave DUART's receiver and the DUART continues to monitor the incoming data for another address character.

The DUART's timers

The first generation of asynchronous receiver/transmitters required external clocks at (typically) 16, 4 or 1 times the rate of the received/transmitted data. Many older systems used an MC14411 baud-rate generator for this function. Newer ACIAs and DUARTs have on-chip baud-rate generators, which both save a component and *provide programmable* baud rates.

The 68681 has an on-chip oscillator which requires a 3.6864 MHz crystal to be wired between its X1 and X2 pins together with the two capacitors shown in Figure 3.15. Alternatively, a 3.6864 MHz signal can be connected to the X1 pin, if such a signal is already available on the module. The baud-rate generator supports 18 commonly used baud rates from 50 to 38 400 baud. The internal clock operates at 16 times the actual signalling rate. Note that *four* different baud rates are available simultaneously (i.e. a transmitter plus a receiver times two channels).

An interface chip ultimately exists to serve one function and that is to maximize the profit of its manufacturer. In order to do this, manufacturers provide chips with as many functions as possible, subject to the limited number of pins. The 68681 is no exception. For example, the baud-rate generator circuit also provides modest timer/counter facilities. A single 16-bit timer/counter can be programmed to operate in one of several modes including a programmable square-wave generator, a real-time clock and a watch-dog timer (i.e. time-out circuit).

The DUART's parallel port

The two parallel ports of the DUART (input bits IP_0 to IP_5 and output bits OP_0 to OP_7) are also marvels of versatility. These ports may operate as simple input and output ports respectively, allowing the 68000 to read parallel data at the input port or to write parallel data to the output port. Both ports have *alternate* functions associated with them. For example, they may be programmed to carry out some of the modem control functions found on first generation ACIAs like the 6850. We will return to the DUART's parallel ports again after we have discussed the DUART's registers and transmitter/receiver functions.

3.3 Registers of the DUART

Although some of the DUART's internal registers will have little meaning at this point in the text, we introduce them to make the reader aware of their existence. The DUART has 32 user-accessible registers arranged in pairs as illustrated in Table 3.5.

Register select lines, RS1–RS4, determine the address of each register pair. Table 3.5 gives register addresses in terms of their offset with respect to the base address of a memory-mapped DUART. The address of a register is the base address of the memory-mapped DUART plus the register number times two. The factor two is included because consecutive registers are aligned on *word* (not byte) boundaries.

A glance at Table 3.5 reveals that two or more registers may share the same address. As we have pointed out in Chapter 2, the manufacturers of the DUART have employed the R/W* input to distinguish between two registers at the same address. One register of a pair is made read-only and the other write-only. For example, the interrupt status register, ISR, can be read at the base address plus $0A. Writing to the same address accesses the interrupt mask register, IMR. Note that the IMR can *never* be read by the programmer.

Another method of increasing the number of addressable registers has been adopted by the DUART. Two registers, *channel A mode register one* and *channel A mode register two* (MR1A and MR2A) share the same address. Following a hardware reset operation (i.e. RESET* pulsed low), the MR1A register is accessed by reading from, or writing to, the DUART base address

TABLE 3.5 The 68681 DUART's internal registers

OFFSET	READ ACCESS (R/W* = 1)		WRITE ACCESS (R/W* = 0)	
0	Mode register A	(MR1A, MR2A)	Mode register A	(MR1A, MR2A)
2	Status register A	(SRA)	Clock-select register A	(CSRA)
4	Not used (do not read)		Command register A	(CRA)
6	Receiver buffer A	(RBA)	Transmitter buffer A	(TBA)
8	Input port change register	(IPCR)	Auxiliary control register	(ACR)
A	Interrupt status register	(ISR)	Interrupt mask register	(IMR)
C	Counter mode: counter MSB	(CUR)	Counter/timer upper register	(CTUR)
E	Counter mode: counter LSB	(CLR)	Counter/timer lower register	(CTLR)
10	Mode register B	(MR1B, MR2B)	Mode register B	(MR1B, MR2B)
12	Status register B	(SRB)	Clock-select register B	(CSRB)
14	Not used (do not read)		Command register B	(CBR)
16	Receiver buffer B	(RBB)	Transmitter buffer B	(TBB)
18	Interrupt-vector register	(IVR)	Interrupt-vector register	(IVR)
1A	Input port (unlatched)		Output port configuration register	(OPCR)
1C	Start counter command		Output port Bit set command	
1E	Stop counter command		Register (OPR) Bit clear command	

plus 0. In order to select MR2A, the base address plus 0 is accessed a second time. In other words, the address DUART + 0 represents either MR1A or MR2A, depending on the state of an internal flag called the *reset pointer*. Similarly, channel B mode registers (MR1B and MR2B) share the same address (offset plus $10).

Although the DUART has so many registers, it is not particularly complex to use. Its operating mode or configuration is selected according to the intended function of the DUART. Once this has been decided, most of its registers are programmed by the initialization software and then forgotten about. All that then remains to be done is to load data into the transmitter register or to read it from the receiver buffer register and then deal with any errors in the received data.

3.3.1 Transmitter and receiver functions of the DUART

Figure 3.17 shows the transmitter/receiver section of the DUART from the point of view of the programmer. For convenience, only channel A is shown, as channel B is identical apart from one tiny difference in the programming of the baud-rate generator.

Basically a character is transmitted by loading it into the *transmitter buffer register*, TBA, and a character is received by reading it from the *receiver buffer register*, RBA. The RBA is arranged as a first-in first-out queue (FIFO), three

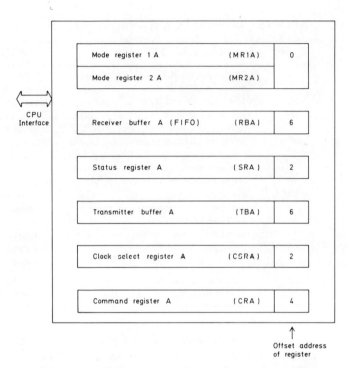

FIGURE 3.17   The transmitter/receiver registers of the DUART

characters deep. Note that the receiver buffers four characters, because there is also a receiver shift register in addition to the FIFO. To transmit the character in register D0 of a 68000, we can execute a MOVE.B D0,DUART + 6 operation and to receive a character we execute a MOVE.B DUART + 6,D0. It's as simple as that – well almost.

Before the DUART can be used to transmit and receive data, it must be initialized and the following registers set up: the channel mode registers 1 and 2 (MR1A, MR2A), the clock select register (CSRA), the auxiliary control register (ACR) and the command register (CRA). Together, these registers provide the systems designer with an amazing number of options. Let us look at MR1A first.

Channel A mode register 1

The channel A mode register 1, MR1A, is accessed at the base address after the DUART has been reset or after a reset pointer command has been issued. Table 3.6 illustrates the structure of MR1A. Register MR1A defines the size of transmitted and received characters (channel A only of course), the type of parity in use, the receiver error mode, receiver IRQ* control and receiver RTSA*

TABLE 3.6 The format of channel A mode register 1 (MR1A)

Bit	7	6	3	4 5 2	1 0
Function	RxRTS control	RxIRQ* select	Error mode	Parity select	Word length

MR1A_1	MR1A_0	Bits per character
0	0	5
0	1	6
1	0	7
1	1	8

MR1A_4	MR1A_3	MR1A_2	Parity
0	0	0	Even parity
0	0	1	Odd parity
0	1	0	Force low parity bit
0	1	1	Force high parity bit
1	0	0	No parity
1	0	1	No parity
1	1	0	Multidrop mode – data character
1	1	1	Multidrop mode – address character

MR1A_5	Receiver error mode
0	Character mode – error status applies to top of FIFO
1	Block mode – error status applies to all characters in FIFO

MR1A_6	Receiver IRQ* function
0	Rx interrupt on character received
1	Rx interrupt on FIFO full

MR1A_7	Channel A RTS output (OP_0)
0	RTSA* set or cleared under programmer control
1	RTSA* asserted on receipt of start bit if FIFO_A full

control. RTS* (request to send) performs a flow control function. Flow control in a data transmission system performs similar functions to traffic lights, one-way streets and traffic police on the roads. Data transmission systems employ flow control to limit the flow of data to levels at which the system can cope. When asserted by the *receiver*, RTS* indicates to external equipment that the receiver is in an active (operational) mode. When the receiver negates RTS*, it indicates to the remote transmitter that the receiver is busy. The RTS* output from the receiver is usually connected to the CTS*, clear to send, input of the remote transmitter. The channel A RTS* output is written *RTSA** to distinguish it from the channel B equivalent – RTSB*.

The character word length is determined by MR1A_0 and MR1A_1, permitting 5-bit to 8-bit characters. Three bits of MR1A, MR1A_2 to MR1A_4, control parity and provide enough options to satisfy the most fussy designers. Note that *force even/odd parity* means that the parity bit is independent of the character and is forced to a zero or a one.

The last two parity select options in Table 3.6 refer to the DUART's multidrop mode and configure the transmitter to send address characters or data characters.

MR1A_5 determines the way in which the receiver reports errors. When MR1A_5 = 0, the receiver error status bits in status register A, SRA, apply only to the character at the top of the FIFO – that is, the next character to be read. When MR1A_5 = 1, the error status in SRA applies to *all* characters which have reached the top of the FIFO since the last *reset error* command was issued to channel A. This so-called *block mode* option provides advance warning that there is an error in the characters already received and permits the system to ask for retransmission immediately.

MR1A_6 controls the way in which the receiver generates interrupts (if it is operating in an interrupt-driven mode). When MR1A_6 = 0, a receiver interrupt is generated whenever a new character is received (as indicated by the RxRDY status bit in SRA). When MR1A_6 = 1, an interrupt is generated only when the FIFO is full, allowing the system to operate in a *block* mode, fetching characters when a batch of four has been assembled.

MR1A_7 controls the receiver's request to send (RTSA*) output. One of the output port's pins, OP_0, can be defined as a channel A request to send, RTSA*. When MR1A = 0, the state of RTSA* is under programmer control and RTSA* is set or cleared by accessing the output port as described later. When MR1A_7 = 1, RTSA* is negated upon the detection of a valid start bit if channel A's FIFO is full, and indicates to the remote device that channel A can no longer receive data. RTSA* is reasserted when a position in the FIFO becomes free foillowing a read by the microprocessor.

Channel A mode register 2

The channel A mode register 2, MR2A, is accessed at the base address after MR1A has been accessed. Further accesses to the same address continue to select MR2A. MR1A can be accessed again only by resetting the channel A *mode register pointer* to point at MR1A by either a hardware reset or by a **reset pointer** command to the auxiliary control register. The format of MR2A is given in Table 3.7.

Bits MR2A_0 to MR2A_3 provide 16 possible lengths of the stop bit which separates consecutive characters. I find that a stop bit of one element duration is suitable for many systems.

TABLE 3.7 The format of channel A mode register 2 (MR2A)

Bit	7	6	5	4	3	2	1	0
Function	Channel mode		Transmitter RTS control	Transmitter CTS control	Stop bit length			

MR2A_3 to MR2A_0				Stop bit code (6–8 bits/character)	
				6–8 bits/char	5 bits/char
0	0	0	0	0.563	1.063
0	0	0	1	0.625	1.125
0	0	1	0	0.688	1.188
0	0	1	1	0.750	1.250
0	1	0	0	0.813	1.313
0	1	0	1	0.875	1.375
0	1	1	0	0.938	1.438
0	1	1	1	1.000	1.500
1	0	0	0	1.563	1.563
1	0	0	1	1.625	1.625
1	0	1	0	1.688	1.688
1	0	1	1	1.750	1.750
1	1	0	0	1.813	1.813
1	1	0	1	1.875	1.875
1	1	1	0	1.938	1.938
1	1	1	1	2.000	2.000

MR2A_4	Channel A clear to send control (CTSA*)
0	CTSA* has no effect on the transmitter
1	CTSA* high stops transmission

MR2A_5	Channel A RTS* OUTPUT (OP_0)
0	RTSA* set/cleared under programmer control
1	RTSA* cleared when all data transmitted

MR2A_7	MR2A_6	Transmitter/receiver operating mode
0	0	Normal mode (full duplex)
0	1	Automatic echo of received data
1	0	Local loopback
1	1	Remote loopback

MR2A_4 determines the way in which the channel A clear to send input (CTSA*) is handled by the transmitter. Parallel port input pin, IP_0, acts as the CTSA* input if it is so programmed. When MR2A_4 is zero, the state of the CTSA* input has no effect on the operation of the transmitter. When MR2A_4 = 1, the transmitter checks the status of the CTSA* input before transmitting a character. If CTSA* is asserted, the character is transmitted. If it is negated, the transmission is delayed until CTSA* is asserted, which allows the remote device to control the operation of the transmitter. Clearly, the state CTSA* = 'electrical high' corresponds to the condition 'remote receiver busy'. It should now be clear that connecting the RTS* output of a receiver to the CTS* input of a transmitter implements the flow control system we described when we discussed the receiver's RTS* output. The transmitter sends information as long as RTS* from the remote receiver is asserted. If the receiver becomes busy, it negates RTS* and the transmitter is forced to wait.

MR2A_5 controls the request to send output (RTSA*) from the channel A transmitter. When MR2A_5 = 0, the RTSA* output (i.e. OP_0) is set or cleared under program control by setting or clearing bit OP_0 of the output port. When MR2A_5 = 1, RTSA* is automatically negated after the transmitter has sent its last character and has nothing more to send (because it is waiting for further data from the microprocessor). The automatic negation of RTSA* can be used to disable the remote receiver at the end of a message. Don't be confused by the *two* RTSA*s. The *receiver* RTSA* is an output inviting the remote transmitter to go ahead, while the *transmitter* RTSA* is an output that tells the remote receiver whether it has further data to send.

The two most-significant bits of MR2A select channel A's operating mode (i.e. normal, automatic echo, local loopback, remote loopback). In normal, full-duplex, mode both MR2A_6 and MR2A_7 are zero. Switching between modes should take place when the receiver is disabled.

Before describing other registers of the DUART, it is worthwhile taking a break and showing how MR1A and MR2A are programmed. The following fragment of assembly language code demonstrates how MR1A and MR2A might be set up.

```
DUART  EQU    $FF0001          Base address of DUART
MR1A   EQU    0                Offset for channel A mode register 1
MR2A   EQU    MR1A             MR2A has the same offset as MR1A
PAR1   EQU    %00100011        Eight bits per character, even parity
*                              block error mode,
*                              no Rx-controlled RTSA* deactivation.
PAR2   EQU    %00010111        One stop bit, enable Tx CTSA* input,
*                              disable Tx RTSA* output, normal
*                              operating mode.
       LEA.L  DUART,A0         A0 points at DUART base address
       MOVE.B #PAR1,MR1A(A0)   Setup MR1A
       MOVE.B #PAR2,MR2A(A0)   Setup MR2A
```

The clock select registers (CSRA and CSRB)

The format of the channel A clock select register, CSRA, is illustrated in Table 3.8 together with the corresponding channel B equivalent, CSRB. CSRA serves

TABLE 3.8 The format of the clock select registers CSRA and CSRB

Clock-select register A (CSRA)

RECEIVER-CLOCK SELECT				Baud rate Set 1 ACR bit 7 = 0	Baud rate Set 2 ACR bit 7 = 1	TRANSMITTER-CLOCK SELECT				Baud rate Set 1 ACR bit 7 = 0	Baud rate Set 2 ACR bit 7 = 1
Bit 7	Bit 6	Bit 5	Bit 4			Bit 3	Bit 2	Bit 1	Bit 0		
0	0	0	0	50	75	0	0	0	0	50	75
0	0	0	1	110	110	0	0	0	1	110	110
0	0	1	0	134.5	134.5	0	0	1	0	134.5	134.5
0	0	1	1	200	150	0	0	1	1	200	150
0	1	0	0	300	300	0	1	0	0	300	300
0	1	0	1	600	600	0	1	0	1	600	600
0	1	1	0	1200	1200	0	1	1	0	1200	1200
0	1	1	1	1050	2000	0	1	1	1	1050	2000
1	0	0	0	2400	2400	1	0	0	0	2400	2400
1	0	0	1	4800	4800	1	0	0	1	4800	4800
1	0	1	0	7200	1800	1	0	1	0	7200	1800
1	0	1	1	9600	9600	1	0	1	1	9600	9600
1	1	0	0	38400	19200	1	1	0	0	38400	19200
1	1	0	1	Timer	Timer	1	1	0	1	Timer	Timer
1	1	1	0	IP4-16X	IP4-16X	1	1	1	0	IP3-16X	IP3-16X
1	1	1	1	IP4-1X	IP4-1X	1	1	1	1	IP3-1X	IP3-1X

Note: Receiver clock is always a 16X clock except when CSRA bits 7 through 4 equal 1111.

Note: Transmitter clock is always a 16X clock except when CSRA bits 3 through 0 equal 1111.

Clock-select register B (CSRB)

RECEIVER-CLOCK SELECT				Baud rate Set 1 ACR bit 7 = 0	Baud rate Set 2 ACR bit 7 = 1	TRANSMITTER-CLOCK SELECT				Baud rate Set 1 ACR bit 7 = 0	Baud rate Set 2 ACR bit 7 = 1
Bit 7	Bit 6	Bit 5	Bit 4			Bit 3	Bit 2	Bit 1	Bit 0		
0	0	0	0	50	75	0	0	0	0	50	75
0	0	0	1	110	110	0	0	0	1	110	110
0	0	1	0	134.5	134.5	0	0	1	0	134.5	134.5
0	0	1	1	200	150	0	0	1	1	200	150
0	1	0	0	300	300	0	1	0	0	300	300
0	1	0	1	600	600	0	1	0	1	600	600
0	1	1	0	1200	1200	0	1	1	0	1200	1200
0	1	1	1	1050	2000	0	1	1	1	1050	2000
1	0	0	0	2400	2400	1	0	0	0	2400	2400
1	0	0	1	4800	4800	1	0	0	1	4800	4800
1	0	1	0	7200	1800	1	0	1	0	7200	1800
1	0	1	1	9600	9600	1	0	1	1	9600	9600
1	1	0	0	38400	19200	1	1	0	0	38400	19200
1	1	0	1	Timer	Timer	1	1	0	1	Timer	Timer
1	1	1	0	IP2-16X	IP2-16X	1	1	1	0	IP5-16X	IP5-16X
1	1	1	1	IP2-1X	IP2-1X	1	1	1	1	IP5-1X	IP5-1X

Note: Receiver clock is always a 16X clock except when CSRB bits 7 through 4 equal 1111.

Note: Transmitter clock is always a 16X clock except when CSRB bits 3 through 0 equal 1111.

one simple function – it determines the baud rate at which both the receiver and transmitter ports of channel A operate. Thirteen different baud-rates are selected by programming CSRA_0 to CSRA_3 (transmitter) and CSRA_4 to CSRA_7 (receiver). Note that the state of bit ACR_7 in the auxiliary control register, ACR, distinguishes between two sets of baud rates.

In addition to the 13 preprogrammed baud rates of Table 3.4, CSRA can be programmed to select either baud rates generated internally by the DUART's timer or baud rates applied to the appropriate pins of the input port. For example, by setting CSRA_7, CSRA_6, CSRA_5, CSRA_4, to 1,1,1,0, the receiver timing is obtained from an external clock applied to parallel port input pin IP_4. The signal at this pin should have a frequency of 16 times the intended baud rate of the data. The channel B clock select register behaves exactly like the channel A equivalent except that the external baud rates are applied to different pins of the input port.

Channel A command register

The channel A command register, CRA, is used to apply certain commands to channel A. The corresponding channel B register, CRB, behaves in exactly the same way as CRA. Table 3.9 gives the format of CRA. Only seven bits have defined functions, as CRA_7 serves no purpose. Bits CRA_0 to CRA_3 are used to enable or to disable the transmitter or receiver and require little further explanation. Note that if the receiver is disabled, it stops receiving immediately, whereas the transmitter finishes sending the current character before it is disabled.

Bits CRA_4 to CRA_6 allow eight *command* operations to be applied to channel A and are defined as follows.

Operation *Action*
0. (000)   No command (i.e. no change in operating mode)
1. (001)   *Reset mode register pointer* The channel A mode register pointer is reset to point at MR1A.
2. (010)   *Reset receiver* The reset receiver command acts like a hardware reset – the receiver is disabled and the FIFO flushed (i.e. all data lost). The RxRDY and FFULL bits in status register A, SRA, are also cleared. This command is used to force the receiver into a known state.
3. (011)   *Reset transmitter* The reset transmitter command acts like a hardware reset – the transmitter is immediately disabled and the TxRDY and TxEMT bits in SRA are cleared. All other registers are unaltered.
3. (100)   *Reset error status* The received break (RB), parity error (PE), framing error (FE) and overrun error (OE) flags in the status register are all cleared by this command.
5. (101)   *Reset channel A break change interrupt* This command causes the

TABLE 3.9 Format of the channel A command register (CRA)

Bit	7	6	5	4	3	2	1	0
Function	Not used	Miscellaneous commands			Transmitter commands		Receiver commands	

CRA_1	CRA_0	Receiver commands
0	0	Receiver remains in present mode
0	1	Receiver enabled
1	0	Receiver disabled
1	1	Do not use this code (forbidden)

CRA_3	CRA_2	Transmitter commands
0	0	Transmitter remains in present mode
0	1	Transmitter enabled
1	0	Transmitter disabled
1	1	Do not use this code (forbidden)

CRA_6	CRA_5	CRA_4	Miscellaneous commands
0	0	0	No command (no change)
0	0	1	Reset MR pointer to MR1
0	1	0	Reset receiver
0	1	1	Reset transmitter
1	0	0	Reset error status
1	0	1	Reset channel's break change interrupt
1	1	0	Start break
1	1	1	Stop break

channel A break detect change bit in the interrupt status register, ISR, to be cleared to zero.

6. (110) *Start break* The start break command forces the transmitter output, TxDA, into its low (space) condition. A break will not be transmitted until any character in the DUART has been sent. Note that the transmitter must be enabled for this command to be accepted.

7. (111) *Stop break* The stop break command terminates a break and brings TxDA high (mark) for at least one bit time before the next character is transmitted.

The channel A command register must be set up after a hardware reset in order to enable channel A. For example, loading CRA with %00000101 enables both the receiver and the transmitter and also issues a *no command* operation.

Channel A status register (SRA)

At last we seem to be getting somewhere, because we now come to a register that is actually concerned with transmitting or receiving information, rather than with simply setting up the DUART! The channel A status register, SRA, can be read at any time and indicates the state of channel A. The corresponding SRB register behaves in exactly the same way. Table 3.10 gives the format of the 8 bits of the SRA. Each bit has a single status function and these are defined below.

TABLE 3.10   Format of channel A status register (SRA)

Bit	SRA_7	SRA_6	SRA_5	SRA_4	SRA_3	SRA_2	SRA_1	SRA_0
Function	RB	FE	PE	OE	TxEMT	TxRDY	FFULL	RxRDY

These apply to the top of the FIFO	Global bits apply to all channel A

SRA_0 RxRDYA   The receiver ready bit indicates that a character has been received and is in the FIFO waiting for the microprocessor to read it. It is cleared when there are no more characters is the FIFO to read.

SRA_1 FFULLA   The FIFO full bit is set when the receiver FIFO is full and is clear when there is one or more free positions in the FIFO. Note that RxRDY is set when there is one or more characters waiting to be read, while FFULL is set only when there are four characters waiting to be read. It is reset when the microprocessor reads a character (unless there is already a character waiting in the receiver shift register).

SRA_2 TxRDYA   This is the transmitter equivalent of RxRDYA. When set, TxRDYA indicates that the transmitter holding register is ready to be loaded with a new character. TxRDYA is cleared when a character is loaded into the transmit holding register by the microprocessor. It is also cleared when the transmitter is disabled.

SRA_3 TxEMTA   This is the transmitter equivalent of FFULLA and indicates that both the transmit holding register and the transmit shift register are empty. It is cleared when the transmit holding register is loaded by the microprocessor or when the transmitter is disabled. When TxEMTA is set, the transmitter can be said to be in an *under run* condition because there is a gap in the data stream.

SRA_4 OE   When set, the overrun error bit indicates that one or more characters in the received data stream have been lost because they were overwritten before the microprocessor read them. It is set when the FIFO is full, the receive shift register contains a character *and* a new character is received. The overrun bit is cleared by a reset error status command to the channel A control register.

SRA_5 PE   The parity error bit is set when the *with parity* or *force parity* modes have been selected and the received character has incorrect parity. PE is valid only when the RxRDYA bit is set.

SRA_6 FE   The framing error bit is set when a character is incorrectly framed by a start bit and a stop bit, and indicates a transmission error or the transmission of a break. FE is valid only when the RxRDYA bit is set.

SRA_7 RB   The received break bit, RB, is set when the received signal, RxDA, remains at the space level (i.e. break) for the duration of a character. Only a single position in the FIFO is occupied when a break is received. When RB is set, the channel A change in break bit in the interrupt status register (ISR_2) is also set. Note that ISR_2 is also set at the end of a break condition *as well as its beginning*.

Note that bits SRA_5 to SRA_7 (PE, FE, RB) of the status register apply to the character at the top of the FIFO. The other bits of the SRA apply to the transmitter or the receiver *globally*.

3.4 Programming the DUART

We have now accumulated enough information to show how the DUART can be operated in a basic mode. By *basic* I mean without using the modem or *flow control* features provided by the input/output ports, without interrupt-driven I/O and without error detection and error recovery features. If this seems rather limited, don't worry. Many microprocessors handle serial I/O in this very basic mode and assume that errors will be handled by higher-level software.

The software required to control the DUART in this mode consists of a setup procedure, an input procedure and an output procedure. An example of the setup, input and output procedures is as follows. Procedure SETUP is called after a system reset and sets up or initializes the DUART. The procedure RECEIVE transfers a character from the DUART to D0, and TRANSMIT transmits the character in D0.

```
DUART    EQU    $FF0001          DUART base address
MR1A     EQU    $00              Address offset for MR1A
MR2A     EQU    MR1A             MR1A has same address as MR2A
CSRA     EQU    $02              Offset for clk select register
```

```
SRA        EQU    CSRA          Offset for status register
CRA        EQU    $04           Offset for command register
RBA        EQU    $06           Offset for Rx buffer
ACR        EQU    $08           Offset for auxiliary control reg
TBA        EQU    RBA           Same address for Tx buffer
TxRDY      EQU    2             TxRDY = bit 2 of status reg
RxRDY      EQU    0             RxRDY = bit 0 of status reg
SET_MR1A   EQU    %00000011     MR1A initialization
*                               ; Rx_RTS* controlled by OPR_0
*                               ; Rx interrupt on RxRDY
*                               ; Char error mode, even parity
*                               ; 8 bits per character
SET_MR2A   EQU    %00000111     MR2A initialization
*                               : Normal mode
*                               ; Tx_RTS* controlled by OPR_0
*                               ; CTS* not used, one stop bit
SET_CSRA   EQU    %10111011     CSRA initialization
*                               ; 9.6 Kbaud Rx and Tx data rate
SET_CRA    EQU    %00000101     CRA initialization
*                               ; Enable Rx and Tx
SET_ACR    EQU    %00000000     Set 1 of CSR, disable change
*                               ; of state detectors
*
SETUP      LEA    DUART,A0              A0 points to the base address
           MOVE.B #SET_MR1A,MR1A(A0)    Setup MR1A
           MOVE.B #SET_MR2A,MR2A(A0)    Setup MR2A
           MOVE.B #SET_CSRA,CSRA(A0)    Setup CSRA
           MOVE.B #SET_CRA,CRA(A0)      Setup CRA – enable Rx and Tx
           RTS
*
RECEIVE    LEA    DUART,A0
POLL_RX    BTST.B #RxRDY,CSRA(A0)       Does Rx have data for reading?
           BEQ    POLL_RX               Repeat until data received
           MOVE.B RBA(A0),D0            Read data
           RTS
*
TRANSMIT   LEA    DUART,A0
POLL_TX    BTST.B #TxRDY,CSRA(A0)       Is Tx ready for data?
           BEQ    POLL_TX               Repeat until ready for data
           MOVE.B D0,TBA(A0)            Transmit data
           RTS
```

3.5 The input/output ports of the DUART

In the best of all possible worlds, DUARTs would have a number of special serial interface pins associated with each channel (i.e. modem control functions), and parallel I/O ports which users can apply as they see fit. In this world, we are limited by the pin-out constraint on chips – there are simply not enough pins for both parallel ports and serial channel control functions. The manufacturers of the 68681 DUART have compromised and provided two parallel ports that can also carry out channel control functions. Clearly, these activities cannot take place at the same time and the user of the DUART is given the choice of dedicating parallel port pins to simple bit I/O or to serial channel control functions.

3.5.1 Programming the input port

Figure 3.18 shows the 6-bit parallel input port, its control registers and the labelling of the input functions. All input pins can be treated as simple inputs (i.e. IP_0 to IP_5) and the signal at the pins read by reading the contents of the input port at base address plus offset $1A (e.g. MOVE.B $1A(A0),D0). Following a reset, the DUART configures IP_0 to IP_5 as simple inputs. When the 6-bit input port is read, D7 is always read as a logical one and D6 returns the logic level at the DUART's IACK* pin.

Four of the input pins, IP_0 to IP_3, also serve as change of state detectors. A low-to-high transition or a high-to-low transition at one of these pins lasting for at least 50 μs sets the corresponding bit in the input port change register, IPCR. Bits 4 to 7 (IPCR_4 to IPCR_7) of the read-only input port change register are set if there is a change of state at inputs IP_0 to IP_3 respectively. Bits 0 to 3 (IPCR_0 to IPCR_3) of the IPCR reflect the actual level of IP_0 to IP_3 respectively at the time the IPCR is read. As it is possible to program the DUART to generate an interrupt on a change of state condition, we have a powerful means of recognizing some *event* taking place at a channel. For example, we may wish to interrupt the microprocessor if the signal strength on a data link drops below a predetermined level.

Other input functions which can be associated with certain pins of the input port are the clear to send inputs (CTSA*, CTSB*), the clock inputs for receivers or transmitters and the timer/counter clock.

The status of each input pin can always be read by interrogating the input port at address offset $1A. This is true even when the inputs are programmed as alternate functions. Equally, the four change of state detectors on pins IP_0 to IP_3 are always active and the input port change register (IPCR) at offset address $08 can be read to determine which inputs have changed state since it was last read. Reading the IPCR *automatically* clears its change of state bits to zero.

It can be seen from Figure 3.18 that IP_0 and IP_1 are programmed as active-low clear to send inputs (CTSA* and CTSB*) by setting MR2A_4 = 1 and MR2B_4 = 1 respectively. When an input pin is programmed as clear to send, it must be active-low to enable the transmitter. When, for example, CTSA* goes inactive-high, the channel A transmitter is inhibited until CTSA* is asserted.

Input pins IP_2 to IP_5 can be programmed as external clock inputs for

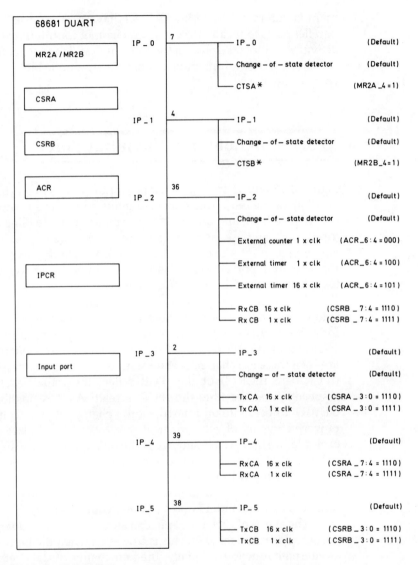

FIGURE 3.18 The 68681's input port

transmitter or receiver clocks for channel A and channel B. In each case, the clock may be programmed at 16 times the serial data rate or 1 times it. Remember that the DUART has an internal baud-rate generator to suit most circumstances and that *few* applications of the DUART should require external clocks. These alternate functions are selected by the appropriate clock select register (CRSA or CRSB) as shown in Figure 3.18. Input IP_2 can also be programmed to act as a clock for the counter/timer by programming bits ACR_4 to ACR_6 of the auxiliary control register, ACR, as shown.

3.5.2 Programming the output port

The parallel output port, OP_0 to OP_7, is byte-wide and, like the input port, its bits function as simple outputs or as control functions associated with the DUART. Figure 3.19 illustrates the parallel input port and shows how its

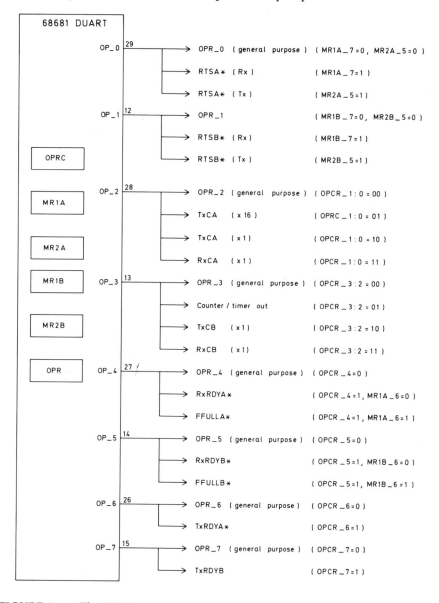

FIGURE 3.19 The 68681's output pins

output pins are configured in terms of the DUART's registers. The output port register occupies *two* addresses, with offsets $1C and $1E. Writing data to the output port is done in a most interesting way. The output port register, OPR, at offset $1C is a *set bit only* port. Writing a one to a bit of this port sets the corresponding output bit. Writing a zero, has no effect on the output.

The output pins of the DUART have invertors between them and the output port register, OPR. That is, the data on pins OP_0 to OP_7 is the complement of that in the output port register.

Similarly, the output port register at offset $1E is a *clear bit only* port. Writing a one (yes!) to a bit at this port clears the corresponding output bit – writing a zero has no effect on the output. For example, if we wish to output the byte $5B (i.e. %01011011) on OP_0 to OP_7, the following code can be used. Note that the output port register must be loaded with the complement of $5B (i.e. $A4 or %10100100).

```
MOVE.B   #%10100100,$1C(A0)   Set bits in OPR
MOVE.B   #%01011011,$1E(A0)   Clear bits in OPR
```

Equally, we could have cleared *all* the bits of the output port before setting those that must be ones.

```
MOVE.B   #$FF,$1E(A0)         Clear all output bits
MOVE.B   #%10100100,$1C(A0)   Set bits in OPR
```

Pins of the output can be treated as simple output bits, associated with a transmitter/receiver control function, used as clock outputs or assigned to the counter/timer port of the DUART. The output port configuration register, OPCR, at offset address $1A defines the operating mode of each output pin. Table 3.11 gives the format of the OPCR and Figure 3.19 shows the programming required to define each bit of the output port.

Output port pins OP_0 and OP_1 differ from other output pins because their functions are determined by the appropriate channel mode register, rather than the output port configuration register.

OP_0 is a simple output bit if MR1A_7 = 0 and MR2A_5 = 0. The alternate function of OP_0 is a channel A request to send output. When MR1A_7 = 1, OP_0 is a request to send output (RTSA*) associated with the *receiver* side of channel A. RTSA* is used to control the flow of data between transmitter and receiver. If a start bit is received when the receiver FIFO is full, RTSA* (i.e. OP_0) is negated. By connecting RTSA* to the remote transmitter's CTS* input, the transmitter is forced to wait until the receiver can handle more data. Once the microprocessor has read data from the FIFO, RTSA* is asserted again to indicate that the transmitter may proceed. Note that OP_1 behaves exactly like OP_0, except that it is associated with channel B.

When MR2A_5 = 1, OP_0 is programmed as the channel A *transmitter-side* request to send output (RTSA*). In this mode, the transmitter automatically negates RTSA* one bit after the transmit shift register and the transmit holding register are both empty. The negation of RTSA* indicates to

TABLE 3.11 The format of the output port configuration register OPCR

Bit	OPCR_7	OPCR_6	OPCR_5	OPCR_4	OPCR_3	OPCR_2	OPCR_1	OPCR_0
Function	OP_7	OP_6	OP_5		OP_3		OP_2	

OPCR_1	OPCR_0	OP_2 function	
0	0	OP_2	(simple output)
0	1	TxCA	16× transmitter clock channel A
1	0	TxCA	1× transmitter clock channel A
1	1	RxCA	1× receiver clock channel A

OPCR_3	OPCR_2	OP_2 function
0	0	OP_3 (simple output)
0	1	Counter/timer output
1	0	TxCB 1× channel B transmitter clock
1	1	RxCB 1× channel B receiver clock

OPCR_4	OP_4 function
0	OP_4 (simple output)
1	RxRDYA or FFULLA

OPCR_5	OP_5 function
0	OP_5 (simple output)
1	RxRDYB or FFULLB

OPCR_6	OP_6 function
0	OP_6 (simple output)
1	TxRDYA

OPCR_7	OP_7 function
0	OP_7 (simple output)
1	TxRDYB

the remote receiver that the transmitter currently has no further data to send. OP_1 performs the RTSB* function associated with channel B and is controlled by MR2B_5.

Output OP_2 is controlled by bits OPCR_1 and OPCR_0 of the output port configuration register as indicated in Figure 3.19. OP_2 can be configured as a simple output or as a transmitter or receiver clock output. These auxiliary functions are provided because some equipment used in data transmission or storage requires access to a clock at the same rate (or 16 times the rate) as the transmitted or received data.

Output OP_3 behaves like OP_2 except that it is associated with channel B and that in one of its modes it provides an output from the counter/timer.

Output OP_4 is programmed as a simple output when OPCR_4 = 0. When OPCR_4 = 1, it is programmed as a channel A RxRDYA* output if MR1A_6 = 0 and as a channel A FFULLA* output if MR1A_6 = 1. The difference between RxRDYA* and FFULLA* (receiver ready A and FIFO full A) is that the RxRDYA* output is asserted whenever the receiver has a character ready for reading by the microprocessor, and FFULLA* is asserted when the FIFO is full and a batch of four characters are ready to be read. When OP_4 is an RxRDYA*/FFULLA* output, it is driven by an open-collecter buffer and can be used as an IRQ* input to the host microprocessor.

Why should OP_4 be programmed to indicate receiver ready or FIFO_full? OP_4 is (in this mode) an interrupt request output and may be connected to one of the microprocessor's interrupt request inputs. Thus, whenever the DUART has data for reading, the microprocessor can be interrupted. OP_4 can request service *independently* of the DUART's own IRQ* output.

Output OP_5 behaves exactly like OP_4 except that its dedicated function is related to channel B (i.e. RxRDYB* or FFULLB*).

Output OP_6 and OP_7 are both available as simple outputs by clearing OPCR_6 and OPCR_7 respectively. Alternatively, they can be configured as open-drain, active-low interrupt request outputs like OP_4 and OP_5. When OP_6 is configured as an interrupt request output, TxRDYA*, it goes active-low whenever the transmitter is ready for a new character from the microprocessor. Similarly, OP_7 acts as channel B's transmitter-side interrupt output, TxRDYB*.

Now that we have dealt with the DUART's parallel input and output ports, it is worthwhile reminding the reader that these ports can be dealt with in three ways:

1. They may be entirely ignored and the DUART operated as a basic two-channel serial I/O port.
2. They may be used partially or wholly to provide simple parallel I/O. Some systems require only, say, three or four lines of I/O to control an external interface. Consequently, the DUART saves the cost of an additional special-purpose parallel interface.
3. They may be programmed as indicated in the text to provide clock inputs or outputs, channel flow-control signals or dedicated interrupt requests.

3.6 Interrupts and the DUART

The 68681 DUART has an interrupt structure which is fully compatible with the 68000's own vectored interrupt system. The DUART has a single active-low composite IRQ* which is asserted to inform the host microprocessor that service is requested. Up to eight events can be programmed to request an interrupt. Note that outputs OP_4 to OP_7 are also available for use as interrupt requests. These are not composite interrupt requests and each output is asserted only in response to a particular event.

Four registers, IMR (interrupt mask register), ISR (interrupt status register), ACR (auxiliary control register) and IVR (interrupt vector register), are associated with the DUART's interrupt control structure and these are illustrated in Figure 3.20. These registers are common to both channels of the

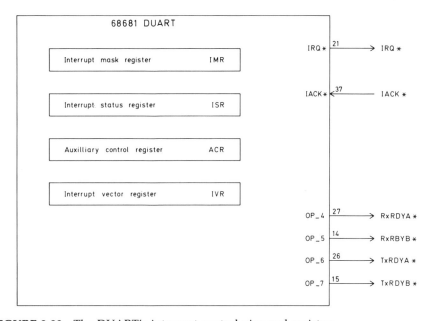

FIGURE 3.20   The DUART's interrupt control pins and registers

DUART. The write-only interrupt mask register, IMR, at address offset $0A determines which of the eight possible events are *permitted* to assert the IRQ* output when they occur. The bits of the IMR are defined below. These bits are all set or cleared under programmer control and are cleared after a hardware reset.

Bit	Mnemonic	Function
IMR_0	TxRDYA	When set, the DUART asserts IRQ* when the channel A transmitter is ready for data from the microprocessor.
IMR_1	RxRDY/FFULLA	When set, the DUART asserts IRQ* when the channel A receiver has data for the microprocessor to read. Bit MR1A_6 of the channel A mode register 1 determines whether the interrupt is generated by a RxRDY or a FFULLA condition.
IMR_2	Delta break A	When set, the DUART asserts IRQ* when either the start of a break condition is detected by channel A or the end of a break is detected.
IMR_3	Counter/timer rdy	When set, the DUART asserts IRQ* when the counter/timer generates an interrupt.
IMR_4	TxRDYB	This is the channel B equivalent of IMR_0.
IMR_5	RxRDY/FFULLB	This is the channel B equivalent of IMR_1.
IMR_6	Delta break B	This is the channel B equivalent of IMR_2.
IMR_7	Input port change	When set, the DUART asserts IRQ* when one of the inputs with change of state detectors undergoes a logical transition and the appropriate bit of ACR has been set.

If, for example, the programmer wishes to generate an interrupt request whenever the channel A receiver has data for the microprocessor or whenever the channel A receiver detects the start or end of a break condition, the IMR must be loaded with %00000110.

The interrupt status register, ISR, has the same address as the IMR (offset $0A), but is read-only. The format of the ISR is exactly the same as that of the IMR. Whenever an event capable of generating an interrupt takes place, the appropriate bit of the ISR is set. An interrupt on IRQ* is generated only if the corresponding bit in the IMR is set.

Interrupt mask bits have no effect on the reading of the ISR. Following a hardware reset, all bits of the ISR are cleared to zero.

The interrupt vector register (IVR) at offset address $18 provides an interrupt vector number during an IACK cycle. The programmer must load the IVR with the appropriate vector number during the DUART's initialization routine. Following a hardware reset, the IVR is loaded with $0F which is the 68000's uninitialized interrupt vector number.

Four bits of the auxiliary control register, ACR, at address offset $08 influence the interrupt structure. These mask the change of state detectors at input pins IP_0 IP_3. Their format is given in Table 3.12. For example, if we wish to detect changes of state on IP_1 and IP_0 *only*, the least-significant four bits of the ACR would be loaded with %0011. Consequently, a change of state in IP_1 or IP_0 would set the input port change bit (i.e. ISR_7) of the interrupt status register. If IMR_7 were set, the IRQ* output would also be asserted.

TABLE 3.12 The interrupt control bits of the auxiliary control register

Bit	ACR_3	ACR_2	ACR_1	ACR_0
Function	Delta IP_3	Delta IP_2	Delta IP_1	Delta IP_0

Consider the following example. Suppose we wish to configure the DUART to generate an interrupt output if any of the following conditions occur:

1. Channel A Tx is ready for new data
2. Channel A Rx has received a character
3. Channel A Tx CTS input changes state

The DUART's response to an interrupt acknowledge cycle is to provide the interrupt vector number $60.

```
INT_MASK   EQU     %10000011          TxRDYA, RxRDYA, CTSA interrupt enable
INT_VEC    EQU     $60                Vector number supplied in IACK cycle
ACR_SET    EQU     %00000001          Enable IP_0/CTSA for change of state
*
           LEA     DUART_BASE,A0
           MOVE.B  #INT_MASK,IMR(A0)  Setup interrupt mask register
           MOVE.B  #INT_VEC,IVR(A0)   Setup interrupt vector
           MOVE.B  #ACR_SET,ACR(A0)   Setup auxiliary control register
```

3.7 The counter/timer function of the DUART

The 68681 DUART also has a primitive counter/timer. In the timer mode, a square wave is produced at a frequency determined under program control. In the counter mode, a counter is started or stopped in response to an external signal. Therefore it is possible to determine the time interval separating two events by reading the accumulated count. Chapter 4 also looks at timers and counters, the reader may therefore wish to read Chapter 4 before continuing with this section.

Two registers are associated with the counter/timer: the counter/timer register (CTUR/CTLR) and the auxiliary control register (ACR). The counter/timer register is 16 bits wide and therefore takes up two locations. Address offset $0C corresponds to the most significant byte of the register (CTUR and address offset $0E corresponds to the least significant byte. Both CTUR and CTLR are write-only registers and they may be loaded with any value from $0002 to $FFFF.

Three bits of the auxiliary control register, ACR_4 to ACR_6, determine the operating mode of the counter/timer and its source of clock signal. Table 3.13 shows the function of these three bits.

TABLE 3.13   The counter/timer control bits of the auxiliary control register

ACR_6	BITS ACR_5	ACR_4	MODE	CLOCK SOURCE
0	0	0	Counter	External clock applied to IP_2
0	0	1	Counter	TxCA – the 1× clock of channel A Tx
0	1	0	Counter	TxCB – the 1× clock of channel B Tx
0	1	1	Counter	Crystal clock scaled by 16
1	0	0	Timer	External clock applied to IP_2
1	0	1	Timer	External clock/16 applied to IP_2
1	1	0	Timer	Crystal clock
1	1	1	Timer	Crystal clock scaled by 16

Note: The crystal clock may be at the freqency of the crystal wired between the X1 and X2 pins or it may be at the frequency of an external clock connected to the X1 pin.

In the timer mode, the counter/timer runs continuously. The 16-bit value loaded into the counter register (CTUR and CTLR) is decremented at each cycle of the clock. When the counter contents reach zero, the counter is reloaded with its maximum value. Each time the counter reaches zero, the logical level at parallel output pin OP_3 is toggled (if OP_3 is programmed as counter/timer output). The signal at OP_3 is therefore a square wave, whose period is determined by the value loaded into CTUR, CTLR and the frequency of the clock selected by the ACR. The period is given by: $2 \times [\text{CTUR:CTLR}] \times \text{clock}$ period. The factor '2' appears because the output is toggled once for each clock period.

The counter ready status bit, ISR_3, is set at the end of each cycle of the square wave. If the corresponding interrupt mask bit, IMR_3, is also set, a continuous stream of interrupts can be generated by the DUART. An unbroken stream of interrupts allows the DUART to be used as a simple real-time clock (see Chapter 4). The counter ready status bit, ISR_3, is reset by a stop counter command (i.e. a read to DUART + $1E). Note that this does not stop the counter. The counter values in CUR and CLR should not be read when the DUART is in the timer mode.

In the counter mode, the counter counts down from the number stored in the 16–bit counter register. Counting begins with a start command to DUART + $1C and the counter reinitializes itself with its preprogrammed value (stored in CTUR;CTLR). When the counter reaches zero, the *terminal count*, the timer/counter ready interrupt bit, ISR_3, is set. The counter *rolls over* from $0000 to $FFFF and continues past the terminal count. Counting continues until the microprocessor issues a stop command to DUART + $1E.

If OP_3 has been programmed as the timer/counter output, OP_3 remains high until the terminal count is reached and then it goes low. When a stop command is issued, the output returns high and ISR_3 is cleared. The count value in CUR/CLR should be read only when the counter is stopped.

3.8 Applying the DUART

The circuit diagram of MICI's serial interface is given in Figure 3.21. The DUART is memory mapped at address $020000 and generates level 3 interrupt requests to the 68000. Serial ports A and B are buffered by RS232C converters and flow-control signals RTS* and CTS* are implemented for both channels.

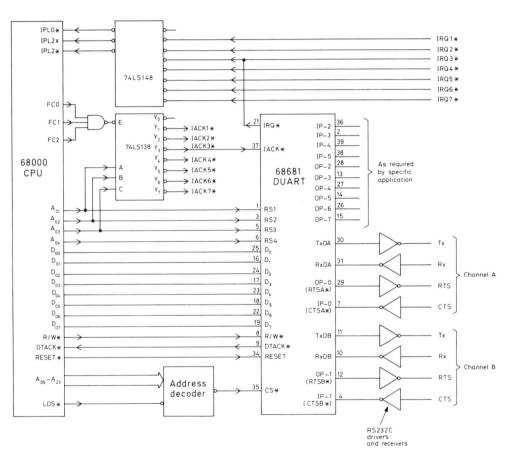

FIGURE 3.21   The circuit of a serial interface using the 68000 and the 68681 DUART

The remaining parallel input and output lines (IP_2 to IP_5 and OP_2 to OP_7) are left unconnected and may be applied as the user sees fit. Once more, I would like to remind the reader just how simple the circuit of Figure 3.21 is. The interrupt control and address decoding logic already exists on MICI because this logic serves other purposes. The only new components required to implement the serial interface are the DUART itself, the line drivers and receivers and the quartz crystal.

Summary

In this chapter we have examined one of today's more sophisticated asynchronous serial interface chips. The 68681 DUART replaces earlier ACIAs which had only one channel and required external baud-rate generators. Unfortunately, this new generation of advanced interface chips are not as easy to understand and to program as their predecessors. However, they do permit the design of low-cost microprocessor systems with remarkably few components.

Chapter 4

The Real-Time

Clock

Now that we have looked at the two most popular microprocessor interfaces, the parallel interface chip and the serial interface chip, we are going to examine another important peripheral, the real-time clock (RTC). Real-time clocks perform a range of functions, varying from the generation of periodic interrupts to maintaining a copy of the *time of day*.

When a student first encounters the term *real time*, he or she can be forgiven for wondering if there is such a thing as *unreal time*, *false time* or even *imaginary time*. After all, time is time and it does not come in different varieties. What we are really interested in is the relationship between time, the computer and external events. An *external event* is something that happens outside the computer and is usually a request for attention by a peripheral (i.e. an interrupt request). Let us consider two examples which demonstrate the relationship between a computer and events that happen outside the computer. First, an engineer submits a program written in FORTRAN to a computer bureau. The program simulates a data transmission system and has to generate a million data elements, transmit them and then receive them. Running such a program may take minutes or even hours on a large mainframe. The program might be run overnight to produce an output for the engineer the next day. Here, there are two *events*: the submission of the program by the engineer and the delivery of the results of the calculations by the computer. Note that the element of time comes into this process in a rather vague and imprecise way. The interval of time between the start of the program and its end depends on many factors, not least of which is the number of other jobs being run at the same time. As long as the results are available tomorrow, the engineer is happy.

Now consider a computer-controlled proximity warning device in an aircraft, which measures the aircraft's height above the terrain by means of a radio altimeter based on radar. At the same time that the height is being measured, the aircraft's forward speed is determined by measuring the air pressure at a small nozzle positioned in the airflow. Using these two measurements, the computer estimates the height of the aircraft at some point in the future. If the computer determines that there is a probability of collision, should the ground continue to rise or the aircraft descend, a warning message is issued to the pilot – usually a synthesized voice saying 'pull up, pull up'. In this example of a real-time system, there is an important relationship between the two events (i.e. the measuring of the height and airspeed, and the transmission of the warning message). The computer's response to the time-varying input must take place fast enough to give the pilot sufficient time to react.

Real-time systems are those that react to events within an *appropriate* time interval. A computer operating a nuclear reactor may demand a guaranteed response time of several milliseconds, while a computer controlling the climate in a large greenhouse may find a response time of several minutes perfectly acceptable. In other words, the precise meaning of *real time* is dependent on the specific application of the real-time system.

Designing a single function real-time system, such as the proximity warning device described above, is not difficult. The computer reads data, processes it and yields a result (i.e. warning or no warning). As long as the software–hardware combination is adequately fast, there is no further problem.

However, some real-time systems have many inputs, outputs and computational processes. A computer in a chemical factory may be sampling the temperature, pressure and other variables at 100 points and be controlling 50 motors/valves/heaters, etc. Clearly, some scheduling is involved here and the computer must deal with critical events (e.g. the sudden build up of pressure in a reaction vessel) more rapidly than with less important events.

Real-time systems are not only found in control applications. Many databases are also real-time systems. A customer in a New York office wishing to reserve a seat on a flight from London to Paris expects the system to respond within a reasonable period of time which, in this case, might be one to three minutes.

The design of real-time systems belongs largely to the field of operating systems and is almost entirely the province of the software engineer. Hardware aspects of real-time systems are relatively small and are largely related to the CPU rather than to external hardware. As a microprocessor involved in a real-time system has to switch rapidly and efficiently between a number of tasks, it should have a suitable mechanism to carry out the switching and, if possible, should provide some measure of protection against one task interfering with another. The 68000 is an excellent microprocessor for use in real-time systems, and its user/supervisor modes provide a suitable basis for task protection.

Task switching in a real-time system is frequently performed by means of an interrupt mechanism. A high-priority interrupt is generated every *T* seconds, forcing the microprocessor to invoke an interrupt-handling routine that is responsible for scheduling the various tasks and for responding to events that must be serviced urgently.

In principle, all the hardware designer has to do is to implement a suitable circuit that asserts an interrupt request line periodically. Some early systems (*c.* 1976) simply wired the microprocessor's interrupt request input to the 60 Hz power line (via a suitable filter). Today, many peripherals provide a more convenient source of timing. For example, we have already seen that the 68681 DUART has a counter/timer that can be programmed to generate an interrupt every, say, 10 ms.

In this section we are going to look at a more interesting real-time clock, the 146818, which does much more than merely provide a source of interrupts. Real-time systems often require access to the actual time of day. For example, a chemical plant must delay certain operations to prevent them taking place between two shifts, or an airline database may delete flights from its files after their scheduled time of departure has passed.

Of course, the time of day can be calculated by counting the number of interrupts in a real-time system (assuming that the switch-on time is known). Several time-of-day clocks once used this technique. Unfortunately, if the system is powered down, the time-of-day counter must be manually updated each time the computer is restarted. We will now look at a device that records the time of day even when the host computer is switched off.

4.1 The 146818 RTC

Many of today's real-time clocks such as the 146818 provide periodic interrupts to a host microprocessor at a predetermined rate and also have time-of-day clocks that run independently of the host microprocessor and which operate even when the host system is powered down. These RTCs are inevitably fabricated with CMOS technology because of its exceptionally low power consumption and are backed up by small batteries. The major features of the 146818 real-time clock are as follows:

1. It provides a time-of-day clock which counts seconds, minutes, hours, day of the week, day of the month, month and year. That is, it records both time and date. The 146818 automatically takes account of the number of days in each month and also corrects for leap years.
2. It operates in either BCD or natural binary modes. The actual operating mode is programmed by setting or clearing a bit in one of its internal registers.
3. It has a programmable square wave output that can also be programmed to

generate frequencies in binary steps (i.e. 2, 4, 8, . . .) in the range 2 Hz to 32.768 kHz.

4. It is able to generate interrupts under three circumstances. An *alarm* interrupt can be generated at rates from once per second to once per day. Periodic interrupts can be generated with intervals between 30 μs and 500 000 μs. Finally, it can be programmed to generate an interrupt at the end of every *update-ended* period. Each type of interrupt can be turned on or off (i.e. masked) under software control. Furthermore, it is possible to determine the source of an interrupt by reading the appropriate register of the RTC.

5. The 146818 uses low power CMOS technology and, in addition to its RTC function, has 50 bytes of general-purpose read/write memory available for use by the programmer. As the RTC is normally kept running while the host system is powered down, the 50 bytes of RAM can be used to store important system constants.

4.2 The RTC support circuitry

Unlike most interface chips, the RTC lacks any substantial *peripheral-side* interface apart from a square wave output pin and a few miscellaneous control pins. Figure 4.1 gives the pin-out of the 146818 with microprocessor-side connections on the left.

The 146818 has very few pins that are not directly devoted to supporting its RTC-microprocessor interface. The following pins of the RTC are those that belong to the user- or application-side interface.

OSC1, OSC2

A quartz crystal of 4.194 304 MHz, 1.048 576 MHz or 32.768 kHz can be wired between the OSC1 and OSC2 pins of the RTC to provide it with a stable timebase from which it derives all its timing signals. It is also possible to leave the OSC2 pin open-circuit and to apply an external timebase to the OSC1 pin. A 4.194 304 MHz crystal provides a more accurate timebase than a 32.768 MHz crystal, but, unfortunately, the higher-frequency crystal consumes a greater current than the lower-frequency crystal during the RTC's battery backed-up standby mode (600 μA compared with 100 μA).

CKOUT, CKFS

The CKOUT (clock output) pin provides a buffered clock signal that may be used by any other part of the microprocessor system. The frequency of the signal at the CKOUT pin is either that of the crystal connected to the OSC1,

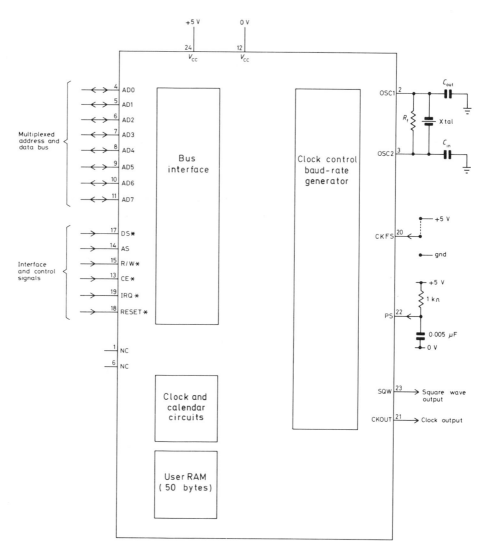

FIGURE 4.1 The pin-out of the 146818 RTC

OSC2 pins or it is one-quarter that frequency. If the CKFS (clock out frequency select) input pin is connected to a logical one, the frequency at CKOUT is the same as the crystal frequency. If CKFS is connected to a logical zero, the frequency of CKOUT is (clock frequency)/4.

SQW

The SQW (square wave) output pin provides the user with a square wave whose frequency is programmable, as we shall see shortly.

PS

The PS (power sense) input pin controls the state of the VRT (valid RAM and time) bit of register D. When the PS pin is low, the VRT bit is cleared. When power is applied to the RTC, the PS pin must be held low for at least $5\,\mu s$. The VRT bit is set by reading the contents of register D (provided that the PS pin is high). The VRT bit and the PS pin can be used by the host microprocessor to verify that the RTC is functioning in its powered up mode.

4.3 The RTC-microprocessor interface

In order to maximize the applications of the 146818, its manufacturers have endowed it with a multipurpose microprocessor interface called *MOTEL* (derived from MOTorola and inTEL). The MOTEL interface makes it easy to connect the 146818 to either a 6800 microprocessor or to an 8080 micro-processor. Note that the address and data buses, AD0–AD7, are multiplexed to reduce the chip's pin count. However, despite the multiplexed address and data bus the 146818 appears to the host microprocessor exactly like a bank of memory locations. In other words, it has all the characteristics of read/write RAM and can be memory mapped like any other peripheral.

The read cycle timing diagram of a 146818 is given in Figure 4.2. Four control inputs to the RTC, CE*, AS, DS* and R/W*, are involved in a read or a write cycle. The active-low chip enable (CE*) input must be asserted for the duration of a read or a write cycle. The multiplexed address strobe, AS, is used to latch an address on AD0–AD7 into the RTC. Do not confuse the RTC's *AS* input with the 68000's *AS** output! The active-low data strobe input, DS*, forces the RTC to place data on AD0–AD7 in a read cycle. The RTC's DS* input is not related to the 68000's data strobes (LDS*/UDS*) and is really equivalent to the output enable (OE*) input pin of a memory component. Note also that I have labelled this DS* to be consistent with its active-low operation, although it is labelled DS in the 146818 data sheet. The R/W* input is high in a read cycle and latches data into the RTC in a write cycle when it is low.

Figure 4.2 shows that an RTC read cycle is divided into two parts: a latch address phase which selects the appropriate register in the RTC and a read data phase which interrogates the selected register. In the latch address phase, an address on AD0–AD7 is latched by the falling edge of AS. The address must be valid t_{ASL} seconds before and t_{AHL} seconds after the falling edge of AS. The minimum value of t_{ASL} and t_{AHL} are 50 ns and 20 ns respectively.

Once the address has been latched and R/W* held high, DS* is asserted to place the data from the RTC on AD0–AD7. Data becomes valid no more than t_{DDR} seconds after the falling edge of DS* and remains valid until t_{DHR} seconds

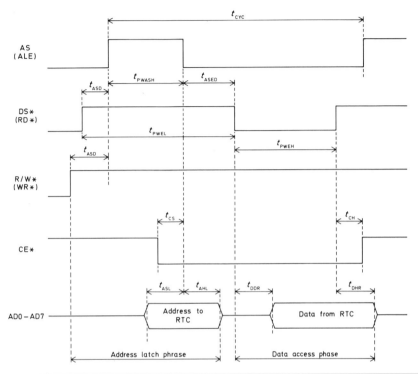

FIGURE 4.2 The read-cycle timing diagram of the 146818 RTC

Symbol	Parameter	Value
t_{cyc}	Cycle time	953 ns min.
t_{ASD}	DS* or E high to AS high	50 ns min.
t_{PWASH}	AS high pulse width	135 ns min.
t_{ASED}	AS low to DS* low	90 ns min.
t_{PWEL}	Pulse width DS* high	300 ns min.
t_{PWEH}	Pulse width DS* low	325 ns min.
t_{CS}	Chip enable setup time before AS low	55 ns min.
t_{CH}	Chip enable hold time	0 ns min.
t_{ASL}	Address valid to AS low	50 ns min.
t_{AHL}	Address hold time from AS low	20 ns min.
t_{DDR}	Data output delay from DS* low	240 ns max.
t_{DHR}	Read data hold time	100 ns max.

after the negation of DS*. The maximum value of t_{DDR} is given as 240 ns and the value of t_{DHR} as 10 to 100 ns.

The write cycle of the RTC is illustrated in Figure 4.3 and begins with an address latch phase which is identical to the address latch phase of a read cycle. During the write data phase, DS* is high and R/W* is low. Data from the host microprocessor on AD0–AD7 is latched by the rising edge of R/W*. The data

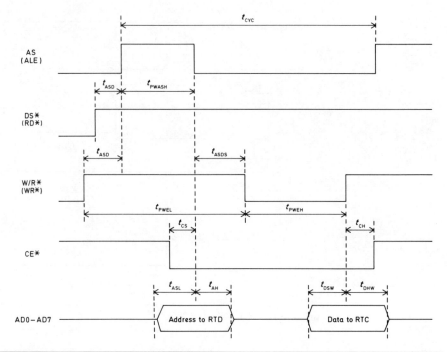

FIGURE 4.3 The write cycle timing diagram of the 146818 RTC

Symbol	Parameter	Value
t_{cyc}	Cycle time	953 ns min.
t_{ASD}	DS* or E high to AS high	50 ns min.
t_{PWASH}	AS high pulse width	135 ns min.
t_{ASED}	AS low to DS* low	90 ns min.
t_{PWEL}	Pulse width DS* high	300 ns min.
t_{PWEH}	Pulse width DS* low	325 ns min.
t_{CS}	Chip enable setup time before AS low	55 ns min.
t_{CH}	Chip enable hold time	0 ns min.
t_{ASL}	Address valid to AS low	50 ns min.
t_{AHL}	Address hold time from AS low	20 ns min.
t_{DSW}	Peripheral data setup time	200 ns min.
t_{DHW}	Peripheral data hold time	0 ns min.

must be valid t_{DSW} (200 ns minimum data setup time) before the rising edge of R/W* and remain valid for t_{DHW} (0 ns minimum data hold time) after the rising edge.

4.3.1 Interfacing the 146818 to the 68000 microprocessor

In principle, it is possible to connect the 146818 to the 68000's address and data buses in such a way that a 68000 read or write cycle is transformed into a 146818 two-phase read or write cycle. However, this approach is messy, as it involves dividing the 68000 memory access into an address latch phase and a read or write phase.

A simple, but not particularly elegant, way of connecting the 146818 RTC to a 68000 is to treat the RTC as a memory-mapped peripheral which has two addresses: an address port location and a data port location. Instead of fitting the two-phase cycle of the RTC into a single 68000 memory cycle, two separate 68000 memory cycles must be used.

In order to access the RTC, a 68000 write cycle is first made to the RTC's address port to latch the address of the register to be accessed in a subsequent read or write to the RTC's data port. Then, the data port is read from, or written to, using the register address already in the RTC.

Figure 4.4 gives the circuit diagram of a possible interface between the 146818 and a 68000 microprocessor. In this example, the RTC's source of timing is a 4.194 304 MHz quartz crystal, and a battery backed-up power supply is provided. Whenever the system V_{cc} supply falls below $V_{backup} + 0.6$, diode D1 becomes reverse-biased and the RTC is isolated from the system power supply. During the power-down mode, germanium diode D2 is forward biased and the RTC is supplied from the on-board battery, which is frequently a 3.9 V NiCad rechargeable cell. When the system power is on, the cell recharges through resistor R1 at a current not more than $C/10$, where C is the capacity of the cell.

The RESET* input from the 68000 is connected to the RESET* input of the RTC via two inverting buffers in series. The invertor connected to the RTC has an open-collector output up to V_{backup} by an 18 kΩ resistor. Therefore, during the power-down mode, the RTC's RESET* input is inactive-high.

The CE* timing requirements are easy to satisfy as, according to the 146818's data sheet, CE* can be permanently strapped active-low when the RTC is in its normal mode. CE* should be brought inactive-high whenever the RTC is in its power-down mode. This condition is satisfied by driving CE* from POR* (i.e. active-low power-on-reset which is asserted when the 68000 is first powered up) with an open-collector driver and by pulling CE* up to V_{backup} by means of an 18 kΩ pull-up resistor. When CE* is high, all address, data, DS*, AS and R/W* inputs to the 146818 are internally disconnected.

The multiplexed address and data bus from the RTC is connected to D_{00} to D_{07} from the 68000.

The three read/write access control input signals to the RTC (AS, DS*, R/W*) are generated by a 74LS139 two-line to four-line decoder from LDS*, A_{01}, R/W* and chip-select from the 68000. During an access to the RTC's memory

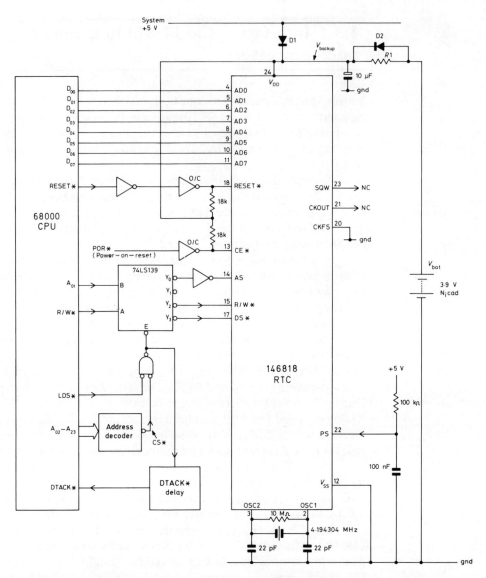

FIGURE 4.4.   The circuit diagram of an interface between a 68000 and a 146818 RTC

space in which LDS∗ is asserted, the decoder is enabled by a suitable chip-select signal from an address decoder driven by A_{02} to A_{23}.

Figure 4.5 illustrates a write cycle to the address latch port address of the RTC at the RTC's base address (i.e. $A_{01} = 0$). The write access sets up the RTC's internal register pointer ready for an access to the data port. The data on D_{00} to D_{07} from the 68000, corresponding to the register in the RTC to be accessed, is latched on the rising edge of AS. There are no particular timing problems, as

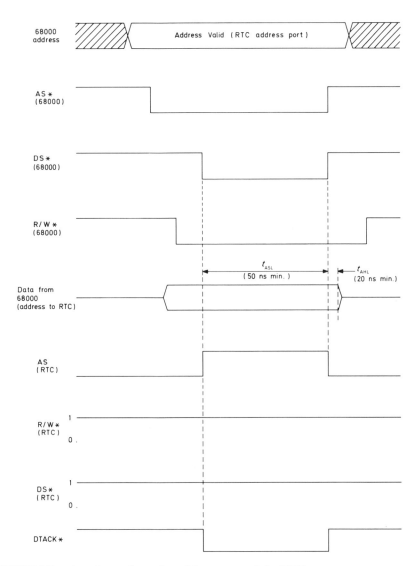

FIGURE 4.5. A write cycle to the address port of the RTC

the multiplexed address setup time required by the RTC is only 50 ns in the address latch phase. A read access can be executed any time after the appropriate register address has been latched into the RTC, as described above.

Consider now a read access to the RTC. There is no restriction on the maximum time between setting up the RTC's address and then reading from or writing to it. During a read access to the RTC, illustrated in Figure 4.6, a 68000 read cycle is carried out at the RTC base address + 2 (i.e. $A_{01} = 1$). When the RTC is accessed at this address, DS* goes low to enable the RTC's output buffers,

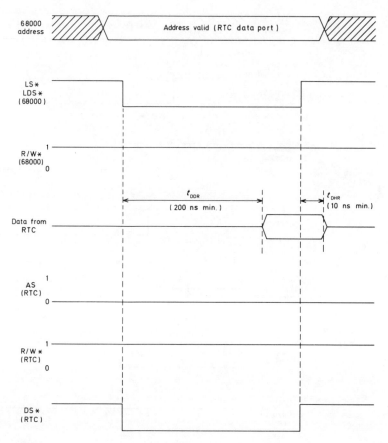

FIGURE 4.6   A read cycle to the data port of the RTC

and data is available on D_{00} to D_{07} no more than t_{on} (220 ns) from the falling edge of DS*.

It is just about possible to operate a 68000 with a 146818 RTC at 8 MHz without the insertion of wait states. However, we certainly cannot operate the RTC in a write cycle without the introduction of wait states. I leave the analysis of the write cycle as an exercise for the student.

4.4 The programmer's model of the 146818 RTC

In contrast to many of today's peripherals, the 146818 RTC is very easy to program. Table 4.1 gives the address map of its 64 internal registers. Locations $00–$09 provide the timer and alarm registers, $0A–$0D are the control

TABLE 4.1 The address map of the 146818 RTC

Address Register

			7	6	5	4	3	2	1	0
00	Seconds									
01	Seconds alarm									
02	Minutes									
03	Minutes alarm									
04	Hours									
05	Hours alarm									
06	Day of week	→								
07	Day of month									
08	Month									
09	Year									
0A	Register A	→	UIP	DV2	DV1	DV0	RS3	RS2	RS1	RS0
0B	Register B	→	SET	PIE	AIE	UIE	SQWE	DM	24/12	DSE
0C	Register C	→	IRQF	PF	AF	UF	0	0	0	0
0D	Register D	→	VRT	0	0	0	0	0	0	0
0E ⋮ 3F	50 bytes of read/write memory									

Note: The *address* refers to the address latched into the RTC in a *latch address* phase. The RTC itself is memory-mapped as two consecutive odd bytes

Day of week → Sunday = 1, Monday = 2, etc.

Day of month (i.e. 1, 2, . . . 28,29,30,31)

Register bit mnemonics

UIP	Update in progress	DM	Data mode (binary/BCD)
DV0–DV2	Division ratio select	24/12	Select 24-hour or 12-hour
RS0–RS3	Interrupt rate select	DSE	Daylight saving enable
SET	Set time	IRQF	Interrupt request flag
PIE	Periodic interrupt enable	PF	Periodic interrupt flag
AIE	Alarm interrupt enable	AF	Alarm interrupt flag
UIE	Update ended interrupt enable	UF	Update ended interrupt flag
SQWE	Square-wave output enable	VRT	Valid RAM and time bit

registers and \$0E–\$3F furnish the 50 bytes of read/write memory available for use by the programmer. The 146818's data sheet refers to the control register at address \$0A as *register A*, the register at address \$0B as *register B* and so on. We will follow the same convention.

The timer registers at locations \$0, \$2, \$4, \$6, \$7, \$8 and \$9 hold the current time and date which are available in either binary or BCD form, depending on the state of the DM bit (DM = data mode) in register B. If DM = 1, the data is in binary form and, if DM = 0, it is in BCD form. For example, the sequence of registers R9, R8, R7, R6, R4, R2, R0 may hold the values: 87,12,13,01,11,34,15 in BCD which is equivalent to 57,0C,0D,01,0B,22,0F in binary. Both these values represent 11.34 am on Sunday, 13 December 1987.

The three alarm bytes (locations $1, $3, $5) allow the programmer to specify the time of day at which an alarm is generated. The *alarm interrupt enable bit* (AIE in register B) must be set to one to enable the alarm. When the contents of the seconds, minutes and hours registers (locations $00, $02, $04) match those of the respective alarm registers, the alarm interrupt flag (AF in register C) is set and the IRQ* output asserted if AIE = 1. The AF flag is cleared automatically by reading register C or by asserting RESET*.

If, however, the two most significant bits of an alarm byte are set by loading the byte with any code from $C0 to $FF, that alarm byte is made a *don't care* value. A don't care value does not take part in the generation of an alarm. For example, if the hour alarm byte is loaded with $FF, an alarm is generated at the same time every hour. Similarly, an alarm can be generated every minute or every second.

4.4.1 Setting up the RTC

Assuming that the time and date registers have already been initialized, the RTC is set up by loading appropriate constants in registers A and B. Register A matches the timebase used by the RTC to the user-supplied crystal frequency by means of bits DV_0 to DV_2, as indicated in Table 4.2. For example, if DV_0 to DV_2 is set to 0,0,0, the RTC is programmed to operate with a 4.194 304 MHz crystal.

TABLE 4.2 Selecting the RTC's timebase

REGISTER A DIVIDER BITS			TIME BASE FREQUENCY	MODE
DV_2	DV_1	DV_0		
0	0	0	4.194 304 MHz	Run
0	0	1	1.048 576 MHz	Run
0	1	0	32.768 kHz	Run
1	1	X	—	Halt

Note: Other combinations of DV_0 to DV_2 are not permitted.

In addition to timed interrupts, the RTC is able to generate an interrupt every *T* seconds. Bits RS_0 to RS_3 of register A select the period between successive interrupts and the frequency of the square wave at the SQW output pin. Note that it is not possible to program these two values independently. The relationship between RS_0 to RS_3 and the interrupt rate and SQW frequency is given in Table 4.3. There are two sets of values, depending on whether the RTC has a 4.194 304/1.048 576 MHz crystal or a 32.768 KHz crystal.

TABLE 4.3 Programming the RTC's interrupt rate and SQW output frequency

SELECT BITS REGISTER A				4.194 304 OR 1.048 576 MHz TIMEBASE		32.768 kHz TIMEBASE	
RS3	RS2	RS1	RS0	PERIODIC INTERRUPT RATE	SQUARE-WAVE OUTPUT FREQUENCY	PERIODIC INTERRUPT RATE	SQUARE-WAVE OUTPUT FREQUENCY
0	0	0	0	None	None	None	None
0	0	0	1	30.517 μs	32.768 kHz	3.906 25 ms	256 Hz
0	0	1	0	61.035 μs	16.384 kHz	7.812 5 ms	128 Hz
0	0	1	1	122.070 μs	8.192 kHz	122.070 μs	8.192 kHz
0	1	0	0	244.141 μs	4.096 kHz	244.141 μs	4.096 kHz
0	1	0	1	488.281 μs	2.048 kHz	488.281 μs	2.048 kHz
0	1	1	0	976.562 μs	1.024 kHz	976.562 μs	1.024 kHz
0	1	1	1	1.953 125 ms	512 Hz	1.953 125 ms	512 Hz
1	0	0	0	3.906 25 ms	256 Hz	3.906 25 ms	256 Hz
1	0	0	1	7.812 5 ms	128 Hz	7.812 5 ms	128 Hz
1	0	1	0	15.625 ms	64 Hz	15.625 ms	64 Hz
1	0	1	1	31.25 ms	32 Hz	31.25 ms	32 Hz
1	1	0	0	62.5 ms	16 Hz	62.5 ms	16 Hz
1	1	0	1	125 ms	8 Hz	125 ms	8 Hz
1	1	1	0	250 ms	4 Hz	250 ms	4 Hz
1	1	1	1	500 ms	2 Hz	500 ms	2 Hz

The *UIP* (update in progress) bit of register A is automatically set or cleared by the RTC and, when set, indicates that an update cycle is active. An *update cycle* occurs once a second when the RTC increments the time by one second. At the end of an update cycle, the alarm bytes are compared with the time bytes and the alarm interrupt flag is set if the alarm and time bytes match. During the updating period, the timer registers of the RTC should not be read, as their values are undefined. When the UIP bit is a logical zero, an update cycle is not in progress and will not begin for at least 244 μs. When UIP is a logical one, an update cycle is either in progress or is about to begin. UIP is a read-only bit and is unaffected by a reset. The programmer should test the UIP bit *before* reading the time. If UIP = 0, the time may be read from the appropriate registers of the RTC. If UIP = 1, the UIP bit must be polled until it is cleared by the RTC before the time can be reliably read.

The *SET* bit of register B controls the update process of the RTC. Writing a logical one to SET, stops the update process. The programmer may initialize the RTC while SET is a logical one, in order to avoid spurious update cycles during the initialization process. When SET is loaded with a logical zero, update cycles may take place. Typical clock setting routines invite the operator to enter the date and time and then to start the clock by hitting any key. This action is carried out by forcing SET to 1, loading the time and date registers with the appropriate user-supplied data and then clearing SET when a key is struck.

The *periodic interrupt enable* (PIE) bit of register B is set or cleared under programmer control. When cleared, the IRQ* output is not asserted by a periodic interrupt – even though the periodic flag (PF) is still set at the appropriate periodic rate. The PIE bit is automatically cleared by a reset. When PIE is set, the IRQ* output is asserted at the rate determined by bits RS_0 to RS_3 in register A.

The *alarm interrupt enable* (AIE) bit of register B determines whether the alarm circuits assert IRQ* when an alarm is generated. If AIE = 0, an alarm interrupt is inhibited. If AIE = 1, an alarm interrupt is generated when the three alarm bytes match the time of day. A reset clears AIE.

The *update-ended interrupt enable* (UIE) bit of register B determines whether an interrupt takes place when an update cycle has been ended. Clearing UIE masks the interrupt, and setting it enables the interrupt. Note that the update-end flag (UF) is set at the end of an update cycle whether UIE is set or not. UIE is cleared by a reset.

The *square-wave enable* (SQWE) bit of register B controls the SQW output pin. When SQWE = 0, the SQW pin is forced low. When SQWE = 1, a square wave is output on the SQW pin at a frequency determined by RS_0 to RS_2 in register A. SQWE is cleared by a reset.

The *data mode* (DM) bit of register B determines whether the time and calendar values are stored as binary or BCD values. Setting DM = 1 forces binary mode, and setting DM = 0 forces BCD mode. A reset has no effect on the state of DM.

The *24/12* control bit in register B determines whether the RTC operates in a 24-hour mode or in a 12-hour mode. When 24/12 = 1, the 24-hour mode is selected. When 24/12 = 0, the 12-hour mode is selected and the hours counter ranges (in BCD) from $01 to $12 (am) and from $81 to $92 (pm). Note that in the 12-hour mode the most-significant bit of the hour-time is set to indicate pm. Similarly the 12-hour mode ranges from $01 to $0C (am) or $81 to $8C (pm) in the binary data mode. In the 24-hour mode the hours range is $00–$23 (BCD) or $00–$17 (binary). The 24/12 bit is modified only under programmer control and is not affected by a reset.

The *daylight savings enable* (DSE) bit of register B is used to enable automatic hour timer increment or decrement to take account of the daylight saving hour. Many countries retard their clocks by one hour during the summer period in order to provide more daylight in the evening and thereby save energy. The DSE bit is provided to enable the RTC to track the *local* time of day throughout the year in the USA. Not all countries apply daylight saving at the same date. When DSE = 0, the clock operates normally. When DSE = 1, the timer jumps from 1:59:59 am to 3:00:00 am on the last Sunday in April. On the last Sunday in October, it jumps from 1:59:59 am to 1:00:00 am. Of course this feature is valid only in those countries that use daylight saving and make the changes on the above mentioned dates. The DSE bit is set or cleared only under programmer control.

The *interrupt request flag* (IRQF) of register C is a composite interrupt request flag and is set whenever the RTC generates an interrupt due to a periodic interrupt, an alarm or an update-ended interrupt. The value of IRQF can be represented by:

IRQF = PF.PIE + AF.AIE + UF.UIE

Note that PIE, AIE, UIE are the three interrupt mask bits and PF, AF, UF correspond to the interrupt flag bits to be described shortly.

The IRQ* output is asserted active-low whenever the IRQF bit is set. All interrupt flag bits in register C are cleared whenever the host microprocessor reads register C or when the RTC is reset.

Register C has three individual interrupt bits, one for each source of interrupt. All three bits are read-only. The periodic interrupt flag, PF, is set whenever a periodic interrupt is generated at the rate determined by the contents of RS_0 to RS_3. The alarm interrupt flag, AF, is set whenever the current time matches the alarm time. The update-ended interrupt flag, UF, is set at the end of each update cycle. This latter interrupt source can be used to generate interrupts at one-second intervals and has the advantage that the time read form the registers is always valid following the interrupt (because the next update cycle is one second away).

The PF, AF and UF bits are always set when triggered by their respective interrupt sources. However, as we have seen, the RTC cannot generate an interrupt request until at least one of the three respective interrupt enable (i.e. interrupt mask) bits, PIE, AIE, UIE are enabled.

Register D contains only a single bit, the valid RAM and time bit, VRT. The VRT bit indicates, when set, that the contents of the RAM and the timer are valid. Whenever the power sense input, PS, goes low, the VRT bit is cleared to indicate that the RAM and timer contents should not be read (or at least VRT should be regarded with great suspicion!) The VRT bit is read-only and is not modified by a reset. It can be set only by reading register D.

4.4.2 Programming the RTC

The RTC is not a difficult device to program. Once the time and date have been loaded into its registers during the RTC's initialization phase, all that is left to do is to read the time and date whenever they are required. All we have to remember is that each read or write access to the RTC consists of two parts: the register selection phase and the read/write access phase. Here, we provide two examples; SET which sets up the RTC, and CLOCK which displays the current time and date on the console.

```
RTC_A      EQU        $00E001         Address of the RTC address latch port
RTC_D      EQU        2               Offset of RTC data port from RTC_A
REG_A      EQU        $A              Offset for register A
REG_B      EQU        $B              Offset for register B
REG_C      EQU        $C              Offset for register C
*          Subroutines
GET_BYTE   EQU        〈address〉       Read hex byte into D0.B
OUT2X      EQU        〈address〉       Print 2 hex chars in D0.B
PSTRING    EQU        〈address〉       Print string pointer at by A4
PSPACE     EQU        〈address〉       Print single space
*
*
*     SET sets up the RTC from user-supplied data
*     We access the sequence of time/date registers by loading
*     a string of pointer nybbles into D1 and then shifting out
*     a nybble each time we access a new register
*

SET        LEA        RTC_A,A0        A0 points to the RTC address latch
           MOVE.B     #REG_A,(A0)     Select register A
           MOVE.B     #$00,RTC_D(A0)  Set register A (4 MHz, no interrupts)
           MOVE.B     #REG_B,(A0)     Select register B
           MOVE.B     #$82,RTC_D(A0)  SET = 1 to halt clock, 24 hour mode, BCD
           MOVE.L     #$0249870,D1    D1 holds sequence of registers to access
           MOVE.W     #5,D2           Six items to set up
SET1       LSR.L      #4,D1           Get next pointer in 1 s nybble
           MOVE.B     D1,D3           Copy RTC register address into D3
           AND.B      #$0F,D3         Mask address to 4 bits
           MOVE.B     D3,(A0)         Send address to RTC address latch
           BSR        GET_BYTE        Get a byte of setup data for RTC
           MOVE.B     D0,RTC_D(A0)    Store the data in the data port
           DBRA       D2,SET1         Repeat until all registers set up
           LEA        MES1,A4         Point to prompt message
           BSR        PSTRING         Invite user to hit key when ready
           BSR        GET_CHAR        Now get the dummy character
           MOVE.B     #REG_B,(A0)        and use it to clear the
           BCLR       #7,RTC_D(A0)       SET bit in Register B.
           RTS
```

```
*
*   CLOCK reads the contents of the RTC and displays them on the
*   console. Note the RTC is polled until the UIP bit is clear
*
CLOCK       LEA         MES2,A4             Point to header string
            BSR         PSTRING               which says 'Time'.
            LEA         RTC_A,(A0)          A0 points to base address of RTC
            MOVE.L      #$0249870,D1        Sequence of RTC's regs to be accessed
            MOVE.W      #5,D2               Six items to read and display
CLOCK1      MOVE.B      #REG_A,(A0)         Send address of register A to latch
CLOCK2      BTST        #7,RTC_D(A0)        Test UIP bit of register A
            BNE         CLOCK2              Read status until UIP clear
            LSR.L       #4,D1               Shift next pointer into 1s position
            MOVE.B      D1,D3               Get address of next register in D3
            AND.B       #$0F,D3             Restrict address to one nybble
            MOVE.B      D3,(A0)             Send register address to RTC
            MOVE.B      RTC_D(A0),D0        Read data from RTC
            BSR         OUT2X               Display it on console
            BSR         PSPACE              Output a space as delimiter
            CMP.W       #3,D2               Test to see if time being printed
            BNE.S       CLOCK3              If not time then skip heading 'Date'
            LEA.L       MES3,A4             Else point to delimiter
            BSR         PSTRING             and print it
CLOCK3      DBRA        D2,CLOCK1           Repeat until all items printed
            RTS
*
MES1        DC.B        'Hit any key to start clock',0
MES2        DC.B        'Time = ',0
MES3        DC.B        'Date = ',0
```

4.5 The ICM7170 real-time clock

Now that we have looked at the 146816 RTC, we can tackle the data sheet of another RTC, the Intersil ICM7170, with little difficulty. As the 7170's data manual is presented in full here, we need say little other than to point out some of the ways in which it differs from the 146816.

From an electrical point of view, the 7170 is easier to interface than the 146816, because the former operates in a non-multiplexed address and data mode which greatly facilitates the design of a 7170 to 68000 interface. Moreover, the 7170 is designed to be connected *directly* to the backup power supply which simplifies the design of the power-down circuitry. The 7170 is a more basic RTC than the 146816, because it lacks some of the latter's features such as user programmable RAM, programmable 12/24 hour modes and programmable binary/BCD modes.

I leave the design of a 7170–68000 interface as a design exercise for the reader.

4.6 The generic counter/timer

The counter/timer is one of the most popular of the peripheral chips and often one of the least understood devices. One reason for this is not hard to find. Because the counter/timer requires few *peripheral-side* pins and is an intrinsically simple device, manufacturers have tended to include timer/counters as parts of other peripheral chips. A result of combining a timer with other interfaces is that the literature describing counter/timers varies widely in its approach and terminology. Contrast this state of affairs with the literature describing the UART or ACIA. We have already encountered two counter/timers in the 68901 MFP and the 146818 RTC.

Here, I intend to discuss the operating modes of a generic or hypothetical counter/timer in order to help the reader to understand real counter/timers. Figure 4.7 demonstrates the logic of a simple timer. At the heart of this circuit

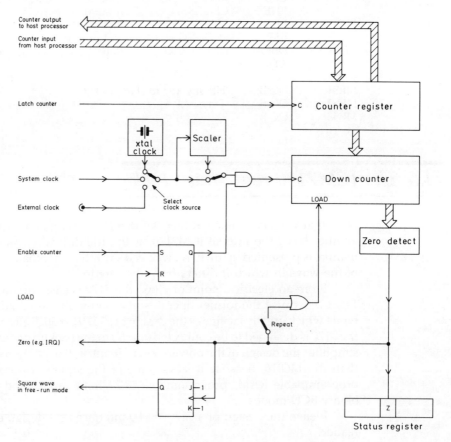

FIGURE 4.7   The logic diagram of a hypothetical timer

lies a binary down-counter. The counter can be preloaded from a counter register, which is itself loaded from the host microprocessor.

Many timers permit the counter to be clocked from one of three sources: an external clock supplied to one of the chip's pins, the system clock, or a clock formed by an on-chip oscillator using a quartz crystal. The external clock source can be selected under programmer control and it is often possible to pass it through a prescaler which, typically, reduces its rate by a factor of sixteen.

When the counter is enabled, either by an external hardware trigger or by a software command, the counter counts down from its preload value towards zero. Eventually the counter reaches zero and the zero-detect bit of an internal status register is set. The zero-detect output also disables the clock and prevents further counting.

The operation of a basic counter is illustrated graphically in Figure 4.8. The counter contents are represented as an *analog* value that steps downwards towards zero. Below the graph of the counter contents is a graph of the zero-detect output, which provides a single pulse when the counter is first enabled. If the counter is preloaded with the value N and the chosen clock has a period T, the length of the zero-detect pulse is NT.

In its basic form, the timer generates a single pulse of predetermined duration, which may be used to control external equipment. Equally the pulse may be used to interrupt the microprocessor at the end of its period. The counter is, of course, acting as a programmable digital *monostable* circuit.

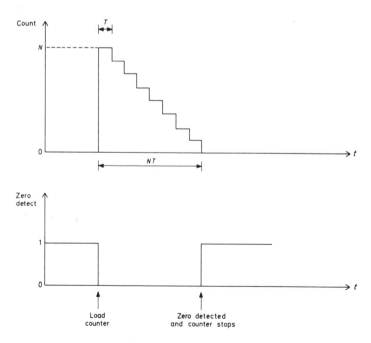

FIGURE 4.8   The operation of Figure 4.7

Suppose now that the simple counter is modified and that the zero-detect output is fed to a JK flip-flop which toggles at each falling edge of the zero-detect signal and that the zero-detect signal is fed back to reload the counter as illustrated by Figure 4.9. That is, the falling edge of the zero-detect pulse *reloads* the counter with its preload value from the preload register. The Q output of the JK flip-flop now provides a square wave output with a period $2NT$ and can be employed as a periodic interrupt (real-time clock) or as a signal for use in an external circuit. In this mode, the counter is acting as a programmable square-wave generator.

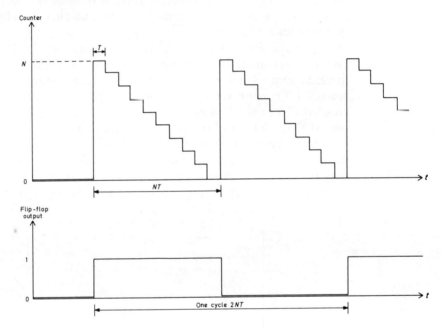

FIGURE 4.9 The counter as a square-wave generator

One variation on the counter/timer theme uses two counter registers which are selected alternately. If one register is preloaded with, say, M and the other with N, the up period of the squarewave is MT and the down period is NT. That is, we have an asymmetric square wave with a period of $(M+N)T$ and a mark:space ratio of $M:N$.

If the counter is triggered by an external signal rather than by a software command, it is possible to measure the elapsed time between the active edge of the external signal and the current time by reading the contents of the counter. For example, if the clock input to the counter has a period of 1 ms and the counter counts up from zero, reading a value of $0104 from the counter indicates an elapsed time of 260 ms.

Although counter/timers perform rather mundane tasks, they free the microprocessor from some very tedious activity. The only way of measuring a period of time without a dedicated timer would be to force the microprocessor itself into a timing loop.

Summary

In this chapter we have looked at the real-time clock and demonstrated how a typical RTC can be interfaced to a 68000 microprocessor system. The real-time clock not only generates signals or interrupts at programmable frequencies, but can also maintain an accurate time-of-day and date. Typical real-time clocks are implemented in CMOS technology which makes it easy to keep them running from small batteries when the host computer is powered down. However, any real-time clock interface has to be designed with care to avoid problems during the change over from system power to battery power.

Appendix: The ICM7170 data sheet

GE Solid State

GENERAL DESCRIPTION

The ICM7170 real time clock is a microprocessor bus compatible peripheral, fabricated using Intersil's silicon gate CMOS LSI process. An 8-bit bidirectional bus is used for the data I/O circuitry. The clock is set or read by accessing the 8 internal separately addressable and programmable counters from 1/100 seconds to years. The counters are controlled by a pulse train divided down from a crystal oscillator circuit, and the frequency of the crystal is selectable with the on-chip command register. An extremely stable oscillator frequency is achieved through the use of an on-chip regulated power supply.

The device access time (t_{acc}) of 300ns eliminates the need for any microprocessor wait states or software overhead. Furthermore, the ALE (Address Latch Enable) input is provided for interfacing to microprocessors with a multiplexed address/data bus. With these two special features, the ICM7170 can be easily interfaced to any available microprocessor.

The ICM7170 generates two types of interrupts. The first type is the periodic interrupt (i.e., 100Hz, 10Hz, etc.) which can be programmed by the internal interrupt control register to provide 7 different output signals. The second type is the alarm interrupt. The alarm time is set by loading an on-chip 51-bit RAM that activates an interrupt output through a comparator. The alarm interrupt occurs when the real time counter and alarm RAM time are equal. A status register is available to indicate the interrupt source.

An on-chip Power-Down Detector eliminates the need for external components to support the battery back-up function. When a power-down or power failure occurs, internal logic switches the on-chip counters to battery back-up operation. Read/write functions become disabled and operation is limited to time-keeping and interrupt generation, resulting in low power consumption.

Internal latches prevent clock roll-over during a read cycle. Counter data is latched on the chip by reading the 100th-seconds counter and is held indefinitely until the counter is read again, assuring a stable and reliable time value.

ORDERING INFORMATION

Part Number	Temperature Range	Package
ICM7170IPG	−40°C to +85°C	24-Pin Plastic Dip
ICM7170IDG	−40°C to +85°C	24-Pin Ceramic
ICM7170IBG	−40°C to +85°C	24-Pin S.O.I.C. (Surface Mount)
ICM7170MDG	−55°C to +125°C	24-Pin Ceramic
ICM7170MDG/883C	−55°C to +125°C	24-Pin Ceramic
ICM7170AIPG	−40°C to +85°C	24-Pin Plastic Dip
ICM7170AIBG	−40°C to +85°C	24-Pin S.O.I.C.
ICM7170AMDG	−55°C to +125°C	24-Pin Ceramic
ICM7170AMDG/883C	−55°C to +125°C	24-Pin Ceramic

"A" Parts Screened to <5 µA I_{STBY} @ 32 KHz

GE SOLID STATE, 10600 RIDGEVIEW COURT, CUPERTINO, CA 95014
Printed in U.S.A. © Copyright 1987, GE Solid State, All Rights Reserved

ICM7170
µP–Compatible Real–Time Clock

FEATURES

- 883B-Rev C Compliant
- 8-Bit µP Bus Compatible
  —Multiplexed or Direct Addressing
- Regulated Oscillator Supply Ensures Frequency Stability and Low Power
- Time From 1/100 Seconds to 99 Years
- Software Selectable 12/24 Hour Format
- Latched Time Data Ensures No Roll-Over During Read
- Full Calendar With Automatic Leap Year Correction
- On-Chip Battery Backup Switchover Circuit
- Access Time Less Than 300ns
- 4 Programmable Crystal Oscillator Frequencies over Industrial Temp Range
- 3 Programmable Crystal Oscillator Frequencies over Military Temp Range
- On-Chip Alarm Comparator and RAM
- Interrupts from Alarm and 6 Selectable Periodic Intervals
- Standby Micro-Power Operation: 2µA Typ. at 3.0V and 32kHz Crystal

APPLICATIONS

- Portable and Personal Computers   • Data Logging
- Industrial Control Systems   • Point Of Sale

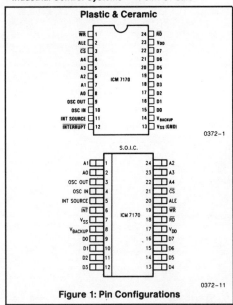

Figure 1: Pin Configurations

GE Solid State

ICM7170

ABSOLUTE MAXIMUM RATINGS

Supply Voltage 8V
Power Dissipation (Note 1)..................... 500mW
Input Voltage (Any Terminal)
(Note 2) .... V_{DD} +0.3V to V_{SS} −0.3V

Operating Temperature .... −40°C to +85°C
Storage Temperature .... −65°C to +150°C
Lead Temperature (Soldering, 10sec) .... 300°C

NOTE 1: T_A = 25°C.

NOTE 2: Due to the SCR structure inherent in the CMOS process, connecting any terminal at voltages greater than V_{DD} or less than V_{SS} may cause destructive device latchup. For this reason, it is recommended that no inputs from external sources not operating on the same power supply be applied to the device before its supply is established, and that in multiple supply systems, the supply to the ICM7170 be turned on first.

NOTE: *Stresses above those listed under "Absolute Maximum Ratings" may cause permanent damage to the device. These are stress ratings only and functional operation of the device at these or any other conditions above those indicated in the operational sections of the specifications is not implied. Exposure to absolute maximum rating conditions for extended periods may affect device reliability.*

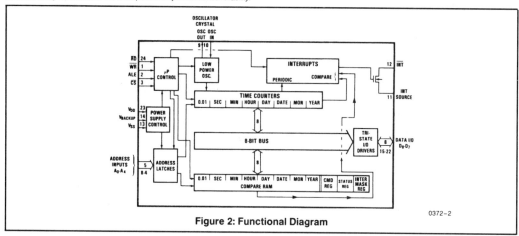

0372−2

Figure 2: Functional Diagram

ELECTRICAL CHARACTERISTICS
DC CHARACTERISTICS

(T_A = −40°C to +85°C, V_{DD} = +5V ±10%, V_{BACKUP} = V_{DD}, V_{SS} = 0V unless otherwise specified)
All I_{DD} specifications include all input and output leakages (7170 and 7170A)

Symbol	Parameter	Test Conditions		Specification			Units
				Min	Typ	Max	
V_{DD}	V_{DD} Supply Range	F_{OSC} = 32kHz		1.9		5.5	V
		F_{OSC} = 1, 2, 4MHz		2.6		5.5	
$I_{STBY(1)}$	Standby Current	F_{OSC} = 32kHz Pins 1−8, 15−22 = V_{DD} V_{DD} = V_{SS}; V_{BACKUP} = V_{DD} − 3.0V For 7170A See General Note (5)	7170		1.2	20.0	μA
			7170A		1.2	5.0	
$I_{STBY(2)}$	Standby Current	F_{OSC} = 4MHz Pins 1−8, 15−22 & 24 = V_{DD} V_{DD} = V_{SS}; V_{BACKUP} = V_{DD} − 3.0V			20	150	μA
$I_{DD(1)}$	Operating Supply Current	F_{OSC} = 32kHz Read/Write Operation at 100Hz			0.3	1.2	mA
$I_{DD(2)}$	Operating Supply Current	F_{OSC} = 32kHz Read/Write Operation at 1MHz			1.0	2.0	mA

"A" Parts Screened to <5 μA I_{STBY} @ 32 KHz

NOTE: All typical values have been characterized but are not tested.

GE Solid State

ICM7170

ELECTRICAL CHARACTERISTICS
DC CHARACTERISTICS

($T_A = -40°C$ to $+85°C$, $V_{DD} = +5V \pm 10\%$, $V_{BACKUP} = V_{DD}$, $V_{SS} = 0V$ unless otherwise specified) (Continued)
All I_{DD} specifications include all input and output leakages (7170 and 7170A)

Symbol	Parameter	Test Conditions		Specification			Units
				Min	Typ	Max	
V_{IL}	Input low voltage (Except Osc.)	$V_{DD} = 5.0V$				0.8	V
V_{IH}	Input high voltage (Except Osc.)	$V_{DD} = 5.0V$		2.4			V
V_{OL}	Output low voltage (Except Osc.)	$I_{OL} = 1.6mA$				0.4	V
V_{OH}	Output high voltage except $\overline{INTERRUPT}$ (Except Osc.)	$I_{OH} = -400\mu A$		2.4			V
I_{IL}	Input leakage current	$V_{IN} = V_{DD}$ or V_{SS}		-10	0.5	$+10$	μA
I_{OL}[1]	Tristate leakage current ($D_0 - D_7$)	$V_0 = V_{DD}$ or V_{SS}		-10	0.5	$+10$	μA
$V_{BATTERY}$	Backup Battery Voltage	$F_{OSC} = 1, 2, 4MHz$		2.6		$V_{DD} - 1.3$	V
$V_{BATTERY}$	Backup Battery Voltage	$F_{OSC} = 32kHz$		1.9		$V_{DD} - 1.3$	V
I_{OL}[2]	Leakage current $\overline{INTERRUPT}$	$V_0 = V_{DD}$	INT SOURCE connected to V_{SS}		0.5	10	μA
$C_{I/O}$	CAPACITANCE $D_0 - D_7$				8		pF
$C_{ADDRESS}$	CAPACITANCE $A_0 - A_4$				6		pF
$C_{CONTROL}$	CAP. $\overline{RD}$, $\overline{WR}$, $\overline{CS}$ ALE				6		pF
C_{IN} Osc.	Total Osc. Input Cap.				3		pF

AC CHARACTERISTICS   ($T_A = -40°C$ to $+85°C$, $V_{DD} = +5V \pm 10\%$, $V_{BACKUP} = V_{DD}$, $D_0 - D_7$ Load
Capacitance $= 150pF$, $V_{IL} = 0.4V$, $V_{IH} = 2.8V$ unless otherwise specified)

Symbol	Parameter	Min	Max	Units
READ CYCLE TIMING				
t_{rd}	READ to DATA valid		250	ns
t_{acc}	ADDRESS valid to DATA valid		300	ns
t_{cyc}	READ cycle time	400		ns
t_{rh}	Read high time	150		ns
t_{rx}	$\overline{RD}$ high to bus tristate		25	ns
t_{as}	ADDRESS to READ set up time	50		ns
t_{ar}	ADDRESS HOLD time after READ	0		ns
WRITE CYCLE TIMING				
t_{ad}	ADDRESS valid to WRITE strobe	50		ns
t_{wa}	ADDRESS hold time for WRITE	0		ns
t_{wl}	WRITE pulse width, low	100		ns
t_{wh}	WRITE high time	300		ns
t_{dw}	DATA IN to WRITE set up time	100		ns
t_{wd}	DATA IN hold time after WRITE	30		ns
t_{cyc}	WRITE cycle time	400		ns
MULTIPLEXED MODE TIMING				
t_{ll}	ALE Pulse Width, High	50		ns
t_{al}	ADDRESS to ALE set up time	30		ns
t_{la}	ADDRESS hold time after ALE	30		ns

NOTE: All typical values have been characterized but are not tested.

GE Solid State

ICM7170

ICM 7170 ELECTRICAL CHARACTERISTICS (TEST SPECIFICATION) FOR MIL-STD-883 COMPLIANCE

ABSOLUTE MAXIMUM RATINGS

Supply Voltage 8V
Power Dissipation (Note 1) 500mW
Input Voltage (Any Terminal)
. . . . V_{DD} + 0.3V to V_{SS} − 0.3V
Operating Temperature . . . . −55°C to + 125°C
Storage Temperature . . . . −65°C to + 150°C
Lead Temperature (Soldering, 10 sec) . . . . 300°C

NOTE 1: T_A = 25°C.

NOTE: *Stresses above those listed under "Absolute Maximum Ratings" may cause permanent damage to the device. These are stress ratings only and functional operation of the device at these or any other conditions above those indicated in the operational sections of the specifications is not implied. Exposure to absolute maximum rating conditions for extended periods may affect device reliability.*

ELECTRICAL CHARACTERISTICS
DC CHARACTERISTICS (V_{DD} = 5V ± 10%, V_{BACKUP} = V_{DD}, T_A = −55°C to + 125°C, unless otherwise specified)
All I_{DD} specifications include all input and output leakages

Symbol	Parameter	Test Conditions		Specification			Units
				Min	Typ	Max	
V_{DD}	V_{DD} Supply Range	F_{OSC} = 32kHz		1.9		5.5	V
		F_{OSC} = 1, 2MHz		2.6		5.5	
$I_{STBY(1)}$	Standby Current	F_{OSC} = 32 kHz Pins 1–8, 15–22 & 24 = V_{DD}	7170		1.2	40.0	μA
		V_{DD} = V_{SS}; V_{BACKUP} = V_{DD} − 3.0V 7170A See General Note (5)	7170A		1.2	5.0	
$I_{STBY(2)}$	Standby Current	F_{OSC} = 2MHz All chip I/O to V_{DD} V_{DD} = V_{SS}: V_{BACKUP} = V_{DD} − 3.0V			30	200	μA
$I_{DD(1)}$	Operating Supply Current	F_{OSC} = 32 kHz Read/Write Operation at 100 Hz			0.3	1.2	mA
$I_{DD(2)}$	Operating Supply Current	F_{OSC} = 32 kHz Read/Write Operation at 1 MHz			1.0	2.0	mA
V_{IL}	Input Low Voltage (Except Osc.)	V_{DD} = 5.0V				0.8	V
V_{IH}	Input High Voltage (Except Osc.)	V_{DD} = 5.0V		2.8			V
V_{OL}	Output Low Voltage (Except Osc.)	I_{OL} = 1.6 mA				0.5	V
V_{OH}	Output High Voltage Except INTERRUPT (Except Osc.)	I_{OH} = 400μA		2.5			V
I_{IL}	Input Leakage Current	V_{IN} = V_{DD} or V_{SS}		− 10	0.5	+ 10	μA
I_{OL}	Tristate Leakage Current (D_0–D_7)	V_{IN} = V_{DD} or V_{SS}		− 10	0.5	+ 10	μA
$V_{BATTERY}$	Backup Battery Voltage	F_{OSC} = 32 kHz		1.9		V_{DD} − 1.5	V
$V_{BATTERY}$	Backup Battery Voltage	F_{OSC} = 2 MHz		2.6	−	V_{DD} − 1.5	V
I_{OL}	Leakage Current INTERRUPT	V_0 = V_{DD} or V_{SS}	INT SOURCE connected to V_{SS}		0.5	10	μA

"A" Parts Screened to < 5 μA I_{STBY} @ 32 KHz

NOTE: All typical values have been characterized but are not tested.

GE Solid State

ICM7170

AC CHARACTERISTICS

$(T_A = -55°C$ to $+125°C$, $V_{DD} = 5V \pm 10\%$, $V_{BACKUP} = V_{DD}$, D_0-D_7 Load Capacitance $= 150$ pF, $V_{IL} = 0.4V$, $V_{IH} = 3.20V$ unless otherwise specified)

Symbol	Parameter	Min	Max	Units
READ CYCLE TIMING				
t_{rd}	READ to DATA Valid		250	ns
t_{ACC}	ADDRESS Valid to DATA Valid		350	ns
t_{cyc}	READ Cycle Time	450		ns
t_{rx}	$\overline{RD}$ High to Bus Tristate		100	ns
t_{as}	ADDRESS to READ Set Up Time	100		ns
t_{ar}	ADDRESS HOLD Time after READ	50		ns
t_{rh}	READ High Time	200		ns
WRITE CYCLE TIMING				
t_{ad}	ADDRESS Valid to WRITE Strobe	100		ns
t_{wa}	ADDRESS Hold Time for WRITE	50		ns
t_{wl}	WRITE Pulse Low Width	125		ns
t_{wh}	WRITE Pulse Width High	325		ns
t_{dw}	DATA IN to WRITE Set Up Time	125		ns
t_{wd}	DATA IN Hold Time after WRITE	50		ns
t_{cyc}	WRITE Cycle Time	450		ns
MULTIPLEXED MODE TIMING				
t_{ll}	ALE Width	50		ns
t_{al}	ADDRESS to ALE Set Up Time	30		ns
t_{la}	ADDRESS Hold Time after ALE	40		ns

NOTE: All typical values have been characterized but are not tested.

GE Solid State

ICM7170

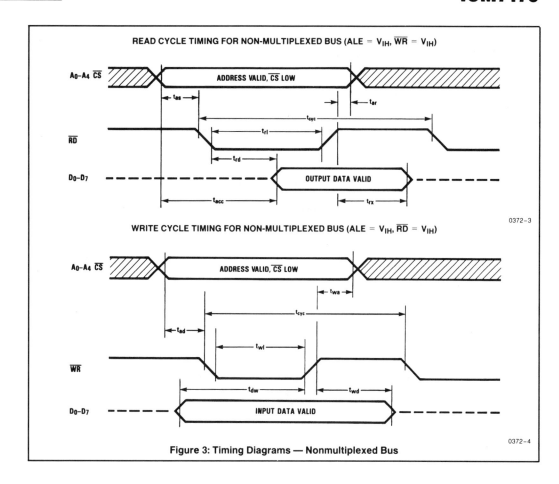

READ CYCLE TIMING FOR NON-MULTIPLEXED BUS (ALE = V_{IH}, $\overline{WR}$ = V_{IH})

WRITE CYCLE TIMING FOR NON-MULTIPLEXED BUS (ALE = V_{IH}, $\overline{RD}$ = V_{IH})

Figure 3: Timing Diagrams — Nonmultiplexed Bus

ICM7170

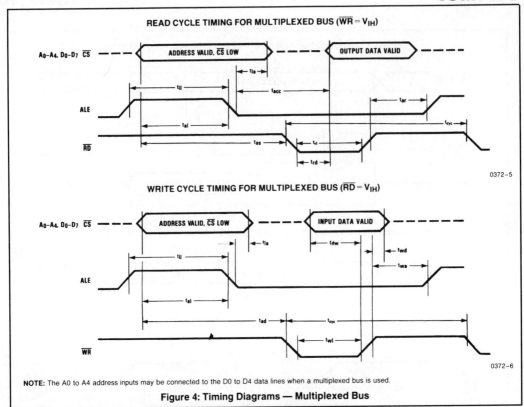

NOTE: The A0 to A4 address inputs may be connected to the D0 to D4 data lines when a multiplexed bus is used.

Figure 4: Timing Diagrams — Multiplexed Bus

Table 1

Signal	Pin	Description
$\overline{WR}$	1	Write input
ALE	2	Address latch enable input
$\overline{CS}$	3	Chip select input
A4-A0	4-8	Address inputs
OSC OUT	9	Oscillator output
OSC IN	10	Oscillator input
INT SOURCE	11	Interrupt source
$\overline{INTERRUPT}$	12	Interrupt output
V_{SS}(GND)	13	Digital common
V_{BACKUP}	14	Battery negative side
D0-D7	15-22	Data I/O
V_{DD}	23	Positive digital supply
$\overline{RD}$	24	Read input

DETAILED DESCRIPTION
Oscillator

This circuit uses a regulated CMOS Pierce oscillator, for maximum accuracy, stability, and low-power consumption. Externally, one crystal and two capacitors are required. One of the capacitors is variable and is used to trim or tune the oscillator output. Typical values for these capacitors are $C_{IN} = 15pF$ and $C_{OUT} = 10-35pF$, or approximately double the recommended C_{LOAD} for the crystal being used. Both capacitors must be connected from the respective oscillator pins to V_{DD} for maximum stability.

The oscillator output is divided down to 4000Hz by one of four selected ratios, via a variable prescaler. The ICM7170 can use any one of four different low-cost crystals: 4.194304MHz, 2.097152MHz, 1.048576MHz, or 32.768kHz. The ICM7170MDG is available with 3 crystal frequency options only. (4.194304 MHz is not avail. with military version.) The command register must be programmed for the frequency of the crystal chosen, and this in turn will determine the prescaler's divide ratio.

Command Register frequency selection is written to the D0 and D1 bits at address 11H and the 12 or 24 hour format is determined by bit D2, as shown in Table 4.

GE Solid State

ICM7170

The 4000Hz signal is divided down further to 100Hz, which is used as the clock for the counters. Time and calendar information is provided by 8 consecutive addressable, programmable counters: 100ths of seconds, seconds, minutes, hours, day of week, date, month, and year. The data is in binary format and is configured into 8 bits per digit. See Table 4 for address information. Any unused bits are held at logic "0" during a read and ignored during a write operation.

Alarm Compare RAM

On the chip are 51 bits of Alarm Compare RAM grouped into words of different lengths. These are used to store the time, ranging from 100ths of seconds to years, for comparison to the real-time counters. Each counter has a corresponding RAM word. In the Alarm Mode an interrupt is generated when the current time is equal to the alarm time. The RAM contents are compared to the counters on a word by word basis. If a comparison to a particular counter is unnecessary, then the appropriate 'M' bit in Compare RAM should be set to logic "1".

The 'M' bit, referring to Mask bit, causes a particular RAM word to be masked off or ignored during a compare. Table 4 shows addresses and Mask bit information.

Periodic Interrupts

The interrupt output can be programmed for 6 periodic signals: 100 Hz, 10 Hz, once per second, once per minute, once per hour, or once per day. The 100 Hz and 10 Hz interrupts have instantaneous errors of $\pm2.5\%$ and $\pm0.15\%$ respectively. This is because non-integer divider circuitry is used to generate these signals from the crystal frequency, which is a power of 2. The time average of these errors over a 1 second period, however, is zero. Consequently, the 100 Hz or 10 Hz interrupts are not suitable as an aid in tuning the oscillator; the 1 second interrupt must be used instead.

See General Note (6).

The periodic interrupts can occur concurrently and in addition to alarm interrupts. The periodic interrupts are controlled by bits in the interrupt mask register, and are enabled by setting the appropriate bit to a "1" as shown in Table 5. Bits D1 through D6 in the mask register, in conjunction with bits D1 through D6 of the status register, control the generation of interrupts according to Figure 5.

The interrupt status register, when read, indicates the cause of the interrupt and resets itself on the rising edge of the RD signal. When any of the counters having a corresponding bit in the status register increments, that bit is set to a "1" regardless of whether the corresponding bit in the interrupt mask register is set or not.

Consequently, when the status register is read it will always indicate which counters have increments and if an alarm compare occurred, since the last time it was read. This requires some special software considerations. If a slow interrupt is enabled (i.e. hourly or daily), the program must always check the slowest interrupt that has been enabled first, because all the other lower order bits in the status register will be set to "1" as well.

Bit D7 is the global interrupt bit, and when set to a "1", indicates that the 7170 did indeed generate a hardware interrupt. This is useful when other interrupting devices in addition to the 7170 are attached to the system microprocessor, and all devices must be polled to determine which one generated the interrupt.

See General Note (6).

Table 2: Command Register Format

COMMAND REGISTER ADDRESS (10001b, 11h) WRITE-ONLY							
D7	D6	D5	D4	D3	D2	D1	D0
n/a	n/a	Test	Global Int Mask	Run	12/24	Freq	Freq

Table 3: Command Register Bit Assignments

D5	Test Bit	D4	Interrupt Enable	D3	Run/Stop	D2	24/12 Hour Format	D1	D0	Crystal Frequency
0	Normal Mode	0	Interrupt disabled	0	Stop	0	12 hour mode	0	0	32.768kHz
1	Test Mode	1	Interrupt enable	1	Run	1	24 hour mode	0	1	1.048576MHz
								1	0	2.097152MHz
								1	1	4.194304MHz

Table 4: Address Codes and Functions

A4	A3	A2	A1	A0	HEX	Function	D7	D6	D5	D4	D3	D2	D1	D0	Value
										Address → **DATA**					
0	0	0	0	0	00	Counter-1/100 seconds	–	.	.	.	.	.	.	.	0-99
0	0	0	0	1	01	Counter-hours	–	–	–	.	.	.	.	.	0-23
						12 Hour Mode	*	–	–	–	.	.	.	.	1-12
0	0	0	1	0	02	Counter-minutes	–	–	.	.	.	.	.	.	0-59
0	0	0	1	1	03	Counter-seconds	–	–	.	.	.	.	.	.	0-59
0	0	1	0	0	04	Counter-month	–	–	–	–	.	.	.	.	1-12
0	0	1	0	1	05	Counter-date	–	–	–	.	.	.	.	.	1-31
0	0	1	1	0	06	Counter-year	–	.	.	.	.	.	.	.	0-99
0	0	1	1	1	07	Counter-day of week	–	–	–	–	–	.	.	.	0-6
0	1	0	0	0	08	RAM-1/100 seconds	M	.	.	.	.	.	.	.	0-99
0	1	0	0	1	09	RAM-hours	–	M	–	.	.	.	.	.	0-23
						12 hour Mode	*	M	–	–	.	.	.	.	1-12
0	1	0	1	0	0A	RAM-minutes	M	–	.	.	.	.	.	.	0-59
0	1	0	1	1	0B	RAM-seconds	M	–	.	.	.	.	.	.	0-59
0	1	1	0	0	0C	RAM-month	M	–	–	–	.	.	.	.	1-12
0	1	1	0	1	0D	RAM-date	M	–	–	.	.	.	.	.	1-31
0	1	1	1	0	0E	RAM-year	M	.	.	.	.	.	.	.	0-99
0	1	1	1	1	0F	RAM-day of week	M	–	–	–	–	.	.	.	0-6
1	0	0	0	0	10	Interrupt Status and Mask Register	+	.	.	.	.	.	.	.	
1	0	0	0	1	11	Command register	–	–	.	.	.	.	.	.	

NOTES: Address 10010 to 11111 (12h to 1Fh) are unused.

'+' Unused bit for Interrupt Mask Register, MSB bit for Interrupt Status Register.

'–' Indicates unused bits.

'*' AM/PM indicator bit in 12 hour format. Logic "0" indicates AM, logic "1" indicates PM.

'M' Alarm compare for particular counter will be enabled if bit is set to logic "0".

Table 5: Interrupt and Status Registers Format

INTERRUPT MASK REGISTER ADDRESS (10000b, 10h) WRITE-ONLY							
D7	D6	D5	D4	D3	D2	D1	D0
Not Used	Day	Hour	Min.	Sec.	1/10 sec.	1/100 sec.	Alarm
	←		Periodic Interrupt Mask Bits			→	Alarm/Compare Mask Bit
INTERRUPT STATUS REGISTER ADDRESS (10000b, 10h) READ-ONLY							
D7	D6	D5	D4	D3	D2	D1	D0
Global Interrupt	Day	Hour	Min.	Sec.	1/10 sec.	1/100 sec.	Alarm
Periodic and Alarm Flags	←		Periodic Interrupt Flags			→	Alarm Compare Flag

NOTE: All typical values have been characterized but are not tested.

GE Solid State

ICM7170

Interrupt Operation

The interrupt output N-channel MOSFET is active at all times when the Interrupt Enable bit is set (bit 4 of the Command Register), and operates in both the standby and battery backup modes.

Since system power is usually applied between V_{DD} and V_{SS}, the user can connect the Interrupt Source (pin #11) to V_{SS}. This allows the Interrupt Output to turn on only while system power is applied and will not be pulled to V_{SS} during standby operation. If interrupts are required only during standby operation, then the interrupt source pin should be connected to the battery's negative side (V_{BACKUP}). In this configuration, for example, the interrupt could be used to turn on power for a cold boot.

Power-Down Detector

The ICM7170 contains an on-chip power-down detector that eliminates the need for external components to support the battery-backup switchover function, as shown in Figure 6. Whenever the voltage from the V_{SS} pin to the V_{BACKUP} pin is less than approximately 1.0V (the V_{th} of the N-channel MOSFET), the data bus I/O buffers in the 7170 are automatically disabled and the chip cannot be read or written to. This prevents random data from the microprocessor being written to the clock registers as the power supply is going down.

Actual switchover to battery operation occurs when the voltage on the V_{BACKUP} pin is within ± 50 mV of V_{SS}. This switchover uncertainty is due to the offset voltage of the CMOS comparator that is used to sense the battery voltage. During battery backup, device operation is limited to timekeeping and interrupt generation only, thus achieving micropower current drain. If an external battery-backup switchover circuit is being used with the 7170, the V_{BACKUP} pin should be tied to the V_{DD} pin. The same also applies if standby battery operation is not required.

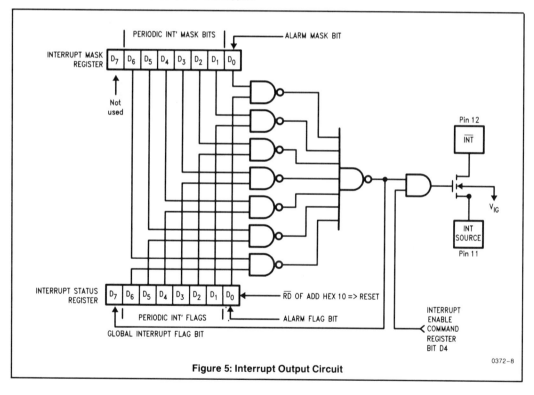

Figure 5: Interrupt Output Circuit

0372-8

GE Solid State

ICM7170

Time Synchronization

Time synchronization is achieved through bit D3 of the Command Register, which is used to enable or disable the 100Hz clock from the counters. A logic "1" allows the counters to function and a logic "0" disables the counters. To accurately set the time, a logic "0" should be written into D3 and then the desired times entered into the appropriate counters. The clock is then started at the proper time by writing a logic "1" into D3 of the Command Register.

Latched Data

To prevent ambiguity while the processor is gathering data from the registers, the ICM7170 incorporates data latches and a transparent transition delay circuit.

By accessing the 100ths of seconds counter an internal store signal is generated and data from all the counters is transferred into a 36-bit latch. A transition delay circuit will delay a 100Hz transition during a READ cycle. The data stored by the latches is then available for further processing until the 100ths of seconds counter is read again. If a read bar signal is wider than 0.01 sec., 100 Hz counts will be ignored.

Control Lines

The $\overline{RD}$, $\overline{WR}$, and $\overline{CS}$ signals are active low inputs. Data is placed on the bus from counters or registers when $\overline{RD}$ is a logic "0". Data is transferred to counters or registers when $\overline{WR}$ is a logic "0". $\overline{RD}$ and $\overline{WR}$ must be accompanied by a logical "0" $\overline{CS}$ as shown in Figures 3 and 4. The 7170 will also work satisfactorily with $\overline{CS}$ grounded. This access also to be controlled by $\overline{RD}$ and $\overline{WR}$ only.

With the ALE (Address Latch Enable) input, the ICM7170 can be interfaced directly to microprocessors that use a multiplexed address/data bus by connecting the address lines A0-A4 to the data lines D0-D4. To address the chip, the address is placed on the bus and ALE is strobed. On the falling edge, the address and $\overline{CS}$ information is read into the address latch and buffer. $\overline{RD}$ and $\overline{WR}$ are used in the same way as on a non-multiplexed bus. If a non-multiplexed bus is used, ALE should be connected to V_{DD}.

Test Mode

The test mode is entered by setting D5 of the Command Register to a logic "1". This connects the 100Hz counter to the oscillator's output. The peak-to-peak voltage used to drive osc. out should not be greater than the oscillator's regulated voltage. The signal must be referenced to V_{DD}.

Oscillator Tuning

Oscillator tuning should not be attempted by direct monitoring of the oscillator pins, unless very specialized equipment is used. External connections to the oscillator pins cause capacitive loading of the crystal, and shift the oscillator frequency. As a result, the precision setting being at-

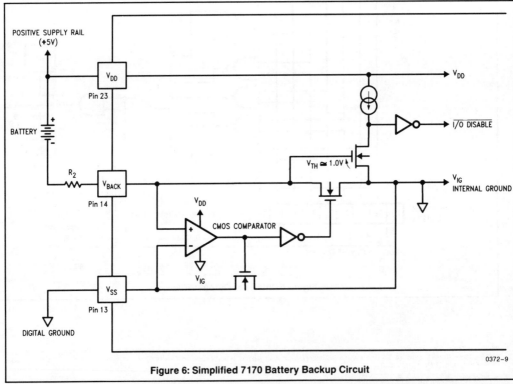

Figure 6: Simplified 7170 Battery Backup Circuit

0372-9

tempted is corrupted. One indirect method of determining the oscillator frequency is to measure the period between interrupts on the Interrupt Output pin (#12). This measurement must be relative to the falling edges of the $\overline{\text{INTERRUPT}}$ pin. The oscillator set-up and tuning can be performed as follows:

1) Select one of 4, readily-available oscillator frequencies and place the crystal between OSC IN (pin #10) and OSC OUT (pin #9).

2) Connect a fixed capacitor from OSC IN to V_{DD}.

3) Connect a variable capacitor from OSC OUT to V_{DD}. In cases where the crystal selected is a 32kHz Statek type ($C_L = 9pF$), the typical value of $C_{IN} = 15pF$ and $C_{OUT} = 5pf-35pF$.

4) Place a 4.7KΩ resistor from the $\overline{\text{INTERRUPT}}$ pin to V_{DD}, and connect the INT SOURCE pin to V_{SS}.

5) Apply 5V power and insure the clock is not in standby mode.

6) Write all 0's to the Interrupt Mask Register, disabling all interrupts.

7) Write to the Command Register with the desired oscillator frequency, Hours mode (12 hour or 24 hour), Run = "1", Interrupt Enable = "1", and Test = "0".

8) Write to the Interrupt Mask Register, enabling one-second interrupts only.

9) Monitor the $\overline{\text{INTERRUPT}}$ output pin with a precision period counter and trim the OSC OUT capacitor for a reading of 1.000000 seconds. The period counter must be triggered on the falling edge of the interrupt output for this measurement to be accurate.

10) Read the Interrupt Status Register. This action resets the interrupt output back to a logic "1" level.

11) Repeat steps 9 and 10 with a software loop. A suitable computer should be used.

PCB DESIGN CONSIDERATION

1) Layout Quartz Crystal traces as short as possible.

2) Keep Crystal traces as far as possible from other traces.

3) PCB should accept both Saronix and Statek 32.768kHz Crystals.

4) Completely surround crystal traces with V_{DD} trace.

5) Try to keep oscillator traces on one side of the PCB.

6) Trimmer capacitor must be accessible from the top of the PCB after it is inserted into the appropriate connector.

7) The fixed and variable oscillator capacitors must be referenced to V_{DD}. V_{SS} is not an AC ground for the oscillator.

8) 1 1k resistor (R2) must be placed in series with the Vbackup pin 14 of the 7170 and the negative side of the battery.

9) See Note 8 for D1 limitations.

APPLICATION NOTES
Digital Input Termination During Backup

To ensure low current drain during battery backup operation, none of the digital inputs to the 7170 should be allowed to float. This keeps the input logic gates out of their transition region, and prevents crossover current from flowing which will shorten battery life. The address, data, $\overline{\text{CS}}$, and ALE pins should be pulled to either V_{DD} or V_{SS}, and the $\overline{\text{RD}}$ and $\overline{\text{WR}}$ inputs should be pulled to V_{DD}. This is necessary whether the internal battery switchover circuit is used or not.

IBM/PC Evaluation Circuit

Figure 7 shows the schematic of a board that has been designed to plug into an IBM PC or compatible computer. It features full buffering of all 7170 address and data lines, and switch selectable I/O block select. A provision for setting the priority level of the 7170 periodic interrupt has also been added.

Since the IBM PC/XT* requires a positive interrupt transition, the 7170's interrupt output transistor has been configured as a source follower. As a source follower, the interrupt output signal will swing between 0V and 2.5V. When trimming the oscillator, the frequency counter must be triggered on the rising edge of the interrupt signal.

Batteries	Crystals
Panasonic	Statek 32kHz CX-1V
Rayovac	SARONIX 32kHz NTF3238

*IBM, IBM PC and IBM XT are registered trademarks of IBM Corporation.

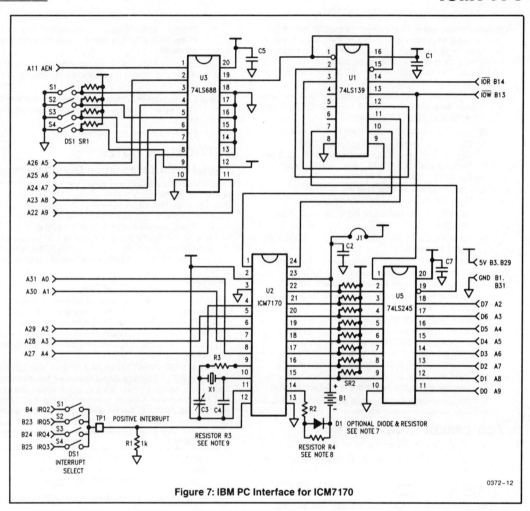

Figure 7: IBM PC Interface for ICM7170

0372-12

GENERAL NOTES:

(1) TIME ACCESS

To access the present time registers (Hex 00–07) the 1/100 register must be read first. The 7 real time counter registers (Hours, Minutes, Seconds, Month, Date, Day, and Year) data are latched only if the 1/100 second counter register is read. The 1/100 seconds data itself is not latched. The real times data will be held in the latches until the 1/100 seconds is again read. See the data sheet section on LATCHED DATA. None of the Rams data is latched since it is static in nature to start with.

(2) REGULATED OSCILLATOR

The oscillator's power supply is voltage regulated with respect to V_{dd}. In the 32 kHz mode the regulators amplitude is $\Sigma Vtn + Vtp$ ($\cong 1.8$). In the 1, 2, and 4 MHz mode the regulators amplitude is $\Sigma Vtn + Vtn + Vtp$ ($\cong 2.6V$). As a result, signal conditioning is necessary to drive the oscillator with an external signal. In addition, it is also necessary to buffer the oscillators signal to drive other external clocks because of its reduced amplitude and offset voltage.

(3) INTERNAL BATTERY BACKUP

When the 7170 is using its own internal battery back-up circuitry, no other circuitry interfaced to the 7170 should be active during standby operation. When V_{dd} (+5V) is turned off (Standby operation), V_{dd} should equal $V_{ss} = 0V$. All 7170 I/O should also equal Gnd. At this time, the Vbackup pin should be 2.8V to 3.5V below Gnd when using a Lithium battery.

(4) EXTERNAL BATTERY BACKUP

The 7170 can be placed on the same battery backed up +5V supply as Ram. When this is the case, the 7170's up Vbackup pin (14) can be used to turn on and off the 7170's I/O. When Vback is switched to V_{dd} (pin 23), I/O is enabled. When switched to V_{ss} (pin 13), I/O is disabled. The signal driving Vback must be able to sink 2 μA–200 μA to support the 7170's standby current drain. During standby operation, RD bar and WR bar control pins must be held to V_{dd} and all other I/O (ALE, CS bar, A0–A4, D0–D7) can be held at either V_{dd} or V_{ss}.

TO AVOID DATA CORRUPTION, when switching between power down or power up, the use of an ICL7665 (power fail detector) is highly recommended. The 7665 can be set to detect if the +5V supply falls to 4.75V and disable I/O to both Ram and the 7170. This is important because many microprocessors can generate spurious write signals when their supply falls below their specified operating voltage limits.

(5) 7170A PART

The 7170A part is binned at final test for a 32.768 kHz maximum current of 5 μA. All other commercial and military specifications remain the same.

(6) INTERRUPTS

For a periodic interrupt to be enabled, both the global interrupt bit (D4) in the command register and at least one mask bit (D1–D6) in the mask register must be set to a 1. When enable, each time a counter receives a clock and has a corresponding bit set in the mask register the interrupt clock will turn on. THE PERIODIC INTERRUPTS STATUS REGISTER BITS TURN ON WHENEVER A COUNTER RECEIVES A CLOCK REGARDLESS OF WHETHER ITS CORRESPONDING STATUS REGISTER BIT IS SET OR NOT. One might think of the periodic status register as a real time bargraph. The interrupt transistor and the status register are reset whenever the status register is read.

For compare or alarm interrupts to be enabled, both the command registers global interrupt bit (D4) and the mask registers bit (D0) must be set to a 1. Each time the 7170's Ram compares to the exact time in the counters the interrupt output N-ch will turn on. In addition, the status register bits D0 and D7 will go high. Reading the status register resets the status register and turns off the interrupt transistor.

(7) VBACKUP DIODE D1 LIMITATIONS

The diode D1 in series with the battery should be used with caution. When the 7170 has system power applied, the N-ch switch in series with the Vbackup pin is turned off (see figure 6). If the diodes leakage is lower than the printed circuit boards leakage, the Vbackup pin (14) can leak close enough to the V_{ss} pin (13) to cause the 7170 to disable its I/O. This possibility can be eliminated by placing a high value resistor (R4) ≥ 2 MΩ across the diode D1.

(8) RESISTOR IN SERIES WITH BATTERY

A 2k resistor (R2) must be placed in series with the battery backup pin of the 7170. The UL laboratories have requested the resistor to limit the charging and discharging current to the battery. The resistor also serves the purpose of degenerating parasitic SCR action. This SCR action may occur if an input is applied to the 7170, outside of its supply voltage range, while it is in the standby mode.

(9) OPTION OSCILLATOR 220K RESISTOR

The resistor in series with oscillator out and the crystal is sometime necessary when using 32 kHz Statek crystals with CL = 9 pF. The resistor of 220k limits the 7170's oscillator inverter gm to 4.5 μmhos. This reduces the possibility of the crystal circuit from operating at an undesirable frequency.

Chapter 5

Analog

Input/Output

All the interfaces between the microprocessor and the world at large described so far have been *digital*. That is, the nature of the signals flowing across the interface between the microprocessor and the external system is identical to that of the signals within the digital system. We now deal with the interface between the digital computer and systems whose signals are said to be *analog* rather than digital. Chapter 5 covers four topics. The first two concern the characteristics of analog signals and their acquisition. The second two examine ways in which digital signals from the microcomputer are converted into analog form, and ways in which analog signals in external systems are converted into digital form for processing by the microcomputer. Examples of digital-to-analog and analog-to-digital converters based on the 68000 are provided.

5.1 Analog signals

It is rather difficult to define a particular signal as digital or analog with any real precision. Indeed, I would argue that an absolute distinction between analog and digital signals does not exist. All signals are discrete (i.e. digital) because of the laws of quantum mechanics. Equally, real digital signals in real circuits share many of the properties of analog signals (e.g. a finite rise-time). For the purpose of this chapter, the following definitions of analog and digital are adequate.

Analog signal

A signal is said to be analog if it falls between two arbitrary levels, V_x and V_y, and can assume any one of an infinite number of values between V_x and V_y. If the analog signal, $V(t)$, is time dependent, it is a continuous function of time, so that dV/dt is never infinity, which would imply an instantaneous change of value.

Analog signals are processed by analog circuitry. The principal feature of an analog circuit is its ability to process an analog signal faithfully, without distorting it. A typical analog signal is the voltage produced at the output terminals of a microphone as someone speaks into it. The voltage varies continuously over some finite range, depending only on the loudness of the speech and on the physical characteristics of the microphone. An amplifier may be used to increase the amplitude of this time-varying signal to a level suitable for driving a loudspeaker. If the gain of the amplifier is A, and the voltage from the microphone $V(t)$, the output of the amplifier is equal to $AV(t)$. The output signal from the op-amp, like the input, has an infinite range of values, but within a range A times that of the signal from the microphone.

Digital signal

A signal is said to be digital if it can assume one of m possible values. Sometimes, the m possible values are called the m symbols of an alphabet. In a binary system there are just two symbols in the alphabet: a one and a zero. Thus, at any instant a binary digital signal can assume one of only two possible values. Therefore, a digital signal is not continuous in value, and is said to be discrete. Equally, it is discrete in time, because the change from one symbol to another is assumed to be instantaneous. Why? Because if there are no intermediate values between two symbols, the change from one to another must be instantaneous. A typical digital system is the Morse code where the alphabet is composed of four symbols: a dot, a dash, the space between dots and dashes within a character, and the space between individual characters. The difference between analog and digital signals is not simply a matter for academic speculation – it affects all aspects of the design of a system.

Because digital signals fall into two ranges (e.g. 0 to 0.4 V for logical low and 2.4 to 5.0 V for logical high levels), small amounts of noise and crosstalk have no effect on digital signals as long as the noise is less than about 0.4 V. Unfortunately, life is much more difficult for the designer of analog systems. Even small amounts of noise in the millivolt (or even microvolt) region can seriously effect the accuracy of analog signals. In particular, the analog designer has to worry about power-line noise and digital noise picked up by analog circuits from adjacent digital circuits.

5.1.1 Signal processing

A system that processes digital signals is called a digital system. It does not seek to preserve the shape of a signal, unlike an analog system. The signal at the input of a digital system is assumed to be one of the m possible values and is processed accordingly. In a binary digital system, the input is always assumed to be a one or a zero. It is this property that accounts for the great interest in digital systems today. Suppose an analog signal is defined as $V(t)$ and is corrupted by an error, $e(t)$, to become $V(t) + e(t)$. When amplified by a factor A, the signal becomes $AV(t) + Ae(t)$. That is, the error, $e(t)$, is amplified along with the desired signal. After this has happened, nothing can be done to remove the error. Consequently, the more an analog signal is processed, the more distorted it becomes.

Now consider a binary digital signal, $V(t)$, which has two possible values A and B, so that at any instant $V(t) = A$ or $V(t) = B$. If this signal is processed, it is also corrupted to become $V(t) + e(t)$. However, when presented to a digital circuit, it is regarded as either A or B. In an ideal system the following rule holds true:

IF V(t) < A + (B − A)/2
     THEN V(t) = A
     ELSE V(t) = B
ENDIF

As long as the magnitude of the error, $e(t)$, is less than $(B - A)/2$, it is always possible to reconstitute a digital signal exactly. Therefore, a digital signal can be processed an infinite number of times without suffering any degradation whatsoever. In a TTL circuit, signals below 0.8 V (i.e. V_{IL}) are guaranteed to be interpreted as low levels, and signals above 2.0 V (i.e. V_{IH}) are guaranteed to be interpreted as high levels. Between these two ranges (i.e. 0.8 V to 2.0 V) lies a forbidden zone of *uncertainty*. Signals falling within this zone will be interpreted as either low or high values because of the digital nature of the circuit. However, the precise threshold between the low and high levels is not specified by the manufacturer. In practical digital systems, it is unlikely that a digital signal will have such a large error component that it is interpreted as an incorrect value.

Applications of digital signal processing

Not very long ago, almost all signal processing involved analog signals and analog techniques. Equipment required to process analog signals was complex, expensive, inflexible and unreliable. Today analog signals are converted to digital form, processed by a digital computer and converted back to analog form for use in the real world. To illustrate the advantages of this approach, let us look at the following two examples.

Example 1

Music from a microphone is converted into a sequence of digital values and fed into a computer; these values are then stored in an array, M. It is also possible to read the consecutive values of M from the array and to convert them back into an analog signal for amplification and presentation to a loudspeaker. Consider the following algorithms.

(a) FOR I = 1 TO K DO
        Output := M(I)
    ENDFOR

(b) FOR I = 1 TO K DO
        Output := A * M(I)
    ENDFOR

(c) FOR I = J + 1 TO K DO
        Output := M(I) + B * M(I − J)
    ENDFOR

(d) FOR I = 1 TO K DO
    a := K4 * M(I − 4)
    b := K3 * M(I − 3)
    c := K2 * M(I − 2)
    d := K1 * M(I − 1)
    e := K0 * M(I)
    Output := a + b + c + d + e
    ENDFOR

In Example 1(a), the digitally stored music is simply reconverted into analog form and all that has happened is that the music has been stored and retrieved. In Example 1(b), it is amplified by a scalar factor A. By changing the value of A, the loudness of the music can be altered. Now we have a digital volume control with no moving parts and which can be programmed to change the sound level at any desired rate.

In Example 1(c), the signal fed to the loudspeaker is composed of two parts. $M(I)$ represents the current value, and $M(I − J)$ the value of the signal J samples earlier, scaled by a factor B. Normally the factor B is less than unity. Where do we get a signal plus a delayed, attenuated value? These features are found in an echo or in reverberation and are of interest to the makers of electronic music. By very simple processing, we are able to generate echoes entirely by digital techniques. To do this with analog signals, very complex and utterly inflexible techniques must be used. For example, to synthesize an echo by analog technique, the analog signal is first converted into sound by a small loudspeaker called a transducer. A spring is connected to the transducer and the acoustic signal travels down it to a microphone at the other end. The output of the microphone represents a delayed version of the original signal – the echo. The length of the delay must be increased by using a longer spring (or delay line). In the digital version, the delay is changed simply by modifying the value of J.

Example 1(d) represents the *linear transversal equalizer* which implements a general-purpose digital filter.

Example 2

Analog-to-digital and digital-to-analog conversion techniques are most commonly found in process control applications. Consider the automatic pilot of an aircraft. At any time the position (height, location and attitude) of an aircraft is measured, together with its performance (speed, rate of climb, rate of turn and engine power). All these values can be converted from analog into digital form and fed into a digital computer. By using these values, the microprocessor can determine the best position for the controls (throttle, elevator, aileron and rudder). The output from the computer corresponding to these quantities is applied to digital-to-analog converters, whose analog outputs operate actuators that directly move the appropriate control surfaces.

5.1.2 Signal acquisition

The conversion of an analog quantity into a digital value requires two separate operations; the extraction of a sample value of the signal to be processed and the actual conversion of that sample value into a suitable digital form. Figure 5.1 gives the block diagram of an analog signal acquisition module. As the analog-to-digital converter (ADC) at the heart of this module may be rather expensive, it is not unusual to provide a number of different analog channels, all using the same ADC.

Each analog channel in Figure 5.1 begins with a transducer that converts an analog signal into an electrical value. Transducers are almost invariably located off-card and are separate from the signal acquisition module proper. A transducer exploits some physical property of matter to perform the conversion process. For example, a typical transducer, called a *thermister*, is composed of a substance whose electrical resistance varies with temperature. By passing a constant known current through a thermister, the voltage across it is a function of its temperature. Sometimes the transducer is a *linear* device, so that a change in the physical input produces a corresponding change in the electrical output. All too often, the transducer is highly non-linear and the relationship between the physical input and the voltage from the transducer is very complex. In such

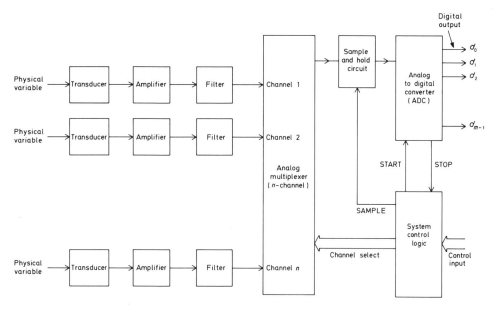

FIGURE 5.1   An analog signal acquisition module

cases it is usual to perform the linearization of the input in the digital computer at a much later stage. It is possible, but not normal, to perform the linearization within the signal acquisition module by means of purely analog techniques.

As the electrical signal from the transducer is frequently very tiny (sometimes only a few microvolts) it must be amplified before further processing, in order to bring it to a level well above the noise voltages present in later circuits.

After amplification comes filtering, which is a process designed to restrict the passage of certain signals through the circuit. For example, if the signal from the transducer contains useful frequency components only, in the range 0 to 20 Hz (as one might expect from an electrocardiogram – ECG), it is beneficial to filter out all signals of a higher frequency. These out-of-band signals represent unwanted noise and have no useful effect on the interpretation of the ECG. Moreover, it is necessary for the filter to cut out all frequencies above one-half the rate at which the analog signal is sampled. The reasons for this are explained later.

The outputs of the filters are fed to a multiplexer which selects one of the input channels for processing. The multiplexer is controlled by the digital system to which the signal acquisition module is connected. The analog output of the multiplexer is applied to the input of the last analog circuit in the acquisition module, the sample and hold (S/H) circuit. The sample and hold circuit has the important function of taking an almost *instantaneous* sample of the incoming analog signal and holding it constant while the analog-to-digital converter is busy determining the digital value of the signal. If the input signal is changing rapidly, the output of an ADC (which takes an appreciable time to perform its conversion) would be meaningless without an S/H circuit to staticize the input.

The analog-to-digital converter transforms the voltage at its input into an m-bit value, where m varies from, typically, 4 to 16 or more. Several types of analog-to-digital converter are discussed later. The remainder of this section considers the relationship between the analog signal and the analog-to-digital conversion process.

5.1.3 Signal quantization

There are two fundamental questions to be asked when considering any analog-to-digital converter. Into how many samples should the input signal be divided and how often should the conversion process be carried out? The precise answer to both these questions is exceedingly complex and requires much mathematics. Fortunately, they both have relatively simple conceptual answers and in many real situations a rule-of-thumb can easily be applied.

When asked how much sugar you want in a cup of coffee, you normally reply: none, half a spoon, one spoon, one and a half spoons, etc. Although a measure of sugar can be quantized right down to the size of a single grain, the practical unit chosen by those who add sugar to coffee is the half-spoon. This unit is both easy to measure out and offers reasonable discrimination between the quanta (i.e. half-spoons). Most drinkers could not discriminate between, say, $\frac{3}{5}$ and $\frac{4}{5}$ of a spoon of sugar. As it is with sugar, so it is with signals. The level of quantization is chosen to be the minimum interval between successive values that carries meaningful information. The reader may ask, 'Why doesn't everyone use an ADC with the greatest possible resolution?' In a 68000 system this implies either a 16- or 32-bit ADC. The answer is perfectly simple. The cost of an ADC rises exponentially with resolution. A 16-bit ADC is very much more expensive than an 8-bit ADC (assuming all other parameters are equal). Therefore, engineers select the ADC with a resolution compatible with the requirements of the job for which it is intended.

The transfer function for a simple, *ideal*, three-bit analog-to-digital converter is given in Figure 5.2. This ADC has a full-scale digital output varying from 000 to 111 for a voltage input in the range 0 V to 7.5 V. Consider the application of a linear ramp input, going from 0.0 V to 7.5 V, to this ADC. Initially the analog input is 0.0 V and the digital output 000. As the input rises, the output remains at 000 until the input passes 0.5 V, at which point the output code jumps from 000 to 001. The output code remains at 001 until the input rises above 1.5 V. Clearly, for each 1.0 V change in the input, the output changes by one unit. Note that the input can change in value by up to 1 V *without* any change taking place in the output code.

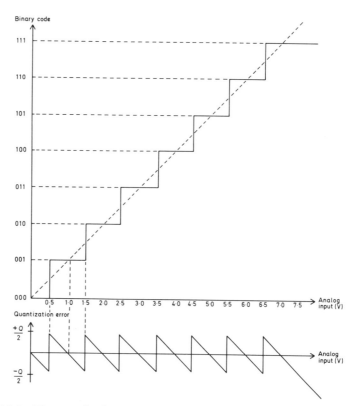

FIGURE 5.2 The transfer function of an ideal 3-bit A/D converter

The resolution of an ADC, Q, is the largest change in its input required to guarantee a change in the output code and is 1.0 V in the above example. The resolution of an ADC is often expressed indirectly by the number of bits in its output code. For example, an 8-bit ADC operating with a bipolar input in the range -4.0 V to $+4.0$ V has a resolution of $8.0\,\text{V}/256 = 0.031\,25\,\text{V} = 31.25\,\text{mV}$. Table 5.1 gives the basic characteristics of ADCs with digital outputs ranging

TABLE 5.1 The performance of ideal analog-to-digital converters

RESOLUTION BITS n	DISCRETE STATES 2^n	BINARY WEIGHT $2^{(-n)}$	VALUE OF Q FOR 10 V FS	S/N RATIO (dB)	DYNAMIC RANGE (dB)
4	16	0.0625	0.625 V	34.9	24.1
6	64	0.0156	0.156 V	46.9	36.1
8	256	0.00391	39.1 mV	58.1	48.2
10	1024	0.000977	9.76 mV	71.0	60.2
12	4096	0.000244	2.44 mV	83.0	72.2
14	16384	0.0000610	610 μV	95.1	84.3
16	65536	0.0000153	153 μV	107.1	96.3

from 4 to 16 bits. The figures in Table 5.1 represent the optimum values for perfect ADCs. In practice, real ADCs suffer from imperfections such as non-linearity, drift, offset error and missing codes, etc. which are described below. Note that an ADC may be *unipolar* and handle a voltage in the range 0 to V, or it may be *bipolar* and handle a voltage in the range $-V/2$ to $+V/2$.

Below the transfer function of a 3-bit ADC in Figure 5.2 is a graph of the error between the input of the ADC and its digital output represented exactly in terms of an analog voltage. For example, if the input is 5.63 V, the output is 110 (representing 6.0 V) and corresponds to an error of 0.37 V. It can be seen from Figure 5.2 that the maximum error between the input and output is equal to $Q/2$. This error is called the quantization error.

When a time-varying analog input is applied to an ADC, its time-varying digital output corresponds to the quantized input, not to the actual input. We have already seen that the three-bit ADC of Figure 5.2 converts a 5.63 V input into a binary value representing an input of 6.00 V, which is equivalent to having an input of 5.63 V corrupted by a noise signal of +0.37 V. In other words, the output from any real ADC can be represented by the output from a *perfect* ADC whose input is equal to the applied signal plus a noise component. The difference between the input and the quantized output (expressed as an analog value) is also a time-varying signal between $+Q/2$ and $-Q/2$ and is called the *quantization noise* of the ADC. The RMS (root mean square) value of the quantization noise is equal to $Q/\sqrt{12}$. Increasing the resolution of the converter reduces the amplitude of the quantization noise.

A figure of merit of any analog system is its signal-to-noise ratio. The signal-to-noise ratio of a system is expressed in decibels and is given by signal:noise (in dB) $= 20\log(V_{\text{signal}}/V_{\text{noise}})$. The signal to noise ratio of an ideal n-bit ADC is given by

$$\frac{S}{N}(\text{in dB}) = 20\log\frac{(2^nQ)}{Q/\sqrt{12}} = 20\log(2^n) + 20\log(\sqrt{12})$$

$$\frac{S}{N}(\text{dB}) = 6.02n + 10.8$$

From this expression it can be seen that the signal-to-noise ratio of the ADC increases by 6.02 dB for each additional bit of precision. Table 5.1 gives the signal-to-noise ratio of ADCs from 4 to 16 bits. An 8-bit ADC has a signal-to-noise ratio similar to that of some low-quantity audio equipment, while a 10-bit ADC approaches the S/N ratio of high-fidelity equipment.

The *dynamic range* of an ADC is given by the ratio of its full-scale range (FSR) to its resolution, Q, and is expressed in decibels by the formula:

Dynamic range (dB) $= 20\log(2^n) = 20n\log 2 = 6.02n$

Table 5.1 also gives the dynamic range of the various ADCs. Once again it can be stated that a 10- to 12-bit ADC is suitable for moderately high-quality audio signal processing. Because of other impairments in the system and the actual behaviour of a real ADC, high quality audio signal processing is normally done with a 16-bit ADC. Today's compact disc players use 14- or 16-bit DACs.

5.1.4 Errors in DACs

Real DACs have characteristics that differ from the ideal relationship between input code and output voltage. Differences between input code and output voltages represent errors, which originate, of course, in the analog circuits of the DAC! Figure 5.3 provides five examples of errors in DACs.

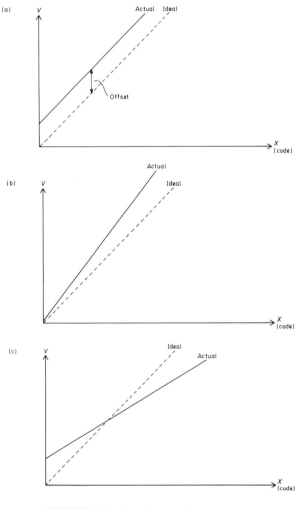

FIGURE 5.3 (*caption opposite*)

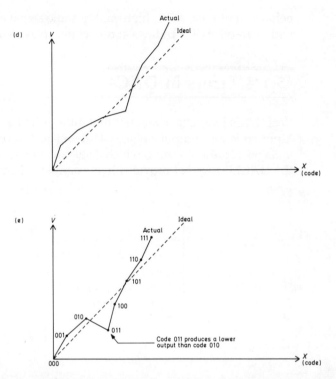

FIGURE 5.3 Errors associated with DACs. (a) The constant offset error. (b) The gain error. (c) The combined effect of offset and gain errors. (d) Non-linearity in ADCs. (e) Non-monotonicity

In Figure 5.3(a), the output voltage of the DAC differs from its ideal value by a constant offset. That is, if the input is a binary value X, the output is equivalent to that of a *perfect* DAC plus a constant error signal E. A constant error is easy to deal with because it can be trimmed out by adding a compensating offset to the output of an operational amplifier.

Figure 5.3(b) illustrates a *gain error* in which the error between the output of the DAC and its ideal value is a linear function of the digital input. The gain error can be removed (i.e. corrected) by passing the output of the DAC through a compensating amplifier. For example, if the gain error is K, the amplifier should have a gain $1/K$.

Real DACs usually have both offset and gain errors as illustrated in Figure 5.3(c). The combined offset and gain errors can both be removed separately by injecting a negative offset and passing the output of the DAC through a compensating amplifier as described above.

A more serious form of error is the non-linear response illustrated in Figure 5.3(d). In this case the change in the output voltage Q for each change in the input code is not constant. Non-linear errors cannot easily be corrected by simple external circuitry. In more brutal terms, make sure that the DAC you buy has an acceptable level of non-linearity. Many DACs are guaranteed to have a maximum linearity less than one-half Q. That is, the error in the analog output of the DAC is always less than $Q/2$ for any input.

Another form of non-linearity is called a non-monotonic response and is illustrated in Figure 5.3(e). *Non-monotonic* means that the output voltage does not always increase with increasing input code. In Figure 5.3(e) it can be seen that the output for an input 011 is *less* than that for an input 010. While this may seem inexplicable to the reader, it can be appreciated when the internal mechanism of DACs is understood. Non-monotonic errors can be dangerous in systems using feedback. For example, if an increasing input produces a decreasing output, the computer controlling the DAC may move the input in the wrong direction.

Analog to digital converters suffer from similar errors to DACs – only the axes of the graphs in Figure 5.3 are changed. There is, however, one particularly interesting form of ADC error which is called the *missing code*. Figure 5.4 provides an example of the transfer function of an ADC that suffers from a missing code. As the input voltage to the ADC is linearly increased, the output steps through its codes one by one in sequence. However, some ADCs step from code X to code $X + 2$ *without* going through code $X + 1$. Therefore, code $X + 1$ is said to be a missing code. In the example of Figure 5.4 the output jumps from 010 to 100 without passing through 011.

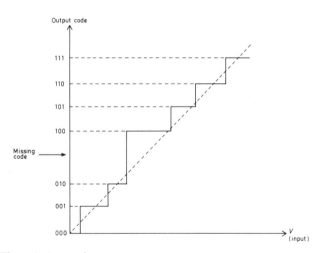

FIGURE 5.4   The missing code

Analog circuits are particularly sensitive to temperature variations which means that errors in DAC or ADC performance are also temperature dependent. Changes in ambient temperature affect both the offset and gain of a DAC. A typical 12-bit DAC may experience a temperature-induced error of $5Q$ (i.e. 5 times the smallest increment) for a temperature change of 30 °C.

5.1.5 Sampling a time-varying signal

We have discussed the need for dividing a signal into an adequate number of discrete values, and the requirement that the signal be effectively constant while it is being sampled. What remains to be considered is the rate at which a signal should be sampled to produce a fair and accurate digital representation of it. We need to know the rate at which a signal must be sampled, because it is best to sample a signal at the minimum permissible rate. By doing so we can use the slowest (i.e. cheapest) ADC and also leave sufficient time between adjacent samples for a digital computer to do the required processing.

Intuitively, we would expect the rate at which a signal must be sampled to be closely related to the rate at which it is changing. For example, a computer controlling the temperature of a swimming pool might need to sample the temperature of the water no more than once every ten minutes. The thermal inertia of the water does not permit sudden changes in temperature. Similarly, if a microcomputer is employed to analyse human speech with an upper frequency limit of 3000 Hz, it is reasonable to expect that the input from a microphone must be sampled at a much greater rate than 3000 times a second, simply because in the space of 1/3000 second the signal can execute a complete sine wave.

Fortunately for the designer of signal acquisition systems, a simple relationship exists between the rate at which a signal changes and the rate at which it must be sampled if it is to be reconstituted from the samples without any loss of information content. The so-called sampling theorem states: 'If a continuous signal containing no frequency components higher than f_c is sampled at a rate of at least $2f_c$, then the original signal can be completely recovered without distortion'.

There are two important points to note about this theorem. The highest frequency component in the signal means just that and includes any noise or unwanted signals present together with the desired signal. If a signal contains speech in the range 300 to 3000 Hz and noise in the range 300 to 5000 Hz, it must be sampled at least 10 000 times a second. One of the purposes of filtering a signal before sampling it is to remove components whose frequencies are higher than the signals of interest, but whose presence would nevertheless determine the lower limit of the sampling rate.

If a signal, whose maximum frequency component is f_c, is sampled at less than $2f_c$ times a second, some of the high-frequency components in it are folded back into the spectrum of the required signal. In other words, sampling a speech signal in the range 300 to 3000 Hz containing noise components up to 5000 Hz at only 6000 times a second would result in some of this noise appearing within the speech band. This effect is called *frequency folding*, and once it has occurred there is no way in which the original, required, signal can be recovered. Figure 5.5 illustrates the effect of frequency folding. In Figure

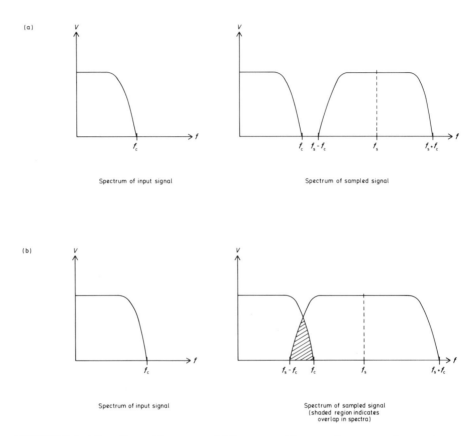

Spectrum of input signal   Spectrum of sampled signal

(b)

Spectrum of input signal   Spectrum of sampled signal
                                                            (shaded region indicates
                                                            overlap in spectra)

FIGURE 5.5   The effect of frequency folding caused by sampling a signal at too low a rate, (a) $f_s > 2f_{cc}$, (b) $f_s < 2f_c$

5.5(a) the input signal consists of a band of frequencies from zero to f_c, sampled at a rate equal to f_s times a second, where f_s is greater than $2f_c$. The spectrum of the sampled signal contains components in the range $f_s - f_c$ to $f_s + f_c$ which do not fall within the range of the input signal.

In Figure 5.5(b) the input has a maximum frequency component of f_c and is sampled at f_s, where $f_s < 2f_c$. Now, some energy in the region $f_s - f_c$ to f_c falls in the range of the input frequency and is represented by the shaded region in Figure 5.5(b). It is difficult to appreciate the full implications of the sampling theorem without an understanding of the mathematics of sampling and modulation. However, all we need say here is that the overlap in spectra caused by sampling at too low a frequency results in unwanted noise in the sampled signal.

Another way of looking at the relationship between a signal and its sampling rate is illustrated by Figures 5.6 and 5.7. Figure 5.6(a) gives the

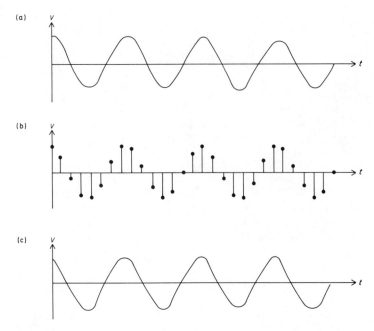

FIGURE 5.6 The aliasing effect ($f_s > 2f_c$). (a) Input signal, (b) sampled signal, (c) reconstituted signal.

continuous input waveform of an analog signal and Figure 5.6(b) its sampled form. These sampled amplitudes are, of course, stored in a digital computer numerically. Figure 5.6(c) shows the output of a circuit, called a filter, fed from the digital inputs of Figure 5.6(b). The simplest way of describing this circuit is to say that it *joins up the dots* of the sampled signal to produce a smooth output. Note that the reconstituted analog signal is virtually a copy of the original analog signal.

Figure 5.7 is similar to Figure 5.6, except that the input signal is sampled at less than $2f_c$. A glance at the sampled values of Figure 5.7(b) is enough to show that much of the detail in the input waveform has been lost. When this sampled signal is reconstituted into a continuous signal, Figure 5.7(c), its frequency is not the same as the input signal. The erroneous signal of Figure 5.7(c) is called an alias. Once more, it must be stressed that if frequencies greater than $1/2f_s$ appear in the input signal they can play havoc with the results of sampling.

Most signal acquisition modules have low-pass filters with a sharp cut-off frequency to attenuate signals and noise outside the band of interest. As it is impossible to construct a perfect filter that passes frequencies in the range 0 to f_c and which attenuates all frequencies above f_c infinitely, it is usual to sample a signal at a much greater rate than $2f_c$ in order to reduce the effects of aliasing to an acceptable level. Typically, a signal may be sampled at up to 5 times the rate of its maximum frequency component.

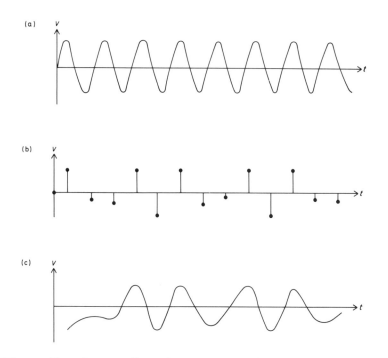

FIGURE 5.7 The aliasing effect (f_c). (a) Input signal, (b) sampled signal, (c) reconstituted signal

Aperture time

In addition to the above consideration of the sampling frequency, we also have to think about the *time* taken by the sampling process itself. It is very unlikely that a real signal acquisition module would have to deal with an entirely static input. Signals of interest are time dependent. One question we should ask is, 'What happens if a signal changes while it is being measured (i.e. digitized)?' Figure 5.8 illustrates the problem of trying to measure a dynamic quantity. Suppose the quantization process takes t_a seconds, which is called the *aperture time*. During this time, the input being measured changes by δV, where δV is given by

$$\delta V = t_a \frac{\mathrm{d}V(t)}{\mathrm{d}t}$$

The change in the input, δV, is called the amplitude uncertainty. A perfect instantaneous digitizer has a zero aperture time and $\delta V = 0$, resulting in a spot sample of the input. In order to get a feeling for the importance of aperture time, let us consider a data acquisition system processing human speech. A

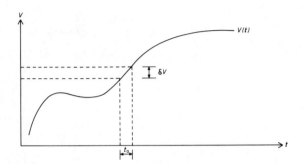

FIGURE 5.8   The effect of a finite measurement time on the A/D conversion process

$$\delta V = \text{amplitude uncertainty} = \frac{dV(t)}{dt} \times t_a$$

where $V(t) =$ signal being sampled and $t_a =$ aperture time

typical system may have an 8-bit analog-to-digital converter and be required to digitize an input with an upper frequency limit of 4000 Hz. We need to know the maximum aperture time necessary to yield an accuracy of one least-significant bit in the digitized output. Assuming a sinusoidal input (i.e. $V(t) = V \sin \omega t$), the amplitude uncertainty is given by

$$\delta V = t_a \frac{d}{dt}(V \sin \omega t) = t_a \omega V \cos(\omega t)$$

The maximum rate of change of $V(t)$ occurs at the zero crossing of the waveform when $t = 0$. Therefore,

$$\delta V = t_a V \omega$$

and

$$\frac{\delta V}{V} = t_a \omega = t_a \times 2\pi f$$

We can substitute $\frac{1}{256}$ for $\delta V/V$ and 4000 Hz for f in the above equation to calculate the desired aperture time as follows:

$$\frac{\delta V}{V} = \frac{1}{256} = t_a \times 2\pi f = t_a \times 2 \times 3.142 \times 4000$$

$$t_a = \frac{1}{256 \times 2 \times 3.142 \times 4000} \text{ seconds}$$

$$= 0.146 \, \mu s$$

An aperture time of $0.146 \, \mu s$ (i.e. 146 ns) is very small, although not too small to be achieved by the fastest current ADCs. However, using a sample and hold circuit to staticize the input enables much slower and cheaper ADCs to perform the conversion. Of course, even a sample and hold circuit is itself subject to the effects of aperture uncertainty. Fortunately, while an aperture time of $1\,\mu s$ is relatively small for an analog-to-digital converter, a sample and hold circuit can achieve an aperture time of 50 ns with little effort.

5.2 Digital-to-analog conversion

A section on digital-to-analog converters, DACs, at this point may seem a little out of place. It is more logical to discuss analog-to-digital conversion first and then deal with the inverse process. There are two reasons for disregarding this natural sequence. The first is that the DAC is very much less complex than the corresponding ADC, and the second is that some analog-to-digital converters, paradoxically, have a digital-to-analog converter at their heart.

Conceptually, the DAC is a very simple device. If a binary value is to be converted into analog form, all we have to do is to generate an analog value proportional to each bit of the digital word and then add these values to give a composite analog sum. Figure 5.9 illustrates this process. An m-bit digital signal is latched by m D flip-flops and held constant until the next value is ready for conversion. The flip-flops constitute a digital sample and hold circuit. Each of the m bits operates a switch that passes either zero or V_i volts to an analog adder, where V_i is the output of the ith switch. The output of this adder is

$$V = d_0 V_0 + d_1 V_1 + \ldots + d_{m-1} V_{m-1}$$

Note that the $\{d_i\}$ in this equation represents binary values zero or one, and the $\{V_i\}$ represent binary powers of the form $(1, \frac{1}{2}, \frac{1}{4}, \frac{1}{8}, \ldots)$.

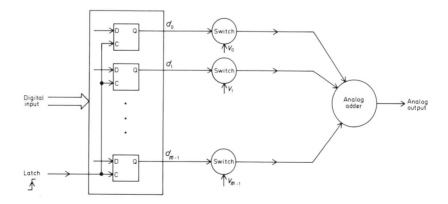

FIGURE 5.9   The digital-to-analog converter; if $d_i = 0$, 0 is passed to the analog adder; if $d_i = 1$, V_i is passed to the analog adder

A possible implementation of a digital-to-analog converter is given in Figure 5.10. The total current flowing into the inverting terminal of the operational amplifier is equal to the linear sum of the currents flowing through the individual resistors. As each of the resistors can be connected to ground or to a precisely maintained reference voltage, V_{ref}, the current flowing through each resistor is either zero or $V_{ref}/(2^iR)$, where $i = 0, 1, 2, \ldots, m-1$. The total current flowing into the operational amplifier is given by

$$\frac{V_{ref}}{R} \sum_{i=0}^{m-1} \frac{d_{m-i-1}}{2^i}$$

where $d(i)$ represents the state of the ith switch.

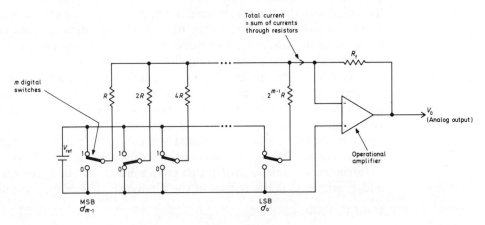

FIGURE 5.10   A possible implementation of the D/A converter

The voltage at the output terminal of the operational amplifier is given by

$$V_o = -2V_{ref}\frac{R_f}{R} [d_{m-1} \times 2^{-1} + d_{m-2} \times 2^{-2} + \ldots + d_0 \times 2^{-m}]$$

In a real digital-to-analog converter, the m switches of Figure 5.10 are, typically, implemented by MOSFETs or JFETs. By switching the control gate of these transistors between two logic levels, the resistance between their source and drain terminals is likewise switched between a very high value (the *off* or *open* state) and a very low value (the *on* or *closed* state). A perfect transistor switch has off and on values of infinity and zero respectively. Practical transistor switches have finite on-resistances which degrade the accuracy of the DAC.

While the circuit of Figure 5.10 is perfectly reasonable for values of m below about six, larger values create manufacturing difficulties associated with the resistor chain. Suppose a 10-bit DAC is required. The ratio between the largest and smallest resistor is $2^{10}:1$ or $1024:1$. If the device is to be accurate to one LSB, the precision of the largest resistor must be at least one-half part in 1024, or approximately 0.05 per cent. Manufacturing resistors to this absolute level of precision is difficult and costly with thin-film technology, and virtually impossible with integrated circuit technology.

The R-2R ladder

An alternative form of digital-to-analog converter is given in Figure 5.11, and DAC relies on the R-2R ladder (pronounced 'R two R' not 'R minus two R'), so called because all resistors in the ladder have either the value R or $2R$. While it is difficult to produce highly accurate resistors over a wide range of values, it is much easier to produce pairs of resistors with a precise 2:1 ratio in resistance.

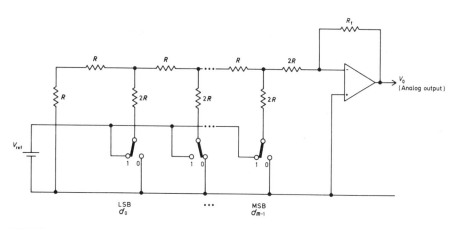

FIGURE 5.11   The R-2R ladder D/A converter

As the current from the reference source flows down the ladder (from left to right in Figure 5.11), it is divided at each junction (i.e. the node between the left R, right R and $2R$ resistors) into two equal parts, one flowing along the ladder to the right and one flowing down the $2R$ shunt resistor. The network forms a linear circuit and therefore the superposition theorem, which states that, 'in a linear system the effect is the sum of all the causes', can be applied. Consequently, the total current flowing into the inverting terminal of the operational amplifier is equal to the sum of all the currents from the shunt (i.e. $2R$) resistors, weighted by the appropriate binary value.

A digital-to-analog converter based on the R-2R ladder has three advantages over the type described in Figure 5.10:

1. All resistors have a value of either R or $2R$, making it easy to match resistors and to provide a good measure of temperature tracking between resistors. Furthermore, the residual *on* resistance of the transistor switches can readily be compensated for.
2. By selecting relatively low values for R in the range 2.5–10 kΩ, it is both easy to manufacture the DAC and to achieve a good response time because of the low impedance of the network.
3. Due to the nature of the R-2R ladder, the operational amplifier always sees a constant impedance at its input, regardless of the state of the switches in the ladder, which improves the accuracy of the operational amplifier circuit.

The R-2R ladder forms the basis of many, if not the majority, of commercially available DACs. Real circuits are arranged slightly differently to that of Figure 5.11 to reduce still further the practical problems associated with a DAC.

DACs based on the potentiometric network

A relatively recent form of digital-to-analog converter found in many commercial products (particularly National Semiconductor's devices) is called the *potentiometric* or *tree* network. A 3-bit arrangement of such a network is given in Figure 5.12. It is only advances in MOS technology that have favoured such converters, as they require a rather large number of switches and resistors.

In Figure 5.12 a chain of n resistors in series is placed between the reference supply and ground. The value of n is given by 2^m, where m is the number of bits to be converted into digital form. In the example of Figure 5.12, $m = 3$ and $n = 8$. An 8-bit converter requires 256 resistors in series. The voltage between ground and the lower end of the ith resistor is given by

$$V = \frac{V_{ref}(i-1)R}{nR} = \frac{V_{ref}(i-1)}{n}$$

Note that the value of the resistors, R, does not affect this equation. All that matters is that the resistors are of equal value. Because the flow of current through the resistors is constant, the effects of resistor heating found in some forms of the R-2R ladder are eliminated.

The switch tree serves only to connect the input terminal of the operational amplifier to the appropriate tap in the resistor network. In fact, this switching network is nothing but an $n:1$ demultiplexer. Moreover, because the switches do not switch a current (as in the case of the R–2R network), the values of their on and off resistances are rather less critical.

A DAC based on a switch tree is also inherently monotonic. That is, as the digital input increases from 00 . . . 0 to 11 . . . 1, the analog output increases for each increment in the input. As we have seen, some DACs suffer from a form of

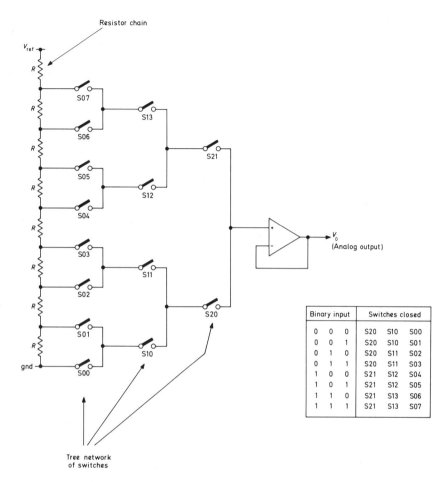

The table in the figure:

Binary input			Switches closed		
0	0	0	S20	S10	S00
0	0	1	S20	S10	S01
0	1	0	S20	S11	S02
0	1	1	S20	S11	S03
1	0	0	S21	S12	S04
1	0	1	S21	S12	S05
1	1	0	S21	S13	S06
1	1	1	S21	S13	S07

FIGURE 5.12   The tree-network D/A converter

error that results in the output voltage from a code X being greater than that due to a code $X + 1$.

5.2.1 A digital-to-analog converter using the MC6890

Choosing a digital-to-analog converter is never an easy task, as there are so many models to choose from. The designer is confronted by a multitude of devices, each characterized by a host of parameters. In general, the parameters of greatest interest are as follows:

1. *Number of bits* The number of bits defines the resolution of the DAC and therefore the DAC's quantization noise level and its dynamic range. The application for which the DAC is intended invariable determines this parameter. Occasionally, it may be economically possible to choose a DAC with a larger number of bits than the minimum required in order to improve accuracy and help overcome other imperfections in the system.

2. *Cost* The best things in life are not only not free but they have an exponential performance versus cost relationship.

3. *Speed* Although most DACs are much faster than the corresponding ADCs, it is sometimes necessary to select a DAC primarily on speed requirements alone. Typically, DACs have conversion times in the range 200 ns to 1 ms.

4. *Ease of interfacing* All digital-to-analog converters have to be interfaced to both the host microcomputer and the external analog system. Sometimes this is very easy if the DAC has the appropriate microprocessor bus interface and most of the analog circuitry on-chip. Sometimes the DAC is little more than the ladder network and switch array and requires both an external bus interface and an operational amplifier.

5. *Power supplies* The simplest microcomputer-based DACs have a single +5 V power supply which is required by the digital circuitry, the internal precision reference voltage and the operational amplifier. Others require multi-level supplies typically +5 V for the digital part of the DAC and −15 V and 15 V for its analog circuits.

The MC6890 8-bit DAC has been chosen to illustrate a practical microcomputer-based D/A converter, as it represents a compromise between ease of use and versatility. Just as importantly, the MC6890 provides a very straightforward interface between the host microprocessor and itself and requires no special attention to detail in its connection to a 68000 (or to most other microprocessors). In fact, the MC6890 looks just like a static write-only memory element to the host microprocessor.

The MC6890 has a moderately fast settling time of typically 200 ns. That is, when new data is latched into the DAC, its output settles to within $\frac{1}{2}$ LSB (i.e. 0.19 per cent full-scale) of its final output value in no more than 200 ns. Therefore, the MC6890 can, theoretically, handle a new input every 200 ns, corresponding to an upper limit of 2.5 MHz at the two samples per hertz required by the sampling theorem.

Like most self-contained DACs today, the MC6890 has an on-chip, low-temperature coefficient, bandgap reference source at 2.5 V. The reference voltage may also be used by external systems, as it is brought out to pin 19. Equally, an external 2.5 V reference may be injected into pin 18 (REF$_{in}$). Note that the reference generator requires a negative supply of between −5 V and −15 V at its V_{EE} input, pin 11.

Unfortunately, the MC6890 does not have an on-chip operational amplifier, making it necessary to convert the output of its programmable current source into a voltage. The operational amplifier must be supplied by the user. However, the feedback resistor between the inverting input of the operational amplifier and its output *is* included on the chip. Interestingly enough, three resistors are provided, connected to pins 13, 15 and 16, as illustrated in Figure 5.13, to allow a wide variety of configurations for this DAC. Figure 5.14 shows the six basic configurations for this DAC. Figure 5.14 shows

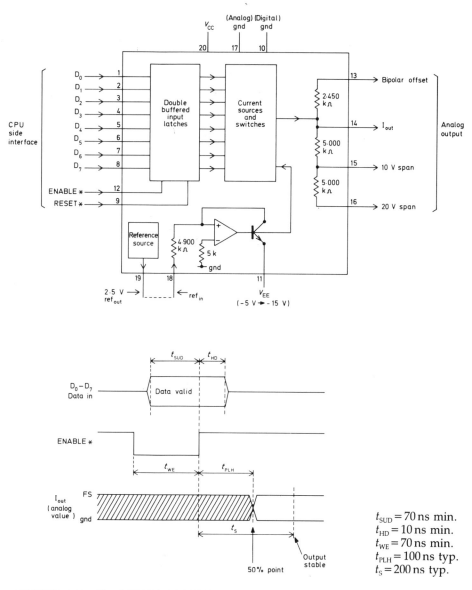

FIGURE 5.13   The MC6890 8-bit D/A converter

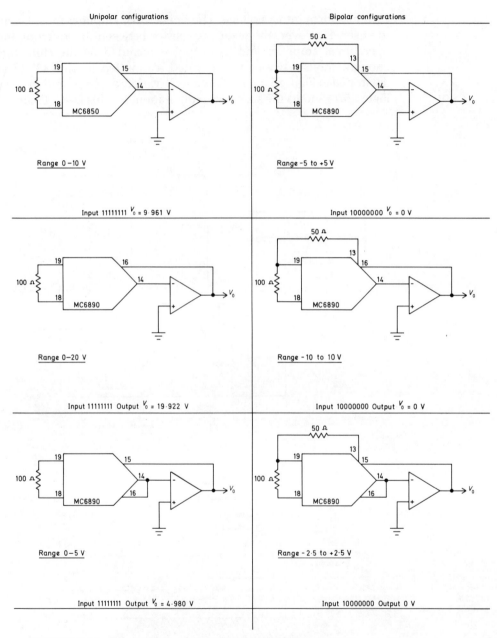

FIGURE 5.14   Six possible configurations of the MC6890 D/A converter

the six basic configurations of the MC6890. Three generate unipolar outputs from zero to 5 V, 10 V and 20 V, and three generate bipolar outputs from -2.5 V to $+2.5$ V, -5 V to $+$ V and -10 V to $+10$ V.

The circuit diagram of a suitable interface between the MC6890 and the

68000 microprocessor is given in Figure 5.15. No surprises are sprung by the microprocessor side of the DAC, and the interface is entirely conventional. The timing diagram of the MC6890 indicates an enable pulse of at least 70 ns, and data setup and hold times of 70 ns and 10 ns respectively. These parameters are satisfied by all versions of the 68000 without wait states. The active-low RESET* input to the DAC can be used to reset the DAC data register to zero by connecting it to the 68000's RESET* pin. Otherwise, the DAC's RESET* input can be connected to a logical one.

The analog side of the DAC requires an external op-amp, which is connected as shown in Figure 5.15, to give a unipolar output in the range 0 V to (nominally) 10 V. A 200 Ω potentiometer is wired between pins 18 and 19 to set the full-scale output of the converter to the desired value.

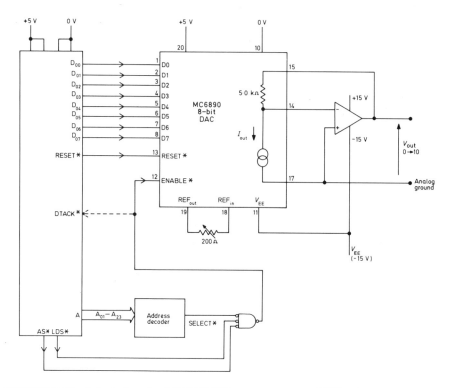

FIGURE 5.15   Interfacing the MC6890 D/A converter to a 68000 microprocessor

Programming the digital-to-analog converter is simplicity itself. It is necessary only to load its input register with the appropriate data using any of the 68000's data transfer instructions. For example, suppose a subroutine is called, periodically, to remove an item from a table and convert it into analog form. The following fragment of code does this. Note that the table of values is circular with the first value following the last value. Each time the routine is called, a single value is taken from the table, converted to analog form and the pointer updated to point at the next value.

```
*                 A0 points to the first location in the data table
*                 A1 points to the next item in the table to be converted
*                 A2 points to the location following the last entry in the table
*
   DAC     EQU      $00F001      Location of memory mapped DAC
           MOVE.B   (A1)+,DAC    Load next item from table into DAC
           CMP.L    A1,A2        Test for end-of-table
           BNE      RETURN       IF not end-of-table THEN return
           LEA      (A0),A1      Reset pointer to table
   RETURN  RTS                   Return to calling program
```

5.3 Analog-to-digital conversion

While converting a digital value into an analog signal is relatively easy, at least for word lengths up to 12 bits, the inverse process of converting an analog quantity into a digital value is frequently rather more involved. In fact, apart from one special type of A/D converter, analog-to-digital conversion is performed in a roundabout way. In this section, three types of A/D converter are described: the parallel converter (the only direct A/D converter), the feedback converter, and the integrating converter.

Before we describe ADCs in detail, we take a close look at the sample and hold circuit used to *freeze* time-varying analog signals prior to their conversion.

The sample and hold amplifier

Like many other analog circuits, the sample and hold amplifier is very simple in principle and very complex in practice. The divergence between theory and practice stems from the effect of second- or even third-order non-linearities of analog circuits. These problems do not affect digital circuits.

The conceptual circuit of a sample and hold amplifier is given in Figure 5.16. If we forget the diode bridge and regard the input resistor, R, as being directly connected to the inverting terminal ($-$ve) of the operational amplifier, we have a simple inverting buffer with unity gain. That is $V_{out} = -V_{in}$. We will also assume that the capacitor C has negligible effect on the circuit.

The diode bridge in Figure 5.16 acts as a simple on/off switch which either connects the analog input to the $-$ve terminal of the op-amp via R, or isolates

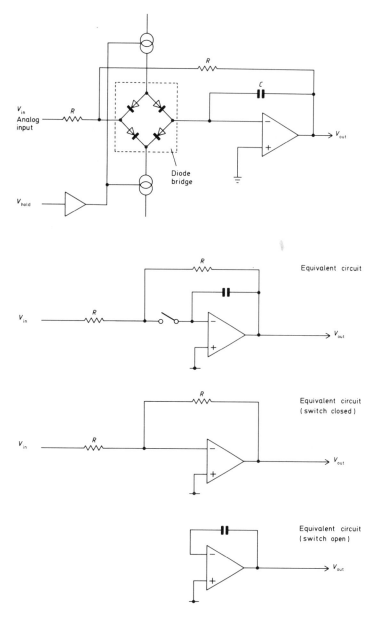

FIGURE 5.16   The sample and hold circuit

the −ve terminal from the input. When the switch is in the closed position, the S/H circuit operates in its sample mode and $V_{out} = -V_{in}$. At the same time, the capacitor, C, is charged up to the output voltage because its other terminal is at ground potential (the −ve terminal of the op-amp is a *virtual ground*).

When the diode switch is opened, the output of the op-amp is held constant by the charge on the capacitor. The capacitor will, of course, gradually discharge and the output will eventually fall to zero. However, in the *short term* the output will remain at the level the input was in at the instant the diode switch was opened.

The timing parameters of a sample and hold amplifier are illustrated in Figure 5.17. At the moment the diode switch is closed and the circuit goes into the sample mode, the capacitor begins to charge up to the level of the input. The period in which the capacitor is charged is called the *acquisition time* and is in the range 3–10 μs for a low-cost S/H circuit. The output now tracks the input up to the maximum slew rate of the S/H circuit.

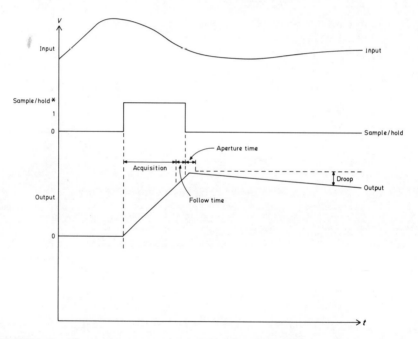

FIGURE 5.17   The timing parameters of the S/H circuit

When the S/H circuit goes into its hold mode and the diode switch is turned off, there is a finite delay during which the capacitor is disconnected from the input. This delay is the aperture uncertainty time of the S/H circuit. We have already met this parameter and it defines the period during which the input must not change by more than, say, a least-significant bit. Aperture times vary from about 50 ns to 50 ps, or less. One ps (pica second) is 10^{-12} seconds.

In the hold mode, the capacitor discharges and the output begins to droop. Droop rates vary, typically, between $5\,\mu$V/μs to $0.01\,\mu$V/μs. The parameters of the S/H circuit are often interrelated and optimizing one parameter sometimes worsens the values of other parameters.

Note that the type of capacitor used in a sample and hold circuit is critical. The capacitor should have a low dielectric absorption factor. Polystyrene or polycarbonate type capacitors are recommended for use in S/H circuits because of their low dielectric absorption coefficients.

Sample and hold circuits are vital when analog-to-digital converters with appreciable conversion times are to be connected to time varying inputs. It is less apparent that sample and hold circuits must sometimes be used with digital-to-analog converters. A sample and hold circuit can be fed from a DAC and used to turn the sequence of analog values from the DAC into a continuous analog signal. In this mode the S/H circuit is called a zero-order hold filter and its output consists of steps between the analog values (see Figure 5.18). Another advantage of the S/H circuit is that it *deglitches* the DAC and removes and glitches (spikes) in its output.

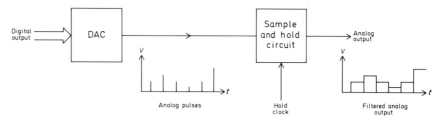

FIGURE 5.18   The S/H circuit as a zero-order filter

5.3.1 The parallel ADC

The parallel A/D converter is also called the *flash converter* because of its great speed of conversion when compared with the two indirect techniques described later. It works by simultaneously comparing the analog input with $2^m - 1$ equally spaced reference voltages. Figure 5.19 illustrates the TDC1014J, a 6-bit flash A/D converter. A chain of equal-valued resistors forms a tapped potentiometer between two reference voltages. The voltage between consecutive taps differs by $1/2^m$ of the full-scale analog input. Each of the $2^m - 1$ taps is connected to the input of a high-speed differential comparator, whose output depends on the sign of the difference between its two inputs. The other inputs of the comparators are all wired together and connected to the analog input of the ADC. Thus, the output of the ith comparator in Figure 5.19 is given by

$$\text{sign}\left[V_{in} - V_{ref}\frac{i}{64}\right]$$

For any given analog input voltage, the outputs of the comparators, whose

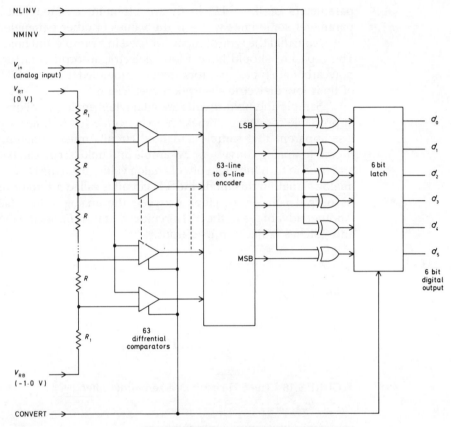

FIGURE 5.19 The flash A/D converter

reference input is above that of the analog input to be converted into digital form, are at a logical one level. All other outputs are at a logical zero. The 63 outputs are fed to a priority encoder which generates a 6-bit output corresponding to the number of logical ones in the input. In the TDC1014J, this 6-bit value is processed by six EOR gates, to enable the converter to directly produce true or inverted outputs, or natural or twos complement outputs.

The parallel A/D converter is very fast – the TDC1014J can digitize an analog signal at up to 30 million samples per second. Such a high conversion rate is required in real-time signal processing in applications such as radar data processing and image processing. For example, we can calculate the total number of samples required to digitize a TV signal in real-time as follows:

samples = pixels per line × lines per field × fields per second

$$= 500 \times 312\tfrac{1}{2} \times 50 = 7\,812\,500 \text{ samples per second (UK)}$$

$$= 500 \times 265\tfrac{1}{2} \times 60 = 7\,875\,000 \text{ samples per second (USA)}$$

Because the flash converter requires so many comparators, it is difficult to produce with greater than about 8 bits precision. Even 6-bit flash ADCs are relatively expensive.

5.3.2 The feedback ADC

The feedback analog-to-digital converter, paradoxically, uses a digital-to-analog converter to effect the required conversion. Figure 5.20 illustrates the basic principle behind this class of converter. A local digital-to-analog converter transforms a digital value, $D = d_0, d_1, \ldots d_{m-1}$, into an analog voltage, V_{out}. The value of D is determined by the block labelled *control logic* in one of the ways to be described later.

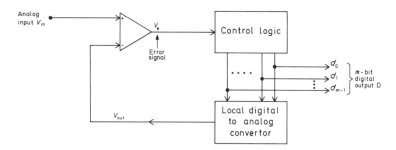

FIGURE 5.20   The basic form of the feedback A/D converter

$V_e = A(V_{in} - V_{out})$

where A = gain of operational amplifier

V_{out} from the DAC is applied to the inverting input of an operational amplifier and the analog input to be converted is applied to its non-inverting input. The output of the operational amplifier corresponds to an error signal, and is equal to A times $(V_{in} - V_{out})$, where A is the gain of the amplifier. The error signal is used by the logic network to modify the digital data, D, in such a way as to minimize the error signal $A(V_{in} - V_{out})$. When the difference between V_{in} and V_{out} is less than that between two quantized signals levels (i.e. Q), the conversion process is complete. In plain English, the digital output is varied by trial and error until the locally generated analog voltage is as close to the analog input as it is possible to achieve. The next step is to examine ways of implementing this *trial and error* process.

The ramp converter

The simplest possible feedback A/D converter is the ramp converter (see Figure 5.21), which uses a binary counter to generate the digital output, D. At the start of a conversion, the binary counter is cleared to zero. A new conversion process starts with the resetting of the RS flip-flop. When Q* goes high following a reset, the AND gate is enabled and clock pulses are fed to the counter causing the output of the counter, D, to increase monotonically from zero (i.e. 0, 1, 2, ... , $2^m - 1$).

The output from the counter is applied to both an m-bit output latch and a D/A converter. As the counter is clocked, the output of the local D/A converter ramps upwards in the manner shown in the timing diagram of Figure 5.21(b). The locally generated analog signal is compared with the input to be converted in a digital comparator, whose output is the sign of the local analog voltage minus the input (i.e. $\text{sign}(V_{out} - V_{in})$). When this value goes positive, the flip-flop is set. At the same time, its Q* output goes low, cutting-off the stream of clock pulses to the counter and its Q output goes high, providing an end of conversion (EOC) output and latching the contents of the binary counter into the output latches.

The ramp feedback A/D converter has a variable conversion time. If the analog input is close to the maximum (i.e. full-scale) value, a total of 2^m clock pulses are required. For an 8-bit ADC the maximum conversion time is 256 times the settling time of the D/A converter plus associated delays in the comparator and counter. The ramp feedback converter produces a *biased error* in its output, as the counter stops only when the local DAC output is higher than the input to be converted. This local analog value is not necessarily closest to the true digital equivalent of the analog input. The advantage of the ramp A/D converter is its great simplicity and low hardware cost.

A modification of the ramp converter is the *tracking converter*, which operates in much the same way as the ramp converter of Figure 5.21, but with the addition of a bidirectional (i.e. up/down) counter and slightly more complex control logic. At the start of each new conversion process, the comparator determines whether the analog input is above or below the feedback voltage from the local DAC. If the analog input is greater, the counter is clocked up, and if it is lower the counter is clocked down. Thus, the counter ramps upwards or downwards until the output of the comparator changes state, at which point the analog input is said to be acquired by the converter.

If the analog input is constant, the conversion time of the counter is effectively zero, once the input has been initially acquired. As long as the input changes slowly with respect to the rate at which the output of the local DAC can ramp upwards or downwards, the tracking counter faithfully converts the analog input into the appropriate digital output. If, however, the analog input rapidly changes its level, the local analog voltage may not be able to track the input, acquisition is lost and the digital output becomes invalid.

The tracking A/D converter is most useful when the input is changing

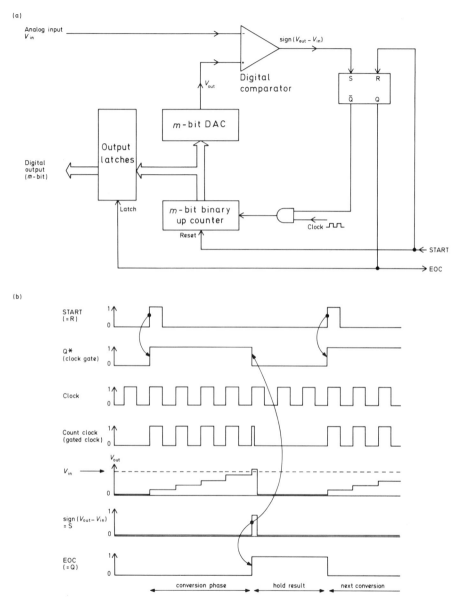

FIGURE 5.21   The ramp feedback A/D converter. (a) the circuit, (b) timing diagram

slowly and is highly auto-correlated. Human speech represents such a signal. If the converter is subject to essentially random inputs (e.g. it is fed from a multiplexer), it offers little or no advantage over a ramp converter.

The successive approximation converter

Intuitively, it would seem reasonable to take very large steps in increasing the analog signal from the local DAC early in the conversion process, and then to reduce the step size as the conversion proceeds and the local analog voltage approaches the analog input. Such an A/D converter is known as the successive approximation A/D converter and uses a binary search algorithm to guarantee an m-bit conversion in no more than m iterations (i.e. clock cycles).

The structure of a successive approximation D/A converter is adequately illustrated by the generic feedback converter of Figure 5.20. It is only the strategy by which the control logic generates successive steps that interests us here. At the start of a new conversion process, the digital logic sets the most-significant bit, MSB, of the input of the local D/A converter to a logical one level, and all other bits to zero. In other words, the first guess is equal to one-half the full-scale output of the converter. If the analog input is greater than half the full-scale output from the local D/A converter, the MSB is retained at a logical one level, otherwise it is cleared. On the second iteration, the next most

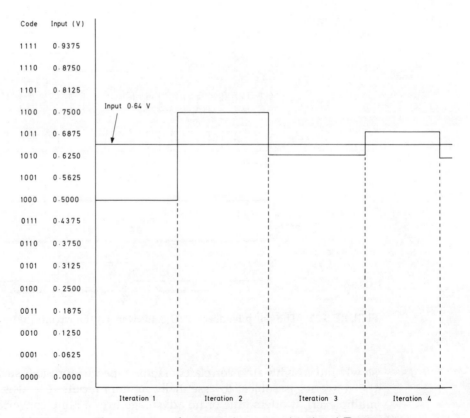

FIGURE 5.22   The operation of a successive approximation A/D converter

significant bit (i.e. d_{m-2} in an m-bit word) is set to a logical one and retained at one if the output of the D/A converter is less than the analog input, or cleared if it is not. This process is repeated m times until the LSB of the D/A converter has been set and then retained or cleared. After the LSB has been dealt with in this way, the process is at an end and the final digital output may be read by the host microprocessor.

Figure 5.22 illustrates the operation of a 4-bit successive approximation A/D converter whose full-scale input is nominally 1.000 V and whose analog input to be converted is 0.6400 V. All the possible sequences of outputs

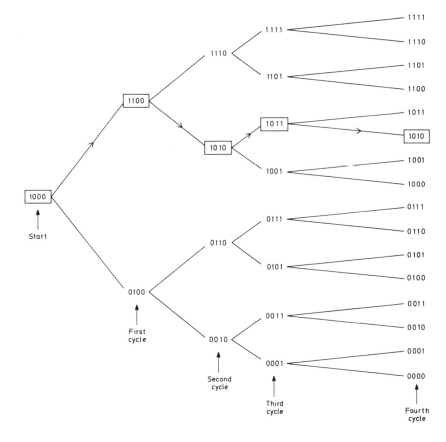

Iteration number	1	2	3	4
D/A converter output (V)	0.5000	0.7500	0.6250	0.6875
Analog I/P–D/A converter O/P	+0.1400	−0.1100	+0.0150	−0.0475
Bit retained	Yes	No	Yes	No
D/A converter output after iteration	1000	1000	1010	1010

FIGURE 5.23   The decision tree for a 4-bit successive approximation DAC

corresponding to a 4-bit successive approximation DAC are given in Figure 5.23, together with the results of converting 0.6400 into digital form described in Figure 5.22.

Practical successive-approximation A/D converters may be bought as single-chip devices with both the DAC and control logic fabricated on the same chip. For greater performance, an off-the-shelf D/A converter can be combined with a successive-approximation register, a device intended to facilitate the design of the control section of the converter. Alternatively, it is possible to use just a D/A converter and a digital comparator, and then implement all control functions in software. This approach is the cheapest but it suffers from a relatively slow conversion rate.

Figure 5.24 illustrates the outline of a simple 68000-controlled successive approximation A/D converter. The microprocesor is connected to a memory-mapped D/A converter which responds only to a write access to the lower byte

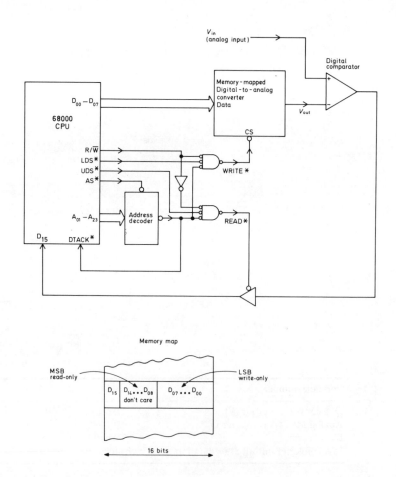

FIGURE 5.24   A 68000-controlled successive approximation A/D converter

of the base address chosen by the address decoder. The analog output of the converter is compared with the unknown input in a digital comparator, whose output is gated onto data line D_{15}, whenever a read access is made to the upper byte of the base address. Table 5.2 gives an example of the software to operate the A/D converter of Figure 5.24.

TABLE 5.2   An example of software-controlled successive-approximation A/D conversion

```
Successive_approximation
    DAC_output:=0
    Increment:=1/2 FSD {100 ... 00}
    FOR I=1 TO Number of bits
        DAC_output:=DAC_output+Increment
        Error_sign:=sign(Vin-DAC_output)
        IF Error_sign negative THEN
                            DAC_output:=DAC_output-Increment
        ENDIF
        Increment:=Increment/2
    ENDFOR
End successive_approximation
```

*			D0 contains the increment
*			D1 is the DAC output
*			D2 is the cycle counter
*			
	ORG	$00F000	Base address of DAC
DAC_IN	DS.B	1	Reserve byte for sign input from DAC
DAC_OT	DS.B	1	Reserve byte for output to DAC
	ORG	$001000	Program origin
CONV	MOVE.B	#$80,D0	Set the half-scale increment
	MOVE.B	D0,D1	Setup initial value for the output
	MOVE.W	#7,D2	We are going to do 8 cycles
AGAIN	MOVE.B	D1,DAC_OT	Transmit output to DAC
	BTST	#7,DAC_IN	Examine output from comparator
	BPL	NEXT	IF positive THEN add next increment
	SUB.B	D0,D1	ELSE remove the increment
NEXT	LSR.B	#1,D0	Increment:=increment/2
	ADD.B	D0,D1	Add increment to output
	DBRA	D2,AGAIN	Repeat for 8 cycles
END	RTS		End of conversion

5.3.3 The integrating ADC

The integrating, or more specifically the dual-ramp converter, transforms the problem of measuring an analog voltage into the much more tractable problem of measuring another analog quantity – time. An integrating operational amplifier circuit converts the analog input into a charge stored on a capacitor, and then evaluates the charge by measuring the time it takes to discharge the capacitor. The block diagram of a dual-slope integrating A/D converter is given in Figure 5.25 and its timing diagram in Figure 5.26.

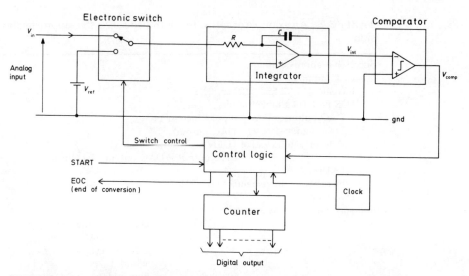

FIGURE 5.25   The integrating A/D converter

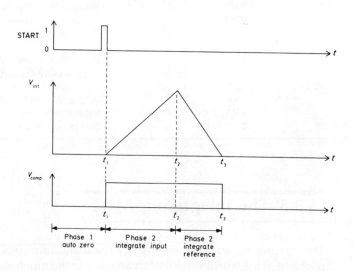

FIGURE 5.26   The timing diagram of the integrating A/D converter

A typical (i.e. commercially available) A/D converter operates in three distinct phases: auto-zero, integrate the unknown analog signal and integrate the reference voltage. The first phase, auto-zero, is a feature of many monolithic IC dual-slope converters and exists to reduce any off-set error in the system. As it is not a basic feature of the dual-slope process, it is not dealt with here. During the second phase of the conversion, the unknown analog input linearly charges the integrating capacitor C. In this phase, the input of the electronic switch connects the integrator to V_{in}.

Figure 5.26 shows how the output from the integrator, V_{int}, ramps upward linearly during phase 2 of the conversion process. At the start of phase 2, a counter is triggered and continues to count upwards from zero to its maximum value $2^n - 1$. At some point, after a fixed period $T_1 = 2^n/f_c$, the counter overflows; f_c is the frequency of the converter's own clock. As soon as the counter overflows, the electronic switch at the input to the integrator connects the input to $-V_{ref}$, the negative reference supply. The output of the integrator now ramps downwards to zero, while the counter runs up from zero. Eventually, the output of the integrator reaches zero and the conversion process stops.

At the end of phase 2 the capacitor is charged up to a level

$$\frac{1}{CR} \int V_{in} \, dt$$

The voltage rise during the second phase is equal to the fall in the third as, of course, the output of the integrator begins at zero volts and ends up at zero volts. Therefore, the following equation holds:

$$\frac{1}{CR} \int_{t_1}^{t_2} V_{in} \, dt = \frac{1}{CR} \int_{t_2}^{t_3} V_{ref} \, dt$$

Assuming that $t_1 = 0$, $t_2 = 2^n/f_c$, $t_3 = t_2 + M/f_c$, we can write

$$\frac{1}{CR} \left[V_{in} t \right]_0^{2^n/f_c} = \frac{1}{CR} \left[V_{ref} t \right]_{2^n/f_c}^{2^n/f_c + M/f_c}$$

or

$$V_{in} 2^n/f_c = V_{ref} M/f_c$$

$$V_{in} = V_{ref} \frac{M}{2^n}$$

This remarkable result is dependent only on the reference voltage and two integers, 2^n and M. The values of C and R and the clock frequency, f_c, do not appear in the equation. Implicit in the equation is the condition that f_c is constant throughout the conversion process. Fortunately, this is a reasonable assumption even for the simplest of clock generators.

The dual-slope integrating A/D converter is popular because of its very low cost and inherent simplicity. Moreover, it is exceedingly accurate and can provide twelve or more bits of precision at a cost below that of some 8-bit DACs.

Because this form of converter requires no absolute value other than V_{ref}, it is possible to fabricate the entire converter in a single 40-pin package.

The conversion time is variable and takes $2^n + M$ clock periods in total. A 12-bit converter with a $1\,\mu$s clock has a maximum conversion time of $2 \times 2^n/f_c$ seconds, since the maximum value of M is 2^n. Using the above figures, the maximum conversion time is equal to $2 \times 4096 \times 1\,\mu$s, or 8.192 ms, which is very much slower than most forms of feedback A/D converter.

Because the analog input is integrated over a period of $2^n/f_c$ seconds, noise on the input is attenuated. Sinusoidal input signals, whose periods are submultiples of the integration period, do not affect the output of the integrator and hence the measured value of the input. This property is exploited by many high-precision converters to remove any unwanted noise at the power line frequency (60 Hz USA, 50 Hz Europe).

5.3.4 An example of a 12-bit ADC

Now that we have looked at some of the principles of ADCs, the next step is to examine the characteristics of a real device and show how it is interfaced to a 68000 microprocessor.

A good example of a single-chip analog-to-digital converter is provided by the Analog Devices Ltd AD574A 12-bit ADC. The AD574A contains *all* the functional parts of a 12-bit successive-approximation analog-to-digital converter (including the clock and the analog reference) on-chip. Even better, the AD574A readily interfaces to 8-bit or to 12-bit microprocessor buses.

Before describing the ADC and its interface to a 68000 microprocessor, we highlight a few of its features.

1. *Power supply* The AD574A requires a TTL supply of +5 V and analog supplies of +12 V and −12 V. It is *critically important* that the power supplies be filtered and well regulated. The power supplies should be decoupled at the ADC with $47\,\mu$F tantalum capacitors in series with $0.1\,\mu$F disk ceramic types. The ADC should be located as far from noise sources as possible and great care taken with the PCB layout.
2. *Errors* The AD574AK has a maximum guaranteed non-linearity of $\pm\frac{1}{2}$ LSB. That is, an analog value falling at the centre of a given code will always result in a correct digital output code. The AD574AK is guaranteed to have no missing codes and that every output code in sequence should be generated as the analog input moves linearly from its minimum value.
3. *Mode* The AD574A operates either in a unipolar mode with a full-scale range of 0 V to +10 V or in a bipolar mode with a full-scale range of −5 V to +5 V.
4. *Bus width* The AD574A has a 12/8* bus-control input pin which defines whether the ADC uses a 12-bit wide bus (12/8* = V_{cc}) or an 8-bit wide bus (12/8* = ground).

Using the AD574A

As the AD574A contains both its digital and analog circuits on chip, very few additional components are required to turn it into a working analog/digital subsystem. It can be seen from the block diagram of Figure 5.27 that the ADC has an almost *standard* microprocessor-side interface, two analog inputs plus a mode control, gain and offset adjustment points and power supply inputs.

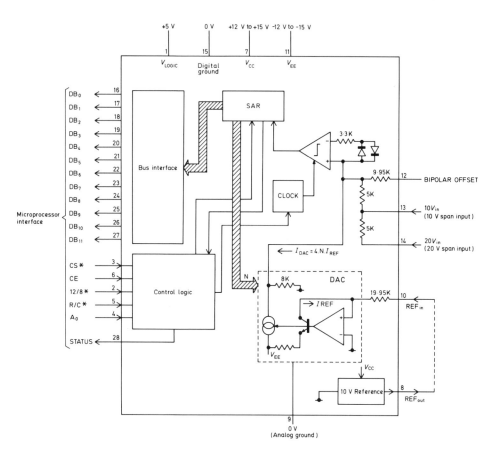

FIGURE 5.27 The AD574A 12-bit ADC

The analog aspects of the AD574A are described in Figure 5.28. Note that there are *two* analog inputs: a 10 V range on pin 13 and a 20 V range on pin 14. The user must select whether to choose a 10 or 20 V full-scale range and connect the appropriate pin to the analog input to be measured. The other pin is left unconnected.

In Figure 5.28(a) the ADC is configured for unipolar mode operation with

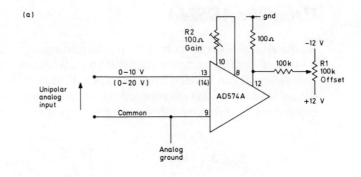

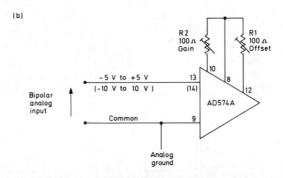

FIGURE 5.28   (a) Configuring the AD574A for unipolar operation
Note: pin 13 for 0–10 V range, pin 14 for 0–20 V range
(b) Configuring the AD574A for bipolar operation
Note: pin 13 for −5 V to +5 V range, pin 14 for −10 V to +10 V range

the bipolar offset pin (BIP$_{off}$) effectively connected to ground potential. The input range is $0-10$ V (or $0-20$ V if the input is connected to pin 14). The offset trim is optional (pin 12 may be directly wired to analog ground – pin 9) and is used to provide $+15$ mV or -15 mV of input offset. The offset can be adjusted to make the first transition from \$000 to \$001 occur when the input level is $+\frac{1}{2}$ Q (i.e. one half LSB) or 1.22 mV on the 10 V range.

The full-scale gain trim is performed by applying the full-scale input *less* $\frac{1}{2}$ LSB (i.e. 9.9963 V on the 10 V range) and adjusting R_2 to give a last transition of \$FFE to \$FFF.

In the bipolar mode of Figure 5.28(b), the input may vary from -5 V to $+5$ V with respect to the analog ground. Setting up is similar to the unipolar mode. A signal $\frac{1}{2}$ LSB above negative full-scale (i.e. -4.9988 V on the 5 V range) is applied and the offset control, R_1, adjusted to give the first transition of \$000–\$001. Then a signal $1\frac{1}{2}$ LSB below positive full-scale (i.e. $+4.9963$ V on the 5 V range) is applied and R_2 is adjusted to give the last transition of \$FFE–\$FFF. Note that the digital output is not signed and varies from \$000 to \$FFF as the input varies from -5 V to $+5$ V.

There are two important points to note about the AD574A. The first is obvious and concerns the power supply. It cannot be emphasized enough that the power supplies must be well regulated and free from noise, and that low impedance grounds must be used. The analog input is referred to the chip's analog ground which is connected to the digital ground at the chip. The second point is that the analogy input to the AD574A is not buffered and the input impedance varies as the successive approximation process is carried out. Therefore, the AD574A should be driven by the low impedance output of an op-amp or a sample and hold amplifier.

A block diagram of the microprocessor side of the AD574A is given in Figure 5.29(a) and Figure 5.29(b) defines the operations of the ADC in terms of its control signals. The ADC is selected when CE = 1 and CS* = 0. An R/C* (read/convert*) input selects either the read mode or the *initiate conversion* mode. A0 is used to select the upper or lower byte in the 8-bit interface mode or it can be used to force a short 8-bit conversion cycle.

According to its data sheet, the AD574A can be interfaced to host microprocessors in one of two modes: a *full control mode* and a *stand-alone mode*. In the full control mode the AD574A looks like a typical memory-mapped peripheral and Figures 5.30 and 5.31 illustrate its 'write' and read timing diagrams respectively. The write cycle is in quotes because it is a dummy write cycle and serves only to force the ADC to carry out a conversion process. Of course, a read cycle cannot take place until the conversion is complete and STS (status) output has returned to a low level.

A glance at the timing control circuit of Figure 5.29(a) tells us that CE and CS* perform, essentially, the same function and that CE may be permanently high or CS* permanently low. However, even if we make, say, CS* permanently low, the timing diagrams of Figures 5.30 and 5.31 require a rather large setup time for the R/C* input. Let us see if the stand-alone mode offers any advantages.

Figures 5.32 and 5.33 illustrate the stand alone mode in which the ADC is permanently enabled with CS* = 0 and CE = 1. Anything that removes the bother of dealing with two control lines cannot be all bad!

In Figure 5.32 R/C* is normally high and is pulsed low to initiate a cycle. The falling edge of R/C* forces a conversion cycle and turns off the data bus buffers. After a suitable delay, the conversion process is complete and the data from the ADC is placed on its output terminals until the next cycle.

In Figure 5.33 R/C* is normally low and is pulsed high to initiate a cycle. In this case, the effect of the read pulse (i.e. R/C* high) is to force a read cycle and to make the ADC look like a read-only memory to the host microprocessor. At the end of the read cycle, the falling edge of R/C* *automatically* triggers the next conversion. In other words, this mode is a *read last result followed by initiate next result* microprocessor. I like this because of its great simplicity.

It is clear from Figure 5.33 that the high R/C* pulse width, t_{HRH}, of 300 ns minimum cannot be achieved with an 8 MHz 68000 without wait states. If R/C* is derived from LDS* or UDS* after inversion, the addition of two wait states

(a)

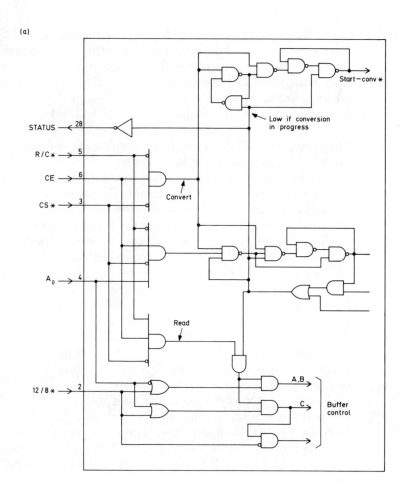

STATUS

R/C∗

CE

CS∗

A₀

12 / 8 ∗

Start−conv ∗

Low if conversion
in progress

Convert

Read

A,B

C

Buffer
control

(b)
Truth table for AD574A's control inputs

CE	CS*	R/C*	12/8*	A0	Operation
0	X	X	X	X	None
X	1	X	X	X	None
1	0	0	X	0	Initiate 12-bit conversion
1	0	0	X	1	Initiate 8-bit conversion
1	0	1	1	X	Enable 12-bit parallel output
1	0	1	0	0	Enable 8 most-significant bits
1	0	1	0	1	Enable 4 least-significant bits

Note :
12 / 8 ∗ input not TTL compatible.
Tie to ground or +5 V

FIGURE 5.29   (a) The digital side of the AD574A. (b)   The AD574A's control signals

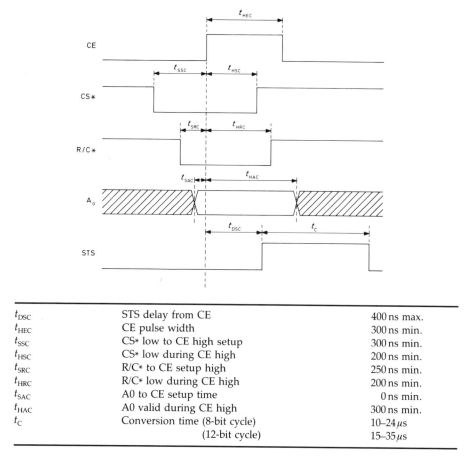

FIGURE 5.30 The AD574As full control mode write cycle

t_{DSC}	STS delay from CE	400 ns max.
t_{HEC}	CE pulse width	300 ns min.
t_{SSC}	CS* low to CE high setup	300 ns min.
t_{HSC}	CS* low during CE high	200 ns min.
t_{SRC}	R/C* to CE setup high	250 ns min.
t_{HRC}	R/C* low during CE high	200 ns min.
t_{SAC}	A0 to CE setup time	0 ns min.
t_{HAC}	A0 valid during CE high	300 ns min.
t_C	Conversion time (8-bit cycle)	10–24 μs
	(12-bit cycle)	15–35 μs

provide a value for $t_{HRH} = t_{DSL} + t_{cyc} = 240$ ns $+ 125$ ns $= 365$ ns. There is enough margin here (i.e. 356 ns $-$ 300 ns $= 65$ ns) to account for delays in the address decoder. The two wait states also take care of the data access time ($t_{DDR} = 250$ ns maximum).

The only worrying aspect of the timing diagram is the relatively long output float delay time. This is the time between the falling edge of R/C* at the point at which the data bus floats and has a quoted maximum of $t_{HL} = 150$ ns. The importance of this normally *trivial* parameter is that no other device may access the data bus while the ADC is actively driving it. In fast systems, a device may be accessing the bus in the next cycle before the ADC has ended the current cycle.

The absolute minimum time separating two successive memory accesses by the 68000 is t_{SH}, the AS*, and LDS* and UDS* high time. For a 68000 at 8 MHz

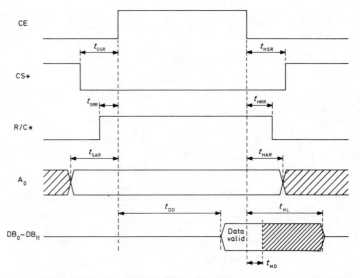

t_{DD}	Access time from CE high	250 ns max.
t_{HD}	Data valid after CE low	25 ns min.
t_{HL}	Output float delay	150 ns max.
t_{SSR}	CS* low to CE high setup time	150 ns min.
t_{SRR}	R/C* high to CE high setup time	0 ns min.
t_{SAR}	A0 to CE high setup time	150 ns min.
t_{HSR}	CS* hold time after CE low	50 ns min.
t_{HRR}	R/C* high after CE low	0 ns min.
t_{HAR}	A0 valid after CE low	50 ns min.

FIGURE 5.31 The AD574A's full control mode read cycle

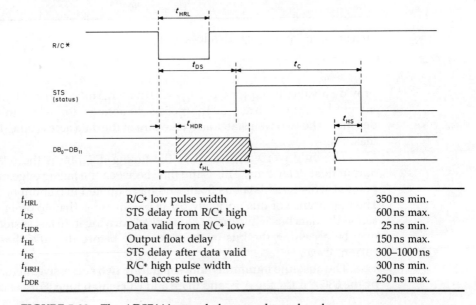

t_{HRL}	R/C* low pulse width	350 ns min.
t_{DS}	STS delay from R/C* high	600 ns max.
t_{HDR}	Data valid from R/C* low	25 ns min.
t_{HL}	Output float delay	150 ns max.
t_{HS}	STS delay after data valid	300–1000 ns
t_{HRH}	R/C* high pulse width	300 ns min.
t_{DDR}	Data access time	250 ns max.

FIGURE 5.32 The AD574A's stand-alone mode read cycle

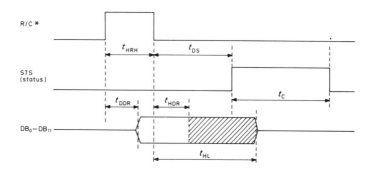

FIGURE 5.33   The AD574A's stand-alone mode write cycle

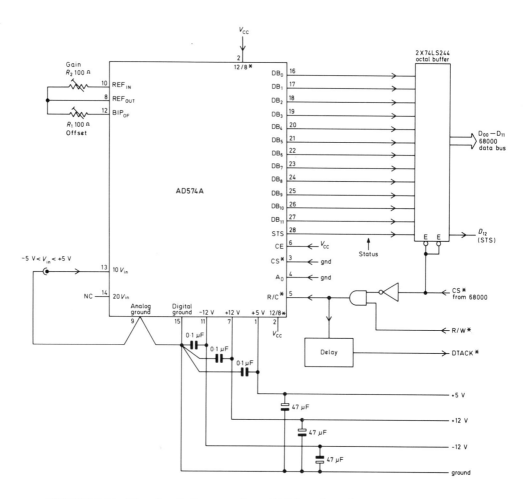

FIGURE 5.34   The circuit diagram of an ADC based on the AD574A

t_{SH} (min) = 150 ns and for a 12.5 MHz it is only 65 ns. It is probably acceptable to connect the AD574A directly to a 68000 data bus and to drive R/C* from LDS* (or UDS*) after qualifying it with R/W* = 1 and chip-select from a suitable address decoder. However, a better solution is to provide the ADC with output buffers having faster turn-off times

The circuit diagram of a complete 12-bit analog-to-digital converter based on the AD574A is given in Figure 5.34. I have chosen the −5 V to +5 V bipolar mode and, of course, taken advantage of the AD574A's 12-bit data bus. The AD574A to 68000 interface operates in the *stand-alone, R/C* pulse high* mode and the data bus is buffered by two 74LS244s. Note that I have returned the ADC's STS output on D15 so that the 68000 can test the converter's status. Although reading the status also forces a rising edge on R/C* it does not trigger a new conversion process until the current conversion is complete.

Summary

In this chapter we have barely scratched the surface of the subject of digital-to-analog conversion and analog-to-digital conversion. The designer of digital-to-analog or analog-to-digital interfaces has to confront special problems not found in purely digital systems. For example, we encounter the sampling theorem, quantization noise and non-linearities, such as missing codes, all of which must be taken into account. As the resolution of the ADC or DAC increases beyond about 8 bits, very great care and special precautions have to be taken with the design and layout of the analog circuits in order to avoid the effect of digital noise getting into analog circuits.

Chapter 6

The CRT

Controller

We are now going to examine the operation of the video display and then show how a CRT terminal or video display terminal, VDT, can be constructed around a CRT controller chip. Unlike many of the other interface chips that we have described, the CRT controller sits at the heart of a *system* and does not simply form the interface between an external device and a host microprocessor. Therefore, we examine not only the CRT controller itself but also include the logic necessary to display alphanumeric text on a CRT.

I first became interested in microcomputer systems design in 1977 when I acquired an early microprocessor development kit. Although I built the kit at home, I was forced to drag it to my laboratory because I had no input/output device. In those days, the 'plain vanilla' computer peripheral was the teletype which produced upper-case only, hard-copy output on paper roll at a snail's pace of 110 baud.

As a student, there was no way that I could afford a teletype of my own and the low-cost VDT had yet to appear. Even if I could, there was hardly room for such a large device at home. So, I decided to build my own CRT terminal.

There was then no CRT controller chip available at an affordable price and, therefore, my VDT had to be constructed from commonly available SSI and MSI TTL devices. The VDT I designed was built and, after debugging, it worked. The most important lesson I learned from this exercise was that much of the conventional digital design I had studied at university was largely irrelevant. I was taught Boolean algebra and all that goes with it, but the problems I encountered in practice were almost always concerned with timing.

Since those days, the design of a CRT controller has been greatly simplified by the introduction of the CRT controller chip, CRTC. The CRTC provides much of, but not all, the control circuitry required by a video display controller. Typically, a CRTC may save the designer between 20 and 50 TTL chips. CRTCs have steadily increased in complexity, with the result that some of today's most sophisticated CRT controllers are considerably more complex than the 68000 itself.

The dilemma facing the author who wishes to write about CRT controllers is whether to choose an old but simple chip or a modern chip which cannot adequately be described in a single chapter. As a compromise, I have decided to concentrate on the Hitachi HD6345. The HD6345 is a relatively recent chip but is really an improved version of the older standard 6845. Both the HD6345 and the 6845 provide all the timing and control circuitry necessary to implement a basic VDT, although they are not as complex as some of the latest generation of CRTCs. Before we consider the CRTC proper, we must examine the operation of the cathode ray tube.

6.1 *The video display*

The most common video display device of the last few decades has been the cathode ray tube (CRT). CRTs are popular because of their low cost, which is probably due to their use in almost all domestic televisions and therefore their mass production. Although the flat-panel liquid crystal display (LCD), a competitor to the CRT, is beginning to appear in the so-called lap portable computer, it is, unfortunately, still relatively expensive. Consequently, we will not deal with the LCD here.

The cathode ray tube is one of the oldest electronic devices and is illustrated in Figure 6.1. A filament at one end of a glass tube heats a cathode which, when hot, gives off electrons. The air inside the CRT is removed to leave a high vacuum that does not impede the flow of electrons. If there were no other electrodes in the CRT, electrons leaving the cathode would fall back, because they are negatively charged and, when they leave the cathode, they cause it to develop a positive charge that attracts them back.

The surface and side of the CRT at the opposite end to the cathode are coated with a conducting material. By connecting this coating to a positive potential with respect to the cathode, electrons are attracted to the screen. As the voltage applied to the coating (the anode) is raised, the electron velocity is also increased and the electron beam hits the screen with considerable kinetic energy. Coating the surface of the screen with certain chemicals called phosphors makes the surface glow where it is bombarded by electrons. The anode potential required to achieve a satisfactory brightness is typically 15 kV more positive than the cathode

Between the cathode and the anode lies a fine wire mesh called the grid. When a negative potential is applied to the grid, electrons from the cathode are

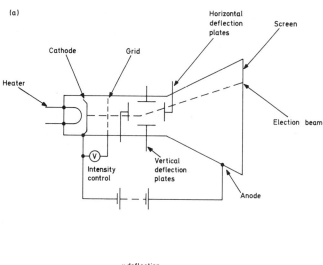

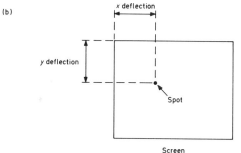

FIGURE 6.1 The cathode ray tube. (a) the CRT structure, (b) the CRT screen

repelled and the beam turned off. Applying a variable potential to the grid modulates the electron beam and therefore the intensity of the spot on the screen. Note that practical CRTs have other electrodes that focus the beam to a small spot.

In some CRTs, the beam passes between two pairs of parallel flat plates. One pair is arranged in the vertical plane and the other in the horizontal plane. By applying a potential difference between a pair of plates, the beam can be deflected in either the horizontal or the vertical axes. Varying the voltage on both pairs of plates simultaneously makes it possible to deflect the beam to any point on the screen. CRTs in modern VDTs and televisions use magnetic deflection rather than electrostatic deflection. Instead of deflecting the beam by means of charged plates, they employ magnetic fields generated by coils placed externally around the neck of the tube.

Now that we have shown how the CRT makes a spot on a screen, the next step is to demonstrate how a moving spot can be used to build up an image. There are two basic ways of operating a CRT tube; one is called a point-plotting display and the other a raster-scan display. Here we are largely concerned with the raster-scan mode which forms the basis of the television display. However, the point-plotting mode will be briefly described before we turn to the raster-scan mode.

6.1.1 The point-plotting display

The block diagram of a point-plotting display is illustrated in Figure 6.2. Both pairs of beam-deflecting plates (or coils) are fed with signals from digital to analog converters. One converter feeds the X-plates and controls the horizontal deflection of the beam and the other feeds the Y-plates and controls the vertical deflection of the beam. Ten-bit DACs permit horizontal and vertical resolutions of 1024 by 1024 dots.

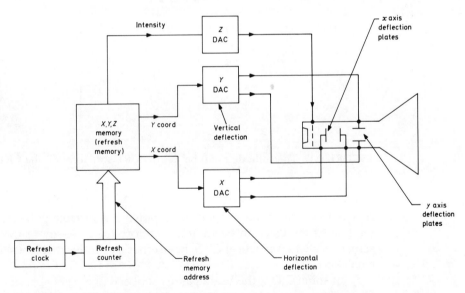

FIGURE 6.2 The point-plotting display

The inputs to the DACs are obtained from a memory (the refresh memory) arranged as a list of X, Y and Z coordinates. By transmitting a sequence of X, Y coordinates to the DACs, a series of dots is drawn on the screen. The position of each dot is determined by its X and Y coordinates and the Z coordinate from the memory determines the spot intensity. A single Z bit allows the beam to be either fully on or fully off (i.e. blanked), while several Z bits provide a so-called grey-scale of intensities between black and white.

Real point-plotting displays require complex analog circuitry to draw lines between points. In principle, the beam moves from point to point *instantaneously* and the screen is dark between consecutive points. By slowing down the movement of the beam (by analog circuitry), it is possible to draw lines of a constant intensity.

6.1.2 The raster-scan display

The raster-scan display does away with the need for *explicit X* and *Y* DACs by transforming the problem of specifying the physical position of a point into the problem of specifying its position in time. Figure 6.3 demonstrates how we do this. A linearly rising *sawtooth* waveform is applied to the *X*-plates, causing the beam to sweep horizontally across the surface of the screen from left to right. When the beam reaches the right-hand edge of the screen, it is rapidly moved back to its starting position on the left-hand side. The beam moves from right to left (its *flyback or retrace* period) in a tiny fraction of the time it moves from left to right. Throughout this chapter, we employ the term *line* to mean a single scan (i.e. a raster) in the horizontal plane and the term *row* to mean a horizontal row of characters. A row of characters is, of course, made up of several lines.

As the beam is scanned in the horizontal plane, it is also scanned in the vertical plane by applying another sawtooth waveform to the *Y*-plates but at a much lower rate than the horizontal scanning. When the beam has moved from the top of the screen to the bottom, it executes its vertical retrace to the top of the screen. Figure 6.3 demonstrates how the beam covers the entire surface of the screen by performing a number of horizontal scans, one below the other.

The scanning process is performed at such a high speed that the human eye perceives a single picture (frame) and does not detect the movement of the spot. In order to avoid flicker, the beam is scanned vertically 60 times a second in the USA and 50 times a second in Europe. A single vertical scan is called a *field*. Field rates of 60 Hz (USA) and 50 Hz (Europe) are chosen to match the power-line frequencies in these countries. Some high-quality displays have vertical scan rates greater than 60 Hz to remove the slightly irritating subliminal flicker of conventional displays.

At the time television systems were first standardized, many of the components now available to designers were unheard of. Consequently, those early standards are now regarded as rather limited in comparison with the level of performance achievable by today's systems. Raster-scan displays built around low-cost television monitors are, therefore, restricted in terms of the number of rows and columns of characters that can be displayed.

One of the problems in devising a television standard is the conflict between the desire to have a high definition (resolution) with as many lines per frame as possible, and to scan at the maximum field rate to avoid irritating

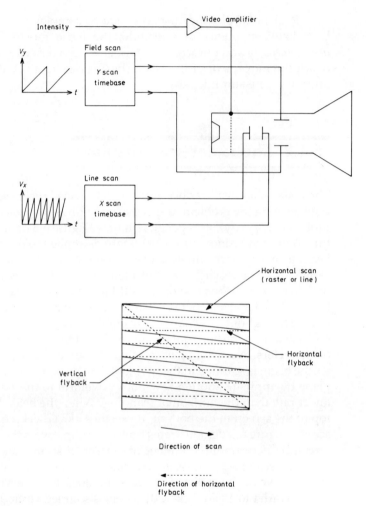

FIGURE 6.3 The raster-scan display

flicker. A solution to this dilemma is to fix the vertical scan rate at 60 Hz to reduce flicker and to settle for a vertical resolution of $262\frac{1}{2}$ lines per field. Unfortunately, a vertical resolution of only $262\frac{1}{2}$ lines is not acceptable for domestic TV. However, by transmitting $262\frac{1}{2}$ *even* lines in one field followed by $262\frac{1}{2}$ *odd* lines in the next field, an *effective* vertical resolution of 525 lines is obtained. This process is called interlacing and is illustrated in Figure 6.4. The European CCIR system interleaves $312\frac{1}{2}$ odd fields with $312\frac{1}{2}$ even fields to obtain an effective vertical resolution of 625 lines.

Interlacing is ideal for normal television displays (i.e. the moving picture), because the eye receives two different fields per frame which the human brain integrates into one composite frame. The viewer, therefore,

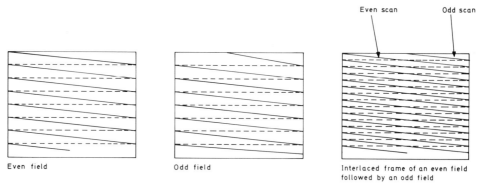

FIGURE 6.4   Interlacing

perceives an acceptable vertical resolution without excessive flicker. Unfortunately, interlacing is not usually possible in VDTs and the number of horizontal scans is limited to $262\frac{1}{2}$ *pairs* of lines. We cannot use interlacing, because the information received by the eye in successive fields is very different and the resulting display appears to flicker horribly. We return to the topic of interlaced displays after the raster-scan, alphanumeric display has been introduced.

6.1.3 Displaying text on a raster-scan display

In order to understand a digital display, we need to introduce the pixel. A pixel is a *picture element* and is the video equivalent of a bit. Like a bit, it is the smallest unit of video information and represents a single spot on the screen. A pixel may be *on* to generate a dot, or *off* to generate an *undot*, which is the absence of a dot. Note that a pixel differs from a bit in at least one way. A pixel can have attributes so that the spot may be white, blue, red or any shade of grey or it may be flashing.

In a conventional monochrome television, the signal representing each line of the display is a time-varying *analog* value that ranges between peak white and black levels. In a raster-scan digital display, the signal representing a line is a time-varying *digital* signal, because each line is subdivided into a number of pixels and each pixel may be on or off. A typical display may have a horizontal resolution of 256, 512 or 1024 pixels and a vertical resolution of 200 pixels. A block of memory, called *video memory* holds a map or *image* of the pixels that are to be displayed on the CRT.

Figure 6.5 illustrates the relationship between a video display and its memory. Each pixel is associated with a single bit (in a monochrome display). The diagram of Figure 6.5 is highly simplified and has a horizontal resolution of

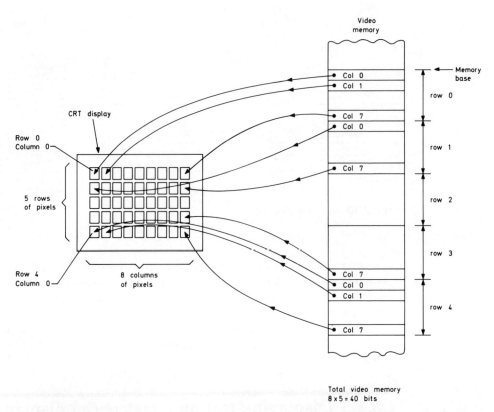

FIGURE 6.5   The video memory and its relationship to the CRTC (5 row × 8 column display shown for simplicity)

eight columns and a vertical resolution of five rows. All a display system has to do is to read the values of the pixels from memory as the beam scans the surface of the screen and then turn the beam in the CRT on or off in sympathy with the pixels. The video memory must be read at exactly the same rate that the beam sweeps across the screen. Note that the bit-mapped scheme of Figure 6.5 is not normally used to display text, as it is relatively inefficient. A 1024 bit by 512 line display would require the storage of $2^{10} \times 2^9 = 2^{19} = 512$ Kbits. Such a display is better suited to bit-mapped *graphics*.

The structure of an alphanumeric (i.e. text) display is given in Figure 6.6. All text is contained within a rectangular display area, surrounded by blanked left, right, upper and lower margins. Margins are required because the CRT display is not exactly square at its corners and most CRTs are not entirely linear devices. Without a margin, some screens would lose part of the display near their edges.

The display area is divided into rows and columns. Each row and column position holds a single character element or no element at all. When the

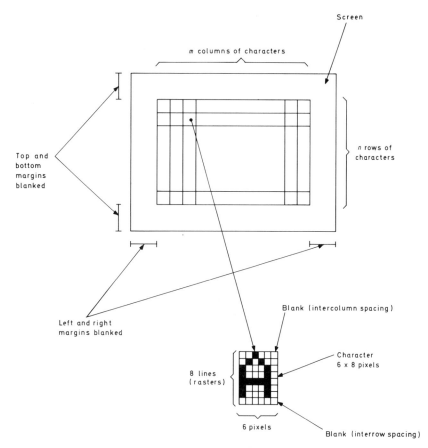

FIGURE 6.6   The structure of an alphanumeric display

character position is blank, it is said to contain a space (ISO character $20). Typical displays have a resolution of 24 rows of 80 columns. For the purpose of this introduction, we assume the characters to be the alphanumeric symbols of the ISO character set, although they could equally be graphics symbols.

A character position is made up of a series of consecutive lines (i.e. horizontal scans) and each line is itself composed of a number of pixels. The character structure is also referred to as a *font*. Typical fonts vary from 6 pixels × 8 lines to 10 pixels × 16 lines.

The logical arrangement of a raster-scan alphanumeric video display is illustrated in Figure 6.7. As the beam sweeps across the CRT from left to right, all the pixels (dots) along one of the lines of a character are drawn (i.e. displayed on the screen). In Figure 6.7, seven horizontal scans form an entire row of characters. For the purpose of illustration, we will imagine that the display is in the act of drawing the line above the central horizontal bar of the left-most letter 'A'.

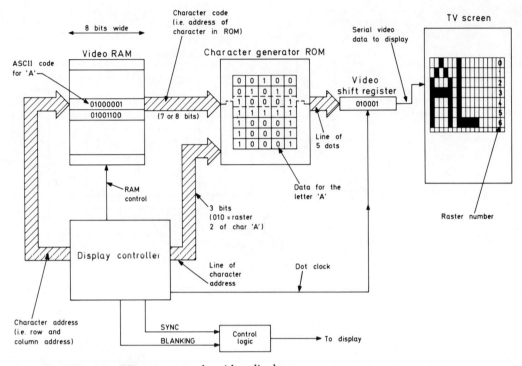

FIGURE 6.7   The structure of a video display

Note: Data in the video shift register is shifted out from the right and the shifted bits are drawn on the screen from *left to right*. Thus, the video data 010001 is displayed as ◼ ☐ ☐ ☐ ◼ ☐.

The pattern of dots making up the seven lines of each character is often stored in read-only memory (the character generator). If, however, read/write memory is used to store the character set, character fonts can be dynamically defined under software control. Figure 6.7 shows the binary pattern in the video RAM corresponding to the character 'A'. The data output from the character generator ROM is one of the seven lines of the selected character and is used to draw the character on the screen. The data output from the ROM is, of course, the 5-bit input to the video shift register that generates the video signal.

The address inputs to the character generator ROM are divided into two fields: a *character address* and a *line-of-character* address. The latter comes from the display controller circuit and the former comes from the video memory. The video RAM contains an *image* of the display in terms of its characters rather than its individual pixels and therefore a typical 24 × 80 column display requires only 1920 bytes of RAM. Each byte contains the code of the character to be displayed.

The output of the character generator ROM is connected to a shift register which holds the seven dots of the current line of the character being displayed plus an undot to provide intercharacter spacing. The contents of the shift register are shifted out at the dot-clock rate, which is the rate at which the dots are drawn on the screen. After a line of a character has been drawn, the shift register is loaded with a line of the next character.

The address input to the video RAM corresponds to the row and column positions of the next character to be displayed and is generated by the display controller which cycles through all the characters of row P and then all the characters of row $P + 1$, etc.

We have now described the essentials of the video display, but have omitted obvious details such as how the characters to be displayed are loaded into the video RAM and the less obvious but rather horrid details of how the whole thing is synchronized with the motion of the beam in the CRT (a major design problem). Characters can be written into the video RAM by multiplexing the RAM between the display system and the host microprocessor. In fact, it is possible for the host microprocessor to take control of the video RAM during the vertical retrace period without affecting the display in any way. The synchronization of all parts of the display are controlled by a single-chip CRT controller. We now look at an example of a CRT controller chip.

6.2 The HD6345 CRT controller chip

The CRT controller chip is responsible for performing most of the timing and control functions of a video display. CRT controllers have typical microprocessor-side interfaces and appear to the host microprocessor as a group of registers. These registers define the format of the display and control features such as scrolling and the cursor. These facilities will be discussed in more detail later.

The *peripheral side* of the CRT controller is not particularly complex and is largely made up of a character address bus, a line-of-character address bus and timing and control signals. Figure 6.8 provides a block diagram of a video display system based on a CRT controller. The designer of a video display has the following four major points to consider: the interface between the CRT controller and the host computer, the multiplexed video RAM and its interface to both the host computer and the display system, the dot-clock and shift register, and the video control circuitry responsible for combining video, blanking and synchronizing signals. We will deal with these in turn.

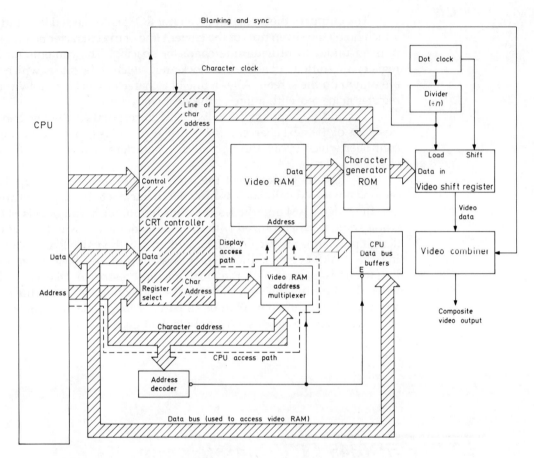

FIGURE 6.8 The block diagram of a video display generator

Note: The dot clock is the highest frequency in the display system (dot clocks are normally in the range 6 MHz to 30 MHz).

6.2.1 The microprocessor-side interface of the HD6345

The HD6345 is a 40-pin chip that interfaces to the host computer through a conventional 8-bit, 6800-type interface. An interface between the HD6345 CRT controller (from now on we will simply call this the CRT controller) and a 68000 is given in Figure 6.9. The HD6345 is connected to the 68000 by means of the latter's synchronous address and data bus. Whenever the 68000 makes a read or a write access to the CRTC's address space, the address decoder asserts the

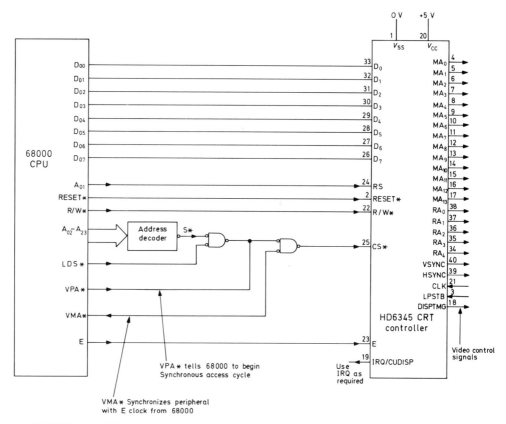

FIGURE 6.9   The interface between an HD6345 CRTC and a 68000 microprocessor

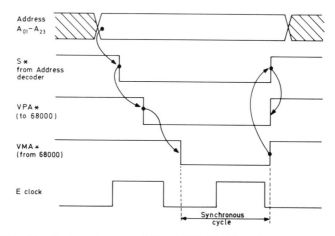

FIGURE 6.10   The timing diagram of the 68000–6345 interface

VPA∗ (valid peripheral address) input to the 68000. The 68000 recognizes the assertion of VPA∗ and executes a synchronous bus cycle by asserting its VMA∗ (valid memory address) output at the appropriate phase in a read/write cycle. The timing diagram of Figure 6.10 illustrates the sequence of events taking place during a synchronous access. VMA∗ is synchronized with the 68000's free running E-clock output operating at a frequency of CLK/10, where CLK is the 68000's own clock input. 6800-series peripherals use the VMA∗ signal from the 68000 to generate, in conjunction with the address coder, a chip-select. These peripherals also use the E-clock for all their internal timing operations.

Note that there is only one address line input to the CRTC, the register select input (RS), which is connected to the 68000's A_{01} output. In order to reduce the number of pins, the manufacturers of this CRT controller have made one register a pointer register and the other register a data register. When RS = 0, the pointer register is selected and the pointer register is loaded with the address of the internal register to be accessed by the host microprocessor. When RS = 1, the internal register pointed at by the contents of the CRT controller's pointer register is selected. The CRT controller has 40 internal registers (in addition to the pointer register). Table 6.1 lists these registers whose functions are looked at in detail later. All we need note here is that most of the registers are set up by the programmer once (and once only) after a reset and that they define the format of the display and the operating mode of the CRTC.

Hitachi have introduced a second version of the HD6345, called the HD6445, that interfaces directly to '8080 type buses'. This device is probably more suitable to the 68000 systems designer because it interfaces directly to the 68000's asynchronous bus. Figure 6.11 provides a timing diagram of the HD6445's read and write cycles and Figure 6.12 shows how it can be interfaced to a 68000.

6.2.2 The video memory

The organization of the video memory that stores the codes of the characters to be displayed is entirely straightforward. To keep the circuit as simple as possible, a single 8-Kbyte static read/write memory component is used to provide 8 Kbytes of character storage, representing over one hundred rows of 80-column text. Video displays operating in a graphics mode by plotting pixels directly (i.e. without using a character generator) require much larger display memories and are invariably forced to use dynamic RAM for reasons of economics.

The circuit diagram of the video memory is provided in Figure 6.13. The byte-wide static video RAM, IC 1, is shared between the 68000 microprocessor and the CRTC. Four 74LS157 quad two-input multiplexers, IC 4 to IC 7,

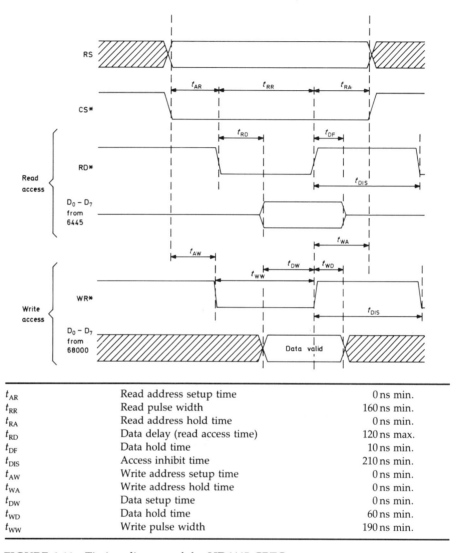

t_{AR}	Read address setup time	0 ns min.
t_{RR}	Read pulse width	160 ns min.
t_{RA}	Read address hold time	0 ns min.
t_{RD}	Data delay (read access time)	120 ns max.
t_{DF}	Data hold time	10 ns min.
t_{DIS}	Access inhibit time	210 ns min.
t_{AW}	Write address setup time	0 ns min.
t_{WA}	Write address hold time	0 ns min.
t_{DW}	Data setup time	0 ns min.
t_{WD}	Data hold time	60 ns min.
t_{WW}	Write pulse width	190 ns min.

FIGURE 6.11   Timing diagram of the HD6445 CRTC

multiplex the memory's 13 address inputs between the address outputs of the CRTC (i.e. MA_0–MA_{12}) and the address outputs of the microprocessor (i.e. A_{01}–A_{13}). Remember that 68000 uses word addressing (i.e. there is no A_{00}) because it has a 16-bit word length. Address output MA_{13} from the CRTC is not required in this application and is simply ignored.

During normal operation, the CRTC has access to the video memory and the output of the address decoder, SELECT*, is inactive-high, disabling the bidirectional data bus transceiver, IC 2. The CRTC scans consecutive video

TABLE 6.1 The registers of the HD6345 CRT controller

CS*	RS	5	4	3	2	1	0	REG. NO.	REGISTER NAME	PROGRAM UNIT	SYMBOL	R/W	7	6	5	4	3	2	1	0
																DATA BIT				
1	x	x	x	x	x	x	x	–	–	–	–	–								
0	0	x	x	x	x	x	x	AR	Address register	–	–	W								
0	1	0	0	0	0	0	0	R0	Horizontal total characters	Character	Nht	W								
0	1	0	0	0	0	0	1	R1	Horizontal displayed characters	Character	Nhd	W								
0	1	0	0	0	0	1	0	R2	Horizontal sync position	Character	Nhsp	W								
0	1	0	0	0	0	1	1	R3	Sync width	*	Nvsw, Nhsw	W	Wv_3	Wv_2	Wv_1	Wv_0	Wh_3	Wh_2	Wh_1	Wh_3
0	1	0	0	0	1	0	0	R4	Vertical total rows	Row	Nvt	W								
0	1	0	0	0	1	0	1	R5	Vertical total adjust	Raster	Nadj	W								
0	1	0	0	0	1	1	0	R6	Vertical displayed rows	Row	Nvd	W								
0	1	0	0	0	1	1	1	R7	Vertical sync position	Row	Nvsp	W								
0	1	0	0	1	0	0	0	R8	Interlace mode and skew	–	–	W	C_1	C_0	D_1	D_0			V	S
0	1	0	0	1	0	0	1	R9	Maximum raster address	Raster	Nr	W								
0	1	0	0	1	0	1	0	R10	Cursor 1 start	Raster	Ncs_1	W		B_1	P_1					
0	1	0	0	1	0	1	1	R11	Cursor 1 end	Raster	Nce_1	W								
0	1	0	0	1	1	0	0	R12	Screen 1 start address (H)	Address†	–	R/W								
0	1	0	0	1	1	0	1	R13	Screen 1 start address (L)	Address†	–	R/W								
0	1	0	0	1	1	1	0	R14	Cursor 1 address (H)	Address†	–	R/W								
0	1	0	0	1	1	1	1	R15	Cursor 1 address (L)	Address†	–	R/W								
0	1	0	1	0	0	0	0	R16	Light pen (H)	–	–	R								
0	1	0	1	0	0	0	1	R17	Light pen (L)	–	–	R								
0	1	0	1	0	0	1	0	R18	Screen 2 start position	Row	–	R/W								

TABLE 6.1 (*continued*)

							Reg	Description			R/W	Bit fields
0	1	0	0	0	1	1	R19	Screen 2 start address (H)	Address†	–	R/W	
0	1	0	0	1	0	0	R20	Screen 2 start address (L)	Address†	–	R/W	
0	1	0	0	1	0	1	R21	Screen 3 start position	Row	–	R/W	
0	1	0	0	1	1	0	R22	Screen 3 start address (H)	Address†	–	R/W	
0	1	0	0	1	1	1	R23	Screen 3 start address (L)	Address†	–	R/W	
0	1	0	1	0	0	0	R24	Screen 4 start position	Row	–	R/W	
0	1	0	1	0	0	1	R25	Screen 4 start address (H)	Address†	–	R/W	
0	1	0	1	0	1	0	R26	Screen 4 start address (L)	Address†	–	R/W	
0	1	0	1	0	1	1	R27	Vertical sync position adjust	Raster	Nvad	W	
0	1	0	1	1	0	0	R28	Light pen raster	–	–	R	DP
0	1	0	1	1	0	1	R29	Smooth scrolling	Raster	Nss	R/W	
0	1	0	1	1	1	0	R30	Control 1	–	–	W	VE VS IB IL SY TV SP_1 SP_0
0	1	0	1	1	1	1	R31	Control 2	–	–	W	SS_4 SS_3 SS_2 SS_1 RI
								Status	–	–	R	AI E SB SL
0	1	1	0	0	0	0	R32	Control 3	–	–	W	CM C_2 CW_1 CW_2 MW TC DR
0	1	1	0	0	0	1	R33	Memory width offset	Character	Nof	R/W	
0	1	1	0	0	1	0	R34	Cursor 2 start	Raster	Ncs_2	W	B_2 P_2
0	1	1	0	0	1	1	R35	Cursor 2 end	Raster	Nce_2	W	
0	1	1	0	1	0	0	R36	Cursor 2 address (H)	Address†	–	R/W	
0	1	1	0	1	0	1	R37	Cursor 2 address (L)	Address†	–	R/W	
0	1	1	0	1	1	0	R38	Cursor 1 width	Character	Ncw_1	R/W	
0	1	1	0	1	1	1	R39	Cursor 2 width	Character	Ncw_2	R/W	

Notes: (1) *: Vertical:raster/Horizontal:character
(2) †: Address = address within video RAM

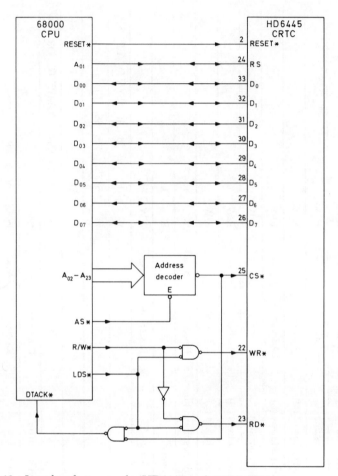

FIGURE 6.12   Interface between the HD6445 and 68000 CPU

Note: The 6445 requires a write pulse (WR∗ low) of 190 ns. As WR∗ is derived from LDS∗, which is low for 115 ns in a write cycle, DTACK∗ must be delayed during a write access.

display (i.e. column) addresses and places the corresponding memory address on MA_0–MA_{13}. The address on MA_0–MA_{13} accesses the video RAM and the resulting code of the character to be displayed is applied to the input of an 8-bit latch, IC 3. The latch is required to cater for the memory access delay. If the output of the video memory were fed directly to the video circuits of the dot generator, it would be possible that, due to the access time of the RAM plus circuit delays, the data might change at the moment the dots were being drawn on the screen. Therefore, the output of the video RAM is staticized by a latch. Figure 6.14 provides a timing diagram for Figure 6.13 during CRTC accesses.

Whenever the CRTC accesses the video memory, it reads characters and

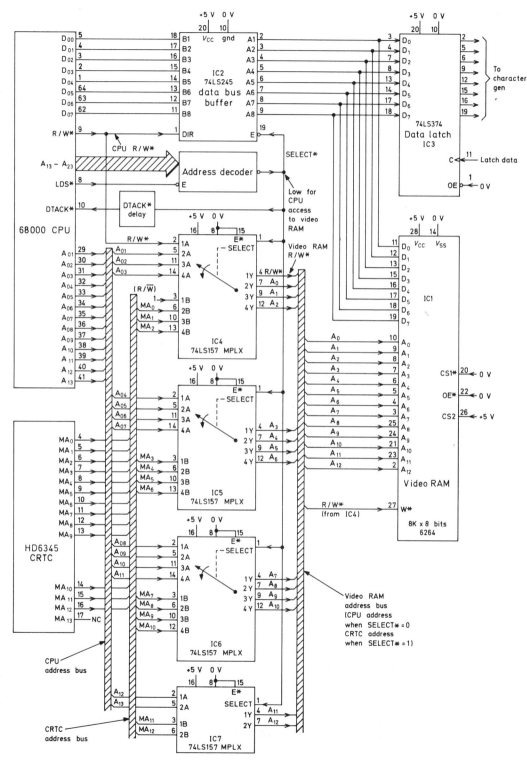

FIGURE 6.13 The circuit of a video RAM and its interface to a CRTC/microprocessor

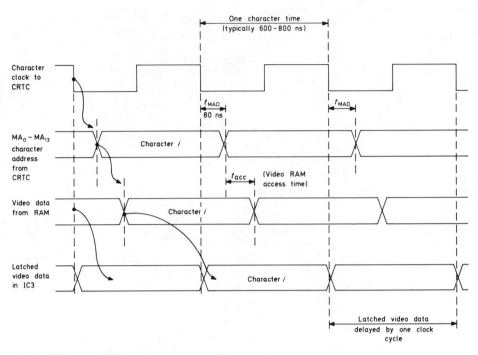

FIGURE 6.14   The timing diagram of Figure 6.13

therefore the memory's R/W* input must be electrically high. The R/W* input of video RAM IC 1 is multiplexed between an electrical high when SELECT* = 1 and R/W* from the microprocessor when SELECT* = 0.

Suppose the microprocessor wishes to access the video RAM. When the 68000 generates the valid address of a lower-order byte falling within the video RAM's address space, the output of the address decoder, SELECT*, goes active-low. A low level on SELECT* has three effects. First, the address inputs of the video RAM are connected to the address outputs of the microprocessor instead of those from the CRTC. Second, the W* input to the RAM is connected to the microprocessor's R/W* output so that the RAM executes a read or a write cycle depending on the type of microprocessor access. Third, the SELECT* output from the address decoder enables the 74LS245 tri-state buffer, IC 2, between the microprocessor's data bus and the RAM's data bus. The direction of data transfer is determined by connecting the 74LS245's DIR input to the 68000's R/W* output.

Note that the microprocessor has unconditional access to the video memory and may read from or write to the memory at any time. If the CRTC is reading the video RAM when the 68000 accesses the RAM, the CRTC's access is aborted and the data sent to the character generator is determined by the 68000. This data is, effectively, random and causes a glitch in the display, which appears as a speckle on the screen lasting only $\frac{1}{60}$ of a second. However, a burst of microprocessor accesses can prove visually irritating and it is better either to blank the display during a microprocessor access or to perform all accesses during the retrace period when the display is already blanked. We can restrict the time during which the host computer is permitted to access the video RAM to the vertical retrace period, because the CRTC can be programmed to interrupt the microprocessor at the start of the vertical retrace blanking period. Equally, the microprocessor can poll the CRTC to determine whether it is actively displaying a line or is in its blanking mode.

6.2.3 The dot generator circuit

The HD6345 CRTC, like many of its contemporaries, generates only character timing signals and users must design their own video circuits to handle signals at the dot-clock rate. The production of the video signal has been omitted from the first generation of video controllers because LSI technology was not able to handle signals at dot-clock rates of 8 MHz or more until the mid 1980s.

The CRTC continually scans the video display memory in sympathy with the raster-scan display to generate the address, on MA_0–MA_{13}, of the next character to be displayed. We have seen how this address is used to interrogate the video RAM and how the corresponding character code is clocked into a latch. We now show how this character code is employed to produce a video signal.

Figure 6.15 gives the circuit diagram of a possible arrangement that takes a character code from the video RAM and converts it into the dots making up the character. The character code from the video RAM is clocked in the octal, positive-edge triggered latch, IC 1, by a character clock, whose frequency is the character rate. Figure 6.16 provides a timing diagram for the circuit of Figure 6.15.

The output of the octal latch is applied to the character-select inputs of the character generator ROM, IC 2. Row address lines RA0 to RA3 from the CRTC, IC 8, are also applied to the character generator to select the line of the character to be displayed. The output of the character generator, representing a line of seven dots, is applied to an eight-input shift register, IC 3. The eighth dot input, D_h, is permanently connected to ground to provide a single-dot intercharacter spacing. Dots are clocked out of the shift register by the free running dot-clock, IC 7. The serial output of the shift register, IC 3, is a stream of dots and is used to create the actual video signal to be fed to the TV display.

The dot-clock is divided by eight in synchronous counter IC 6 to generate a character clock at a rate of dot-clock/8 at the Qc output of IC 6. The character clock serves two functions: it clocks the CRTC and it latches data from the video RAM into the octal latch.

After the eight dots of a character have been clocked out of IC 3, the shift

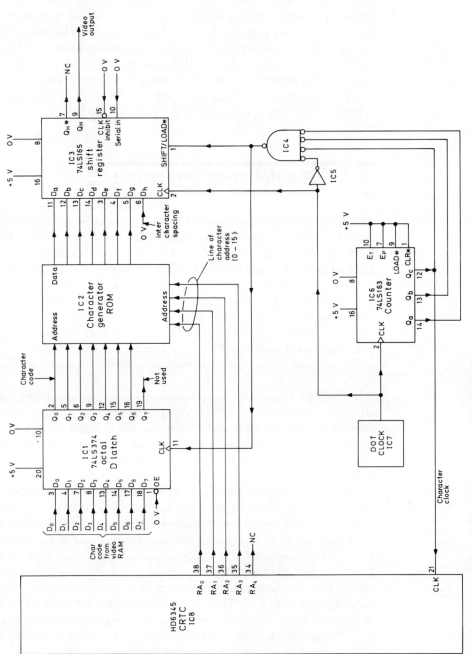

FIGURE 6.15 Converting the character code into a dot pattern

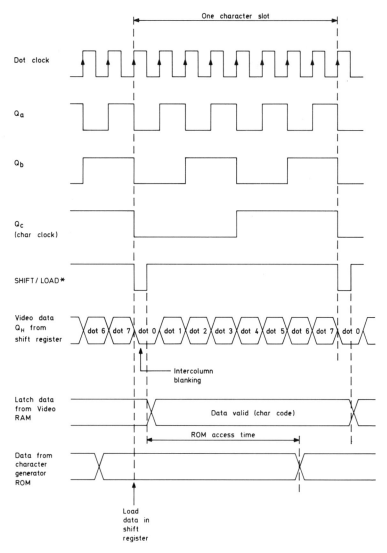

FIGURE 6.16 The timing diagram of the dot generator

register is loaded with the eight dots of the next character. The SHIFT/LOAD*
input to IC 3 is generated by detecting the first half-cycle of a series of eight dots
(ICs 4 and 5). SHIFT/LOAD* is the logical AND (negative logic) of the
inverted dot clock, Qa, Qb and Qc from IC 6.

At first sight, the function of the octal latch, IC 1, in Figure 6.15 might not
be clear. Latches, or more correctly *pipeline latches*, are required in digital
systems to hold data constant and to stop it changing while it is being used as

an input to some process. Figure 6.17 demonstrates why the pipeline register is required in a video display.

The CRTC also generates the horizontal and vertical synchronization pulses required by the CRT display to synchronize its scanning with the CRTC. Sync pulses can be fed to the display system directly or they can be combined

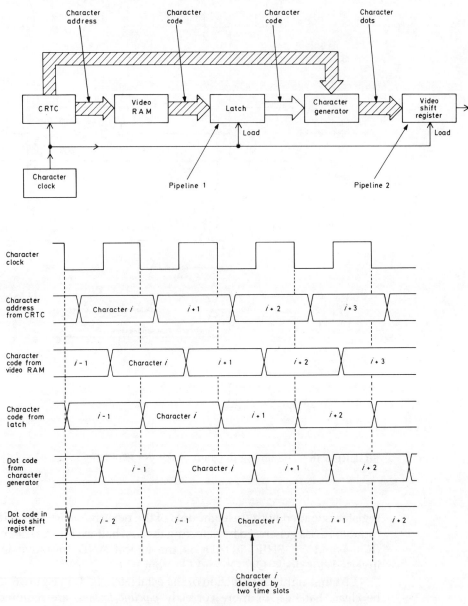

FIGURE 6.17   Use of pipeline registers in video displays

with the video signal to give what is called a composite video signal. This composite video signal is later divided into a video signal and separate sync pulses by circuits in the display system. We have now described most of the circuitry of a CRT display based on the HD6345. The next step is to show how the CRTC is programmed.

6.3 Registers of the HD6345 CRTC

The HD6345 CRTC has a total of 40 user-programmable internal registers plus a pointer register. In spite of such a profusion of registers, the HD6345 is easier to program than many apparently simpler devices. As we have already stated, only two registers are directly accessible from the host microprocessor: a pointer register at the base address (i.e. $RS = A_{01} = 0$), and a data register at the base address + 2 (i.e. $RS = A_{01} = 1$). Internal registers, other than the pointer register, are accessed by loading their number into the pointer register (i.e. 0 to 39) and then reading from or writing to the data register.

The 40 user-programmable registers of the CRTC are illustrated in Table 6.1. Like most peripherals, the majority of these registers are set up once by an initialization routine after a reset of the CRTC and are then totally ignored. In the following description we provide a simplified version of this CRTC and omit some of its complexities.

6.3.1 Display format registers

At the beginning of this chapter, we demonstrated how a raster-scan video display divides the screen into rows and columns and then displays each character as a pattern of dots within a character cell. The CRTC's display format registers define the structure of the display in terms of character duration, raster-scan period, rasters per field and field rate. Figure 6.18 shows how some of the CRTC's registers relate to the display format.

Setting up the display is not particularly complex when we realize that, for a standard TV style display, almost all we need to know is that there are $262\frac{1}{2}$ horizontal scans every $\frac{1}{60}$ second ($312\frac{1}{2}$ per $\frac{1}{50}$ second CCIR).

Let us consider an example. Suppose a designer wishes to display 64 characters per line on a domestic television. Experience shows that this is about the highest horizontal resolution possible with a domestic TV. High-bandwidth monitors can readily display 80 to 120 or more characters per line. We will consider a CCIR display with 50 fields of $312\frac{1}{2}$ lines per second. The character font is to be 9 lines by 7 dots within a 12 line by 8 dot matrix.

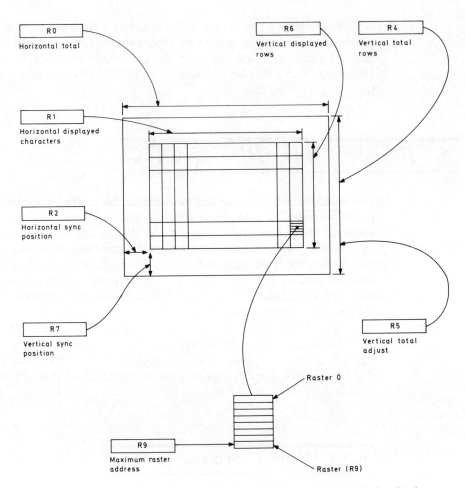

FIGURE 6.18 The relationship between the CRTC's registers and the display

The duration of a single line is $20\,\text{ms}/(312.5) = 64\,\mu\text{s}$. It is tempting to think that each character has a duration of line time/number of characters = $64/64\,\mu\text{s} = 1\,\mu\text{s}$. Unfortunately, the duration of a line must also include the left and right blanked margins plus the retrace period. The time available for the display of the 64 characters is therefore considerably less than the total line time of $64\,\mu\text{s}$.

Assume that a line is made up of exactly n character slots, of which m are actually displayed. A typical TV can readily display about two-thirds of a horizontal line. Therefore, if $m = \frac{2}{3}$ line = 64 characters, the total line contains $n = 96$ character slots. We will now look at the display format registers, one by one, and show how they are programmed to suit the above example.

Controlling horizontal resolution

Register R0

This contains the total number of character positions per line minus one. Note that R0 includes both displayed and blanked characters. Therefore $[R0] = n - 1 = 96 - 1 = 95$. In other words, R0 defines the duration of a line in terms of the character period.

Register R1

This contains the total number of characters to be displayed per line. In this example, $[R1] = m = 64$ by definition.

Register R9

This contains the *maximum raster address* which is defined as the number of lines per character (i.e. per row) minus one, when the CRTC is operating in the *non-interlace* mode considered here. In this case, R9 is loaded with 11. Note that R9 is programmed with the total number of raster lines per character, rather than the raster lines per character font (in this case 9). Only bits 0–4 of R9 are defined and, therefore, the maximum raster address is 31. When the 6345 is operating in the interlace sync and video mode (see later), R9 must be loaded with the number of lines per character minus 2.

Vertical resolution

Having dealt with the horizontal resolution of the display, we must consider the vertical resolution, which is expressed in terms of the number of rows of characters, rather than the number of raster lines. However, the number of raster lines taken up by the display should come to the CCIR standard value of $312\frac{1}{2}$ lines per field.

Register R4

This contains the total number of rows of characters per field (including blanked rows) minus one. As there are 12 raster lines per row, the contents of R4 are given by: $312.5/12 - 1 = 26.04 - 1 = 25.04$. However, R4 contains only the integer part of this value and is therefore loaded with 25.

Register R5

This is called the *total raster adjust register* because it compensates for the fact that R4 contains only the integer part of the rows per field, while a field consists of an exact number of rows plus a few raster-scan lines. The value of R5 can be expressed as

lines/field = total rows × lines/row + total raster adjust

$$= ([R4] + 1) \times ([R9] + 1) + [R5]$$

In this case, we have: $312.5 = 26 \times 12 + [R5]$. Therefore, $[R5] = 0.5$. As the contents of R5 must be an integer, R5 may be loaded with either 0 or 1. Only bits 0–4 of R5 are defined and the maximum vertical total raster adjust is 31.

Register R6

This contains the number of rows of characters displayed. As we know that the maximum number of rows is 26 and that about $\frac{1}{3}$ of this is allocated to retrace and top/bottom margins, the maximum number of rows per field is approximately 17. Therefore, we will select a 16-row display and load R6 with 16.

Sync control

In addition to defining the physical display format, it is necessary to set up the horizontal and vertical synchronizing pulses that synchronize the CRT in the display with the successive fields generated by the CRTC. There are four quantities to be defined here; the width of the horizontal and vertical synchronizing pulses and their position with respect to the raster-scan line and field, respectively. Figure 6.19 illustrates the relationship between the sync pulses and the video waveform.

Register R2

This defines the horizontal synchronizing pulse position. The value in R2 is the position of the synchronizing pulse, measured in units of characters, less one. The contents of R2 determine where the displayed characters fall with respect to the edges of the CRT. In other words, R2 must be chosen to centralize the display in the horizontal plane. The effect of increasing the value in R2 is to shift the display on the screen left. Decreasing R2 shifts the display right.

Register R3

This sets the width of both the vertical and horizontal synchronizing pulses simultaneously. The format of R3 is given in Figure 6.20. The vertical sync width is defined in terms of rasters (scan lines) and the horizontal sync width in terms of characters. Note that a vertical sync pulse width of 16H (i.e. 16 horizontal lines) is provided when V3–V0 = 0,0,0,0. The correct vertical and horizontal sync pulse widths are obtained from the appropriate display

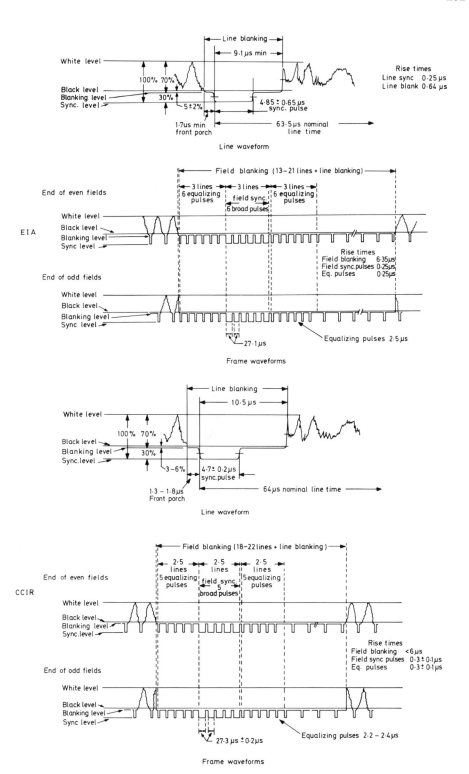

FIGURE 6.19 The composite video signal

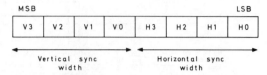

FIGURE 6.20   The format of register R3 – the vertical and horizontal sync pulse width control register

standards (i.e. EIA in the USA and CCIR in Europe). The EIA horizontal synchronizing pulse width is $4.85\,\mu s$ (CCIR = $4.7\,\mu s$) and the vertical synchronizing pulse width is 9 lines (CCIR = 4 lines). However, most displays are fairly tolerant of errors in sync pulse widths. Note that a horizontal sync width of zero is not permitted.

Register R7

This is the vertical counterpart of the horizontal sync pulse position register R2. The contents of R7 minus one define the position of the vertical synchronizing pulse. The value in R7 is expressed in terms of rows. When the contents of R7 are increased, the position of the display is shifted upward.

Register R27

The vertical sync position adjust register is used to fine-tune the vertical sync position within the line set by the vertical sync position register (i.e. R7). Therefore, the vertical sync position is given by $([R7] - 1) \times \text{rows} + [R27] \times \text{rasters}$. Only the five least-significant bits of R27 are defined and therefore the maximum value that can be loaded in R27 is 31. Note that R27 is enabled (i.e. used by the CRTC) only if the SY bit of control register 1 (R30) is set.

6.3.2 The CRTC mode control registers

In addition to defining the physical parameters of the display, the CRTC has mode-control registers that determine the type of display and a status register.

Register R8

This has the format defined by Figure 6.21 and determines three attributes of the CRTC: the scan mode, the cursor skew and the display blanking skew. The least two-significant bits of R8, V and S, select the scan mode as illustrated in Figure 6.21. DISPTMG enables the display (when low DISPTMG blanks the screen to provide upper, lower, left and right margins) and CUDISP is a *cursor enable* output that can be used to highlight a particular position on the display.

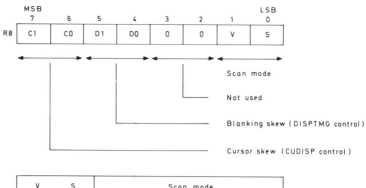

	Bits		Value		Control function	Control effect
C1	C0	0	0	Cursor output	No skew
C1	C0	0	1	Cursor output	Skew by one character
C1	C0	1	0	Cursor output	Skew by two characters
C1	C0	1	1	Cursor output	No cursor output
D1	D0	0	0	Display enable	No skew
D1	D0	0	1	Display enable	Skew by one character
D1	D0	1	0	Display enable	Skew by two characters
D1	D0	1	1	Display enable	No DISPTMG output

FIGURE 6.21   The format of the scan mode, cursor and blanking skew control register, R8

The scan mode selected by V and S of register R8 determines whether or not the display uses interlaced fields. Remember we said that an EIA standard television picture is made up of pairs of fields each of $262\frac{1}{2}$ lines, and that two fields make a frame of 525 lines. Well, this only works because the two successive frames of a TV picture carry very *similar* information. The slight difference between the pairs of fields is put together by the eye (the brain) to increase the effective resolution.

Unfortunately, if text is displayed in the interlaced mode, the successive fields vary so much in content that the character update rate becomes effectively 30 Hz and is very unpleasant to the eye. Consequently, it is unusual to operate CRTCs with full interlacing and with 525 raster-scan lines. Instead, the display is treated as $262\frac{1}{2}$ pairs of lines which carry identical information. Now there is no real difference between successive fields and the flicker is removed at the cost of a vertical resolution of only $262\frac{1}{2}$ lines, permitting about

16–24 rows of text. Full interlacing can be used if the field rate is increased or if the CRT has a long-persistence coating which retains the image.

Figure 6.22 relates the scan modes of the CRTC to the displayed text. In the non-interlaced mode or the interlaced mode with identical fields, the resolution provides twice the resolution of a single field. In the interlaced sync and video mode, interlacing provides twice the resolution of a single field.

Bits D1 and D0 of R8 control the display timing signal skew, DISPTMG, from the CRTC, and bits C1 and C0 control the cursor display skew, CUDISP, as illustrated in Figure 6.21. DISPTMG enables the display (when low

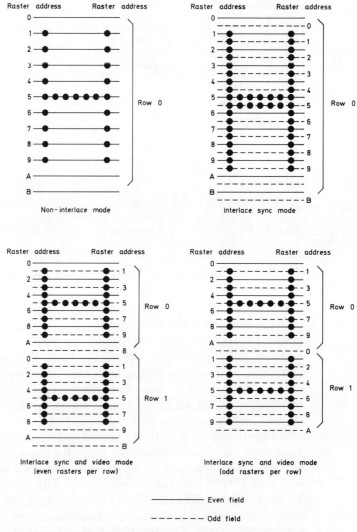

FIGURE 6.22   The effect of the HD6345 scan modes on displayed text

DISPTMG blanks the picture to provide margins) and CUDISP enables the cursor to highlight a particular position on the display. Control bits C1, C0 and D1, D0 are not as complex as they appear – they simply delay either the cursor output or the display enable output from the CRTC. The older 6845 lacks this function and any delays must be supplied by external hardware.

Why then do we need these delays? These delays are related to the problems of timing and video pipelining mentioned earlier. When I first built my own display from random logic, it worked, but the first column of text was filled with gibberish and the last column was missing. After thinking about the problem, the solution was quite simple. As soon as the column display counter generates the address of the first column, the display is unblanked (i.e. enabled). At the same time the column address is applied to the video RAM, the contents of the video RAM at this address are applied to the character generator ROM and the output of the ROM is loaded into the video shift register. Of course, all these actions take time to execute, and the video output for character i is not available during the ith time slot. Therefore the video data in my display was *undefined* at the moment the display was enabled in column zero. My solution to this problem was very simple – I delayed the display enable signal in a D flip-flop to give the video signal time to catch up.

The manufacturers of the HD6345 provide programmable delays (or *skews*) of 0, 1 or 2 character periods. The skew may be between the characters being displayed and the DISPTMG output of the CRTC, or the skew may be between the character being displayed and the cursor control output, CUDISP. A typical value for the contents of R8 is C1,C0 = 0,1 (one character skew in display enable timing), D1,D0 = 0,1 (one character skew in cursor display control) and V,S = 0,1 (non-interlace video with interlaced sync). These values give [R8] = 0101xx01 = \$51.

Register R30

This is called control register 1 and its 8 bits are used to perform four functions: external sync control, interrupt control, vertical sync control and screen partition control. The structure of register R30 is illustrated in Figure 6.23.

The 2-bit screen partition field of R30 (P0, P1) enables the CRTC to display 1, 2, 3 or 4 screens. These screens are *logical* screens and should not be confused with the CRT screen which is a *physical* screen. Remember that a CRTC generates memory addresses that map characters in the video RAM onto a CRT screen. Consequently, a CRTC can map the contents of any contiguous block of memory onto the physical screen. The HD6345 goes one step further than first generation CRTCs and permits up to four *separate* regions of the memory to be displayed on the screen at any time. Therefore, we can maintain up to four independent displays (on the same CRT screen).

The way in which the HD6345 maintains these screens is rather rudimentary. Figure 6.24 provides examples of split-screen displays. In Figure 6.24(a) all four screens are displayed at the same time, while in Figure 6.24(b)

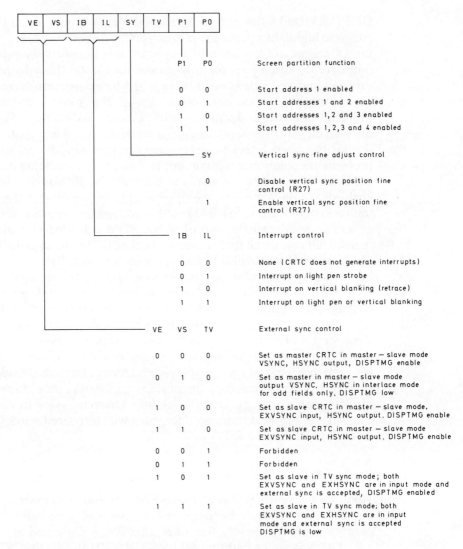

FIGURE 6.23   The structure of register R30 – the control register 1

only screens 1 and 4 are displayed and in Figure 6.24(c) only screens 1, 4 and 2 are displayed. The starting positions for split-screens 2, 3 and 4 are defined by the CRTC's registers R18, R21 and R24 respectively. Split-screen 1 always starts from row zero. These three registers hold the starting address (i.e. row) of the corresponding screen as demonstrated in Figure 6.25. According to Figure 6.23, the four screens cannot be turned on or off individually, as bits P1 and P0 permit only four choices of split-screen displays. The options available are screen 1, screens 1 and 2, screens 1, 2 and 3, and screens 1, 2, 3 and 4. Screen 1 is the basic screen and cannot be turned off. Figure 6.26 shows the relationship

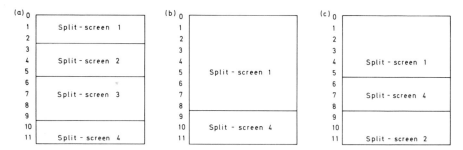

FIGURE 6.24 The relationship between physical and logical screens. (a) All screens displayed Screen 2 start register = 2, Screen 3 start register = 5, Screen 4 start register = 9. (b) Screens 2 and 4 displayed Screen 4 start register = 8, Screen 2 start register ⩾ 11, Screen 3 start register ⩾ 11. (c) Screens 1, 4 and 2 displayed Screen 2 start register = 8, Screen 4 start register = 5, Screen 3 start register ⩾ 11

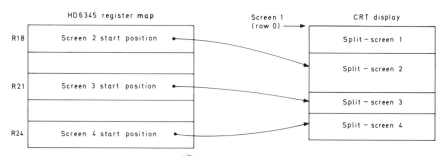

FIGURE 6.25 The CRT's screen start position registers; the starting position of a screen is always one more than the value stored in a start position register; split-screen 1 always starts at row 0

between the video display, the video memory and the CRTC. Remember that the video memory is loaded by the host microprocessor and is under the control of the programmer.

The CRTC contains four pairs of registers: R12,R13; R19,R20; R22,R23; and R25,R26. These define the starting address in the RAM of each of the screens. Start address registers are 14 bits wide with the register at the *lower* address providing bits MA_8–MA_{13} and the register at the higher address providing bits MA_0–MA_7. R12 and R13 determine the start of screen 1, R19 and R20 determine the start of screen 2, R22 and R23 determine the start of screen 3 and R25 and R26 determine the start of screen 4.

Screen 1 starts at the top right-hand corner of the display and fills the display if it is the only screen enabled. The other screens start at the points indicated by the three 8-bit start position registers (register R18 for screen 2, R21

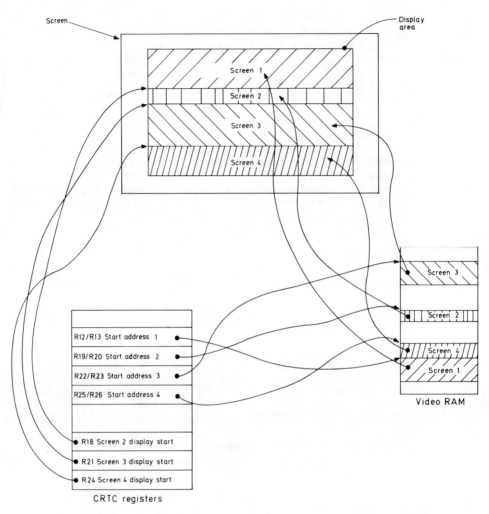

FIGURE 6.26   Relationship between the CRTC's screens, registers and video RAM

for screen 3 and R24 for screen 4). Now admit it, you are confused by the *screen start address* and the *screen start position* registers. The *screen start address* is the location of the screen image in the video RAM; it is a 14-bit memory address and it has no effect on the presentation of the display. The *screen start register* tells the CRTC where the screen goes (i.e. starts) on the display and is measured in rows from the top of the screen.

These screens are crude versions of the windows associated with operating systems like GEM or Microsoft's Windows. For example, it is possible to devote screen 1 to a program listing, screen 2 to the run-time output of the program and screen 3 to input commands. Of course, it is not necessary to control screens by hardware in the same way that the HD6345 does it. Split-screens can be handled entirely by software techniques by moving data into the video RAM. However, screens manipulated by hardware can be switched on or off or moved around much more rapidly than software screens.

The *vertical sync position fine adjust function* field of control register 1, R30, has a simple function. When SY = 0, the vertical sync position fine adjust register (i.e. R27) is disabled and when SY = 1 it is enabled.

The *interrupt control field* of control register 1, bits IB and IL, is used to enable or to mask interrupts. The CRTC can be programmed to generate an interrupt by asserting its active-high IRQ output under two circumstances. The first is when the CRTC begins its vertical blanking period. As this is a relatively long period in comparison with the microprocessor's cycle time, the microprocessor can update the video RAM during the time that the display is blanked and so avoid contention between the microprocessor and the CRTC for the memory.

The HD6345's IRQ output, pin 19, is a multifunction pin and can be programmed as a *combined* cursor display enable output, CUDISP, and IRQ output, or it can be programmed as a dual-port memory, DPRAM, access-inhibit output. Figure 6.27 shows how the IRQ/CUDISP output pin is used to generate interrupts to the host CPU. IRQ/CUDISP is asserted *both* during the cursor display period *and* the vertical retrace period. Fortunately, it is easy to distinguish between these two functions, because CUDISP is active only when the display enable output, DISPTMG pin 18, is active-high and IRQ is active only when DISPTMG is low. A D flip-flop is required to synchronize IRQ with the character clock to avoid hazards (glitches) due to the almost simultaneous logic transitions on DISPTMG and IRQ/CUDISP. Figure 6.27 also provides a timing diagram for the IRQ/CUDISP circuit. Note that IRQ is cleared during the retrace period by reading the contents of the status register, R31.

The second possible interrupt source is a light pen. A light pen is so called because it looks like a pen and can be pressed against the screen. It is, in fact, a light-sensitive diode which generates a pulse when the raster passes underneath it. Registers R16 and R17 are loaded with the 14-bit address in video RAM of the character at the position of the light pen. R16 contains the 6 higher-order bits of the light pen address and R17 contains the 8 lower-order bits. When an interrupt is generated by the light pen, the microprocessor can read R16/R17 to determine where the pen is located on the surface of the CRT. In this way the system is able to interact with the user. For example, a menu of functions can be displayed on the screen and the operator invited to select an option by pressing the light pen against the appropriate option.

Synchronizing the display to TV displays

The *external sync function* field of R30 has three bits, VE, VS and TV, which are used to control the CRTC's external synchronization and DISPTMG output.

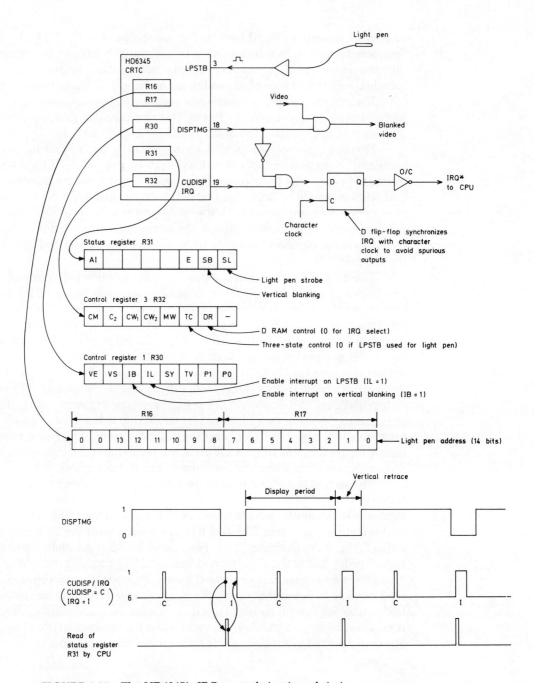

FIGURE 6.27 The HD6345's IRQ control circuit and timing

We have already said that the video signal sent to a CRT display must include synchronizing information to keep the beam in step with the controller. Now suppose it is necessary to display text on the same screen as a normal television picture – the picture may come from an off-air receiver, a video cassette recorder or a camera. A special problem arises when we attempt to display two or more pictures from *independent* sources on the same CRT. The problem is that it is not possible to *add* video signals like audio signals, because two independent video signals are not synchronized. The solution adopted by the HD6345 is to operate in a slave mode and to accept *external* synchronizing signals.

Figure 6.28 shows how the CRTC can be synchronized to a display. The horizontal and vertical sync pulses from the master display generator are applied to the EXHSYNC and EXVSYNC inputs of the CRTC. In this mode VE = 1 and TV = 1. The CRTC's own DISPTMG (display enable) output may be enabled or disabled by setting or clearing the VS bit of R30. Note that in Figure 6.28, the clock input to the CRTC must be manually synchronized by forcing the counter to zero at the start of each horizontal synchronizing pulse. Only vague details of the HD6345's external synchronization modes are provided here; further information is provided in its data sheet.

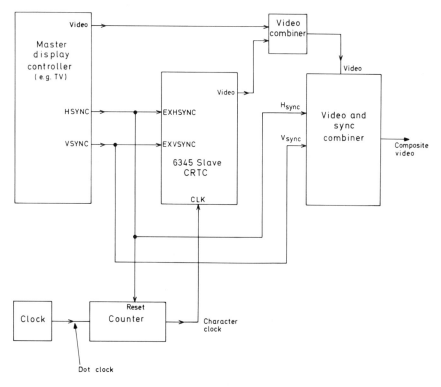

FIGURE 6.28 Synchronizing the HD6345 CRTC with an external system

6.3.3 The cursor control registers

A cursor is a *marker* displayed on a screen which serves to indicate the current *active position*. We use the expression *active position* to indicate the place at which the next character will be displayed. The cursor may take one of many forms. It may be a white square, an underscore, or the current character in reverse video (i.e. black on white instead of white on black). The cursor may be steady or it may blink on and off. Without a cursor, the video display would be difficult for a human operator to use, because he or she would not be able to 'visualize' where the next character would go, especially if a series of spaces or new lines had been entered. As text or control characters are entered, the cursor is automatically moved to reflect the current active position. Of course, the cursor movement is carried out by software running on the host computer and not by the CRTC itself.

The HD6345 devotes five registers to the control of a cursor. R10 and R11 define the size of the cursor, R14 and R15 define the position of the cursor on the display and R38 defines the cursor's width. The cursor start register, R10, performs a dual role. Two bits, B1 and P1 define the cursor display mode as indicated in Figure 6.29. The options provided by B1 and P1 are cursor off, cursor on and cursor blinking. When blinking, the cursor is on for 16 fields and off for 16 fields or on for 32 fields and off for 32 fields.

The least-significant 5 bits of R10 determine the raster (i.e. line) at which the cursor begins. Remember that R9 contains the number of rasters per row less one and the rasters are numbered 0 to [R9] starting at the top. Figure 6.30 illustrates the relationship between R9, R10 and R11 (R11 contains the address of the end of the cursor). From Figure 6.30 it can be seen that any subset of a character area can be defined as a cursor.

The position or address of the cursor is expressed as a 14-bit value and is held in R14 and R15, with R14 holding the most significant 6 bits. The address of the cursor is loaded into R14 and R15 by the host computer. That is, the CRTC does not determine the cursor position itself. As each new character is loaded in the video RAM, the cursor position is updated by the appropriate software.

The cursor width register, R38, defines the width of the cursor in terms of characters. Writing a zero to R38 defines a cursor of zero width which, of course, disables the cursor. In general, the vast majority of displays define the cursor width as one single character. Note that R38 is not active until control bit 5 (CW1) of control register 3 (R32) is set.

Unlike most first generation CRTCs, the HD6345 provides two cursors: cursor 1 is defined as above and cursor 2 is defined by the contents of R34, R35 (cursor 2 start, end), R36, R37 (cursor 2 address) and R39 (cursor 2 width). The cursor 2 width register, R39, is enabled when CW2 (bit 4 of control register 3, R32) is set. When the CRTC is in the DPRAM mode, R39 has a different function

R10   Cursor 1 start register

B1	P1	Cursor display mode
0	0	Display cursor without blinking
0	1	No cursor displayed
1	0	Cursor blinks in 16 - field sync
1	1	Cursor blinks in 32 - field sync

R11   Cursor 1 end address

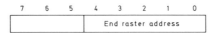

R14, R15   Cursor address

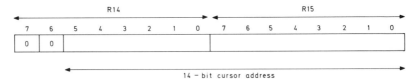

FIGURE 6.29 Format of the cursor control registers

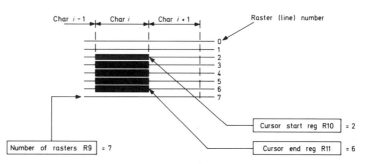

FIGURE 6.30 The relationship between R9, R10 and R11

and cursor 2 cannot be displayed. Figure 6.31 demonstrates how the HD6345 supports two active cursors at the same time. Note that the cursors can take different forms and widths. Once again, it must be stressed that we can have as many software cursors as we like merely by writing the appropriate symbol at the desired point in the video RAM.

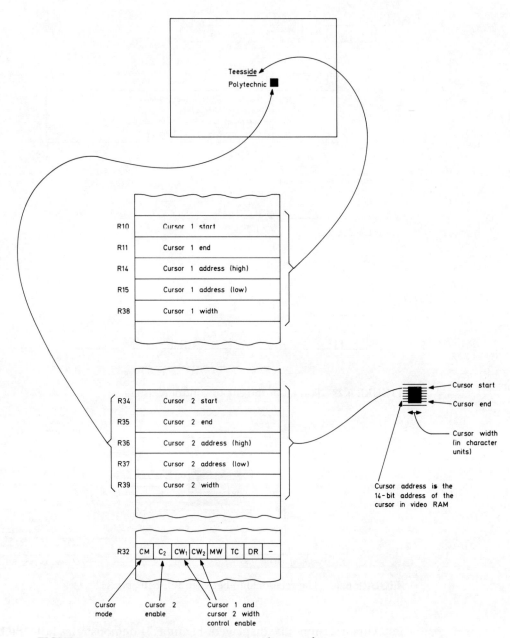

FIGURE 6.31 Displaying two cursors simultaneously

As the CRTC scans a physical screen line by line, the CUDISP (cursor display) output can be used by an external video circuit to generate the actual cursor as illustrated in Figure 6.32. Whenever, the CUDISP output is active-high, the EOR gate IC 4a inverts the video signal to provide a reverse-video cursor. Note that the CUDISP output can be delayed by 0, 1 or 2 character times with respect to the current character address from the CRTC, as we have already explained. Figure 6.33 demonstrates the effect of CUDISP in both normal and reversed video modes.

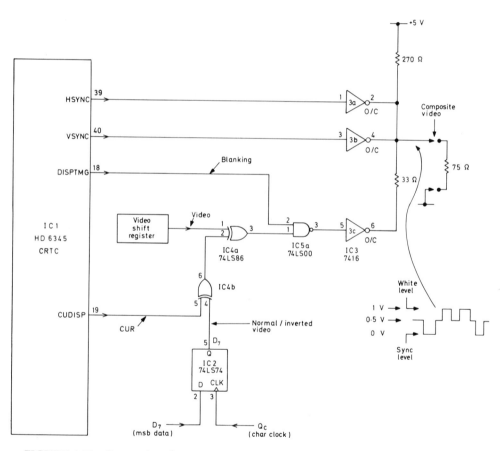

FIGURE 6.32 Generating the cursor

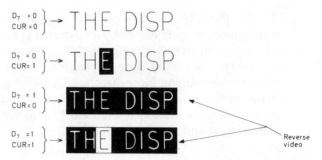

FIGURE 6.33 The effect of CUDISP on both normal and reverse video displays

Combining video and sync signals

In Figure 6.32 we have also included the final part of the video circuit required to create a VDT. IC 2, a 74LS74 D flip-flop, delays the most-significant bit from the video RAM by one character period. This bit is used in conjunction with EOR gates IC 4a and IC 4b to provide reverse video whenever $D7 = 1$. Open-collector buffers ICs 3a, 3b and 3c combine the video, HYSYNC and VSYNC signals to provide a composite 3-level video signal suitable for use with a video monitor.

6.3.4 Smooth scrolling registers

The HD6345 supports a facility known as *smooth scrolling*. Whenever text is entered on a display, successive characters are added from left to right and successive rows from top to bottom – in exactly the same way as English is written or printed. When the bottom line of a display has been entered, no new text can be accepted *without* overwriting existing text. The usual procedure for handling this situation is called scrolling, because it mimics the way people used to read scrolls before the invention of books. The current top row of the display is lost and all other rows move up by one row to create a new blank line at the bottom of the display. In other words, we discard the *oldest* line to make way for the *newest*. The majority of first and second generation displays move rows up in one discrete operation resulting in a disconcerting jump. Displays with smooth scrolling are much kinder on the eyes of the viewer than conventional row-at-a-time scrolling. Smooth scrolling is available on the HD6345 in the non-interlace mode and the interlace sync mode, but not in the interlace sync and video mode.

The HD6345 has a smooth scroll register, R29, that defines the starting address of the raster with a row of characters. In normal operation R29 is loaded with zero and the first line of a row starts at raster address zero. By starting a row of characters with a raster address other than zero, the row of characters can be moved up with respect to the row boundaries. In other words, the character is no longer centralized within the imaginary boundaries of the row. Figure 6.34 shows how R29 is used to implement smooth scrolling. By incrementing the contents of R29 each row of characters is moved up by one line (i.e. raster). Note that the CRTC scrolls by one line at a time and that it is the job of the controlling software to execute a sequence of one line scrolls until a whole row has been moved up one position. The number of one line scrolls to be executed is, of course, equal to the number of lines per row.

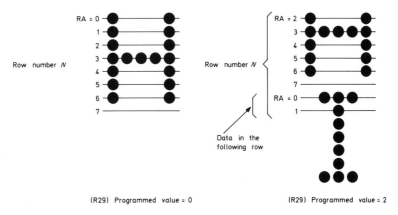

FIGURE 6.34   Smooth scrolling

Smooth scrolling in the vertical direction can be accomplished by changing the start raster address in a character row. Whether scrolling in each split-screen is available or not can be selected. Selected split-screens scroll in the same way up to four split-screens simultaneously.

Smooth scrolling is performed by bits SS1–SS4 of the control 2 register (R31), and the smooth scrolling register (R29).

Smooth scrolling can be used in the non-interlace mode and the interlace sync mode, but not in the interlace sync and video mode.

Control register 2 (R31)

Register R31 is a dual-purpose control/status register. When written to, R31 behaves as control register 2 and controls the smooth scrolling and raster interpolation functions. Figure 6.35 provides the layout of R31.

Before smooth scrolling can be applied to a *logical* screen, the appropriate smooth scrolling bit of R31 must be set. For example, if we wish to scroll screens 1 and 4 we must set bits 4 and 7 respectively of R31.

The raster interpolation bit, RI, selects double-height characters when

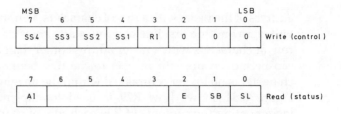

FIGURE 6.35 Control register 2 (R31) (the control and status register)

Control bits
SS1–SS4 = Smooth scrolling enable bits for screens 1–4
        Setting SS*i* to 1 enables screen *i*

RI   = Raster interpolation bit
        RI = 0 enable normal operation
        RI = 1 display double-length character

Status bytes
AI   = Access inhibit status
        AI = 0 Video memory can be accessed
        AI = 1 Video memory cannot be accessed

E   = Display field status
        E = 0 odd field
        E = 1 even field

SB   = Vertical blanking status (SB = 1 = vertical blanking)

SL   = Light pen status
        SL = 0 Light pen strobe not detected
        SL = 1 Light pen strobe detected

RI = 1. All raster interpolation does is to *repeat* each raster so that the number of lines per row is doubled. In normal use, RI = 0. Raster interpolation is available only in the non-interlace and interlace sync modes.

Whenever the control/status register is read by the host microprocessor, its three least-significant bits (E, SB, SL) and its most-significant bit, AI, provide status information. The E-bit (even-bit) is zero during the display of an odd field or when the CRTC is in the non-interlace mode. E is one whenever an even-numbered field is being displayed.

As we have already stated, the SB bit defines the *vertical blanking* status. When SB = 0 a screen is being displayed. When SB = 1 the CRTC is in the vertical blanking mode. During this blanking period, the video RAM can be accessed by the host computer without causing a video memory contention problem.

The light pen status bit, SL, is set to one whenever a pulse is received at the CRTC's light pen strobe input, LPSTB. The SL bit is cleared automatically following a reset or a read operation on R31. That is, SL is *self-clearing*. When a light pen is in use, the host microprocessor polls the SL bit until it is set by a signal on LPSTB. Once LPSTB has been detected asserted, the contents of R16 and R17 can be read to determine the location of the light pen at the moment the strobe was generated.

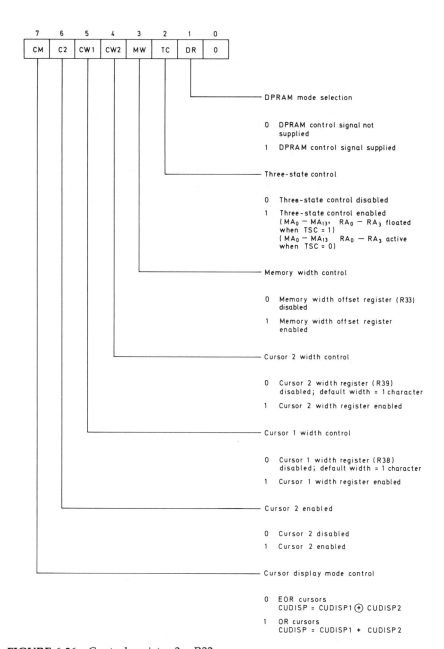

FIGURE 6.36   Control register 3 – R32

The light pen raster register R28 provides a fine position address for the light pen. When the light pen strobe, LPSTB, goes high the current raster address (i.e. line of the row) is written into bits 0–4 of R28. The most significant bit of R28, DP, is a flag bit which is set when the light pen raster register is written to during the display period (i.e. LPSTB is asserted during the display period). The DP flag is zero if the LPSTB strobe occurred during the display blanking period.

6.3.5 Miscellaneous functions of the CRTC

Control register 3 (R32)

Control register 3 controls the cursors and performs the three miscellaneous functions illustrated in Figure 6.36: DPRAM mode control, three-state control and memory width control. The cursor control bits of R32 are almost all self-explanatory. CW1 and CW2 control the width of cursor 1 and cursor 2 respectively. If CW1 = 0, the width of cursor 1 is one character. However, if CW1 = 1, the width of cursor 1 is expressed in units of one character and is given by the contents of R38. Similarly, if CW2 = 1, the width of cursor 2 is given by the contents of R39. The cursor 2 enable bit, C2, enables cursor 2 when C2 = 1. Note that cursor 1 is *permanently* enabled and cannot be turned off.

DPRAM Control

The CRTC operates in a so-called dual-port memory mode, whenever the DR bit of R32 is set. Dual-port memory, DPRAM, has two access ports enabling it to be shared between two devices (e.g. the CPU and the CRTC). There is nothing special about DPRAM – it is nothing more than a block of read/write RAM with internal address and data multiplexers. DPRAM is discussed further in Chapter 8 when we look at its role in multiprocessor systems. The CRTC supports DPRAMs by generating an access control inhibit signal, ACI, that indicates whether the CPU or the CRTC is to have control of the DPRAM.

Figure 6.37 illustrates the general arrangement of DPRAM and Figure 6.38 provides the timing diagram of the 6345's ACI output. In the DPRAM mode, the 6345 automatically switches the video memory between the CPU and the CRTC. The 6345 uses its multifunction IRQ/CUDISP/ACI output pin to generate an active-high access inhibit output whenever the CPU may access the video RAM. Note that when the DPRAM mode is selected, two penalties must be paid: the IRQ function and the cursor 2 function are both unavailable in the DPRAM mode. This is an operational limitation of the 6345 and comes about because of the restrictions on pins and the number of internal registers.

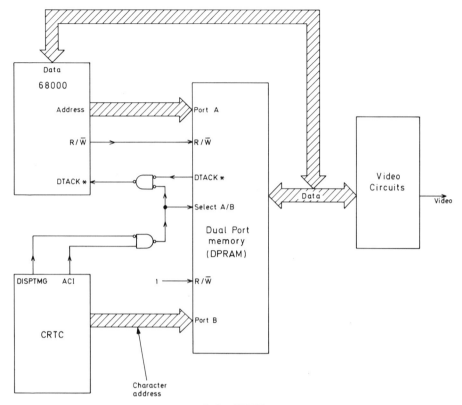

FIGURE 6.37   DPRAM memory and the CRTC

The CRTC determines which device gets control of the video RAM. During normal display operations, the CRTC selects port B. When the CRTC is performing a retrace, its ACI (access inhibit) output is low and DISPTMG is high. ACI high and DISPTMG low is used to select port A and give the 68000 access during the retrace time. DTACK* to the 68000 has been ANDed with the video memory's own DTACK* and with the port select signal in order to force the 68000 to wait if it attempts to access the video RAM during the time it is 'owned' by the CRTC.

Whenever the 6345 is programmed for the DPRAM mode, the CUDISP/ACI pin goes active-high during the retrace period. Figure 6.37 demonstrates that we can distinguish between CUDISP and ACI signals because ACI is active only when the DISPTMG output is active-low. Note that ACI is asserted R39 clock periods after the beginning of the display period.

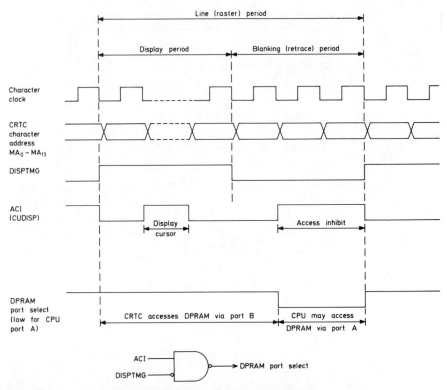

FIGURE 6.38   The HD6345's DPRAM mode timing diagram

Three-state control

The HD6345's LPSTB/TSC input pin can be programmed as a three-state control input by setting the TC bit of control register 3. In the three-state control mode, we lose the CRTC's light pen function but win the ability to design a rather simpler video display controller.

Because both the CRTC and the CPU access the video RAM, we are forced either to use special dual-port RAM or to multiplex the address inputs to the RAM between the CPU and CRTC. Typical address multiplexer circuits require either three or four 74LS157 quad two-input multiplexers. The three-state mode of the 6345 avoids the need for address multiplexers by turning off the CRTC's address outputs on MA_0–MA_{13} as illustrated in Figure 6.39.

Whenever the CPU accesses the video RAM, the active-high TSC signal from the address controller is fed to the CRTC's TSC input and has the effect of tri-stating the MA_0–MA_{13} (and also RA_0–RA_4 outputs. At the same time, the address buffers from the CPU's address bus are enabled to permit the CPU to access the video RAM. Once the CPU has finished its access, the address

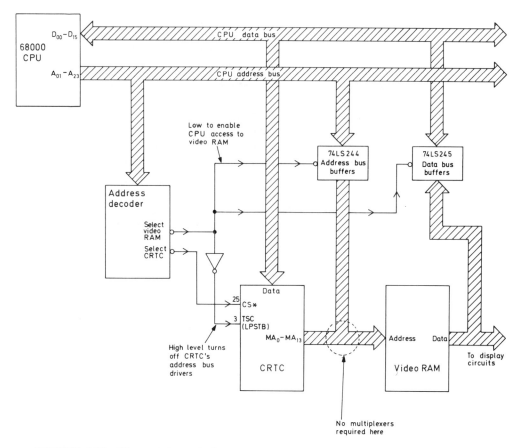

FIGURE 6.39   Three-state control

When the address decoder detects an address within the video RAM, it enables the 68000's address and data buffers. These buffers permit the 68000 to execute a read or a write access to the video RAM. The active-low video RAM chip select signal is also connected to the CRTC's TSC∗ input and has the effect of tristating the CRTC's address outputs on MA_0–MA_{13}. Consequently, the address inputs of the video RAM can be connected to both the address outputs of the CRTC and the address bus buffers from the 68000 without danger of bus contention. This arrangement avoids, typically, three or four quad two-input address multiplexers.

buffers are disabled, TSC negated and the CRTC once more supplies addresses to the video RAM.

Memory-width control

Whenever the MW (memory width enable) bit of R32 is clear, the 6345 operates in a mode in which the *width* of the video display is the same as the width of the display memory. By this, I mean that the video display generates rows of *n* characters and the memory maintains a table of rows, each of which is exactly *n* characters wide. Figure 6.40(a) demonstrates the situation in which a block of video RAM is mapped onto a display. The width of the display is defined by the contents of R1 and the register pair R12,R13 contains the starting address of the video display. We can scroll the video display up or down by incrementing the contents of R12,R13 by the contents of R1 (i.e. one row).

If we set the MW bit (Figure 6.40(b)), the width of the display memory can be made wider than the display itself. In this mode, the width of the video RAM is given by the contents of R1 (the display width) *plus* the contents of R33 (the offset value). For example, if R1 = 80 and R33 = 42, the *displayed* row contains 80 characters and the *stored* row contains 132 characters. Each new row in the video RAM is 132 characters onward from the start of the previous row. If we wish to scroll the display by one row, we must add or subtract 132 to the contents of R12,R13.

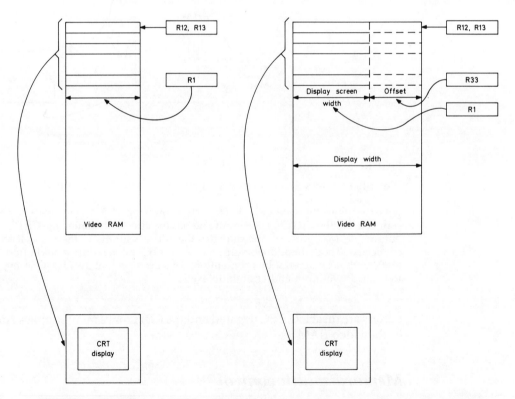

FIGURE 6.40 Memory width offset. (a) MW = 0 Memory width control disabled, (b) MW = 1 Memory width control disabled, (b) MW = 1 Memory width control enabled and offset in R33

Figure 6.41 demonstrates the effect of setting MW = 1 and using a wider memory width than the displayed width. The displayed portion of the memory is a window that can be moved up or down or *left or right*. In other words, we can scroll the display horizontally as well as vertically. Adding one to R12,R13 has the effect of moving the window one place right. Horizontal scrolling is useful when we wish to edit documents whose width is greater than that of the CRT display.

6.3.6 Resetting the HD6345 CRTC

Like almost all peripherals, the HD6345 has a RESET∗ input that is used to place it in a known state after the power-up sequence. Note that RESET∗ is interpreted by the CRTC only when the light pen strobe, LPSTB, is at its inactive-low level. In practice, RESET∗ is invariably connected directly to the 68000's own RESET∗ output pin.

Unlike other peripherals of a similar complexity, the HD6345 is not reset by loading all its registers with default values and a reset has little effect on the contents of most of the CRTC's internal registers. The contents of R1–R39 must be set up under programmer control and, apart from R30–R32, are not modified by the CRTC itself during a hardware reset.

A hardware reset switches between the HD6345's '6845' mode and its '6345' mode. Following a reset, the HD6345 behaves like a conventional 6845 CRTC. In the mode, only registers R0–R17 are active and the enhancements of the 6845 (e.g. split-screen operation, dual cursors, smooth scrolling and memory width control) are not available.

After a reset, the programmer is free to access control registers R30–R32 to set up any new feature offered by registers R18–R39. A reset clears all bits of control register 1 (R30), the SB and SL bits of control register 2 (R31), and all bits of control register 3 (R32).

6.4 A video display module for the 68000

The complete circuit diagram of an alphanumeric display system based on the HD6345 CRTC is given in Figure 6.42. This circuit is entirely conventional and is nothing more than a compilation of the individual circuits that have already been described.

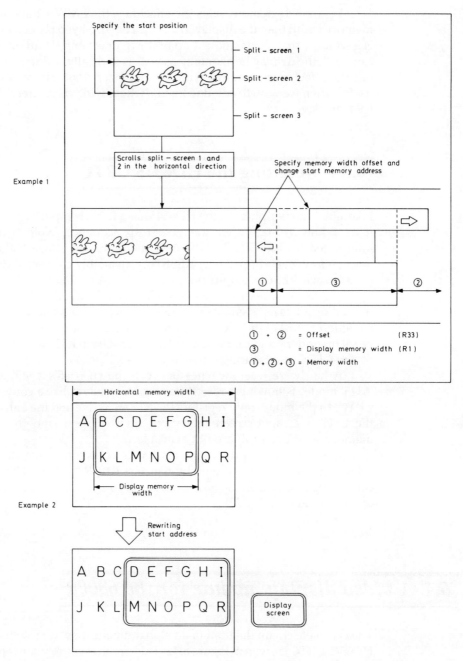

FIGURE 6.41 Using memory width control to scroll

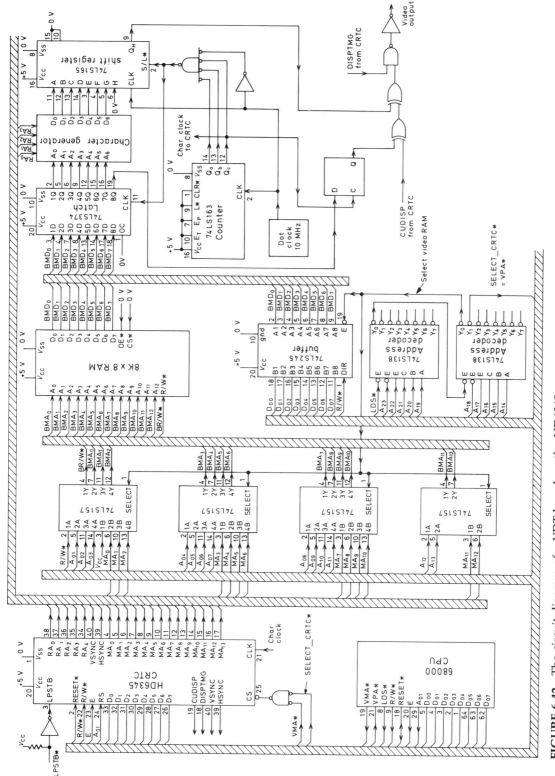

FIGURE 6.42 The circuit diagram of a VDT based on the HD6345

6.4.1 Programming the HD6345

Now that the CRTC and the construction of the display system interfaced to a 68000 microprocessor have been described, the next step is to write some software to drive the CRTC. The software consists of two parts: the initialization routine that sets up the CRTC and permits the display of data on the CRT screen, and the driver routines that control where data is to be displayed on the screen. For the sake of simplicity, we shall operate the HD6345 in its '6845' mode to make this software compatible with other CRTCs of the 6845 variety.

6.4.2 Initializing the CRTC

I always find programming a CRTC a rather tricky exercise and adopt an *iterative* approach. That is, I make some rule-of-thumb calculations and then refine them to produce final values. For the purpose of this example, we will assume that the CRTC is going to control a television. Consequently, the number of horizontal characters is limited to no more than 64 (due to the bandwidth of the receiver). The display is to be the CCIR format with a line duration of $64\,\mu s$ and a field duration of 20 ms. Interlacing will not be used and we will assume that there are 312 lines per field. The character font is to be 9 lines by 7 dots in a display area of 12 lines by 8 dots.

Figure 6.43 illustrates some of the fundamental parameters of the display. Suppose we choose the active display portion of a line to be 75 per cent of the available display time. This gives us a display period of $48\,\mu s$ for 64 characters, or $48\,\mu s/(64 \times 8) = 0.0937\,\mu s$ per dot, corresponding to a dot rate of 10.667 MHz.

Now let us try a second iteration using a standard dot clock value of 10 MHz. The duration of a character is $8 \times 100\,ns = 0.8\,\mu s$ and the 64-character segment of a line has a duration of $64 \times 0.8\,\mu s = 51.2\,\mu s$. The undisplayed portion of a line is $64\,\mu s - 51.2\,\mu s = 12.8\,\mu s$, or $12.8\,\mu s/0.8\,\mu s = 16$ character periods (note this is an integer value – we have juggled the figures nicely).

The next step is to determine the key vertical parameters. Given 312 lines vertical resolution, the number of lines available is approximately 75 per cent of this value, or 234. Dividing this by 12, we get 19.5 which is close enough to 20 – a reasonable value for the number of displayed rows.

Twenty displayed rows requires $20 \times 12 = 240$ lines, leaving $312 - 240 = 72$ lines for the vertical retrace and top and bottom margins. These 72 lines correspond to $72/12 = 6$ rows.

The final step is to calculate the 16 values to be loaded into the CRTC's registers R0–R15 during the initialization phase. Some of these values are

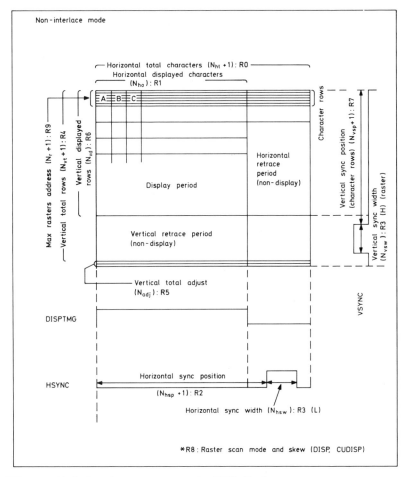

FIGURE 6.43   Defining the parameters of a CRT display

'guesstimates' and might require modifying when the display is up and running on the bench. The data to be loaded into registers R0–R15 is as follows.

R0 Horizontal total characters register = total chars/row − 1 = 64 + 16 − 1 = 79
R1 Horizontal displayed characters register = displayed chars/row = 64
R2 Horizontal sync position register = 72
R3 Sync width register: horizontal sync = 4 ms = 6 characters
                    vertical sync = 4 lines
                       Therefore, R3 = 0100 0110 = \$46
R4 Vertical total rows register = total rows − 1 = 20 + 6 − 1 = 25
R5 Vertical total adjust register = 0 (because 12 × 26 = 312 exactly)
R6 Vertical displayed rows register = 20
R7 Vertical sync position register = 22

R8   Interlace mode and skew register: CUDISP skew = 2

                                                      : DISPTMG skew = 2

                                                      : Non-interlace video mode

                                                      : Therefore, R8 = 10100000 = $A0

R9   Maximum raster address = max lines/row − 1 = 12 − 1 = 11

R10 Cursor 1 start register = 0 (cursor to start at top of cell)

R11 Cursor 1 end register = 11 (cursor to end at bottom of cell)

R12 Screen 1 start address high = $00

R13 Screen 1 start address low = $00

R14 Cursor 1 start address high = $00

R15 Cursor 1 start address low = $00

The data to be loaded into the CRTC's registers is normally stored in the initialization routine as a define constant statement, that is

CRT__DATA DC.B 79,64,72,$46,25,0,20,22,$A0,11,0,11,0,0,0,0

We have selected the screen 1 start address as $0000, which means that the first character (i.e. the character at the lowest address) in the video RAM is mapped onto the top left-hand position in the display. Similarly, the cursor has been moved to its *home* position (column zero on row zero).

6.4.3 The display software

The display software presented below in pseudocode form provides an indication of the type of routines required to support a memory-mapped video display. All the software does is to accept a new ISO (ASCII) encoded 7-bit code, analyse it and display it if necessary. Control characters are interpreted and printing (alphanumeric) characters are displayed. In the interest of simplicity, the only control characters to be handled here are: carriage return, line feed, back space, cursor up, cursor down, cursor left, cursor right, home, clear screen. All other control characters will be ignored. Scrolling is performed by physically moving up or down the screen in memory. Such an activity is not necessary with the 6345 CRTC, because scrolling can be carried out simply by modifying the contents of the screen start address register.

```
Initialize
      Load R0 to R15 with initialization data
      Home
End initialize

CRTC_driver
      Get character
      CASE OF:
                  Carriage-return
                  Line feed
                  Back space
                  Cursor up
                  Cursor left
                  Cursor right
                  Home
                  Clear screen
                  Printing character
      END CASE
End CRTC_driver

Define data: Base_address     {Start of video RAM}
             Cursor_address   {Address of cursor in RAM}
             Current_row      {Current row counter}
             Current_col      {Current column counter}
             Max_row = 19     {0–19 rows of characters}
             Max_col = 63     {0–63 columns of characters}

Carriage_return {Move cursor to column zero on same row}
      Cursor_address := cursor_address − current_col
      Current_col := 0
End carriage_return

Line_feed {Move cursor down by one row}
      Cursor_address := cursor_address + (max_col + 1)
      Current_row := current_row + 1
      Scroll_up {Deal with scrolling if at bottom}
End line_feed

Back_space {Move cursor one place left}
      Cursor_address := cursor_address − 1
      [Cursor_address] := space {store space at cursor position}
      Current_col := current_col − 1
      IF Current_col := −1 THEN
                  BEGIN {Move to end of line above}
                  Current_col := Max_col
                  Current_row := Current_row − 1
                  Scroll_down
                  END
End back_space
```

Cursor_up {Move the cursor up by one row}
    Cursor_address := cursor_address − (Max_col + 1)
    Current_row := current_row − 1
    Scroll_down {Deal with problem of falling off top}
End cursor_up

Cursor_left {Move the cursor left without destroying chars}
    Cursor_address := cursor address − 1
    Current_col := current_col − 1
    IF Current_col := −1 THEN
                    BEGIN
                    Current_col := Max_col
                    Current_row := Current_row − 1
                    Scroll_down
                    END
End cursor_left

Cursor_right
    Cursor_address := cursor_address + 1
    Current_col := current_col + 1
    IF Current_col > Max_col THEN
                    BEGIN
                    Current_col := 0
                    Current_row := current_row + 1
                    Scroll_up
                    END
End cursor_right

Home {Move cursor to top left-hand of screen}
    Cursor_address := Memory_start
    Current_col := 0
    Current_row := 0
End home

Print_character
    [Cursor_address] = character {store new char at current cursor}
    Cursor_address := cursor_address + 1
    Current_col := current_col + 1
    IF Current_col > Max_col THEN
                    BEGIN
                    Current_col := 0
                    Current_row := current_row + 1
                    Scroll_up
                    END
End print_character

```
Scroll_up
    IF Current_row > Max_row THEN
        BEGIN
        FOR I = 1 TO Max_row {Start at top row}
            FOR J = 0 TO Max_col {Move a row at a time}
                [Base_address + (I − 1)*(Max_col + 1) + J]:=
                    [Base_address + I*(Max_col + 1) + J]
            ENDFOR
        ENDFOR
        FOR I = 0 TO Max_col {Clear the bottom row}
            [Base_address + (Max_col + 1)*Max_row + I]:= space
        ENDFOR
        Cursor_address:= cursor_address − (Max_col + 1)
        Current_row:= Max_row
        END
    ENDIF
End scroll_up

Scroll down
    IF Current_row < 0 THEN
        BEGIN
        FOR I = Max_row−1 DOWNTO 0
        {Move a row of characters down one row}
            FOR J = 0 TO Max_col
                [Base_address + (I + 1)*(Max_col + 1) + J]:=
                    [Base_address + I*(Max_col + 1) + J]
            ENDFOR
        ENDFOR
        {Clear contents of top row}
        FOR I = 0 TO Max_col
        [Base_address + I]:= space
        Current_row:= 0
        Curso_address:= cursor_address + (Max_col + 1)
        ENDFOR
    ENDIF
End scroll_down
```

Summary

Not very long ago, designing a CRT controller was a far larger task than designing a microprocessor system itself. In those days dedicated CRT controller chips did not exist and the designer had to make up a circuit with 50 or more SSI and MSI TTL chips. In this chapter we have looked at how a CRT display can be controlled by a moderately simple-to-use chip, the HD6345, which is an improved version of the 6845 CRT controller.

Unfortunately, the 6345 does not concern itself with units of information smaller than the character, and the designer is still left to provide the dot generator circuits. These circuits are relatively straightforward and the only real problem with the generation of video signals is the need to take care with timing requirements at such high bit rates.

We have also looked at the programming model of the 6345. It is programmed by setting up its control registers to suit the format of the required display during its initialization phase following a system reset on power-up. Many CRT displays controlled by the 6345 and similar chips use character-mapped displays in which the video memory contains a video image of the display at the character level. We have provided a pseudocode program to emulate a simple terminal.

Chapter 7

The Disk Drive

and its Interface

The history of the microcomputer is every bit as much the history of the development of its associated peripherals, as it is of the microprocessor itself. While the microprocessor has attracted almost all the glamour, it is the proliferation of low-cost peripherals that have turned it into the microcomputer found in the home and the office. More specifically, the dramatic growth of the microcomputer industry has been achieved by the development of the dot-matrix and daisy-wheel printers, and the floppy disk drive. In this section we examine the floppy disk subsystem and its interface to a microprocessor. Throughout this chapter we shall employ the term *floppy disk* or more simply *disk*, although the term *diskette* is probably more correct.

7.1 Data encoding

7.1.1 Non-return to zero encoding

One of the most popular classes of recording code is non-return to zero, NRZ. There are several variants of this code, of which NRZ1 is the most widespread. NRZ1 is frequently found in multi-track tape drives in medium recording density systems. The encoding algorithm used by NRZ1 is very simple; a logical one is recorded as a change of flux and a logical zero as no change. Figure 7.1 illustrates NRZ1 encoding. NRZ1 encoding requires a maximum of one flux transition per recorded bit and therefore has an efficiency of 100 per cent.

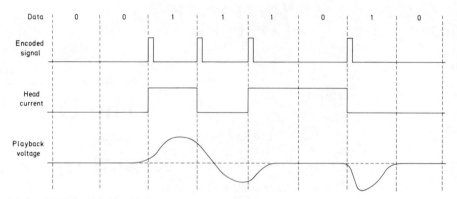

FIGURE 7.1   NRZ1 encoding

As a series of zeros is represented by no change of flux, this code is not self-clocking and it is very difficult to divide the data stream into individual bits. NRZ1 also has a very poor low-frequency response caused by long strings of zeros. For this reason, NRZ1 is not used in disk systems, even though it is efficient and is easy to implement.

7.1.2 Biphase encoding (single-density or FM encoding)

Another popular class of encoding techniques is biphase encoding. Included in this class are phase encoding (PE), also called Manchester encoding, and frequency modulation (FM), also called single-density encoding. These codes are characterized by having two flux transitions per bit, and therefore their efficiency is only 50 per cent, or half that of NRZ1.

The details of the classic form of phase encoding are provided in Figure 7.2. A flux change occurs in the centre of each data cell; if the data to be recorded

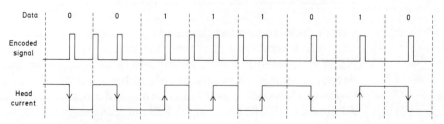

FIGURE 7.2   Phase encoding

is a logical one, the flux change is positive, and if it is a logical zero the flux change is negative. Where two or more ones or zeros occur in succession, it is necessary to force a flux transition at the cell boundary. Because there is always a flux change in the centre of a cell, this code is self-clocking and it is relatively easy to derive a timing signal from the recorded data. Unlike NRZ1, there is no d.c. component in a phase encoded signal, making the design of the signal processing circuits much easier.

Although phase encoding achieves a lower efficiency than NRZ1, its self-clocking properties, its lack of a d.c. component and its good immunity to noise make it a popular choice for both synchronous data transmission systems and for magnetic tape of disk drives.

The encoding technique chosen by many disk systems is a modest variation of the phase encoding arrangement of Figure 7.2 and is called frequency modulation (FM) or single-density encoding. FM encoding is described in Figure 7.3. The recorded flux changes state at each cell boundary. If the cell contains a logical one, there is an additional flux change in the centre of the cell, otherwise there is no flux change in the centre. A glance at Figure 7.3

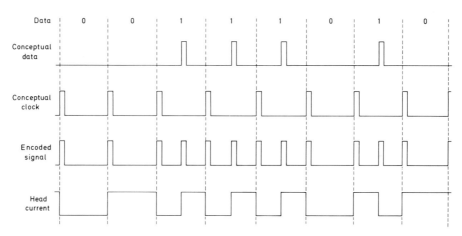

FIGURE 7.3   Single-density (FM) encoding

should demonstrate why this encoding process is also called frequency modulation, because a string of zero results in a flux change at a frequency F, while a string of ones results in a flux change at a frequency $2F$.

All the basic properties of FM encoding (efficiency, bandwidth, its self-clock nature, etc.) are identical to those of phase encoding.

7.1.3 Miller encoding (double-density or MFM encoding)

Frequency modulation is largely associated with the first generation of floppy disk systems based on the IBM 3740 standard. Although a few systems still use FM encoding, it has largely been superseded by double-density encoding. Strictly speaking, this is Miller encoding, but is normally referred to as modified frequency modulation MFM. The term MFM is used in what follows.

MFM is an attempt to raise the efficiency of FM encoding to the level of NRZ1, while maintaining FM's self-clocking properties. Referring to Figure 7.3, it can be seen that the encoded FM signal may be divided conceptually into two separate signals: a timing signal consisting of a pulse at each cell boundary, and a data signal consisting of a pulse at the centre of each data cell containing a logical one. It is tempting to ask if we can remove the clock signal, as it carries no useful information.

Figure 7.4 shows how a data signal is encoded by MFM. The encoded signal consists of a pulse in the centre of each data cell containing a logical one. There is no pulse between the boundaries of adjacent cells, unless a zero is followed by another zero. Thus, a clock signal is introduced only when it is needed – at the boundary of two consecutive cells containing no data pulse. Figure 7.4 also demonstrates how the MFM signals can be split into separate data and clock components.

Floppy disk drives store information at a constant bit rate, so MFM provides twice the storage capacity of FM, because the clock pulses of FM have been replaced by data pulses in MFM. The ability of MFM to store twice as much data as FM is not clear from Figures 7.3 and 7.4, as their scales are

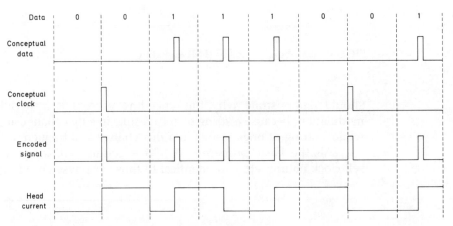

FIGURE 7.4   Double-density (MFM) encoding

TABLE 7.1   Parameters of a $5\frac{1}{4}$ inch family of floppy disk drives
Data capacity (Normal density mode)

RECORDING METHOD		FM	MFM
Data transfer rate (Kbits/s)	Speed mode I (300 rpm)	125	250
	Speed mode II (360 rpm)	150	300
tracks/disk		160	160
Innermost track flux density (frpi)		2961	5922
Innermost track flux density (frpi)		5922	5922
Data Capacity	Unformatted Kbytes/track	3.125	6.25
	Kbytes/disk	500	1000
	Formatted 16 sectors/track Kbytes/sector	0.128	0.256
	Kbytes/track	2.048	4.096
	Kbytes/disk	327.68	655.36

Data capacity (High density mode)

RECORDING METHOD		FM	MFM
Data transfer rate (Kbits/s)		250	500
Tracks/disk		154 (160)	154 (160)
Innermost track bit density (bpi)		4823 (4935)	9646 (9870)
Innermost track flux density (frpi)		9646 (9870)	9646 (9970)
Data capacity	Unformatted Kbytes/track	5.208	10.416
	Kbytes/disk	802	1604
F o r m a t t e d	26 sectors/track Kbytes/sector	0.128	0.256
	Kbytes/track	3.328	6.656
	Kbytes/disk	512.5 (532.5)	1025.0 (1065.0)
	15 sectors/track Kbytes/sector	0.256	0.516
	Kbytes/track	3.840	7.680
	Kbytes/disk	591.4 (614.4)	1182.7 (1228.8)
	8 sectors/track Kbytes/sector	0.512	1.024
	Kbytes/track	4.096	8.192
	Kbytes/disk	630.8 (655.4)	1261.6 (1310.7)

Note: Up to 80 cylinders are available for the FDD. The figures in the brackets are for 80 cylinder's operation (160 tracks).

intrinsically different. Figure 7.5 presents the same data waveforms for FM and MFM on identical time scales. It can now be appreciated that MFM stores twice the information on the same surface area. For a $5\frac{1}{4}$ inch disk drive, FM data cells are $8\,\mu s$ wide and MFM cells $4\,\mu s$ wide. The greater recording density of MFM has important implications when system reliability is considered, because of the greater susceptibility of MFM to pulse-crowding and imperfections in the magnetic medium. Table 7.1 provides the parameters of the TEAC-55 series of $5\frac{1}{4}$ inch floppy disk drives.

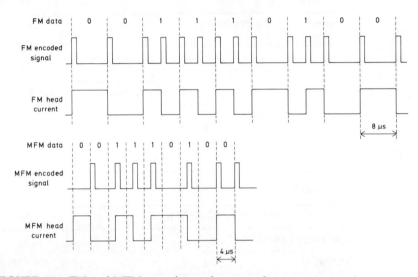

FIGURE 7.5   FM and MFM waveforms drawn to the same time scale

7.1.4 Data and clock pulse separation

For all practical purposes, data encoding prior to recording does not fall within the province of the computer designer. Both the floppy disk controller chip and the disk drive itself are bought off-the-shelf, leaving the systems designer with little freedom of choice other than to pick single- or double-density, or to adopt an entirely do-it-yourself approach as found, for example, in the Apple IIe microcomputer. The inverse process, in which the composite signal from the disk drive in demodulated to extract a data signal and a separate clock signal, provides the computer designer with more room to manoeuvre.

Broadly speaking, the demodulation techniques used in a disk system largely determine the soft error rate of the playback process. A good demodulator should achieve a soft error rate of less than one error in 10^9 bits read. A soft error is dealt with by re-reading the offending sector. If the soft error rate rises substantially above one error in 10^9 bits, a considerable amount of time is wasted by re-reading sectors.

One of the earliest floppy disk controllers, the Western Digital 1771, included on-chip data separation circuits for FM. Unfortunately, the decoding process was substantially poorer than that achieved by random logic decoders. Consequently, most 1771 users abandoned its internal demodulator in favour of an external circuit. As time has passed, single-chip demodulators such as the FDC9216 have appeared, and the current range of floppy disk controllers (described in the next section) now includes more reliable demodulators. Typical clock and data pulse separation circuits are illustrated in Figure 7.6.

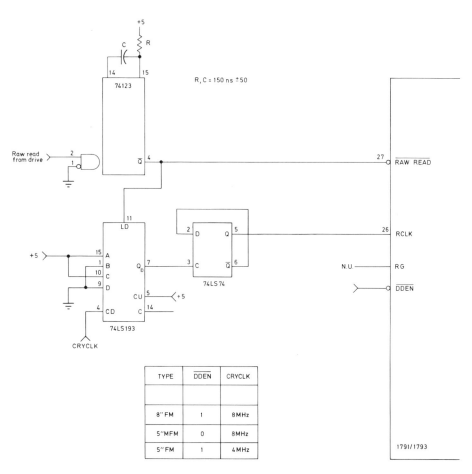

TYPE	$\overline{DDEN}$	CRYCLK
8" FM	1	8 MHz
5" MFM	0	8 MHz
5" FM	1	4 MHz

FIGURE 7.6 Typical clock and data pulse separator circuits (*continued*)

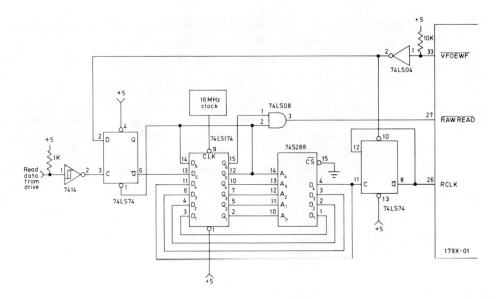

74S288 programming table		
Address	Data	Action taken
00	01	None
01	01	Retard by 1 count
02	02	
03	03	
04	03	Retard by 2 counts
05	04	
06	05	
07	06	
08	0B	Advance by 2 counts
09	0D	
0A	0C	
0B	0E	
0C	0F	
0D	0F	Advance by 1 count
0E	00	
0F	01	
10	01	Free run
11	02	
12	03	
13	04	
14	05	
15	06	
16	07	
17	08	
18	09	
19	0A	
1A	0B	
1B	0C	
1C	0D	
1D	0E	
1E	0F	
1F	00	

FIGURE 7.6   (*continued*)

7.2 *The organization of data on disks*

Although there are an almost infinite number of ways in which digital data may be arranged (i.e. organized or formatted) on a disk, there are only two really respectable ways of formatting the data. These have both been developed by IBM and are referred to as IBM 3740-compatible single-density recording, and IBM System 34-compatible double-density recording. I chose the word *respectable* above because the proliferation of *ad hoc* formats does not benefit the world of computing generally. From the end-user's point of view, the free exchange of software between computers is highly beneficial. At the same time, from the software distributor's point of view, the choice of a non-standard format certainly makes it difficult for others to copy their software. Equally, it often forces the user of such non-standard equipment to remain dependent on one or two suppliers.

Floppy disk formatting techniques fall into one of two classes: hard-sectored and soft-sectored. Hard-sectored disks have 32 holes arranged round their circumference, which are detected by an LED/photocell pair in the disk drive. A pulse from the photocell denotes the beginning of a new sector. Although hard-sectored disks store approximately 23 per cent more data than soft-sectored disks, they are not widely used, as they do not support IBM 3740 or System 40 compatible formats. Therefore hard-sectored disks are not considered further.

A soft-sectored disk is so called because the beginning of a sector is identified by a code written on to the disk rather than by a physical tag such as a hole. To be precise, a soft-sectored disk has a single index hole to locate the beginning of the sectors making up a track. It is best to think of a soft-sector as a vehicle for transporting data. This vehicle is a form of data structure (like an array or matrix in a high-level language). A consequence of soft-sectored disk formatting is that the disks must be formatted before they can be used. Formatting a disk consists of writing information on to each track in order to let the controller know when to start reading or writing information. That is, a disk is formatted by writing a series of sector headers followed by empty data fields that can later be filled with data as required.

Figure 7.7 gives the typical arrangement of a single track of a disk formatted according to the IBM 3740 single density format with 128 bytes of user data per sector. Figure 7.7 is much less complex than it looks. A track consists of an index gap plus 16 sectors ($5\frac{1}{4}$ inch) or 26 sectors (8 inch). The number and size of sectors varies widely from operating system to operating system. Each of the sectors is made up of an identity field (ID field) and a data field. The various information units on the disk are separated by gaps. We now look at the structure of a sector in more detail.

A soft-sectored disk has a single index hole and the start of a track is denoted by the leading edge of a pulse, generated when the index hole passes

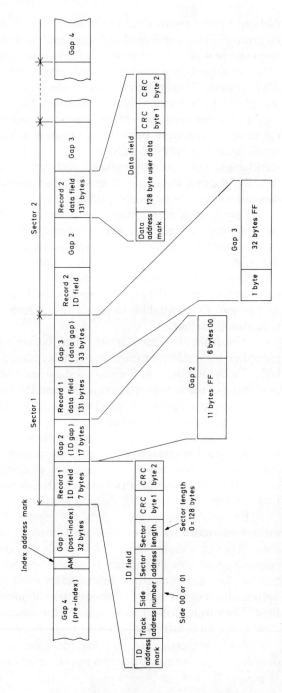

FIGURE 7.7 The IBM 3740 format for single-density recording

between an LED and a photoelectric cell. An index address mark is written on the disk, 46 bytes after the leading edge of the index pulse, to denote the start of the current track. The address mark is a special byte, unlike any other. We have already seen that the FM and MFM recording processes are carried out according to particular algorithms. That is, only certain bit-patterns are valid. By deliberately violating these algorithms and recording a bit pattern that does not conform to the set of valid patterns, certain uniquely identifiable bit patterns can be created to act as special markers. This marker is rather like the opening flag pattern found in synchronous serial transmission systems. Special bit patterns are generated by omitting certain clock pulses.

Following the index gap are 16 sectors, each of which is made up of an ID (identification) address mark, an ID field, gap 2, a data field, and gap 3. The ID field is 7 bytes long, including the ID address mark. The other 6 bytes of the address field are: the track number (0–39 i.e. $00–$27), the side number (0 or 1), the sector address (1–16 i.e. $01–10), the sector length code (0 for 128-byte sectors), and a 2-byte cyclic redundancy code (CRC). The CRC is the 16-bit remainder obtained by dividing the polynomial representing the field to be protected by a standard polynomial called a generator. The 16-bit CRC provides a powerful method of detecting an error in the sector's ID field. Remember that several disk formats are widely used – 35, 40 or 80 track for $5\frac{1}{4}$ of $3\frac{1}{2}$ inch disks. In this chapter we shall assume 40-track disks. A typical 8 inch disk format has 26 sectors numbered from 1 to 26, and 77 tracks numbered from 0 to 76.

MS DOS versions later than 2.0, for example, use nine sectors numbered 1–9. A two-sided IBM disk has a total capacity of 2 sides $\times$ 40 tracks/side $\times$ 9 sectors/track = 720 sectors. As each sector holds 512 bytes, the disk capacity is 512 bytes/sector $\times$ 720 sectors = 368 640 bytes (i.e. 360 K). Modern high-density, 96 t.p.i., double-sided, double-density disks are able to store 2 sides $\times$ 80 tracks $\times$ 8 sectors/track $\times$ 1024 bytes/sector = 1 310 720 bytes (i.e. 1.2 Mbyte).

The beginning of the data field itself is denoted by one of two special markers: a *data address mark* or a *deleted data address mark*. Following the data address mark are 128 bytes of user data, terminated by a 16-bit CRC to protect the data field from error. The data field is bracketed by two gaps, whose purpose is to provide time for the write circuits in the disk to turn on to write a new data field and then turn off before the next sector is encountered. Without gaps 2 and 3, it would not be possible to manufacture a real disk drive. Note that gap 2 must have an *exact* size for correct operation with a floppy disk controller, while gaps 1, 3 and 4 are simply delimiters and must only be greater than some specified minimum.

Figure 7.8 provides the format for IBM 34 format double-density recording with 256 bytes per sector. Because Figure 7.8 is very similar to that of Figure 7.7, additional commentary is not necessary.

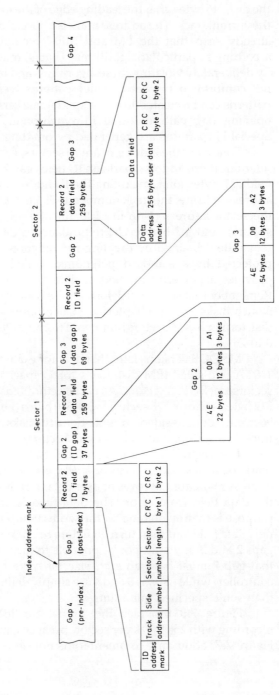

FIGURE 7.8   The IBM System 34 format for double-density recording

7.3 The floppy disk controller (FDC)

The floppy disk controller, FDC, is widely available as a single chip (frequently a 40-pin DIL package), which performs the same function in a disk system as an ACIA does in a serial data transmission system. That is, it forms the interface between the microprocessor and the disk drive itself, saving the computer systems designer a considerable quantity of software and hardware. Hardware is saved because the FDC converts parallel data from the host microprocessor into the encoded serial form required by the floppy disk drive, and because it converts the serial data from the disk drive into the parallel form required by the host computer. The FDC also reduces the amount of software required, because it carries out some relatively complex operations such as reading a track number from the disk and comparing the number with the contents of its own track register.

The role of the FDC in a disk system is illustrated in Figure 7.9. Conceptually, the host microcomputer in Figure 7.9 is organized hierarchically,

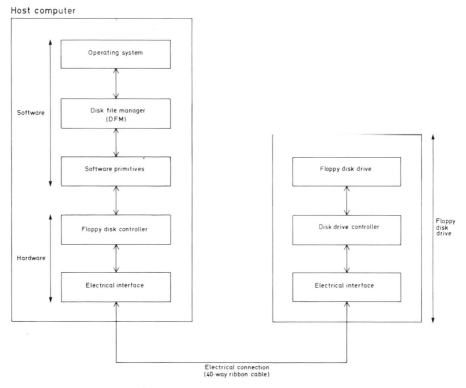

FIGURE 7.9   The role of the FDU and logical structure of a disk subsystem

with the operating system at the top of the diagram and the physical connection to the disk drive at the bottom. Although the disk drive itself can be considered to have a similar but simpler internal organization, it is bought as a complete unit. The designer normally knows little of its internal arrangement; largely because disk drives are highly standardized and have a standard connection (i.e. plug and socket) between themselves and the host microcomputer.

At the microcomputer end of the disk interface, the operating system carries out the applications-oriented transactions such as create or delete a file, list the contents of a disk's directory, and update a file. The disk file manager (DFM) in the operating system is concerned with the physical organization of files on the disks and is responsible for carrying out the actions requested by the operating system. For example, when the operating system wishes to create a file named CLEMENTS.123, the DFM has to find room for the file on the disk and then has to update the directory by putting CLEMENTS.123 in the directory of files.

The software primitives in Figure 7.9 represent the lowest level of software operations that can be carried out by the system. These primitives are used by the DFM to perform basic operations such as the actual reading or writing of a sector on the disk. At this level, certain error recovery actions may be built in. For example, suppose the DFM calls a software primitive in order to read a sector of a particular file. If a read error occurs, the primitive may make, say, five attempts at reading the file before reporting an error to the DFM.

The floppy disk controller of Figure 7.9 is part of the hardware and is used by the software primitives. The FDC is responsible for moving the read/write head in the disk drive to the appropriate track, and for translating the format of the data between that used by the microprocessor for storage in memory and that required by the disk drive for recording on the disk.

At the lowest level in Figure 7.9 is the electrical interface that matches the signals from the FDC to those from the disk drive unit. In general, this is a simple task, as the FDC and disk drive both use TTL-compatible signals. However, the electrical interface is also responsible for a certain amount of processing carried out on the data signal received from the disk drive during a read operation. Fortunately, the latest generation of floppy disk controllers include some signal processing on-chip, considerably simplifying the electrical interface.

Individual microprocessor manufacturers have often designed FDCs for use with their own family of microprocessors. However, one particular series of FDCs has become an industry standard and is found in many different microprocessor systems. These are the Western Digital Corporation controllers which began with the FD177X series. The FD177X family of controllers had a relatively poor access time (i.e. microprocessor read/write cycle time) and required a three voltage power supply. The FD177X series was later replaced by the improved FD179X series, which required a two-rail power supply (+5 V and +12 V) and had a read access time of 350 ns. The WD279X-02 series of FDC is now available with a single supply of +5 V, a read access time of 200 ns and a considerable amount of interface support circuitry built in.

The WD279X-02 series has four members: the 2791, 2793, 2795 and 2797. These four FDCs are very similar, except that the 2793 and 2797 have true data buses. Data is inverted in the 2791 and 2795, which is a relic from the days when many microprocessors had inverted data buses because inverting transceivers were more readily available. Today's transceivers, such as the 74LS245, have made inverted data buses unnecessary. The 2795 and 2797 have a side-select output which is used to control the operation of double-sided disk drives, while 2791 and 2793 are intended for single-sided operation.

Western Digital have come full circle and have now produced a pair of FDCs, the WD1770 and the WD1772, designed to support $5\frac{1}{4}$ inch disk drives only and which include on-chip digital processing of the data from the disk drive like the earlier FD177X series. We describe the WD1770 here because of its great simplicity (unlike most FDCs the 1770 is available in a 28 pin DIL package rather than the more usual 40 pin package). The only difference between the WD1770 and the WD1772 is that the latter has a faster track-to-track stepping rate.

7.3.1 The FDC to host microprocessor interface

Figure 7.10 shows the relationship between the 1770, the host microprocessor, the electrical interface and the disk drive. The pins of the 1770 can be divided into two groups: host microprocessor interface and disk drive interface. We will describe first the 1770 to 68000 interface and then the 1770 to disk interface.

The hardware aspects of the 1770 present little difficulty, or indeed choice, to the systems designer. It is connected to the host microcomputer in the way dictated by its read and write cycle characteristics, and to the disk drive in a thoroughly straightforward way, as most of its disk interface pins match up with the corresponding terminals of the disk drive. The greatest degree of freedom the designer has is in constructing the software to control the FDC.

The interface between the 1770 and host microprocessor is almost entirely conventional. Most circuits built around the 1770 treat it as a simple memory-mapped peripheral with four internal locations selected by two address lines, A0 and A1. The FDC's data lines are labelled DAL0 to DAL7 and are connected to the 68000's lower-order data lines D_{00} to D_{07}. The 1770 has a R/W* input used in conjunction with an active-low chip-select input CS* rather than the separate RD* and WR* inputs found on most of Western Digital's other FDCs. The 1770 is provided with an active-low MR* (master reset) input which is used to abort any command in progress and to clear the status register.

Finally, two outputs from the 1770, interrupt request (INTRQ) and data request (DRQ), allow it to signal the host microprocessor for attention. DRQ is

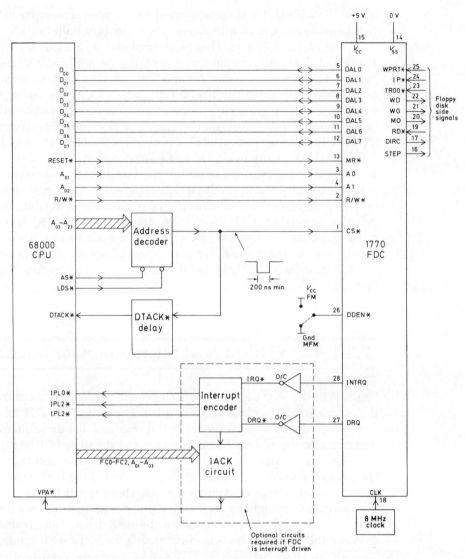

FIGURE 7.10 The relationship between the 1770 FDC, the host microprocessor and the disk drive

active-high and is asserted by the FDC to indicate to the host processor that the data register is full on a read operation or is empty on a write operation. Many systems use DRQ in conjunction with a DMA controller. INTRQ is also an active-high output and is used to interrupt the host microprocessor at the termination of a command. Note that it is not necessary to use either DRQ or INTRQ in all applications of the 1770 – it is perfectly possible to operate the 1770 in a polled data mode.

Figure 7.11 provides brief details of the 1770's relatively uncomplicated read cycle and write cycle timing requirements. All times are minima except the read cycle access time of 200 ns measured from the falling edge of CS*.

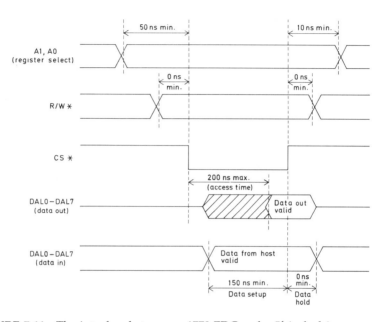

FIGURE 7.11   The interface between a 1770 FDC and a 5¼ inch drive

7.3.2 The FDC-disk drive electrical interface

The connections between the FDC and the disk drive electrical interface are those that directly control the operation of the disk drive, and receive status information back from it. The connections have been largely standardized and all the designer has to do is to connect each disk drive-side pin of the FDC to the appropriate input of the disk drive via a suitable electrical interface as illustrated in Figure 7.12. Below is a list of the disk drive interface-side pins of the 1770 FDC. Note that some pins interface to the disk drive and some are used to control the operating mode of the FDC itself.

CLK

The 1770 FDC requires a free-running CLK (clock) input at a frequency of 8 MHz.

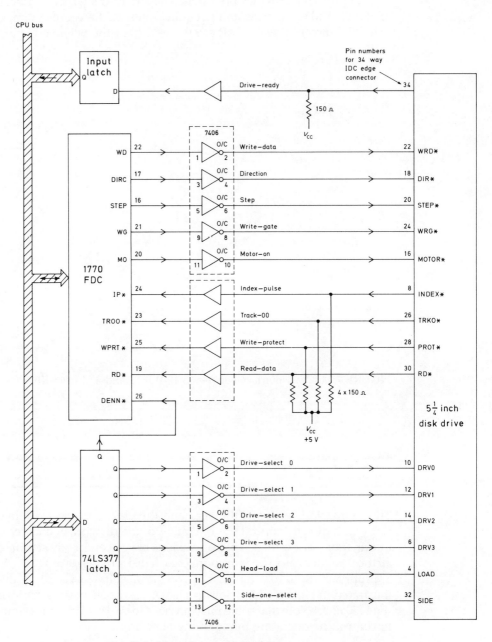

FIGURE 7.12   The disk drive electrical interface

DDEN*

The double-density enable, DENN*, input to the 1770 determines whether the FDC is to operate in the single-density FM mode (when DDEN* = 1) or is to operate in the double-density MFM mode (when DDEN* = 0). DDEN* can be made software selectable if the system is to operate in mixed FM/MFM modes, or can be manually programmed by links if the system is to operate only in FM or only in MFM modes. Some systems connect DDEN* to the TR00* (track 0) output from the disk drive via an inverter to force FM in track 0 and MFM in all other tracks. This apparently bizarre arrangement reduces the probability of errors in track 0 to a very low level and is suited to systems that locate vital information in track 0.

TRACK 00*

The track 0 input to the FDC is active-low, whenever the read/write head is positioned over track 0 and provides the FDC with a confirmation that the head is in the track 0 position.

STEP

The STEP output produces a pulse for each step of the drive's read/write head. The step pulse duration is $8\,\mu s$ in the FM mode and $4\,\mu m$ in the MFM mode.

DIRC

The direction, DIRC, output indicates to the disk drive the direction in which the read/write head is to move. When high, DIRC causes STEP pulses to move the read/write head towards the centre (i.e. step in). When low, DIRC causes the head to move towards the edge of the disk (i.e. step out).

IP*

The index pulse, IP*, input to the FDC indicates that the index hole has been encountered and therefore the read/write head is at the start of the current track.

MO

The motor-on pin of the 1770 is an active-high output that can be employed to switch on or off the disk drive's motor. MO is used to switch off the drive's motor between successive disk accesses to reduce wear on the motor. Not all systems make use of this output.

RD*

The active-low RD* (read data) input receives the raw data from the disk drive and separates it into clock and data pulses. The clock and data separation is performed automatically by the 1770.

WG

The write gate output is asserted by the FDC before it issues write pulses to the disk drive. WG is used by the disk drive to enable its write circuits.

WPRT*

Before the FDC can write to the disk drive, the write protect input to the 1770 must be inactive-high. The disk drive asserts WPRT* whenever a write-protected disk is in position.

WD

The write data output from the FDC consists of the stream of pulses to be written on the disk. The 1770 FDC determines whether the write pulses are FM or MFM encoded according to the state of its DDEN* input.

Figure 7.12 demonstrates that many of the FDC's signals are simply connected directly to the disk drive or via relatively simple buffering. Engineers occasionally design more complex interfaces when they wish to tailor pulses from the FDC exactly to the needs of the disk drive. For example, some interfaces are monostables to produce precise value of the step pulse.

7.4 The programming model of the 1770 FDC

Like many other highly specialized peripherals, the basic suite of operations carried out by the 1770 floppy disk controller is laid down by its manufacturer leaving only slight variations in some of its parameters controllable by the user. All communication between the 1770 and the host microcomputer takes place through four registers, which are selected whenever CS* = 0. The names of these registers and their relationship to the chip's A1 and A0 inputs are given in Table 7.2.

TABLE 7.2 Addressable registers in the 1770 FDC

ADDRESS INPUTS		READ ACCESS R/W∗ = 1	WRITE ACCESS R/W∗ = 0
A1	A0		
0	0	Status register	Command register
0	1	Track register	Track register
1	0	Sector register	Sector register
1	1	Data register	Data register

Note: The status and command registers share the same address (i.e. the low address of the FDC) and the status register is read-only and the command register write-only. The data register serves a dual purpose. In some operations it is loaded with the address of the desired *track* position (as opposed to data to be written to the disk).

7.4.1 The 1770's registers

Each of the 1770's four registers is 8 bits wide. The track, sector and data registers may be written to or read from. The command/status register has a single address but the command register is selected when R/W∗ = 0 and the status register when R/W∗ = 1.

The command register

This holds the command currently being executed. There are eleven different commands arranged in four groups, although most of the commands have slight functional variations. The command register must not be loaded whenever the FDC is busy (as indicated by the status register), unless the new command is a *force interrupt*.

The status register

This is located at the same address as the command register and can only be read from. Its 8 bits reflect the status of the FDC. The status register of some of Western Digital's floppy disk controllers is almost unique in the world of peripherals, as the meaning of its bits depends on the previous commands loaded into the command register.

The track register

This holds the track number of the current read/write head position in the disk drive. The contents of the track register are incremented by one each time the head is stepped in (towards the inner track), and decremented when the head is stepped out (towards track 0). During certain operations of the FDC (i.e. disk read, write and verify), the contents of the track register are compared with the recorded track number in the ID field read from the disk. If the recorded and stored track numbers are not equal (after five attempts), the *record not found* bit of the status register is set. The track register should not be loaded when the FDC is busy.

The sector register

The address of the sector to be accessed by the next command is held in the sector register. The contents of the sector register are compared with the sector number in the ID field during disk read or write operations. The sector register should not be loaded if the FDC is busy.

The 8-bit data register

This is a buffer register used in disk read or write operations. In a read operation, the serial data from the disk is assembled and loaded into the data register a byte at a time. Consequently, it is necessary to read each byte of data before it is overwritten by new data from the disk. Similarly, in a write operation, data is loaded in the data register by the host microprocessor, and serialized by the FDC for presentation to the disk drive.

The data register serves a secondary function. When a seek track operation is executed, the data register is loaded with the address of the desired track position by the host computer. A seek causes the FDC to move the head from its current position (defined by the contents of the track register) to the position specified in the data register.

The eleven commands interpreted by the 1770 are given in Table 7.3, and are grouped into four types in accordance with Western Digital's own convention.

TABLE 7.3   The instruction set of the 1770-series FDC

TYPE	COMMAND	EFFECT
I	Restore	Move the head to track 0
I	Seek	Move the head to the specified track
I	Step	Step to the next track
I	Step-in	Step one track towards track 39
I	Step-out	Step one track towards track 0
II	Read sector	Read the contents of a specified sector
II	Write sector	Write a sector at a specified address
III	Read address	Read the 6-byte contents of the next ID field
III	Read track	Read the entire contents of the current track
III	Write track	Write a track; used in disk formatting
IV	Force interrupt	Specify the conditions that generate an interrupt

It can be seen from Table 7.3, that command types I to III are divided into those that simply move the head and/or verify its position, and those that actually write data to or read data from the disk. For example, to read a given sector, a *restore* may be performed to move the head to track 0, followed by a *seek* to the desired track. The sector register is then loaded with the address of the sector to be read and a *read sector* command issued. Then the data must be read from the FDC as fast as it is gathered from the disk drive. A $5\frac{1}{4}$ inch drive with double-density encoding generates a new byte every $32\mu s$. Fortunately, a data rate of one byte per $32\mu s$ presents no difficulty to a 68000.

The *read track* operation is intended as a diagnostic device, as it reads everything in a track, including all gaps and ID-field information. The corresponding *write track* operation is used only to write an entire track during the initial formatting of a disk.

We are now going to look at the FDC's instruction set in more detail. Table 7.4 provides a list of the FDC's instructions in terms of their bit patterns. Each of these commands is qualified by two or more variable bits, labelled r1, r0, h, V, m, u, E, a0, and I_0–I_3, in Table 7.4. The meaning and effect of these control bits are defined as follows.

TABLE 7.4 Encoding the 1700 FDC's commands

TYPE	COMMAND	7	6	5	BIT 4	3	2	1	0
I	Restore	0	0	0	0	h	V	r1	r0
I	Seek	0	0	0	1	h	V	r1	r0
I	Step	0	0	1	u	h	V	r1	r0
I	Step-in	0	1	0	u	h	V	r1	r0
I	Step-out	0	1	1	u	h	V	r1	r0
II	Read sector	1	0	0	m	h	E	0	0
II	Write sector	1	0	1	m	h	E	P	a0
III	Read address	1	1	0	0	h	E	0	0
III	Read track	1	1	1	0	h	E	0	0
III	Write track	1	1	1	1	h	E	P	0
IV	Force interrupt	1	1	0	1	I3	I2	I1	I0

h = motor-on flag
    h = 0 enables spin up sequence
    h = 1 disable spin up sequence
V = verify flag
    V = 0 no verification performed
    V = 1 verify on destination track
u = update flag
    u = 0 do not update track register
    u = 1 update track register
m = multisector flag
    m = 0 single sector operation
    m = 1 multisector operation

E = enables 30 ms settling delay
    E = 0 no delay
    E = 1 add 30 ms delay head settling time
P = write precompensate
    P = enable write precompensation
    P = 1 disable write precompensation
I_3–I_0 = interrupt enables
    I_0 = not used by 1770
    I_1 = not used by 1770
    I_2 = interrupt on index pulse
    I_3 = interrupt on ready
    I_3–I_0 = 0000 terminate without interrupt

r1,r0

These two bits determine the stepping rate for all type I commands. The figures in Table 7.5 specify the waiting time between successive track-to-track steps by the FDC. When programming the FDC, the values of r1 and r0 are chosen to give the fastest stepping rate appropriate to the disk drive in use. Problems have sometimes arisen when people have replaced disk drives in a micro-computer with others from a different source. If the new drives have slower track-to-track access times and the FDC is programmed for the faster drives, intermittent errors can occur. Once r1 and r0 have been calculated, they are not changed unless the system configuration is altered.

TABLE 7.5 The effect of the r1, r0 bits on the 1770's stepping rate

r1	r0	TRACK TO TRACK STEPPING RATE	
		WD1770	WD1772
0	0	6 ms	6 ms
0	1	12 ms	12 ms
1	0	20 ms	2 ms
1	1	30 ms	3 ms

h (motor-on flag)

The motor-on flag bit, h, permits the programmer to specify a delay between the loading of a command into the command register and the subsequent execution of the command. The delay provides time for the disk to come up to speed. If $h = 0$ (i.e. spin up sequence enabled) and the motor-on output, MO, from the FDC is low, the 1770 will assert its motor-on output to start the disk drive and wait six revolutions before executing the command to provide one second delay for the disk to come up to speed. At the end of the command, the disk drive executes ten revolutions and negates its motor-on output. Should another command be executed while the motor-on output is still high, it is executed immediately without any delay. Note that the symbol h is used as the motor-on flag because the corresponding command bit was used to control head loading in other versions of Western Digital's FDCs.

V (verify)

The verify bit, V, determines whether or not a verify operation takes place at the completion of a type I command. If $V = 0$, the command is completed and either the next command is executed or the FDC returns to its idle state. If $V = 1$, the command is executed and the position of the head is determined by reading the first ID field encountered on the disk. As the head positioning mechanism is open-loop, it is necessary to provide some way of checking that the head is really where it is supposed to be. Setting the V flag of a type I command enables the position of the head to be determined by reading the first ID field read from the track. The track number of the ID field is compared with the contents of the track register in the FDC. If they are the same and the CRC of the ID field is correct, the verify operation is complete and an interrupt request is generated by asserting INTRQ. If there is a match, but the cyclic redundancy check of the ID field is invalid, the CRC error status bit (bit 3 of the status register) is set, and the next ID field encountered on the disk is read in order to perform a verification.

The FDC must find an ID field with a correct track number and a correct CRC within five revolutions of the disk. If a verification cannot be completed satisfactorily, the seek error status bit is set and an interrupt request generated.

u (update)

The update bit is examined during step commands. If $u = 0$, the track register is not updated each time a step is executed. If $u = 1$, the track register is updated each time the head is stepped in or out (i.e. Track:= Track + 1 for step in and Track:= Track - 1 for step out).

E (settling delay)

The E-bit is used by type II and III commands to add a 30 ms delay to the execution of commands. If $E = 0$, the operation begins immediately and if $E = 1$, it is preceded by a 30 ms delay. A settling delay is provided to allow time for the head to settle when it is first loaded against the disk. When the solenoid is energized to push the head against the surface of the disk, the head bounces and data read is invalid during this period. Once the head has been loaded, no further settling delays are required unless the head is retracted and reloaded.

P (enable precompensation)

The P-bit is interrogated during write accesses and is used to determine whether the FDC is to apply precompensation (when $P = 1$) to the data stream. Precompensation is used only during double-density recording and compensates for the effects of pulse crowding. More sophisticated systems permit precompensation to be fine-tuned (i.e. the amount by which pulses are shifted from their nominal time slot is made a user-selectable parameter). The 1770 FDC either advances or delays write bits by 125 ns from their nominal times according to the following algorithm. All other bit patterns are recorded at their nominal centre.

bit_{i-3}	bit_{i-2}	bit_{i-1}	bit_i	Advance/delay bit i
X	1	1	0	advance
X	0	1	1	delay
0	0	0	1	advance
1	0	0	1	delay

a0 (data address mark)

The data address mark is used only during a write sector command and is used to force a special bit pattern to identify the start of a data sector. If a0 = 0, the normal data mark is written. If a0 = 1, the deleted data address mark is written.

m (multiple record flag)

Then m flag in type II commands determines whether the command is to be executed once only, or repeatedly. If m = 0 a single sector is read from or written to, and an interrupt is generated at the completion of the command. If m = 1 multiple sectors can be accessed. After each sector has been read from or written to, the FDC's sector register is automatically updated. This allows an address verification on the next sector read, provided, of course, the V-bit is set. In the multiple sector mode, the FDC continues to read or write records and to update the sector register in numerical ascending sequence until the sector register exceeds the number of sectors on the track, or until the force interrupt command is loaded into the command register. The latter operation is carried out under program control and aborts the multiple sector command.

7.4.2 The 1770's instruction set

We will now look at the 1770's command in more detail. Tables 7.3 and 7.4 reveal that the 1770 FDC has eleven instructions plus their variations, arranged into four basic classes. These classes are: class I – basic read/write head movement; class II – sector read/write; class III – track operations; class IV – force an interrupt. The details of the actual instructions are rather complex and may be found in the 1770 series data sheets in flowchart form. Here, only the basic details of each command are given, for the purpose of brevity.

Type I commands

Restore (seek track 0)

Because the disk drive has an open-loop track seeking mechanism, some form of absolute reference is necessary to ensure that the track over which the head is positioned is the expected track. An absolute positional reference is provided by track 0 (often written Track 00 by convention), the outermost track on the disk, because the TR00* output from the disk drive is asserted when the head is over track zero. Once the head is positioned over track 0, it can be moved to the desired track by stepping the requisite number of tracks. 'Ah!' you say, 'Why don't you determine the position of the head by reading the ID field of the current track?' This can be done, but the restore command is automatically performed after a reset operation to place the system in a known state. In any case, it is necessary to use a restore if the disk has not been formatted. You cannot read a track's ID until it has first been written.

Once a restore op-code has been loaded into the FDC's command register, thre TR00* input from the disk drive is sampled. If TR00* is asserted, the head must already be over track 0 and the command is terminated after the track register has been loaded with zero. If it is negated, the FDC generates stepping pulses at the rate determined by r1,r0 until TR00* goes active-low and then the track register is cleared to reflect the current position of the head. This, and all other commands, are terminated by an interrupt request. Should TR00* not be asserted within 256 stepping pulses, the FDC terminates the operation, generates an interrupt and sets the seek error bit in the status register. The limit of 256 stepping pulses has been imposed to avoid the system hanging up if the disk drive is faulty. Occasionally, the head steps past track 0 and keeps trying to move outwards. Sometimes the head positioning mechanism jumps out of its groove and refuses to move. In these cases operator intervention may be necessary. If the V flag is set, a verification takes place. Similarly, if the h flag is set, the motor-on option is selected at the start of the command. The verify, motor-on option and interrupt on termination actions are common to all type I commands. An interrupt is generated at the completion of a seek.

Seek

The seek command moves the head to the track position specified by the contents of the *data register*. As the head is stepped towards its intended location, the contents of the track register are updated. Note that the track register must contain the current head position before the seek command is executed, as it is updated by recording the number of tracks moved from the initial head position. Remember that in this case the FDC's data register is used to hold command information (i.e. the destination track) rather than data.

When the contents of the track register match the number in the data register, the seek operation is complete.

Step, step-in and step-out

These three commands each cause the head to execute one step to an adjacent track. A *step* moves the head in the same direction as the previous step command, a *step-in* moves it one track in the direction of track 39 and a *step-out* moves it one track in the direction of track 0. In each case, a verification is executed if the V-bit is set, the track register is updated if the u flag is set, and the motor-on option is selected if the h-bit is set.

Type II commands

The 1770 has two type II commands, read a sector and write a sector. As we might imagine, the operation of these commands are very similar.

Read sector

As its name suggests, the read sector command causes the FDC to read the contents of an entire sector byte by byte. Before executing a read (or write) sector, it is necessary to load the sector register with the number of the sector to be read (or written to). When this command is issued, the busy bit of the status register is set and the DRQ, lost data and record not found, RNF, bits are cleared. If the E flag is set, the command is not executed until after a 30 ms delay.

The FDC begins a read or write sector command by locating and reading the first ID field encountered. If the track number in the track register matches with that read from the disk, the sector number in the ID field is compared with the value in the sector register. Successive ID fields are read until the required sector is found. When this occurs, the CRC of the ID field is checked and, if there is no error, the data field is read. If the FDC does not find an ID field with a valid track number, sector number and CRC within five revolutions, the record not found bit of the status register is set and the command is terminated with an interrupt request.

As each byte is obtained from the disk, it is loaded into the data register and the DRQ (data request) output is asserted. If the host microprocessor does not read the data register before the current byte has been overwritten by the next one transferred from the disk, the lost data bit in the status register is set to indicate an overrun condition. The command is completed when the CRC of the data field has been read and verified. If the CRC is valid, the CRC error status bit is cleared. If it is in error, the CRC error status bit is set and the command terminated (even if the multiple sector bit is set). If $m = 1$, multiple records are read and the sector register updated so that address verification can take place on the next record. At the end of a read operation, the type of data and address mark found in the data field is recorded in bit 5 of the status register ($SR\_5 = 0 =$ deleted data mark, $SR\_5 = 1 =$ data mark).

Write sector

The write sector command is almost identical in operation to the read sector. When the appropriate sector has been located, the DRQ (data request) output is asserted and the DRQ bit of the status register is set. If the DRQ is not serviced (i.e. by writing data to the FDC's data register) within 11 bytes (FM) or 22 bytes (MFM), the command is terminated and the lost data flag is set.

If the DRQ is serviced, the write gate (WG) output is asserted and 6 bytes of zeros (FM) or 12 bytes of zeros (MFM) are written to the disk. Then the data address mark is written, followed by the data to be recorded. The host microprocessor must service each DRQ (one for each byte to be written) before the FDC runs out of data to write to the sector. If the FDC does not have data to record, a byte of zeros is written to the disk and the lost data flag is set. Note that this does not terminate the command, as that would lead to an incomplete sector. After the last byte has been written, the FDC computes a 16-bit CRC and writes it to the sector, followed by a byte of all ones. The FDC terminates a write command by negating the WE output and then generating an interrupt.

Type III commands

Read address

The read address command is a diagnostic operation designed to inform the host microprocessor of the current location of the read/write head. On receiving a read address command, the busy status flag is set and the next ID field is read from the disk. The entire 6 bytes of the ID field are treated as *pure data* and transferred to the data register one by one. The format of the ID field is given in Table 7.6.

TABLE 7.6 The format of the ID field

BYTE NO.	1	2	3	4	5	6
Function	Track address	Side no.	Sector Address	Length	CRC1	CRC2

```
00  128 bytes
01  256 bytes
10  512 bytes
11 1024 bytes
```

The two 8-bit CRC words are both transferred to the data register for reading and are also checked for validity internally by the FDC. Any error results in the CRC error status bit being set. Note that the track address read from the track address field of the ID is also loaded into the sector register, which allows easy comparison between the contents of the track register (expected location) and sector register which now contains the actual location of the read/write head. At the end of the read address command, an interrupt is generated and the busy bit cleared.

Read track

This is an almost entirely diagnostic operation and is not used during most normal disk operations. After a read track command has been loaded into the FDC, the busy bit is set and the spin-up sequence is completed. Reading starts with the leading edge of the first encountered index pulse and continues until the next index pulse. All gap, header and data bytes are read from the disk and, of course, a DRQ is generated for each byte read.

No CRC checking is performed by this command. By means of the *read track* operation the entire structure of a track can be obtained and used to look for errors or to deal with a record that has been corrupted.

Write track

The write track command is the inverse operation of a read track. However, unlike the read track command, it is not a diagnostic operation. It forms the heart of the disk formatting procedure. Initially, a virgin disk has nothing written on it at all. By employing the write track command, the basic structure of a track can be laid down on the disk.

Formatting a disk is accomplished by placing the head over each of the tracks in turn and then writing the appropriate track. Upon receipt of the write track command, the same motor-on sequence is executed as for a read track command. Writing starts with the leading edge of the first encountered index pulse and continues until the next index pulse (at which time an interrupt is generated). A data request is issued as soon as the write track command is loaded, but writing does not start until after the first byte has been loaded in the data register by the host microprocessor. If a byte is not in the DR when it is needed, a byte of zeros is written to the disk.

Earlier in this section it was stated that special address and data marks appear on the disk and are recognizable because they have *missing* clock pulses. When certain bytes are loaded into the data register during the execution of a write track command, they force the FDC to generate these special marks or a CRC byte, as shown in Table 7.7.

For example, if a data pattern in the range $F8 to $FB is loaded into the FDC's data register during a write operation when the FDC is in the single density FM mode, the CRC generator is initialized. Each new successive character is then used to build up the value of the CRC. When a $F7 is loaded in the FDC's data register, the accumulated CRC is written to the disk. Figure 7.13 provides two examples of how the special data patterns are generated.

A disk is formatted by successively writing the appropriate information on to each track by means of the write track command. While it is possible to use wide variety of disk formats, the IBM 3740, 128 bytes/sector FM, or IBM System 34, 256 bytes/sector MFM, formats are most suitable as they permit the interchangeability of disks between systems (at least as far as the physical representation of the data is concerned).

Table 7.8 (FM) and Table 7.9 (MFM) provide the sequence of data values that must be written to the disk in order to effect the appropriate IBM format. Once the formatting operation has been executed, the disk is available for normal read/write accesses. It is never reformatted unless it becomes irretrievably corrupted

TABLE 7.7 The effect of special bytes on the FDC during a write track command

DATA PATTERN LOADED IN DR	1770 INTERPRETATION OF DATA WHEN DDEN* = 1 (FM)	1770 INTERPRETATION OF DATA WHEN DDEN* = 0 (MFM)
00–F4	Write 00–F4 with clock = FF	Write 00–F4 in MFM
F5	Not allowed	Write A1 in MFM, preset CRC
F6	Not allowed	Write C2 in MFM
F7	Generate 2 CRC bytes	Generate 2 CRC bytes
F8–FB	Write F8–FB, clock = C7, preset CRC	Write F8–FB in MFM
FC	Write FC with clock = D7	Write FC in MFM
FD	Write FD with clock = FF	Write FD in MFM
FE	Write FE with clock = C7, preset CRC	Write FE in MFM
FF	Write FF with clock = FF	Write FF in MFM

Notes: 1. Clock refers to the clock pattern and is $FF in the single-density mode, because there is a clock pulse between each data pulse.
2. When A1 is written in the MFM mode, the missing clock transition is between bits 4 and 5.
3. When C2 is written in the MFM mode, the missing clock transition is between bits 3 and 4.

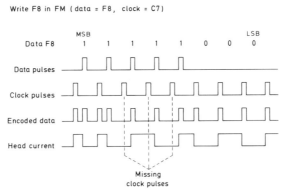

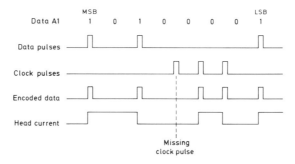

FIGURE 7.13 Special data patterns used as markers

TABLE 7.8 The information to be written to a track to format a disk with 128 bytes/sector FM

NUMBER OF BYTES WRITTEN	DATA VALUE	MEANING (DECIMAL)
40	FF or 00	
6	00	Address sync
1	FE	ID address mark
1	00–27	Track number 00–39
1	00 or 01	Side number 00 or 01
1	01–10	Sector number 01–16
1	00	Sector length 128 bytes
1	F7	Write two address CRCs
11	FF	Data gap
6	00	Data field sync
1	FB	Data address mark
128	E5	Data–initially 'E5'
1	F7	Write two CRCs
10	FF or 00	
369	FF or 00	

Notes: 1. The bracketed field is written 16 times.
2. The data written to the sector during formatting is typically $E5.
3. After the 16 sectors have been written, FFs are written until the FDC generates an interrupt at the end of the track. This gap is approximately 369 bytes long.

TABLE 7.9 The information to be written to a track to format a disk with 256 bytes/sector MFM

NUMBER OF BYTES WRITTEN	DATA VALUE	MEANING (DECIMAL)
60	4E	
12	00	
3	F5	Write A1
1	FE	ID address mark
1	00–27	Track number 00–39
1	00 or 01	Side number 00 or 01
1	01–10	Sector number 01–16
1	01	Sector length 256 bytes
1	F7	Write two CRCs
22	4E	
12	00	
3	F5	Write A1
1	FB	Data address mark
256		Data
1	F7	Write two CRCs
24	4E	
668	4E	

Notes: 1. The bracket field is written 16 times.
2. The data written to the sector during formatting is typically $E5.
3. After the 16 sectors have been written, $4Es are written until the FDC generates an interrupt at the end of the track. This gap is approximately 668 bytes long.

Type IV commands

Force interrupt

The force interrupt command can be loaded into the command register at any time and has the effect of forcing the FDC to generate an interrupt request to the host microprocessor. It is generally used to terminate a multiple sector read or write command, or to force the meaning of the contents of the status register to correspond to a type I command. If a command is currently being executed when a force interrupt command is loaded, the command is terminated and the busy flag bit reset.

The lower-order four bits of this command define the condition or conditions under which the FDC generates an interrupt and are defined in Table 7.5.

The status register of the 1770 FDC

The status register is 8 bits wide and reflects the status of the FDC. Unfortunately, the status register does not provide sufficient status information in 8 bits. Some chip makers would provide one or more auxiliary status

TABLE 7.10 Status register summary

BIT	NAME	MEANING
S7	Motor On	This bit reflects the status of MO output
S6	Write protect	When set, indicates write protect is activated; this bit is an inverted copy of the WRPT input
S5	Record type or spin-up	When set, this bit indicates that the motor spin-up sequence has been completed on type I commands; for type II and III commands this bit indicates record type: 0 = data mark, 1 = deleted data mark
S4	Record not found	When is set, record not found indicates that the desired track, sector or side were not found
S3	CRC error	If S3 is set, an error was found in one or more ID fields, otherwise it indicates an error in the data field
S2	Track 00	When set, indicates read/write head is positioned at track 0; this bit is an inverted copy of the TR00* input
	Lost data	On commands other than type I, S2 is set to indicate that the host processor did not respond to a DRQ in one byte time
S1	INDEX	For type I commands this bit indicates the status of the INDEX input
	Data request	On other commands S1 is a copy of the DRQ output; when set, it indicates that the data register is full on a read access or the data register is empty on a write access
S0	BUSY	When set, command is in progress; when reset, no command is in progress

registers. Not Western Digital. They have decided that the status information varies with the type of command issued, and have applied this information accordingly. For example, bit 5 of the status register corresponds to *spin up sequence complete* during a type I command, and to *record type* during a read sector command. In other words, the status information can only be interrupted with respect to the command currently loaded in the command register. Table 7.10 gives a summary of the interpretation of status bits.

7.5 Interfacing the 1770 FDC to a 68000

We have already covered the electrical interface of the 1770. Here, we are going to briefly look at some of the issues raised by programming the FDC.

Although the 1770 has several commands and variations on commands, all we really require to construct a practical FDC interface at the level of primitive operations are: a restore command, a seek track command, a read sector command, a write sector command and a format disk command. Error handling can either be performed at a *low level* (i.e. within these primitive actions) or at a *high level* by the disk file manager itself. Placing error handling and recovery in higher levels of software means that we can write very simple disk access primitives.

FLEX, a typical first generation operating system written by Technical System Consultants for the 6809 8-bit microprocessor, performs all its disk accesses via the following primitives. Some of the details have been simplified for our present purposes.

Read

Read a specified sector into memory and perform a seek if necessary. Entry parameters are a pointer to the sector buffer, track and sector addresses. Exit parameters are an error status byte from the FDC and a composite error flag (i.e. error/no error). All the primitives return the same status and error information.

Verify

The verify operation checks the last sector written to the disk for CRC errors. No seek is performed by a verify, as the seek is carried out immediately after a write access. No entry parameters are required by a verify operation.

Restore

Restore moves the head to track 0. There are no entry parameters and the exit parameters are the usual status byte and error flag.

Chkrdy

The check drive ready command determines whether the drive is ready to be accessed (i.e. its motor is running). The return parameter is drive ready/drive not ready.

Seek

The seek command seeks the specified track. The only input parameter is the track number.

We are now going to look at how some of these commands might be implemented in pseudocode. Note that in the read/write sector routines we check the busy bit of the 1770's status register to determine whether the FDC has aborted its read/write access before the requisite amount of data has been transferred, because the 1770 terminates a read or write sector operation whenever a fatal error is detected.

```
Read_sector
            Seek {locate the desired track}
            IF Seek_error THEN EXIT ENDIF
            Byte_count: = 256
            Issue read command to FDC
            REPEAT
              IF FDC DRQ_bit = 1 THEN
                                BEGIN
                                Read data byte from FDC
                                Transfer data to buffer
                                Byte_count: = Byte_count − 1
                                END
                                ELSE
                                BEGIN
                                IF FDC Busy_bit = 0 THEN ERROR ENDIF
                                END
              ENDIF
            UNTIL Byte_count = 0
            Return
    ERROR   Mask FDC Status_byte
            Return
End read_sector
```

```
Write_sector
        Seek
        IF Seek_error THEN ERROR ENDIF
        Issue write command to FDC
        Byte_count:=256
        REPEAT
          IF FDC DRQ_bit=1 THEN
                            BEGIN
                            Get byte from buffer
                            Send byte to FDC
                            Byte_count:=Byte_count−1
                            END
                            ELSE
                            BEGIN
                            IF FDC Busy_bit=0 THEN ERROR ENDIF
                            END
          ENDIF
        UNTIL Byte_count=0
        Return
ERROR   Mask FDC Status_byte
        Return
End write_sector

Seek    Seek_error:=false
        Write Track_number to FDC
        Issue seek command to FDC
        REPEAT
          Read FDC Status_byte
        UNTIL FDC Busy_bit=0
        Mask FDC Status_byte
        IF masked status≠0 THEN Seek_error:=true ENDIF
        Return
End seek

Verify
        Issue verify command to FDC {e.g. read command with V=1}
        REPEAT
          Read FDC Status_byte
        UNTIL FDC Busy_bit=0
        Mask FDC Status_byte
        Return
End verify
```

Restore
            Issue restore command to FDC
            REPEAT
                Read FDC Status_byte
            UNTIL FDC Busy_bit = 0
            Mask FDC Status_byte
            Return
End restore

At this stage we can now look at the type of 68000 assembly language that might be written to support the 1770 FDC. Please note that these routines are illustrative and are not intended to be definitive. The entry point to the software is ACCESS which decodes the command type in D3 and makes up to five attempts if an error is reported by one of the primitives called by ACCESS.

```
DRQ            EQU     1                              Data request = bit 1 of SR
BUSY           EQU     0                              Busy = bit 0 of SR
FDC_BASE       EQU     ⟨Base of memory mapped FDC⟩
BUFFER         EQU     ⟨Sector buffer in memory⟩
COM_REG        EQU     0                              FDC command register
STAT_REG       EQU     0                              FDC status register
TRACK_REG      EQU     2                              FDC track register
SECTOR_REG     EQU     4                              FDC sector register
DATA_REG       EQU     6                              FDC data register
RD_CMND        EQU     $84                            Read m = 0, h = 0, E = 1)
WR_CMND        EQU     $A4                            Write (m = 0, h = 0, E = 1, P = 0)
RST_CMND       EQU     $03                            Restore (h = 0, V = 0, r1,r0 = 1,1)
SEEK_CMND      EQU     $13                            Seek (h = 0, V = 0, r1,r0 = 1,1)
VRFY_CMND      EQU     $17                            Verify = seek with V = 1
MASK           EQU     $5C                            Mask status to WRPT, RNF,
*                                                     CRC error, lost data
MASK1          EQU     $18                            Mask to RNF, CRC
*
*              D0 = track register
*              D1 = sector register
*              D3 = command identifier
*              D4 = attempt counter (five tries allowed)
*              D5 = byte count (read/write)
*              D7 = FDC status byte
*
ACCESS         MOVE.W  #4,D4                          5 tries allowed
               LEA     FDC_BASE,A0                    A0 points to base of FDC
ACCESS1        MOVE.B  TRACK,D0                       Setup track register
               MOVE.B  SECTOR,D1                      Setup sector register
               MOVE.B  COMMAND,D3                     Setup command
               CMP.B   #0,D3                          Test for restore command
               BNE     TRY_SEEK
               BSR     RESTORE                        IF restore THEN do it
               BRA     COMPLETION                     and exit
```

```
TRY_SEEK       CMP.B    #1,D3                          Test for seek command
               BNE      TRY_VERIFY
               BSR      SEEK                           IF seek THEN do it
               BRA      COMPLETION                     and exit
TRY_VERIFY     CMP.B    #2,D3                          Test for verify command
               BNE      TRY_READ
               BSR      VERIFY                         IF verify THEN do it
               BRA      COMPLETION                     and exit
TRY_READ       CMP.B    #3,D3                          Test for write command
               BNE      TRY_WRITE
               BSR      READ                           IF read THEN do it
               BRA      COMPLETION                     and exit
TRY_WRITE      CMP.B    #4,D3                          Test for write command
               BNE      NO_CMND                        IF not write THEN invalid command
               BSR      WRITE                          IF write THEN do it
               BRA      COMPLETION                     and exit
*
NO_CMND        RTS                                     Simple return
*
COMPLETION     TST.B    D7                             Any errors?
               BEQ      EXIT_OK                        If no error then return
               DBRA     D4,ACCESS1                     ELSE try again
               BRA      EXIT_FAIL                      Exit after five tries
*
EXIT_OK        RTS                                     These two return points
EXIT_FAIL      RTS                                        may be modified to include
*                                                         any other necessary actions
*
READ           BSR      SEEK                           Perform seek if necessary
               BNE      RDEXIT                         IF seek_error THEN exit
               MOVE.B   D1,SECTOR_REG(A0)              Tell FDC which sector
               LEA      BUFFER,A1                      A1 points to data buffer
               MOVE.W   #255,D5                        Setup byte count
               MOVE.B   #RD_CMND,COM_REG(A0)           Issue read command
RDRPT          MOVE.B   STAT_REG(A0),D7               Read FDC status byte
               BTST.B   #DRQ,D7                        IF data from FDC THEN get it
               BEQ      RD1
               MOVE.B   DATA_REG(A0),(A1)+             Move data from FDC to buffer
               DBRA     D5, RDRPT                      REPEAT UNTIL all data read
               BRA      RDGXIT
RD1            BTST.B   #BUSY,D7                       ELSE test if FDC still busy
               BEQ      RDERROR                        IF not busy THEN error
               BRA      RDRPT                          REPEAT
RDEXIT         AND.B    #MASK,D7                       Mask status
               RTS
RDERROR        AND.B    #MASK,D7                       Mask to error bits
               RTS

WRITE          BSR      SEEK                           Perform seek
               BNE      WRERROR                        IF seek_error THEN exit
               MOVE.B   D1,SECTOR_REG(A0)              Tell FDC which sector
               LEA      BUFFER,A1                      A1 pointer to data buffer
               MOVE.B   #WR_CMND,COM_REG(A0)           Issue write command
               MOVE.W   #255,D5                        Setup byte count
```

```
WRRPT       MOVE.B   STAT_REG(A0),D7        Read FDC status byte
            BTST.B   #DRQ,D7                If FDC ready for data THEN
            BEQ      WR1                       get it ELSE test for not busy
            MOVE.B   (A1)+,DATA_REG(A0)     Move data from buffer to FDC
            DBRA     D5, WRRPT              REPEAT UNTIL all data written
            BRA      WREXIT
WR1         BTST.B   #BUSY,D7               Is FDC still busy
            BEQ      WRERROR                IF not busy THEN error
            BRA      WRRPT                  REPEAT
WREXIT      AND.B    #MASK,D7              Mask status
            RTS
WRERROR     AND.B    #MASK,D7              Mask status byte to error
            RTS

SEEK        MOVE.B   #SEEK_CMND,COM_REG(A0)    Issue seek command
            MOVE.B   D0,TRACK_REG(A0)         Tell FDC which track we want
SEEKWAIT    MOVE.B   STAT_REG(A0),D7          REPEAT
            BTST.B   #BUSY,D7                 Read FDC status register
            BNE      SEEKWAIT                 UNTIL FDC not busy
            AND.B    #MASK1,D7               Mask status to error bits
SEEKEXIT    RTS

VERIFY      MOVE.B   #VRFY_CMND,COM_REG(A0)   Issue verify command
VRFYLOOP    BTST.B   #BUSY,STAT_REG(A0)       REPEAT Read FDC status
            BNE      VRFYLOOP                 UNTIL FDC not busy
            AND.B    #MASK1,D7               Mask status to error bits
            RTS

RESTORE     MOVE.B   #RST_CMND,COM_REG(A0)    Issue restore command
RSTLOOP     BTST.B   #BUST,STAT_REG(A0)       REPEAT Read FDC status
            BNE      RSTLOOP                  UNTIL FDC not busy
            AND.B    #MASK1,D7               Mask status to error bits
            RTS
```

Disk formatting

There is, unfortunately, no simple way of formatting disks with the WD1770 FDC. It is necessary to set up in memory an *image* of the tracks to be formatted and then to use the write track command to write each track to disk.

Starting at track 0, the image of a complete track is stored in RAM. This image includes all gaps, the ID address mark, the track and sector numbers, dummy data, the data address mark and the CRC code. Remember that certain codes are interpreted by the 1770's write track commands as special control codes that force the FDC to write a CRC or an address mark etc.

Once the track image has been set up (usually one track at a time is formatted), it is written to the disk using the write track command. Each track is set up and written to disk in the same way (but, of course, with a new track image in memory).

7.6 An introduction to the 68454 intelligent multiple disk controller

If I were asked to name the peripherals that had grown most in complexity and sophistication over the decade 1975–85, I would choose the CRT controller and the floppy disk controller. The 1770 that we have just described is a linear descendant of Western Digital's first generation of floppy disk controllers. Here we are going to outline some of the features of the Signetics SCN68454 Intelligent Multiple Disk Controller, IMDC. Unfortunately, it is impossible to do the IMDC justice in a relatively short space. Equally, it is impossible to describe the IMDC in detail, because of its sheer complexity.

The key features of the IMDC are its ability to support up to four rigid Winchester disks and floppy disks in any combination, its very high performance (data transfer rates up to 10 Mbits/s) and its amazing flexibility (i.e. programmability).

The 68454 to 68000 interface

It is moderately easy to interface the IMDC to a 68000, because the IMDC has been designed to be compatible with the 68000. In other words, the IMDC fully supports the 68000's asynchronous data bus. Moreover, the IMDC has an on-chip DMA controller and is able to execute DMA data transfers.

One of the problems facing the designers of peripherals is the need for more and more internal (i.e. on-chip) control and data registers to hold the large volume of control and status data required by today's peripherals. The IMDC neatly avoids the difficulties created by putting a large number of registers on chip. Indeed, the IMDC has fewer on-chip registers than some very old peripherals!

The IMDC locates the vast majority of its registers *off-chip* in the system memory. While freeing the IMDC from the tyranny of a limited number of registers, it raises the problem of how the IMDC goes about accessing its own registers. The answer to this dilemma is simple. The programmer (i.e. operating system) loads the IMDC's registers in memory with their appropriate values and then loads the IMDC with a *pointer* to these off-chip registers. A command is next issued to the IMDC to trigger its DMA controller. Now the IMDC uses its own DMA controller to request the bus from the host 68000 and thereby access its registers in memory.

Figure 7.14 shows how the IMDC maintains its data structures. Two 16-bit registers hold the *event control area pointer* that points to a block of four longwords in memory called the *event control area*. The event control area (ECA) consists of four longword pointers, each of which points to the event control area block belonging to one of the disks. Note that the IMDC maintains up to four ECA blocks, one for each disk drive. More basic chips like the 1770 can deal with only one drive at a time because it is necessary to reload their track and sector registers each time a new drive is accessed. The ECA blocks hold all the parameters necessary to access the associated disks.

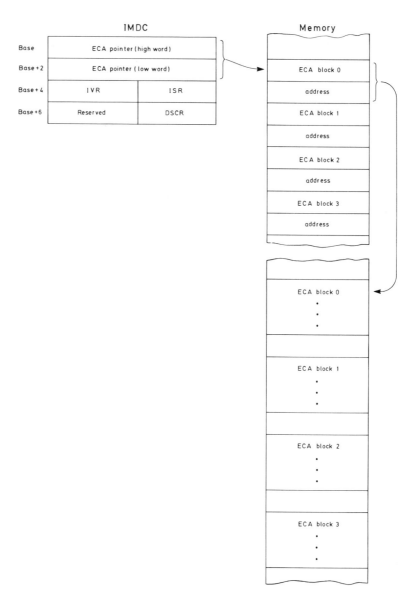

FIGURE 7.14 The IMDC's data structure

The other on-chip registers of the IMDC are an 8-bit *interrupt vector register,* an 8-bit *interrupt source register* an 8-bit *drive status and configuration register,* DSCR. The DSCR determines whether the IMDC operates in an 8-bit or a 16-bit data transfer mode and permits the programmer to activate the disk drive. By setting one of the DSCR's disk busy bits to 1, the IMDC makes a DMA request and accesses the associated event control area block to perform the action (previously loaded into the ECA block).

An indication of the type of hardware required to support the IMDC is provided in Figure 7.15. Although the IMDC is tailored to the 68000 bus, it requires latches and bidirectional data transceivers to implement its DMA

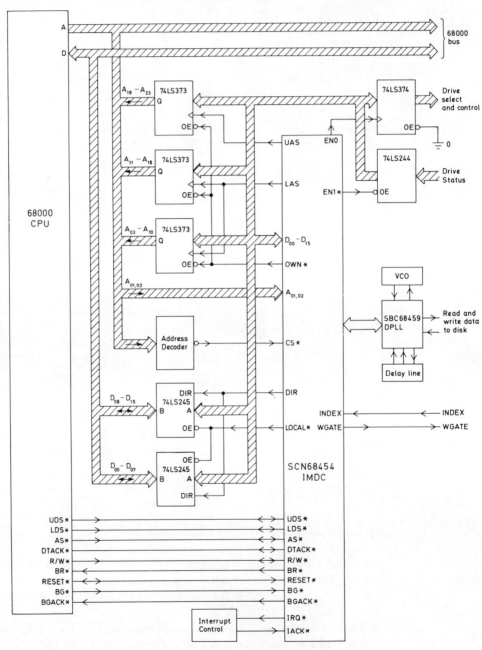

FIGURE 7.15   Hardware required to support the IMDC

interface. Whenever it is accessed by the host 68000, its CS* input goes low and its registers are written to or read from in the normal way. Whenever it is triggered by setting a busy bit in its command and status register, it uses the three bus arbitration lines to gain control of the bus and access memory through its multiplexed address and data bus.

The disk side of the IMDC is more complex than that of earlier FDCs, because it requires a relatively complex external data and clock pulse separator if it is able to operate at the 10 Mbits/s data transfer rate supported by rigid disks.

The operating parameters of the IMDC are governed by the contents of the ECA block as listed in Table 7.11. It is not my intention to define the meaning of the 45 words of an event control area, but to demonstrate the range of attributes provided in an ECA block. For example, complex disk drives are supported and the parameters of the track structure are user definable (words 16 to 18 of the ECA block).

TABLE 7.11 The structure of the IMDC's ECA block

WORD NO.	15	8	7	0	
00	Command code		Main status		
01	Extended status				
02	Max no. of retries		Actual no. of retries		
03	DMA count		Command options		
04	Buffer address most significant word				
05	Buffer address least significant word				
06	Buffer length request				
07	No. of bytes transferred				
08	Cylinder number				*
09	Head number		Sector number		*
10	Current cylinder position				
11	PRP command control word				†
12	Location of SCWT, most significant word				†
13	Location of SCWT, least significant word				†
14	Scan terminator		Reserved		†
15	Maximum record length − 1				†
16	N0 – pre-index gap		N1 – post-index gap		‡
17	N2 – sync byte count		N3 – Post-ID gap		‡

(continued)

TABLE 7.11 (*continued*)

WORD NO.	15	8	7	0	
18	N4 – Post-data gap		N5 – address mark cnt		‡
19	Reserved				‡
20–22	ECC mask (3 words)				
23	Motor on delay		No. of heads		
24	Ending sector no.		Stepping rate		
25	Head setting time		Head load time		
26	Seek type		Phase count		
27	Low write current boundary track				
28	Precompensation boundary track				
29–31	ECC remainder (3 words)				§
32	Maximum number of cylinders per surface				
33	Sector length/first sector		Flag byte		
34–35	B – tree pointer (2 words)				†
36–45	IMDC working area 10 words				

* Physical starting sector number.
† Programmable record processing parameters.
‡ Track format fields.
§ ECC remainder will be aligned to the MSB byte of this field.

Note that the ECA block does not include a *data area*. Data destined for a disk in a write operation or data read from a disk in a read operation is stored in the buffer whose address is given by words 4 and 5 of the ECA block and whose length is indicated by the word 6.

The IMDC executes a set of commands that are not particularly different from those of the 1770. However, the IMDC can also execute some rather sophisticated commands. Not only can the IMDC format a disk, it can search a disk for a particular string. Words 12 and 13 of the ECA block point to the *scan control word table*, SCWT, in memory which defines the parameters required by the search. For example, the IMDC can be instructed to locate a specified string of characters within a logical data block. After the string has been located, the IMDC can be programmed to retrieve and store the contents of the logical data block. These facilities of the IMDC are quite complex but are very efficient because they free the host processor from much tedious processing.

We are clearly observing a trend towards FDCs that behave in a more and more autonomous fashion. Each new generation of FDCs takes on more of the functions that were once performed by the operating system. Perhaps future generations of FDC will actually put the file-handling part of an operating system on-chip and the instruction set of the FDC will include operations of the form, 'open a file, update a file, read a file, delete a file'.

7.7 Disk data structures

Up to now we have considered only the structure of information stored on disk at the track and sector level. The large-scale structure of information on disks belongs to the realm of operating systems. However, now that we have got so far, it would be churlish to end without saying something about files.

There are many ways of organizing files on disk and any particular method has its own peculiar advantages and disadvantages. Conceptually, we can imagine that a disk file system might require three data structures: a list of the sectors available for use by the filing system (i.e. the free sectors) a directory or catalogue of files and the files themselves.

7.7.1 The free sector list

A simple, crude, but quite effective method of dealing with the allocation of sectors to files is to provide a bit-map (usually in track 0, sector 1). Each bit of the bit-map represents one of the sectors on the disk, and is clear to indicate a free sector and set to indicate an allocated sector. *Free* means that the sector can be given to a new file and *allocated* means that the sector already belongs to a file. If all bits of the bit-map are set, there are no more free sectors and the disk is full. Figure 7.16 illustrates the free sector list.

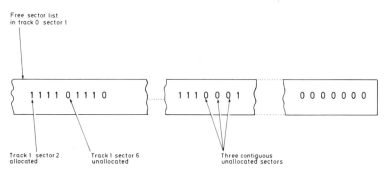

FIGURE 7.16   The free sector list

A disk with 40 tracks of 16 sectors has a total of $40 \times 16 = 649$ sectors. If we assume that the free sector list is written in FM, the bit-map sector contains 128 bytes or 1024 bits. Disks with a greater number of sectors may require two or more sectors for the bit-map.

Clusters

It is not necessary to allocate a bit to each sector on the disk. Some operating systems associate each bit of the bit-map with a *cluster* of, say, eight sectors. Using a cluster-map rather than a bit-map reduces the number of bits required in the map and is more efficient because it reduces the number of times that the operating system has to search the map for new sectors. However, the cluster-map increases the *granularity* of files because they are forced to grow in minimum increments of a whole cluster. If sectors hold 1024 bytes, eight-sector clusters mean that the minimum increment for a file is 8×1024 bytes $= 8$ Kbytes. If the disk holds a large number of files, the total wasted space can be quite considerable.

Whenever the disk file manager wishes to create a file, it searches the bit-map for free sectors and allocates them to the file. Similarly, when a file is deleted, its sectors are once more returned to the free pool by clearing the appropriate bits in the bit-map. Note that the sectors comprising the file are not overwritten or deleted when the file is deleted by the operating system. For this reason, it is often possible to recover 'deleted' files as long as they have not been overwritten since they were removed from the directory and their sectors returned to the pool of free sectors.

The MS DOS operating system does not maintain a bit-map (or cluster-map) as such. MS DOS maintains a cluster-map in which each entry points to the location of the next cluster used by the file containing the current cluster. This data structure is termed a *file allocation table*, FAT. A simplified version of FAT might look like the following:

```
FAT byte:  2  3  4  5  6  7  8  9  A  B   C   D  . . .
Cluster    4     6        7  8  A     B  FF
```

The file can be represented by the clusters:

| 4 | | 6 | | 7 | | 8 | | A | | B |

Note that the entry $FF in the FAT indicates the last cluster in a file.

Logical and physical sectors

The physical sectors on a disk are numbered 1, 2, . . up to the maximum number of sectors per disk. Equally, the logical sectors making up a file are also numbered 1, 2, . . . At first sight it might seem sensible to make the physical and logical numbering of sectors the same. After all, if a file has logical sector numbers . . . , 6, 7, 8, 9, . . , these sectors can quite happily be mapped onto the contiguous physical sectors numbered, say, . . . 2, 3, 4, 5 . . . Unfortunately, this simple scheme has a problem. When a sector is read from disk, the operating system must perform various housekeeping functions after each sector has been read (e.g. calculation of the next sector address, data validation, transferring the data to its destination in main memory, etc.). If the logical sectors of a disk are mapped onto contiguous physical sectors, by the time physical sector i has been read and processed, the head might be over, say, physical sector $i+2$. Consequently, contiguous sectors cannot be read consecutively and almost a complete revolution of the disk takes place between each sector read. By *interleaving* the logical sectors, we can greatly reduce access time by arranging that the next logical sector will be the next physical sector to be read. Figure 7.17 demonstrates the effect of sector interleaving.

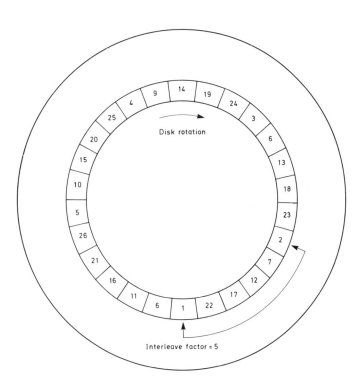

FIGURE 7.17 Sector interleaving

7.7.2 The directory

There is little point in storing data on a disk unless it can be accessed with a minimum of effort. To achieve this objective, a data structure called a *directory* holds information about the nature of each file and where the file can be found. Information in directories varies from the minimum required (the file name plus the location of the first sector of the file) to an extensive description of the file (including attributes such as file ownership or access rights). Figure 7.18 illustrates a possible directory structure.

Name
Extension
Date first created
Date last read
Date last updated
File type (e.g. text, relocatable object, absolute object, compressed text, encoded, etc.
Length of file in sectors
Pointer to list of contents
Access rights (e.g. read-only, invisible, delete protection)

FIGURE 7.18   The directory structure

Before continuing with a discussion of file structures, we need to introduce the concept of a linked list. Figure 7.19 demonstrates a simple linked list in which each sector contains a pointer to the *next* sector in the list. The final sector contains a null pointer (i.e. 0) because it has no next sector to point to. The advantage of a linked list is that the sectors can be randomly organized on the disk (randomization occurs because new files are continually being created and old files deleted). Two bytes are required for each pointer; one for the track number and one for the sector number.

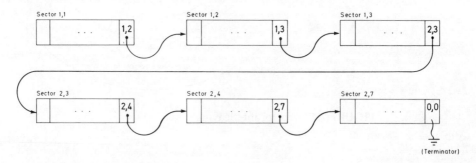

FIGURE 7.19   The linked list

An alternative form of linked list has two pointers per element and is illustrated in Figure 7.20. Each element has a pointer that points to the previous element and a pointer that points to the next element. The advantage of the doubly linked list is that we can move through it in either a forward direction or in a backward direction. Moreover, if one of the links is *damaged*, it is still possible for the operating system to recover the file. If a sector is lost in a single linked list, all successive sectors are lost.

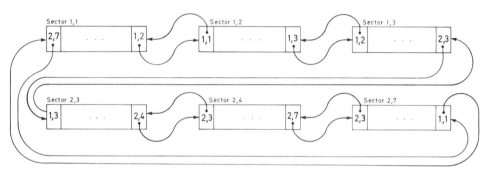

FIGURE 7.20 The doubly linked list

While linked lists can be used to create entire files, they create *sequential access* files rather than *random access* files. The only way of accessing a particular sector in the file is by reading all sectors of the list until the desired sector is located. Such a sequential access is, of course, highly inefficient. If a disk is heavily used, its files may become very fragmented (i.e. their positions randomized). Once the sectors making up the various disk files are located at almost entirely random addresses on the disk, disk accesses become very long because of the amount of head movement required. Programs have been written to clean up disk by reorganizing files to make consecutive *logical* sectors have consecutive addresses. However, sequential access files are very easy to set up and a disk file system designed to implement only sequential files is much easier to design than one that caters for random access files.

An alternative file organization is to maintain a list of sectors belonging to each file (Figure 7.21). Each directory entry contains a pointer to the list of sectors making up that file. Once the operating system has read the sector list, it is able to move to any point in the file without reading the file sequentially. Moreover, the operating system can conveniently increase the size of a file or delete part of it merely by updating a file's sector list (and, of course, the disk's sector map). A table of sectors makes it easy to create random access files.

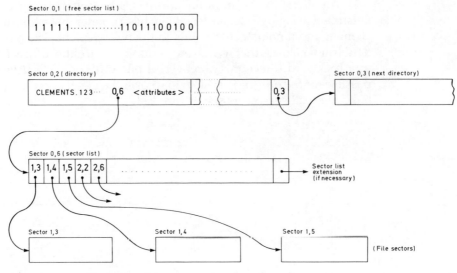

FIGURE 7.21 The sector list

7.7.3 Disk file manager primitives

The DFM performs a set of primitive operations on files just as the FDC software performs a set of primitive operations on individual tracks and sectors. Operations on files include:

DIR   List the files in the current directory
CREATE   Create a new file
DELETE   Remove a file from the directory
RENAME   Change the name of a file
COPY   Copy a file from one source to another
READ   Read the contents of a file
UPDATE   Modify the contents of a file

We can convert some of these commands into pseudocode as follows:

Create
    Locate the directory
    Find first free entry
    Locate bit-map
    Find sufficient free sectors for the file
    Remove these sectors from the bit-map
    Write new file entry in directory
    Create a list of sectors for the file
End create

Read
  Locate directory
  Scan directory to locate file
  IF file_not_found THEN EXIT ENDIF
  Read directory to locate sector list
  Read sector list
  Read sectors into buffer
End read

Many DFMs maintain a data structure in RAM that provides all the necessary details required to access files. This data structure is called a *file control block* (FCB) and a possible FCB for a disk file manager is illustrated in Figure 7.22. Essentially, the FCB provides a buffer area for the sector currently being accessed and the details of the current file. Each time a file is accessed by the DFM, the FCB is updated.

Function code (i.e. operation request to DFM)
Status returned to DFM
Directory information : name extension attributes address of sector list
Last sector accessed
Current sector being accessed
Next sector to be accessed
Next free sector available for file
Sector buffer (typically 256 bytes)

FIGURE 7.22   The file control block –FCB

Summary

We have now looked at all the significant aspects of a floppy disk subsystem for a microcomputer. Although the disk subsystem is quite complex, the average engineer designing a system has only to worry about the processor to FDC interface, the FDC to disk drive interface and the primitive routines that may need to be written to interface the FDC to the existing operating system.

Chapter 8

Multiprocessor

Systems

In a multiprocessor system two or more processors work together to achieve a greater throughput than is possible with one processor alone. I use the word *processor* in the previous sentence rather than *microprocessor* or *CPU*, because it is not necessary to combine identical processors to create a multiprocessor system. Indeed, there is sometimes an advantage in using several different types of processor, each optimized for the tasks to be run on it. Generally speaking, the term *processor* can be applied to any device with the characteristics of a central processing unit, CPU. That is, a processor should be able to read instructions from memory and then execute them (although some processors do not themselves read instructions from memory but rely on some other device to transfer data to them). A true multiprocessor system contains two or more processors in the *same* housing – the processors are separated by no more than a few tens of centimetres. The physical distance between the processors making up a multiprocessor system is important, because there is a world of difference between a multiprocessor system and the distributed computer system (called a local area network – LAN).

The individual processors in a multiprocessor system operate together on a *logically coherent* task. That is, the various processors of the multiprocessor system co-operate to solve a specific task and are not simply operating on a number of unrelated tasks, as we might find in a typical LAN. The processors communicate intimately with each other and often share the same facilities (either hardware or data). In contrast to the multiprocessor system, the individual processors of a distributed system are separated by distances ranging from a few metres to many kilometres and communication between them is minimal. The LAN is designed to enable users to share resources such as disks and printers that are geographically distributed. This chapter provides an overview of multiprocessor systems and describes some of the techniques that can be used to link together two or more 68000s to create a multiprocessor. In particular, we look at the way in which 68000s are able to communicate with each other via shared memory and by means of the popular VMEbus. Multiprocessing is, of course, a vast subject and here we only scratch the surface of this topic. We are more interested in the way in which the 68000 interfaces with other 68000 microprocessors than with specific applications of multiprocessor systems. High-performance multiprocessor systems with a level of performance ranging from that of the superminicomputer to the supercomputer are based on between 2^6 and 2^{16} processing elements.

8.1 An overview of multiprocessor systems

Multiprocessor systems exist only because a given task can be carried out by means of several low-cost processors operating in parallel, rather than by a single high-cost high-performance processor operating alone. For example, suppose an application requires a throughput equivalent to a single 68000 operating at a clock rate of 60 MHz. Clearly, such a device does not exist and the cost of constructing a system from ECL logic or buying a superminicomputer may be prohibitive. It may be possible to partition the task into subtasks in such a way that, say, ten 68000s operate on the subtasks simultaneously to give an effective throughput equal to that of a single high-performance processor.

Even when a multiprocessor system is not mandatory in a particular arrangement, multiprocessing can provide an economic advantage by increasing the power of a computer for very little additional cost. The economic benefits of multiprocessing arise because the cost of computer hardware lies almost entirely in its memory and peripherals. Often the microprocessor itself represents between 1 per cent and less than 0.01 per cent of the retail price of the system. Therefore, adding extra processors has little effect on the overall cost of the hardware. Unfortunately, an extra processor cannot just be plugged into an existing system. The global implications for the system hardware and its software are not trivial, because the individual processors have to share the available resources (i.e. memory and input/output). As with people, a one-person job is dispute free, while a two-person job introduces the possibility of conflict. An effective multiprocessor system must be able to allocate resources to contending processors without seriously degrading the performance of the system.

Another reason for the interest in multiprocessor systems springs from their potential reliability. It can be argued that, if the probability of failure over a given time of a processor is p, then the probability of the simultaneous failure of two processors is p^2. Thus, if $p = 1$ per cent per 10 000 hours for a given microprocessor, the reliability of a dual-processor system is 0.01 per cent per 10 000 hours. Similarly, the reliability of a triple-processor system is 0.0001 per cent per 10 000 hours.

Alas, life is not as simple as the above figures would suggest. The processor represents only a tiny fraction of a computer's total hardware and there is little point in replicating this relatively reliable component alone. A realistic implementation of a highly reliable system replicates memory, control and peripheral elements. To make matters worse, the extra logic needed to detect, report and deal with the failure of a processor reduces the reliability of the system. Consequently, multiprocessor systems can be designed to be highly reliable, but are not necessarily cheap. Such systems are said to offer a *high level of availability* and display *graceful degradation*. The latter term implies that the failure of part of the system results in a reduced level of peformance, but not necessarily its total shut-down.

Some multiprocessor systems are termed *reconfigurable*, which means that the structure of the hardware itself can be modified by the operating system. For example, the way in which memory is distributed between the individual processors can be changed dynamically under software control. Similarly, interrupt handling can be dynamically partitioned between the various processors to maximize efficiency. We do not discuss reconfigurable architectures further here.

While the architecture of a stored-program computer (i.e. a Von Neumann machine) can be defined quite precisely, there is no similar definition of a multiprocessor system. Multiprocessor systems come in many different flavours and a configuration suitable for one particular application is almost useless for another. The only really universal characteristic common to all multiprocessor systems is that they have more than one processor. We shall soon examine the various classes of multiprocessor system.

Along with the advantages of multiprocessor systems come the disadvantages. To be more precise, the disadvantages are really the problems that the systems designer must consider. These are the distribution of tasks between processors, the interconnection of the processors (i.e. the topology of the multiprocessor system), the management of the memory resources, the avoidance of deadlock and the control of input/output resources.

The distribution of tasks between processors is of crucial importance in selecting the architecture of the processor system itself. In turn, the distribution of tasks is strongly determined by the nature of the problem to be solved by the computer. In other words, the architecture of a multiprocessor system can be optimized for a certain type of problem. Conversely, a class of programs that runs well on one multiprocessor system may not run well on another.

A classic problem that often involves multiprocessing belongs to the world of air-traffic control. A radar system receives a periodic echo from the targets (i.e. aircraft) being tracked. Each echo is a function of the bearing and distance of the target. Due to imperfections in the system, there is an uncertainty associated with the echo. Moreover, a new echo is received every few milliseconds. From this constantly changing input, the computer connected to the radar receiver has to calculate the current positions of the targets and then to estimate the future track of each target and report any possible conflicts. Such a system requires very large amounts of computer processing power with relatively little I/O activity or disk access. Obviously it is not unreasonable to try to solve the problem by means of multiprocessing. For example, as one processor is updating a target's current position, another processor can be calculating its future position.

The preceding problem is described as *classic*, because it is so well suited to multiprocessing. There are several ways of allocating the mathematics involved in the radar calculations to the various processors. It is, unfortunately, much less easy to decompose a general task into a number of subtasks that can be run in parallel. Often it is necessary for the *programmer* to write programs in such a way that they involve the greatest amount of parallel activity.

8.1.1 Topics in multiprocessor systems design

The key parameter of a multiprocessor system is its topology, which defines how the processors are arranged with respect to each other and how they communicate. A second important parameter of a multiprocessor system is the degree of coupling between the various processors. We will discuss processor coupling first and then look at multiprocessor topologies.

Processors with facilities for exchanging large quantities of data very rapidly are said to be tightly coupled. Such computers share resources like buses or memory blocks. The advantage of tightly coupled systems is their potential speed, because one processor does not have to wait long periods of time while data is transferred from another. Their disadvantage springs from the complexity of the hardware and software necessary to co-ordinate the processors. If they share a bus or memory, some arbiter is needed to determine which processor is permitted to access the resource at any time. Arbitration may require both complex software and hardware.

Loosely coupled processors transfer data via an I/O channel such as a parallel (or even a serial) port, which offers a much slower data interchange but which simplifies the hardware design.

Although not a problem associated entirely with multiprocessors, the avoidance of deadlock must feature in the design of some classes of multiprocessor. Deadlock is a term most frequently used in the world of multi-tasking systems and describes the situation in which two tasks are unable to proceed because each task holds something needed by the other. In a real-time system, the sequential tasks (i.e. the software) require resources (memory, disk drives, I/O devices, etc), while in a multiprocessor system these resources are required by the individual processors.

Suppose a multiprocessor system has two processors X and Y. In order to complete its task, processor X needs resources P and Q, and processor Y also needs resources P and Q. If X seizes resources P and Q before Y, there is no problem because X continues and Y must wait for the resources to become available. If, however, X seizes P and at the same time Y seizes Q, we have a deadlock. X is waiting for Y to release Q but Y will not release Q until it has used P. Similarly, Y is waiting for X to release P. Therefore, the system halts and goes into an infinite waiting loop; a situation also called the *deadly embrace*.

When designing multiprocessor systems, the problem of deadlock cannot be overlooked and ways of avoiding the situation in which no processor has all the resources it needs must be considered. The avoidance of deadlock falls within the scope of the operating systems designer and is not considered further here.

Every multiprocessor system, like every single-processor system, has facilities for input or output transactions. We therefore have the problem of how I/O transactions are to be treated in a multiprocessor system. Does each processor have its own I/O arrangements? Is the I/O pooled between the processors, with each processor asking for I/O facilities as they are needed? Finally, is it possible to dedicate one or more processors solely to the task of I/O processing?

In a similar vein, the designer of a multiprocessor may need to construct an appropriate interrupt-handling system. When an I/O device interrupts a processor in a single-processor system, there is not a lot to decide. Either the processor services the interrupt or it is deferred. In a multiprocessor system we have to decide which processor will service an interrupt, which in turn begs the question, 'Do we pool interrupts or do we allocate certain types of interrupt to specific processors'? If interrupts are pooled, the interrupt-handling software must also be pooled, as processor A must deal with an interrupt from device X in exactly the same way that processor B would deal with the same interrupt. In addition to interrupts generated by I/O devices, it is possible for one processor to interrupt another processor.

Like any other computer, the multiprocessor requires an operating system. There are two basic approaches to the design of operating systems for multiprocessors. One of the simplest arrangements is the *master–slave* operating system in which a single operating system runs on the *master processor* and all other processors receive tasks that are handed down from the master. The master–slave operating system is little more than the type of operating system found in conventional single-processor systems.

The *distributed* operating system provides each processor with its own copy of the operating system (or at least a processor can access the common operating system via shared memory). Distributed operating systems are more robust than their master–slave counterparts because the failure of a single processor does not necessarily bring about a complete system collapse.

The problems we have just highlighted serve to emphasize that a multiprocessor system cannot easily be built in a vacuum. Whenever we are faced with the design of a multiprocessor system it is necessary to ask, 'Why do we need the multiprocessor system and what are its objectives?' and then to configure it accordingly. In other words, almost all design aspects of a multiprocessor system are very much problem dependent.

8.1.2 Multiprocessor organization

Although there are an endless variety of multiprocessor architectures, we can identify broad groups whose members have certain features in common. One possible approach to the classification of multiprocessor systems, attributed to Flynn, is to consider the type of the parallelism (i.e. architecture or topology)

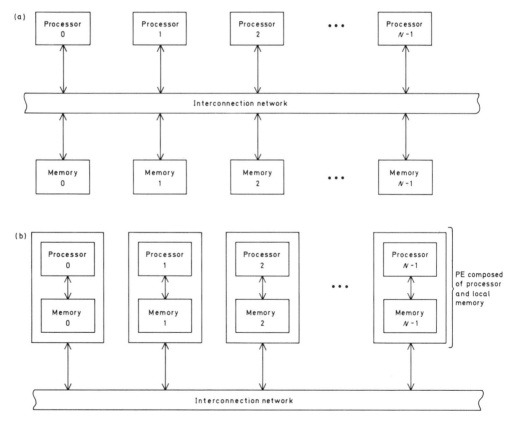

FIGURE 8.1 P to M and PE to PE multiprocessor configurations. (a) Processor to memory structure, (b) PE to PE structure

and the nature of the interprocessor communication. Flynn's four basic multiprocessor architectures are referred to by the acronyms: SISD, SIMD, MISD and MIMD and are described later. However, before continuing, we must point out that Flynn's topological classification of multiprocessor systems is not the only one possible, as multiprocessors may be categorized by a number of different parameters. One broad classification of multiprocessors depends on the processor's relationship to memory and to other processing elements. Multiprocessors can be classified as *processor to memory* (P to M) structures or as *processing element to processing element* (PE to PE) structures. Figure 8.1 describes these two structures. A P to M architecture has N processors, an interconnection network and N memory elements. The interconnection network allocates processor X to memory Y. The more general PE to PE architecture uses N processors, each with its own memory, and permits PE X to communicate with PE Y via an interconnection network. The multiprocessors described in this chapter best fit the PE to PE model.

SISD (single instruction single data-stream)

The SISD machine is nothing more than the conventional single processor system. It is called *single instruction* because only one instruction is executed at a time, and *single data-stream* because there is only one task being executed at any instant.

SIMD (single instruction multiple data-stream)

The SIMD architecture is designed to execute instructions *sequentially*, but on data in *parallel*. The idea of a single instruction operating on parallel data is not as strange as it may sound. Consider vector mathematics, where, for example, the calculation of the inner product of two n-component vectors, **A** and **B**, is frequently required. The inner product of vectors **A** and **B** is defined as

$$s = \mathbf{A} \cdot \mathbf{B} = \sum_{i=0}^{n-1} a_i b_i$$

The inner product is expressed as a single operation (i.e. $s = \mathbf{A} \cdot \mathbf{B}$), but involves multiple data elements (i.e. the $\{a_i b_i\}$). One way of speeding up the calculation of an inner product is to assign a processor to the generation of each of the individual elements, the $\{a_i b_i\}$. The simultaneous calculation of $a_i b_i$ for $i = 0$ to $n - 1$ requires n processors, one for each component of the vector.

Such an arrangement generally consists of a single controller that steps through the program (i.e. the single instruction-stream) and an array of processing elements (PEs) acting on the components of a vector (i.e. the multiple data-stream) in parallel. Often, such PEs are really number crunchers or high-speed ALUs, rather than the type of general-purpose microprocessor we have been considering throughout this text.

The SIMD architecture, or array processor as it is frequently known, has a very high performance/cost ratio, together with a great degree of efficiency, as long as the task running on it can be decomposed largely into vector operations. Consequently, the array processor is best suited to the air-traffic control problem discussed earlier, to the processing of weather information (this involves partial differential equations) and to tomography where the output of a body-scanner is processed almost entirely by vector arithmetic. As the SIMD architecture is generally built around a central processor controlling an array of special-purpose processors, the SIMD architecture is not discussed in any further detail here. However, we provide an example of an SIMD architecture to illustrate one of its applications. This example is taken from 'Large-scale parallel processing systems', by Siegel *et al.* (*Microprocessors and Microsystems*, **11**(1), Jan. 1987.

Figure 8.2 demonstrates the application of an SIMD architecture to *image smoothing* which offers a method of processing the images from *noisy* sources such as spacecraft cameras to yield a relatively noise-free image. Consider an input array, I, of 512×512 pixels which is to be smoothed to produce an output array S. A pixel is an 8-bit unsigned integer representing one of 256 grey levels from 0 (white) to 255 (black). Each pixel $S(i, j)$ in the smoothed array, S, is the average of the grey levels of its eight nearest neighbours. The neighbours of $S(i, j)$ are: $I(i-1, j-1)$, $I(i-1, j)$, $I(i-1, j+1)$, $I(i, j-1)$, $I(i, j+1)$, $I(i+1, j-1)$, $I(i+1, j)$ and $I(i+1, j+1)$. The top, bottom, left and right edge pixels of S are set to zero, since their corresponding pixels in I do not have eight adjacent neighbours.

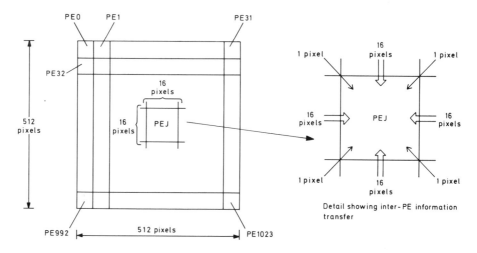

FIGURE 8.2 Applying the SIMD architecture to image smoothing

Assume that an SIMD array has 1024 PEs logically arranged as an array of 32×32 PEs as shown in Figure 8.2. Each PE stores a 16×16 pixel sub-image block of the 512×512 pixel image I. For example, PE 0 stores a 16×16 pixel sub-image block composed of columns 0–15 and rows 0–15, PE 1 stores the pixels in columns 16–31 of rows 0–15, etc. Each PE smooths its own sub-image, with all PEs operating on their sub-images concurrently. At the edges of each 16×16 sub-image, data must be transferred between PEs in order to calculate the smoothed value. The necessary data transfers for PE j are shown in Figure 8.2. Transfers between different PEs can take place simultaneously. For example, when PE $(j - 1)$ sends its upper right corner pixel to PE j, PE j can send its own upper right corner pixel to PE $(j + 1)$, and so on.

To perform a smoothing operation on a 512×512 pixel image by the parallel smoothing of 1024 sub-image blocks of 16×16 pixels, 256 parallel smoothing operations are executed. However, the neighbours of each sub-image edge pixel must be transferred between adjacent PEs and the total number of parallel data transfers required is $(4 \times 16) + 4 = 68$ (i.e. 16 for each of the top, bottom, left and right side edges and four for the corners). The corresponding serial algorithm needs no data transfers between PEs but $512^2 = 264\,144$ smoothing calculations must be executed. If no data transfers were needed, the parallel algorithm would be faster than the serial algorithm by a factor of $262\,144/256 = 1024$. If the inter-PE data transfer time is included and it is assumed that each parallel data transfer requires at most as much time as one smoothing operation, then the time factor improvement is $262\,144/324 = 809$. The inter-PE transfer time approximation is a conservative one. Thus, the overhead of the 68 inter-PE transfers that must be performed in the SIMD machine is negligible compared to the reduction in smoothing operations.

The last step is to set to zero the edge pixels of S. This creates an additional (although negligible) overhead which is to enable only the appropriate PEs when the zero values are stored for these edge pixels (only enabled PEs execute the instructions broadcast to the PEs). Serially, this would require $(4 \times 512) - 4 = 2044$ stores, and in the SIMD machine only $(4 \times 16) = 64$ parallel stores. It should be clear from the above description that SIMD architectures can be implemented by means of arrays of relatively primitive processing elements (e.g. ALUs). It is not usually necessary to make each processing element as complex as a CPU.

MISD (multiple instruction single data-stream)

The MISD architecture performs multiple operations concurrently on a single stream of data and is associated with the pipeline processor. A pipeline processor is best described in terms of an analogy with an automobile assembly line, where a single stream of components is operated on by a number of sequential processes to produce the finished automobile. For example, four cars may be in the pipeline at any instant with a different operation being applied to each car. A complete car is produced after a car has passed through each of the stages in the pipeline and has been operated on at each stage. In multiprocessor terms, the various processors are arranged in-line and are synchronized so that each processor accepts a new input every t seconds. If there are n processors, the total execution time of a task is nt seconds. At each epoch, a processor takes a partially completed task from a downstream processor and hands on its own task to the next upstream processor. As a pipeline processor has n processors operating concurrently and each task may be in one of the n stages, it requires a total of $nt + (K - 1)$ time slots to process K tasks.

The RISC (reduced instruction set) microprocessor uses pipelining to achieve a high throughput. At each clock cycle, one stage of the pipeline of the processor is fetching an instruction, one stage is decoding an instruction, one stage is executing an instruction and one stage is storing the operand from the previous execution stage. MISD systems are highly specialized and require special-purpose architectures and are not discussed further here. In fact, MISD architectures have never been developed to the same extent as SIMD and MIMD architectures.

MIMD (multiple instruction multiple data)

The MIMD architecture is really the most general-purpose form of multi-processor system and is represented by systems in which each processor has its own set of instructions operating on its own data structures. In other words, the processors are acting in a largely autonomous mode. Each individual processor may be working on a subsection of the main task and does not necessarily need to get in touch with its neighbours until it has finished its subtask. The PE to PE architecture described in Figure 8.1 can be thought of as a generic MIMD machine.

Because of the generality of the MIMD architecture, it can be said to encompass the relatively tightly coupled arrangements to be discussed shortly, and the very loosely coupled geographically distributed LANs.

In one sense, we have already encountered a MIMD architecture. Although most people do not regard it as a multiprocessor, any arrangement of a microprocessor and a floppy disk controller chip is really a loosely coupled MIMD. The floppy disk controller is really an autonomous processor with its own microprocessor, internal RAM and ROM. Because the FDC has all these resources on one chip and communicates with its host processor as if it were a simple I/O port, it is considered by many to be a simple I/O port. If it were not for the fact that the FDC is available as a single chip, engineers would be designing *true* multiprocessor systems to handle disk I/O. Figure 8.3 provides a graphical illustration of the classification of multiprocessor systems according to Fathi and Krieger (*Computers*, March 1983, 'Multiple Microprocessor Systems: What, Why and When').

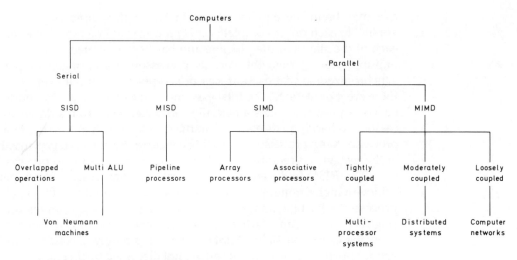

FIGURE 8.3   Multiprocessor systems

8.2 MIMD architectures

While the array or pipeline processor is likely to be constructed from very special units, the more general MIMD architecture is much more likely to be built from widely available devices like the 68000. Therefore, the major design consideration in the production of such a multiprocessor concerns the topology of the system, which is a measure of the way in which the communications paths between the individual processors are arranged.

Figures 8.4 to 8.8 depict the five classic MIMD topologies, which are (apart from the hypercube) incidentally the same as those available to the designer of local area networks. Multiprocessor structures are described both by their topology and by their *interconnection level*. The level of interconnection is a measure of the number of *switching units* through which a message must pass when going from processor X to processor Y. The four basic topologies are the

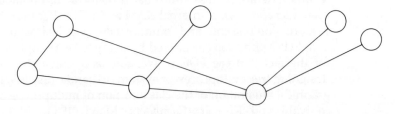

FIGURE 8.4   The unconstrained topology

unconstrained topology, the bus, the ring and the star, although, of course, there are many variants of each of these pure topologies. The principal features of each of these arrangements are defined as follows.

The unconstrained topology

The unconstrained topology is so called because it is an *ad hoc* arrangement in which a processor is linked directly to each other processor with which it wishes to communicate (Figure 8.4). It takes very little thought to appreciate that the unconstrained topology is not really practicable for any but the simplest of systems. Clearly, as the number of processors grows, the number of interconnections (i.e. buses) becomes prohibitive. The advantage of such a system is the very high degree of coupling that can be achieved. As the buses are dedicated to communication between only two processors, there is no conflict between processors waiting to access the same bus.

The bus

The bus is the simplest of topologies because each processor is connected to a single common bus (Figure 8.5). The bus is a simple topology not least because it avoids the problem of how to route a message from processor X to processor Y. In fact, the interprocessor bus is little more than an extension of the bus (back-plane) found in any conventional computer. Indeed, it is entirely possible to use the existing bus of many microcomputers to create a multiprocessor system. All that is required is a mechanism enabling control to be passed from one microprocessor to another.

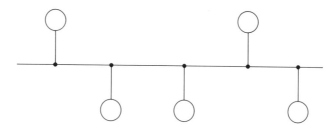

FIGURE 8.5 The bus

The disadvantage of the bus as a method of implementing a multi-processor system lies in the problem of controlling access to the bus. As only one processor at a time can use the bus, it is necessary to design an arbiter to determine which processor may access the bus at any time. Arbitration between two or more contending processors slows down the system and leads to bottlenecks. A bus offers a relatively high degree of coupling but is more suitable for schemes in which the quantity of data exchanged between processors is small. Because of the economic advantages of the bus, we concentrate on the MIMD bus architecture. Later in this chapter we consider the design of a suitable MIMD architecture for the 68000 microprocessor.

The ring

The ring topology of Figure 8.6(a) is arranged so that each processor is connected only to its two nearest neighbours. One neighbour is called the *upstream neighbour* and the other the *downstream neighbour*. A node receives

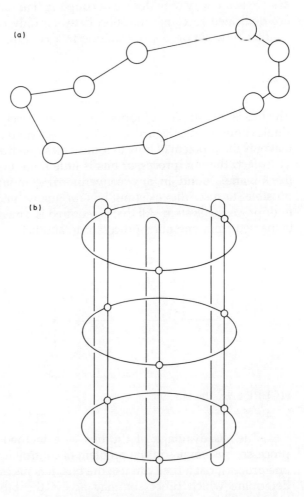

FIGURE 8.6   (a) The ring. (b) The two-dimensional ring

information from its upstream neighbour and passes it on to its downstream neighbour. In this way, information flows round the ring in one direction only, and a packet of information passes through each of the processors in the ring. The information passed to a node contains a destination address. When a node receives a packet, it checks the address and, if the packet address corresponds to the node's own address, the node reads the packet. Similarly, a node is able to add packets of its own to the stream of information flowing round the ring.

The ring topology offers certain advantages for some classes of loosely coupled multiprocessor network and represents one of the most popular forms of local area network. It is less widely used as a method of interconnecting processors in a tightly-coupled MIMD architecture. It is, in fact, possible to construct two-dimensional ring networks. Figure 8.6(b) demonstrates a two-dimensional ring with nine processing elements and three horizontal plus three vertical rings. The two-dimensional ring offers multiple paths between nodes and is not catastrophically affected by the failure of a single node.

The star

The star topology of Figure 8.7 employs a central processor as a switching network, rather like a telephone exchange, between the other processors which are arranged logically (if not physically) around the central node. The advantage of the star is that it reduces bus contention, as there are no shared communication paths and it does not require the large number of buses needed by unconstrained topologies.

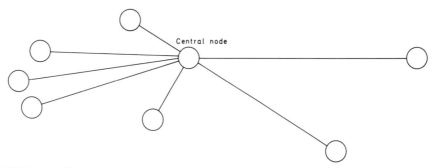

FIGURE 8.7 The star

On the other hand, the star network is only as good as its central node. If this node fails, the entire system fails. Consequently, the star topology does not display any form of graceful degradation. Moreover, the central network must be faster than the nodes using its switching facilities if the system is to be efficient. In many ways, the star topology is a configuration better suited to local area networks, where the individual signal paths are implemented by serial data channels, rather than by the parallel buses of the tightly coupled multiprocessor.

The hypercube

An n-dimensional hypercube multiprocessor connects together $N = 2^n$ processors in the form of an n-dimensional binary cube. Each corner (vertex or node) of the hypercube consists of a suitable processing element and its associated memory. Because of the topology of a hypercube, each node is directly connected to exactly n other neighbours. Figure 8.8 illustrates the hypercube topology for $n = 1$, 2, 3 and 4.

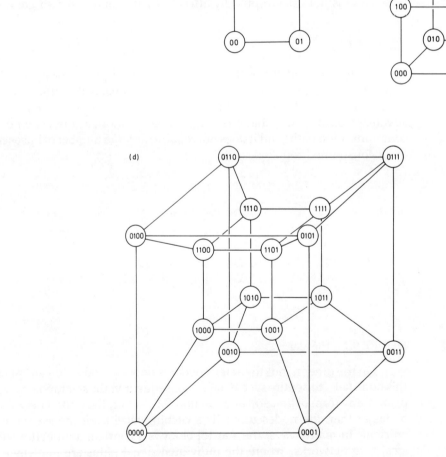

FIGURE 8.8 The hypercube. (a) Hypercube $n = 1$, (b) Hypercube $n = 2$, (c) Hypercube $n = 3$, (d) Hypercube $n = 4$

Each processor in a hypercube has an n-bit address in the range $0 \ldots 00$ to $1 \ldots 11$ (i.e. $0-2^n - 1$) and each of the n nearest neighbours of a particular node has an address that differs from the node's address by only 1 bit. For example, if $n = 4$ and a node has an address (0100), its four nearest neighbours have addresses (1100), (0000), (0110) and (0101).

A hypercube of dimension n is constructed recursively by taking a hypercube of dimension $n - 1$ and prefixing all its node addresses by 0 and adding to this another hypercube of dimension $n - 1$ whose node addresses are all prefixed by 1. In other words, a hypercube of dimension n can be subdivided into two hypercubes of dimension $n - 1$, and these two subcubes can, in turn, be divided into four subcubes of dimension $n - 2$ and so on.

The hypercube is of interest because it has a topology that makes it relatively easy to map certain groups of algorithm onto a hypercube topology. In particular, it is well suited to problems involving the evaluation of fast Fourier transforms (FFTs). The first practical hypercube multiprocessor was built at Caltech in 1983. This was called the Cosmic Cube and was based on 64 6086 microprocessors plus 8087 floating-point coprocessors.

Hybrid topologies

In addition to the above *pure* network topologies, there are very many *hybrid* topologies, some of which are described in Figures 8.9 to 8.12.

Figures 8.9(a) and 8.9(b) both illustrate the dual-bus multiprocessor, although this topology may be extended to include any number of buses. In Figure 8.9(a) the processors are split into two groups, with one group connected to bus A and one to bus B. A switching unit connects bus A to bus B and therefore allows a processor on one bus to communicate with a processor on the other. The advantage of the dual-bus topology is that the probability of bus contention is reduced, because both buses can be operated in parallel (i.e. simultaneously). Only when a processor connected to one bus needs to transfer data to a processor on the other does the topology become equal to a single-bus topology.

The arrangement of Figure 8.9(b) also employs two buses, but here each processor is connected directly to both buses via suitable switches. Two communication paths always exist between any pair of processors; one using bus A and one using bus B. Although the provision of two buses reduces the bottleneck associated with a single bus, it requires more connections between the processors and the two buses, and more complex hardware is needed to determine which bus a processor is to use at any time.

Another possible topology described in Figure 8.10 is the so-called *crossbar* switching architecture, which has its origin in the telephone exchange where it is employed to link subscribers to each other.

The processors are arranged as a single column (processors P_{c1} to P_{cm}) and a single row (processors P_{r1} to P_{rn}). That is, there are a total of $m + n$ processors.

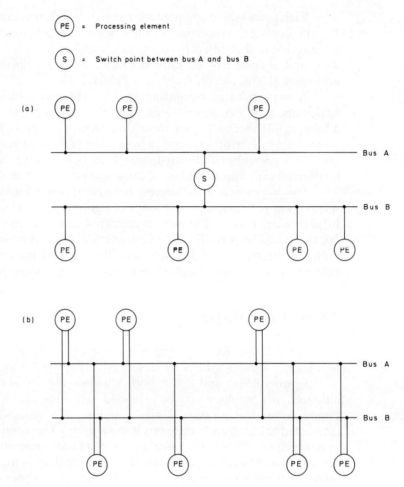

FIGURE 8.9 (a) The twin-bus multiprocessor – version 1. (b) The twin-bus multiprocessor – version 2

Each processor in a column is connected to a horizontal bus and each processor in a row is connected to a vertical bus. A switching network, $S_{r,c}$, connects the processor on row r to the processor on column c. Note that there are $m \times n$ switching networks for the $m + n$ processors.

The advantage of the crossbar matrix is the speed at which the interconnection between two processors can be set up. Furthermore, it can be made highly reliable by providing alternative connections between nodes should one of the switch points fail. Reliability is guaranteed only if the switches are *fail safe* and always fail in the off or no-connection position.

If the switches at the crosspoints are made multi-way (vertical to vertical, horizontal to horizontal or horizontal to vertical), we can construct a number of

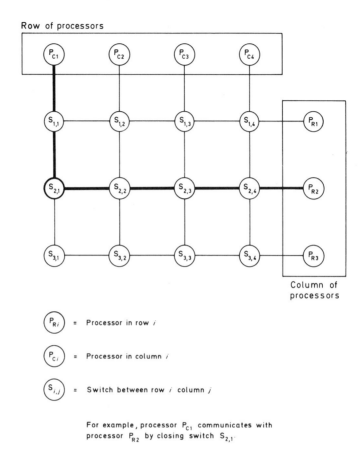

Row of processors

Column of processors

$\left(\begin{smallmatrix} P \\ Ri \end{smallmatrix}\right)$ = Processor in row *i*

$\left(\begin{smallmatrix} P \\ Ci \end{smallmatrix}\right)$ = Processor in column *i*

$\left(\begin{smallmatrix} S \\ i,j \end{smallmatrix}\right)$ = Switch between row *i* column *j*

For example, processor P_{C1} communicates with processor P_{R2} by closing switch $S_{2,1}$.

FIGURE 8.10 The crossbar switching network

simultaneous pathways through the matrix. The provision of multiple pathways considerably increases the bandwidth of the system.

In practice, the crossbar matrix is not widely found in general-purpose systems, because of its high complexity. Another penalty associated with this arrangement is its limited expandability. If we wish to increase the power of the system by adding an extra processor, we must also add another bus, together with its associated switching units.

An interesting form of multiprocessor topology is illustrated in Figure 8.11. For obvious reasons this structure is called a *binary tree*, although I am not certain whether it is really a special case of the unconstrained topology of Figure 8.4, or a trivial case of the star topology (using three processors), repeatedly iterated.

Any two processors (nodes) in the tree communicate with each other by traversing the tree right-to-left until a processor common to both nodes is

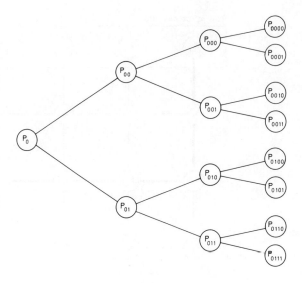

Example P_{0110} in communication with P_{0100}

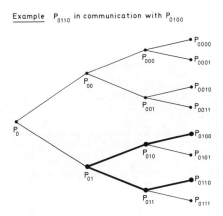

FIGURE 8.11   The binary tree topology

found, and then traversing the tree left-to-right. For example, Figure 8.11 shows how processor P_{0110} communicates with processor P_{0100}, by establishing backward links from P_{0110} to P_{01} and then forward links from P_{01} to P_{010} to P_{0100}.

The topology of the binary tree has the facility to set up multiple simultaneous links (depending on the nature of each of the links), as the whole tree is never needed to link any two points. In practice, a real system would implement additional pathways to relieve potential bottlenecks and to guard against the effects of failure at certain switching points. Note that the failure of a switch in a right-hand column causes the loss of a single processor, while the failure of a link at the left-hand side immediately removes half the available processors from the system.

In some ways, the structure of Figure 8.11 can be found to exhibit interesting properties. However, due to its complexities, it is likely to remain an intriguing topology and almost never to raise its head above the pages of somebody's PhD thesis.

Finally, and more down-to-earth, Figure 8.12 illustrates the cluster topology which is a hybrid star-bus structure. The importance of this structure lies in its application in highly reliable systems. Groups of processors and their local memory modules are arranged in the form of a cluster. Figure 8.12 shows three processors per cluster in an arrangement called *triple modular redundancy*. The output of each of the three processors is compared with the output of the other two processors in a *voting network*. The output of the voting circuit (or majority logic circuit) is taken as two-out-of-three of its inputs, on the basis that the failure of a single module is more likely than the simultaneous failure of two modules. Although the clusters in Figure 8.12 communicate with each other via a bus, it is possible to use any other suitable mechanism to link them.

The design of a clustered triple modular redundancy system is not as easy as might be first thought. One of the major problems associated with modular redundancy arises from a phenomenon called *divergence*. Suppose that three identical processors have identical hardware and software and that they receive identical inputs and start with the same initial conditions at the same time. Therefore, unless one processor fails, their outputs are identical, as all elements of the system are identical.

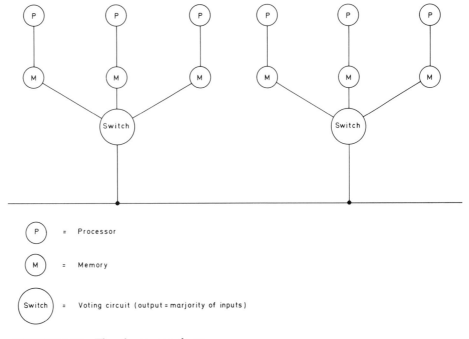

FIGURE 8.12 The cluster topology

In actual fact, the above statement is not true. In order to create truly redundant systems, each of the three processors in a cluster must have its own independent clock and I/O channels. Therefore, events taking place externally will not be 'seen' by each processor at exactly the same time. If these events lead to conditional branches, the operation of a processor in the cluster may diverge from that of its neighbours quite considerably after even a short period of operation. In such circumstances,. it becomes very difficult to tell whether the processors are suffering from divergence or whether one of them has failed.

The problem of divergence can be eliminated by providing synchronizing mechanisms between the processors and by comparing their outputs only when they all wish to access the system bus for the same purpose. Once more it can be seen that, although the principles behind the design of multiprocessor systems are relatively straightforward, their detailed practical design is very complex due to a considerable degree of interaction between hardware and software. As we have already pointed out, topologies for multiprocessor systems are legion. Figure 8.13 provides examples of three further topologies – just to provide food for thought.

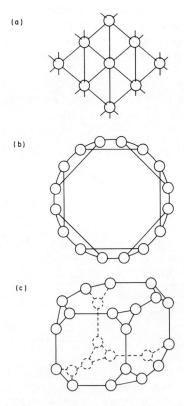

(a)

(b)

(c)

FIGURE 8.13 Three further topologies. (a) Systolic array, (b) chordal ring, (c) tricyclic cube

8.3 Interprocessor communication

Up to now we have been looking at the topology of multiprocessor systems with little or no consideration of the nuts and bolts of the actual connections between the processors. Here we describe some of the ways in which processors are linked together and examine the various issues involved in linking them.

8.3.1 Coupling

We have already met the concept of coupling between processors. Possibly more than any other factor, the required degree of coupling between processors in a multiprocessor system determines how the processors are to be linked. A tightly coupled multiprocessor system passes data between processors either by means of shared memory or by allowing one processor to access the other processor's data, address and control buses directly. When shared memory, sometimes called *dual-port RAM* or *DPRAM*, is employed to couple processors, a block of read/write memory is arranged to be common to both processors. One processor writes data to the block and the other reads that data. Data can be transferred as fast as each processor can execute a memory access. Later we look at the design of DPRAM and the problem arising when both processors try to access the same block of memory simultaneously.

The degree of coupling between processors is expressed in terms of two parameters: the transmission bandwidth, and the latency of the interprocessor link. The transmission bandwidth is defined as the rate at which data is moved between processors and is expressed in bits per second. For example, if a 68000 writes a byte of data to an 8-bit parallel port every $4\,\mu s$, the bandwidth of the link is 8 bits/$4\,\mu s$ or 2 Mbits/s. However, if a 16-bit port is used to move words at the same rate, the bandwidth rises to 4 Mbits/s.

The latency of an interprocessor link is defined as the time required to initiate a data transfer. That is, latency is the time that elapses between a processor requesting a data transfer and the time at which the transfer actually takes place. A high degree of coupling is associated with large transmission bandwidths and low latencies. As might be expected, tightly coupled microprocessor systems need more complex hardware than loosely coupled systems.

The way in which processors are linked can be listed in order of their degree of coupling as follows:

1. A serial data link
2. A parallel data link

3. A parallel data link with FIFO buffers between processors
4. A DMA channel
5. A shared bus
6. Shared memory common to each processor

Serial data link

Figure 8.14 illustrates the most loosely coupled form of data link in which the two processors are linked by means of a serial transmission path, which may be either a synchronous or an asynchronous link. Each processor sees the other

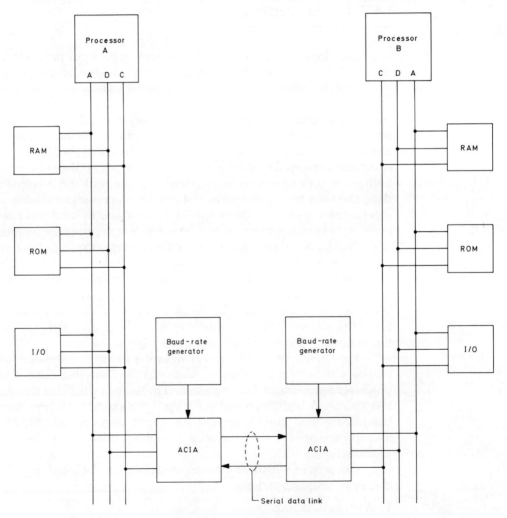

FIGURE 8.14   Processors linked by a serial data link

processor as a simple I/O port to which data is transmitted or from which data is received. The transmission bandwidth of a serial data link is low. For example, at a baud rate of 9600 bits/s with an asynchronous data link using one start bit, parity and stop bit per byte, the transmission bandwidth is $9600 \times \frac{8}{11} = 6982$ bits/s. Even with synchronous serial data transmission at 76.8 Kbaud, the bandwidth only just approaches 76.8 Kbits/s. In spite of its low bandwidth, the serial data link is preferred in geographically distributed systems. As far as the conventional MIMD architecture is concerned, it is a non-starter.

Parallel data link

Figure 8.15 shows a parallel data link between two processors. Figure 8.15 is almost identical to Figure 8.14 except that the ACIA of Figure 8.14 has been replaced by a 68230 parallel interface/timer (PI/T), configured as dual unidirectional 8-bit ports. One 8-bit port transfers data from processor A to processor B and the other from processor B to A. An interlocked handshaking data transfer mode is selected and H2 of the output port is connected to H1 of the input port and vice versa.

Because of the double buffering of the parallel ports and the automatic interlocked data transfer procedure, it is possible to move data between processors at the same rate that the PI/T can be accessed by a processor.

A possible data transfer loop may be written:

```
BUFFER  EQU      $100000        Block of data to be transferred
PIT     EQU      $800000        Location of the PI/T
*
        LEA      BUFFER,A0      A0 points to the data to be moved
        LEA      PIT,A1         A1 points to its destination – the PI/T
        MOVE.W   #BATCH,D0      Move BATCH+1 bytes
*
LOOP    MOVE.B   (A0)+,(A1)     (12 cycles) Move a byte from buffer
        DBRA     D0,LOOP        (10 cycles) Repeat until buffer empty
```

The above instructions move data pointed at by register A0 to the PI/T, whose address is in register A1. To speed up the transfer process, a DBRA implements the looping mechanism, with D0 acting as the cycle counter. As each time round the loop takes 22 clock cycles, an 8 MHz 68000 achieves a bandwidth of $1/22 \times 125$ ns) $\times 8 = 3$ Mbits/s (approximately). This bandwidth should be regarded as a target figure, as the scheme suggested by the above program fragment will not work over an extended period, because it is almost certain that one processor will eventually transfer data at such a rate that the other processor will lose some. Two non-synchronized devices, *both* working flat out, cannot remain in step for any extended period with nothing more than a double buffer to take up slack in the system.

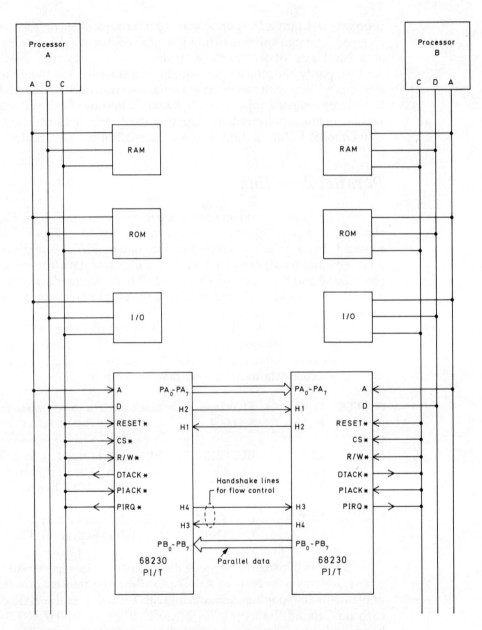

FIGURE 8.15   Processors linked by a parallel data link

A parallel data link with a FIFO buffer between processors

Figure 8.16 illustrates a logical extension of the simple parallel data link in which a pair of first-in first-out buffers (FIFOs) is placed in the data path between the two processors. Figure 8.16 shows how the FIFOs (two per channel) are inserted between the outputs of the PI/Ts, in an arrangement almost identical to that of Figure 8.15. The FIFO is a memory component arranged as a parallel shift register of n words by m bits and configured to operate as a first-in first-out queue. Typical commercially available FIFOs are organized as 64 words by 4 bits. FIFOs can be operated in series to increase the number of words stored (i.e. depth of the queue) or in parallel to increase the word length.

Figure 8.16 also illustrates the external connections to a FIFO. The data to be written into a FIFO is applied at the left by strobing its SI (shift in) input, which causes the word at its input terminals to enter and to ripple through empty positions in the queue until it appears at the end of the queue waiting to leave. The FIFO has an IR (input ready) output that is negated whenever the FIFO is full. Whenever the IR output is negated, no further data must be entered.

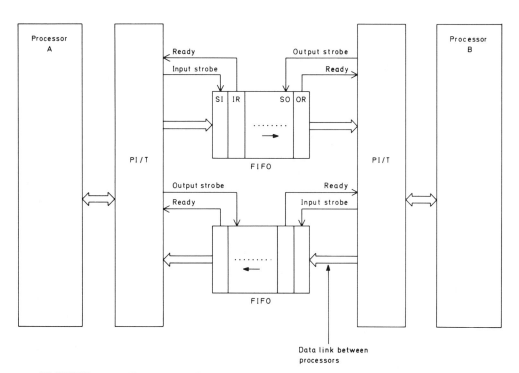

FIGURE 8.16 Processors linked by a parallel link with FIFO buffering

When data is removed from a FIFO, the SO (shift out) line is strobed and the data read from its output terminals. Reading from the FIFO causes all the entries in its internal queue to move one place towards the output. If the OR (output ready) output of the FIFO is negated, all its data has been read and its queue is empty.

The advantage of coupling processors by means of FIFOs is that the processor transmitting information can send it at its maximum rate without any fear of losing data. The receiving processor may then read the data at its leisure. Of course, the transmitting processor must stop and wait if its FIFO is full. That is, the FIFO is best suited to the transmission of relatively short bursts of data, rather than to long data blocks (e.g. entire files or digitized speech).

DMA data link

Another possible way of linking processors is by means of a DMA channel. Each processor has its own DMA controller and treats the other processors and their memory as I/O ports. The advantage of this approach is that the DMA controller is an autonomous device and can effect a data transfer without the explicit intervention of a microprocessor. As a DMA controller sets up transfer addresses and counts the quantity of data transferred entirely by means of hardware, this approach can have a very large bandwidth. Links between processors based on DMA are not often seen, possibly because the DMA controller and its associated hardware is very much more complex and expensive than a PI/T. Moreover, the DMA controller method is not well suited to arrangements where more than two processors share data and is much more complex than shared bus techniques.

A shared bus

One of the most popular ways of tightly coupling processors is to permit two or more processors to share the same bus in an arrangement of time division multiplexing. That is, the bus is allocated to a processor only for a fraction of the available time.

When only two processors share the same bus, we have essentially the same type of arrangement described by the above systems. However, it is possible to permit more than two processors to share the same bus, allowing the general bus topology to be realized. It is for this reason that the shared bus is so popular. It should be immediately apparent that if a number of processors do try to access the common bus all the time, the throughput of the individual processors will be very low.

Figure 8.17 shows how a shared bus system is arranged. Each of the three processors, A, B and C, has its own local buses through which it accesses its own local memory and, possibly, I/O ports. For much of the time the processors

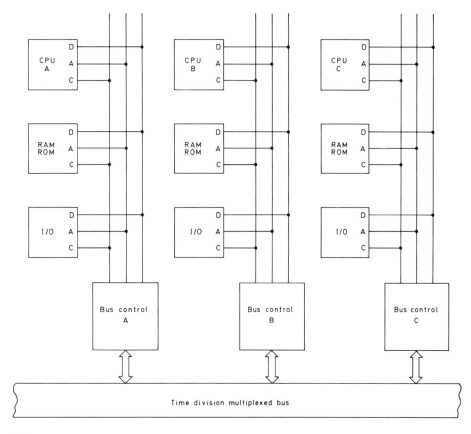

FIGURE 8.17 Processors linked by a shared bus

execute programs stored in their local memory and operate on their own data. When one processor wishes to communicate with another, it takes control of the system bus through its bus control unit. Now it can access the resources of another processor by controlling the system bus. In Section 8.5 we shall see how the 68000 uses its bus control facilities (BR*, BG*, BGACK*) to simplify the design of multiprocessor systems.

Shared memory

The final method of linking two processors, to be discussed here, employs a block of memory common to both processors. As we have already stated, common memory is often called dual-ported RAM (DPRAM) and is illustrated in Figure 8.18. It is, in fact, possible to have n-ported RAM that is shared between n processors. Because multiprocessor systems based on shared

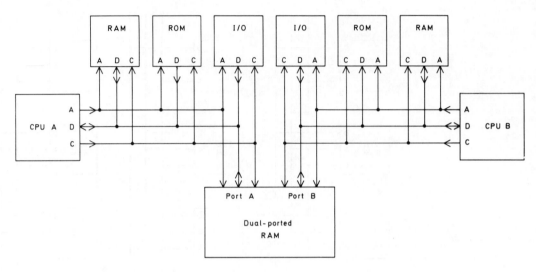

FIGURE 8.18   Processors linked by a block of shared memory common to both processors

memory have very low latencies due to their tight coupling, we will look at the design of multiprocessors with shared memory.

8.4 Designing multiprocessors with shared memory

In this and the next section, two types of multiprocessor based on the 68000 are examined. Both are tightly coupled and can be regarded as typical examples of MIMD architecture. They may form parts of larger multiprocessor systems with topologies as complex or as simple as any of those described in the previous section.

The first arrangement to be described is one that links two processors by means of shared memory, as it follows on naturally from the last section. Only a dual-processor shared memory arrangement is described, although it is possible to assign as many processors to a block of shared memory as the designer sees fit.

The second arrangement uses a common time-shared bus to link two or more processors. A bus link has been chosen because it is implemented by the popular VMEbus and is therefore widely supported in both hardware and software. Furthermore, this approach demonstrates the application of the 68000's bus arbitration facilities (BR*, BG*, BGACK*).

We are now going to look at an example of a dual-processor system using shared memory. In the example of Figure 8.18, the two processors have entirely separate buses together with their own local memory and I/O resources as appropriate. However, each processor is also able to read from or write to a block of dual-ported memory common to both their address spaces. Figure 8.19 provides further details of the arrangement of this memory. For the sake of simplicity, byte selection details are not included here.

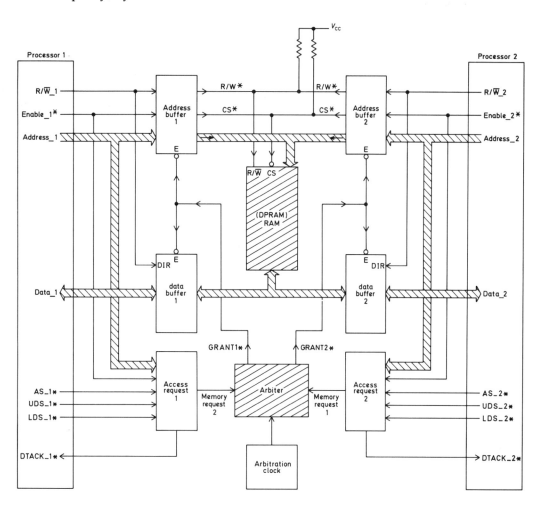

FIGURE 8.19   The structure of a multiprocessor using shared memory

Each processor in Figure 8.19 has its own data and address bus buffered on to the DPRAM's buses by means of two pairs of tri-state buffers. Processor 1 accesses the dual-ported memory when ENABLE_1* is asserted and processor 2 accesses the DPRAM when ENABLE_2* is asserted. As the outputs of the buffers are connected together, only one set of buffers at a time may be enabled. Therefore, both processors cannot access the memory simultaneously.

The CS* and R/W* inputs to the DPRAM are also buffered by tri-state bus drivers. However, in this case it is necessary to pull-up both CS* and R/W* when neither processor is accessing the bus, in order to avoid spurious memory accesses.

Arbitration

So far so good. The real problem in designing a shared memory system lies in the selection of a suitable mechanism by which a processor is granted access to the shared memory. Each processor in Figure 8.19 may attempt to access the DPRAM by asserting its AS*, UDS* and LDS* lines and by placing the appropriate address on A_{01}–A_{23}. The access requests from both processors are fed to an arbiter circuit to decide which processor will be granted access to the shared memory block. Some arbiters have a clock input (not necessarily the system clock) that determines the points at which the request inputs are sampled. That is, the requests are sampled periodically by a sampling clock. This clock has important implications for the reliability of the system as we shall soon see.

If one processor requests the memory and the other does not, the requesting processor is granted access. Equally, once a processor has been granted access, the other is locked out and must wait until the memory becomes free. When both processors request a memory access almost simultaneously, the arbiter must decide which processor may proceed and which must wait.

The arbiter is an interesting device, not least because it is *impossible* to design a *perfect* arbiter. It is an asynchronous device because a processor may request a memory access at *any* instant, if its clock is independent of the arbiter's clock. Therefore, there is a finite probability that a processor may request access at the exact moment (in practice a finite sampling window) that the arbiter is making a decision. In this case, the state of the system is undefined. No matter how well an arbiter is designed, the problem of a simultaneous access request and sampling clock edge can never be eliminated. The effect of simultaneous changes at a flip-flop's data and clock inputs is called *metastability*. The problem can, however, be reduced to *acceptable* limits. For example, an arbiter may be designed that fails once every, say, fifty years. A mean time between failure of 50 years represents, of course, a high degree of reliability by everyday standards. We should note that a failure due to a metastability problem is a soft failure.

Another problem associated with shared memory, although it is common to almost all forms of multiprocessor systems, is in ensuring reliable communication between the processors via the shared memory. Suppose one processor, call this processor A, writes a block of data to the DPRAM for the other to read. Processor A will want exclusive use of the shared memory for the duration of this operation. As processor A cannot lock out processor B by a hardware technique, it is necessary for A to pass a message to B, telling B that processor A wishes to have sole access to the memory.

Typically a flag bit, called for historical reasons a semaphore, forms one of the memory locations and, when set, indicates to a processor that the memory is in use by another processor and is therefore unavailable.

In order for A to take control of the shared memory, it first reads the semaphore. Remember that both processors can physically access memory, subject only to the state of the arbiter. If the semaphore is set, A must wait, as B is already using the memory. If the semaphore is clear, A may take control of the shared memory by setting the semaphore and thereby locking out B.

Simple? Well, not really. Assume that processor A reads the semaphore and finds the semaphore clear. Processor A will then perform a write operation to set the semaphore and to gain possession of the shared memory. Now suppose that infinitesimally after processor A requests the memory, processor B does the same. Processor B will read the semaphore after A has read it and it too will find the semaphore clear. Therefore, both processors A and B will set the semaphore, each thinking that it has sole possession of the shared memory.

The above is not a theoretical, abstract or irrelevant problem. It has serious consequences in multiprocessor systems. For example, in a geographically distributed system a travel agent may ask for a seat on a certain flight. The computer system interrogates the database and finds, say, a single seat free. The client then books this seat. But suppose in another town a second client also requests a seat on the same flight. He or she may be told that the flight is free because the first client has not yet booked the seat. The outcome is that the seat becomes double booked. Fortunately, most databases have software that avoids this dilemma. Once a client has asked if a seat is available, that section of the database cannot be read by another user until the original transaction is fully completed.

The 68000 microprocessor has a special instruction, test and set (TAS), designed entirely for multiprocessor applications. A TAS ⟨ea⟩ instruction reads the contents of the specified effective address and, if clear, sets the least-significant bit of the byte tested in one indivisible operation. That is, it does not release the memory between the action of reading the semaphore and that of setting it. The action carried out by a TAS instruction is called an indivisible read, modify and write operation.

Figure 8.20 provides the timing diagram of a TAS instruction, which lasts a minimum of 20 clock states and includes a conventional write access followed by a conventional read access. Like any other memory access, both read and write operations can be extended by delaying DTACK* as required. However, unlike other read-followed-by-write cycles, the address strobe is not negated between the read and the write accesses. Therefore, in any multiprocessor using shared memory, the arbiter must be arranged so that it will never rescind a processor's access to the shared memory, as long as its AS* is asserted. In the next section, we consider the design of a shared memory system.

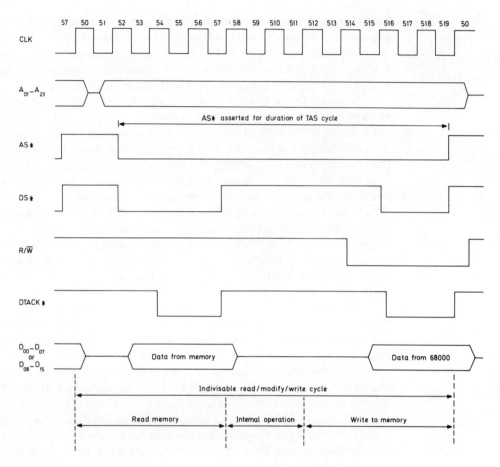

FIGURE 8.20   The timing diagram of an indivisible test and set (TAS) instruction

8.4.1 Memory arbitration

The possible arrangement of a practical dual-port RAM with 64 Kbytes of shared memory is given in Figure 8.21. Two 32K by 8 bit chips provide the 32 Kwords of shared memory and eight bus drivers form the electrical interface between the RAM and processor 1 or processor 2. Processor data lines are buffered by 74LS245 bidirectional transceivers, whose data direction inputs are controlled by the R/W* signal from the processor bus to which they are connected. The data buffers are enabled by ENABLE_1* when processor 1 has access to the memory and by ENABLE_2* when processor 2 has access.

Address lines A_{01}–A_{15} from processor 1 are buffered by two 74LS244 octal

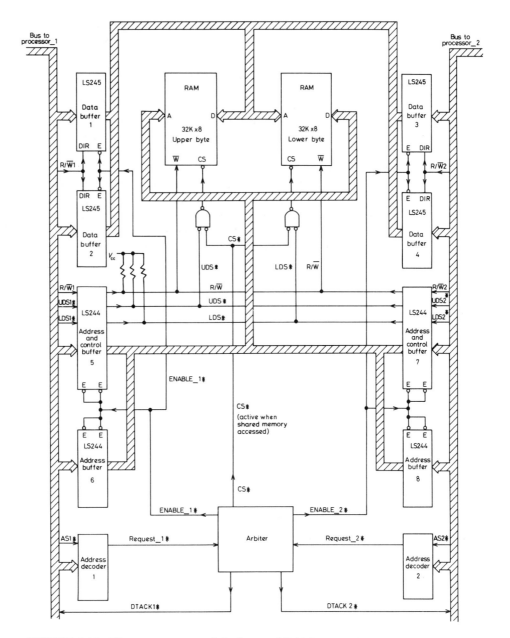

FIGURE 8.21 The arrangement of dual-ported RAM in a multiprocessor system

tri-state bus drivers enabled by ENABLE_1*. A_{01}–A_{15} from processor 2 are similarly buffered and enabled by ENABLE_2*.

Three 74LS244 tri-state buffers are required to buffer the 15 address lines and the R/W*, UDS* and LDS* control lines from the processors (only two are shown in Figure 8.21). Each of these three control lines is pulled up to a logical one state (on the RAM side of the buffers) by resistors, to avoid accessing the RAM when neither ENABLE_1* nor ENABLE_2* is asserted.

Two OR gates (AND gates in negative logic terms) permit the processors to perform byte or word accesses to the RAM. These gate UDS* with CS* from the arbiter to select the upper byte, and LDS* with CS* to select the lower byte.

Address decoder 1 and decoder 2 are driven from processors 1's and processor 2's address bus respectively. Each decoder is enabled by its own processor's address strobe. For example, if processor 1 requests a memory access by addressing the 32K block selected by address decoder 1, the decoder output, REQUEST_1*, is asserted. Assuming processor 2 does not require the bus, the arbiter asserts ENABLE_1* and buffers 1, 2, 5 and 6 are enabled. This permits processor 1 to access the memory exactly as in any other access to static RAM. Note that CS* from the arbiter is asserted to enable the RAM if either ENABLE_1* or ENABLE_2* is asserted. Should processor 2 request the RAM, the action is identical to that above, except that buffers 3, 4, 7 and 8 are enabled by ENABLE_2*.

The circuit diagram of a possible arbiter for the dual-ported RAM is given in Figure 8.22, and is taken from Motorola's application note AN 881. Each processor employs its address bus together with AS* and UDS*/LDS* to

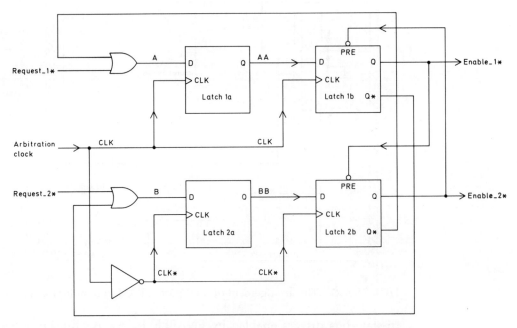

FIGURE 8.22   The circuit diagram of a two-input asynchronous arbiter
Latch 1a and latch 1b are clocked by CLK, and latches 2a and 2b are clocked by CLK* to ensure that the two request inputs (REQUEST_1* and REQUEST_2*) are not sampled at the same time.

generate a memory access request whenever it wishes to write to or read from the shared memory. The memory requests, REQUEST_1* and REQUEST_2*, are sampled by two positive-edge triggered latches. The latch to be clocked first locks out the other latch, so that the latter cannot respond to a request at its input. The secret of the arbiter is its use of an antiphase clock to provide different sampling points for the request inputs.

Figure 8.23 provides a timing diagram for the case in which both processors request the bus simultaneously. As we can see, processor 2 *wins* the

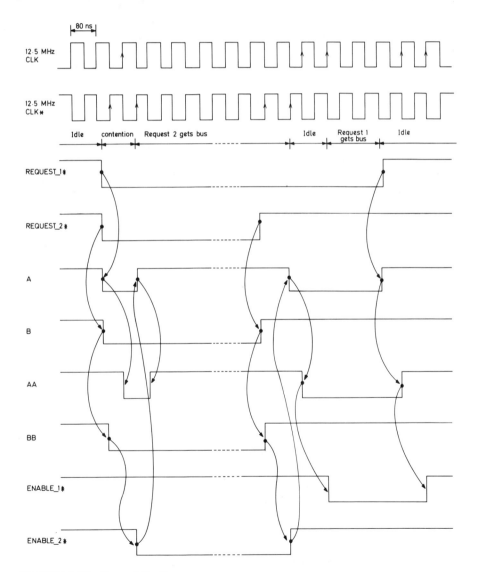

FIGURE 8.23   Bus arbitration

request and processor 1 must wait until processor 2 has relinquished the bus. That is, processor 1 does not have to *try again*, it simply waits for the memory to become free. Processor 1 determines that the bus is once more free by the eventual assertion of its DTACK*.

Initially, the arbiter is in an idle state with both request inputs inactive-high. Therefore, both D inputs to latches 1a and 2a are high, and in a steady state condition. Outputs AA, BB, ENABLE_1* and ENABLE_2* are all high.

Suppose that REQUEST_1* and REQUEST_2* are asserted almost simultaneously when the clock is in a high state. This results in the outputs of both OR gates (A and B) going low simultaneously. The cross-coupled feedback inputs to the OR gates (ENABLE_1* and ENABLE_2*) are currently both low.

On the next rising edge of the clock, the Q output of latch 1a (i.e. AA) and the Q output of latch 2a (i.e. BB) both go low. However, as latch 2a sees a rising edge clock first, its Q output goes low one-half a clock cycle (40 ns) before latch 1's output also goes low.

Earlier, it was stated that when a latch is clocked at the moment its input is changing, it goes into a metastable state in which its Q output is indeterminate. The metastable state can last for up to about 75 ns before the output of the latch settles into one state or the other. For this reason a second pair of latches are used to sample the input latches after a period of 80 ns.

Thus, 80 ns (one clock cycle) after REQUEST_2* has been latched and output BB forced low, the output of latch 2b, ENABLE_2*, goes low. Its complement, ENABLE_2, is fed back to OR gate 1, forcing input A high. After a clock cycle AA also goes high. Because ENABLE_2* is connected to latch 1b's active-low preset input, latch 1b is held in a high state.

At this point, ENABLE_1* is negated and ENABLE_2* asserted, permitting processor 2 to access the bus. The access is completed by the generation of a DTACK_1* and by the negation by processor 2 of its AS* and UDS*/LDS* outputs.

When processor 1 relinquishes the memory, REQUEST_2* becomes inactive-high, causing first B, then BB and finally ENABLE_2* to be negated as the change ripples through the arbiter. Once ENABLE _2* is high, ENABLE_2 goes low, causing the output of OR gate 1 (i.e. A) to go low. This is clocked through 1a and 1b to force ENABLE_1* low and therefore permit processor 1 to access the memory. Of course, once ENABLE_1* is asserted, any assertion of REQUEST_2* is ignored.

The remaining aspect of the dual-ported RAM to be considered is the generation of DTACK_1* and DTACK_2* by the arbiter. Many circuits which produce a DTACK* response to the assertion of the processor's address strobe following a valid address would not be suitable for a dual-ported RAM. A glance at Figure 8.20, the timing diagram of a TAS instruction, reveals the difficulty unique to TAS. TAS is the only instruction that requires *two* handshake cycles (one to acknowledge the read cycle and one to acknowledge the write cycle) while AS* is continually asserted.

Figure 8.24 shows how DTACK_1* for processor 1 is generated from UDS1* (or LDS1*), REQUEST_1*, and ENABLE_1* from the arbiter. Basically, DTACK_1* is generated in the normal fashion by holding a shift register (74LS164) in a clear state whenever REQUEST_1* (i.e. CS1*) is inactive-high, and then using the shift register to shift a clock pulse along when it is enabled. In this case, the shift register is also reset when UDS1* and LDS1* are negated. Consequently, the circuit generates the two consecutive DTACK_1*s required during a TAS operation. Figure 8.25 provides a timing diagram for the DTACK* generator. Note that DTACK_2* is generated in an identical way, except that the shift clock is derived from the complement of the arbiter clock.

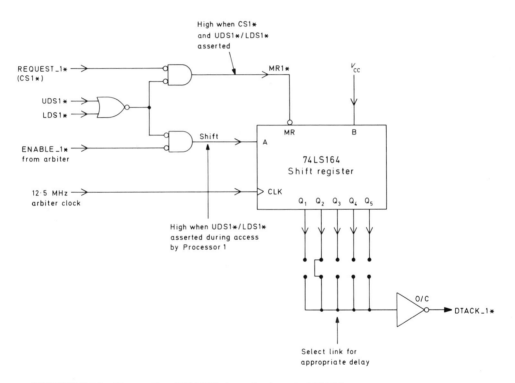

FIGURE 8.24   Generating DTACK* in a dual-ported RAM

We have now completed the hardware design of a dual-ported RAM. In use it may be accessed by a processor as follows:

```
SHARED-MEMORY    EQU    $F00000           Location of memory block
SEMAPHORE        DS.W   1                 First word = semaphore
                  .
                  .
                  .
                 LEA    SEMAPHORE,(A0)    Point to semaphore
```

WAIT	TAS	(A0)	Test and set semaphore
	BMI	WAIT	Repeat until semaphore set
	:		)
	:		)Critical section
	:		)
	CLR.B	(A0)	Clear semaphore

The address of the semaphore is loaded into A0 and the TAS/BMI loop repeated until the semaphore is found to have its bit 7 clear (i.e. BMI WAIT not taken). When bit 7 of the semaphore is clear it is set by the TAS to enable the processor to take control of the shared memory.

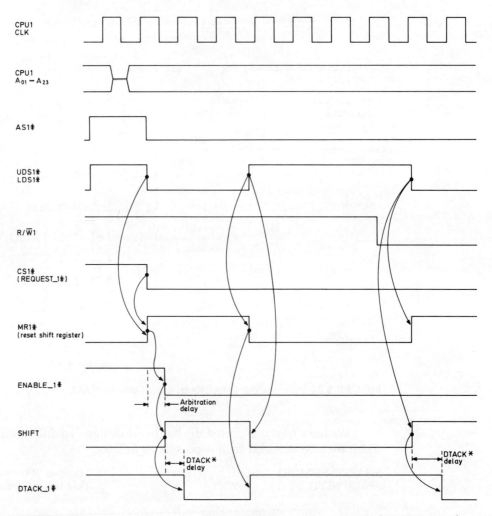

FIGURE 8.25 The timing diagram of the DTACK* generator during the execution of a TAS instruction

Note: Arbitration and DTACK* delay not to scale

The next part of the program is called the *critical section* because it is the region that must be executed to completion without any other processor accessing its data. Once the critical section has been completed, the shared memory is de-allocated by CLR.B (A0) which resets the semaphore.

The 74LS764 DRAM controller

Modern semiconductor technology is very good at killing two birds with one stone. Few devices illustrate this old maxim better than the 74LS764 DRAM controller which includes the arbitration logic for dual-port memory and the controller and interface to a block of dynamic RAM.

Figure 8.26 provides a block diagram of the 74LS764. REQ1* and REQ2* are the *access request* inputs from ports 1 and 2, and SEL1* and SEL2* are the corresponding *access grant* outputs. All other inputs and outputs are largely self-explanatory. A typical timing diagram of an access by processor 1 is

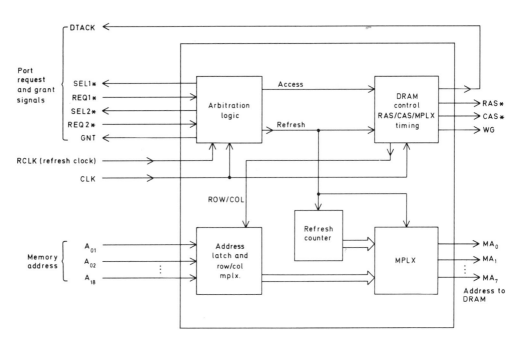

FIGURE 8.26   Block diagram of the 74LS764 DRAM controller

provided by Figure 8.27. Figure 8.28 gives the circuit diagram of a dual-68000 system based on the 74LS764.

A microprocessor requests access to the DRAM by asserting the appropriate REQ* input. If a DRAM refresh cycle is not in progress and the other request input is not active, the SEL* output corresponding to the active

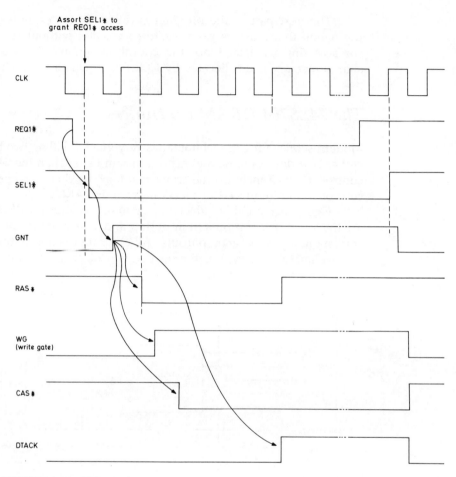

FIGURE 8.27   Timing diagram of a 74LS764 arbitration sequence

REQ* will go low to indicate that the access will be granted. The GNT output then goes high and its low-to-high transition indicates that a memory cycle is about to begin. If an access or refresh cycle is in process and the other processor has not requested access by asserting its REQ*, the SEL* output corresponding to the active REQ* input will go low to indicate that access will be granted. However, GNT will not go high until the current cycle has been completed. After the completion of the current cycle, GNT will automatically be asserted high.

If access to the DRAM is requested by *both* processors, the initial arbitration phase will determine which processor is to gain access to the memory by asserting the appropriate SEL* output. This arbitration takes place irrespective of whether or not a refresh cycle is in progress at the time the access is requested. REQ* contention is arbitrated, as we discussed earlier, by sampling the REQ* inputs on opposing phases of the arbiter's clock.

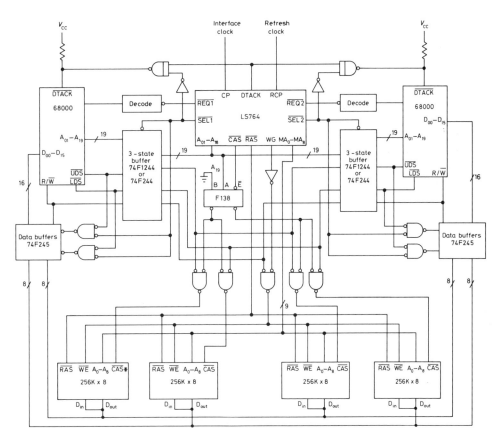

FIGURE 8.28   Circuit diagram of a dual-68000 system using the 74LS764

When GNT becomes active-high, the A_{01}–A_{18} address inputs are latched by the 74LS764 and the A_{01}–A_{09} signals propagated to the MA_0–MA_8 row address outputs. One half a clock cycle later, the column address inputs on A_{10}–A_{18} are propagated to MA_0–MA_8 and the active-low column address strobe, CAS*, asserted. Once CAS* is asserted, the controller will wait three clock cycles before negating RAS*, making RAS* four clock cycles in duration. At the time that RAS* is negated, the DTACK output becomes active-high to indicate that data on the DRAM data lines is valid (or that the proper access time has been met). All controller outputs are held in their *final* state until the processor accessing the DRAM negates its REQ*. When the request is negated, all controller outputs assume their inactive states and any impending refresh cycles are serviced.

A refresh cycle is triggered by internally generated refresh requests. The refresh clock is divided by 64 to produce periodic refresh cycles and then arbitrated with the SEL* outputs in the second stage of arbitration. Refresh cycles always take priority over processor accesses. At the start of a refresh cycle, the 9-bit refresh address is placed on MA_0–MA_8 for one-half clock cycle and then RAS* is asserted for four clock cycles, followed by three cycles inactive-high. The inactive-high period of RAS* allows time for the DRAM's precharge period. Now that we have looked at multiprocessor systems based on dual-ported memory, we are going to look at the popular VMEbus which links together microprocessors in a card-based modular system.

8.5 Multiprocessors and the VMEbus

We have already indicated that the bus topology offers the simplest approach to multiprocessor design. While this statement is true, it is not true that the design of a multiprocessor system based on a common bus is a trivial task. In fact, the design of any high-speed bus, be it a simple bus in a single-processor system or a contention bus, is much more complicated than it might appear. Many of the problems in bus design arise from the electrical effects associated with high-speed pulses on transmission lines.

Probably the best approach to designing a bus-based microcomputer is to choose one of the popular and standardized commercially available buses – unless, of course, the volume of production justifies the design, development and manufacture of a custom bus. Here we are going to examine the VMEbus that has now become a standard for many 68000-based microcomputers. As this is not a course on microprocessor systems design, we examine the VMEbus from the point of view of its application to multiprocessor systems. The bibliography provides sufficient references for those who wish to learn more about the VMEbus. However, a short introduction to the VMEbus is provided to put it in context.

8.5.1 The VMEbus

The VMEbus was originally designed and supported by three major manufacturers: Motorola, Mostek and Signetics. Today it is supported by a wide range of manufacturers and is in the process of becoming an international standard (IEEE 1014 and IEC 821). Although originally intended for 68000-based microcomputers, the VMEbus is suited to other advanced 16- or 32-bit microprocessors.

Physically, the VMEbus is a typical backplane bus with plug-in cards of either 233.35 mm × 160 mm (i.e. 9.2 inches × 6.3 inches) or 100 mm × 160 mm (i.e. 3.9 inches × 6.3 inches) (so-called single height 3U Eurocards and double height 6U Eurocards). The cards are connected to the VME bus by means of two-part 96-way DIN 41612 standard plugs and sockets. These connectors are relatively expensive but are highly reliable.

There are, in fact, two VMEbuses. In minimal systems a J1 bus with 96 lines provides all the facilities required to support a 16-bit data bus and a 23-bit address. A second bus, called J2, expands the J1 bus to cater for processors with 32-bit data and 32-bit address buses. The majority of tracks on the J2 bus are user defined. Table 8.1 defines the pinout of the VMEbus.

TABLE 8.1   Pinout of the VMEbus
(a) J1/P1 pin assignments

PIN NUMBER	ROWa SIGNAL MNEMONIC	ROWb SIGNAL MNEMONIC	ROWc SIGNAL MNEMONIC
1	D_{00}	BBSY*	D_{08}
2	D_{01}	BCLR*	D_{09}
3	D_{02}	ACFAIL*	D_{10}
4	D_{03}	BG0IN*	D_{11}
5	D_{04}	BG0OUT*	D_{12}
6	D_{05}	BG1IN*	D_{13}
7	D_{06}	BG1OUT*	D_{14}
8	D_{07}	BG2IN*	D_{15}
9	GND	BG2OUT*	GND
10	SYSCLK	G3IN*	SYSFAIL*
11	GND	BG3OUT*	BERR*
12	DS1*	BR0*	SYSRESET*
13	DS0*	BR1*	LWORD*
14	WRITE*	BR2*	AM5
15	GND	BR3*	A_{23}
16	DTACK*	AM0	A_{22}
17	GND	AM1	A_{21}
18	AS*	AM2	A_{20}
19	GND	AM3	A_{19}
20	IACK*	GND	A_{18}
21	IACKIN*	SERCLK	A_{17}
22	IACKOUT*	SERDAT*	A_{16}
23	AM4	GND	A_{15}
24	A_{07}	IRQ7*	A_{14}
25	A_{06}	IRQ6*	A_{13}
26	A_{05}	IRQ5*	A_{12}
27	A_{04}	IRQ4*	A_{11}
28	A_{03}	IRQ3*	A_{10}
29	A_{02}	IRQ2*	A_{09}
30	A_{01}	IRQ1*	A_{08}
31	-12 V	+5 V STDBY	+12 V
32	+5 V	+5 V	+5 V

(continued)

TABLE 8.1 *(continued)*
(b) J2/P2 pin assignments

PIN NUMBER	ROWa SIGNAL MNEMONIC	ROWb SIGNAL MNEMONIC	ROWc SIGNAL MNEMONIC
1	User defined	+5 V	User defined
2	User defined	GND	User defined
3	User defined	RESERVED	User defined
4	User defined	A_{24}	User defined
5	User defined	A_{25}	User defined
6	User defined	A_{26}	User defined
7	User defined	A_{27}	User defined
8	User defined	A_{28}	User defined
9	User defined	A_{29}	User defined
10	User defined	A_{30}	User defined
11	User defined	A_{31}	User defined
12	User defined	GND	User defined
13	User defined	+5 V	User defined
14	User defined	D_{16}	User defined
15	User defined	D_{17}	User defined
16	User defined	D_{18}	User defined
17	User defined	D_{19}	User defined
18	User defined	D_{20}	User defined
19	User defined	D_{21}	User defined
20	User defined	D_{22}	User defined
21	User defined	D_{23}	User defined
22	User defined	GND	User defined
23	User defined	D_{24}	User defined
24	User defined	D_{25}	User defined
25	User defined	D_{26}	User defined
26	User defined	D_{27}	User defined
27	User defined	D_{28}	User defined
28	User defined	D_{29}	User defined
29	User defined	D_{30}	User defined
30	User defined	D_{31}	User defined
31	User defined	GND	User defined
32	User defined	+5 V	User defined

Logically the VMEbus can be divided into four sub-buses: a data transfer bus (DTB), an arbitration bus, an interrupt bus and a utilities bus. The *data transfer bus* is a conventional non-multiplexed address and data bus that enables information to be transferred between a *bus master* and a *bus slave*. At this point we should note that the VMEbus operates in a master–slave mode so that at any instant only one device (e.g. 68000 microprocessor or DMA controller) may access a slave connected to the bus. The *arbitration bus* provides the VMEbus with multiprocessor facilities by enabling control to be passed from one master to another in an orderly fashion. The *interrupt bus* enables an interruptor to signal its need for attention and an interrupt handler to deal with the interrupt request. Figure 8.29 illustrates the structure of the VMEbus. The *utilities bus* provides several miscellaneous functions not catered for by the other buses such as a 16 MHz clock and a system failure line.

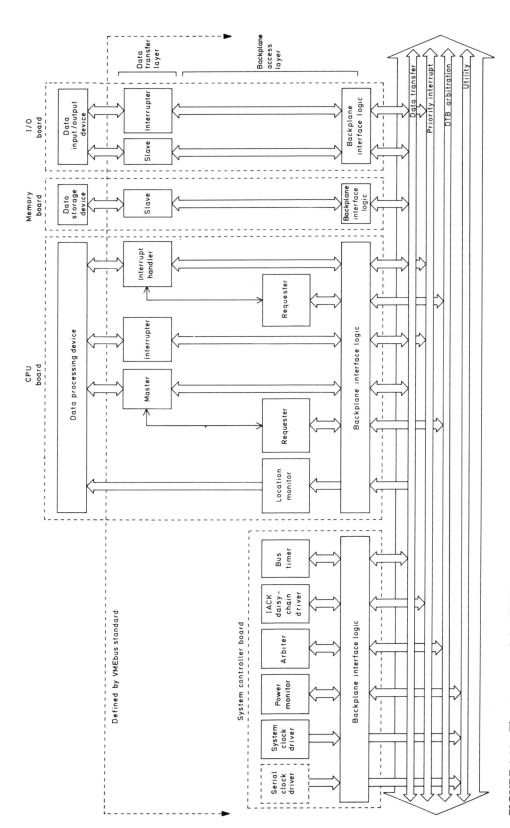

FIGURE 8.29 The structure of the VMEbus

8.5.2 The data transfer bus (DTB)

The data transfer bus of the VMEbus is based on the 68000's own address, data and control bus. Figure 8.30 illustrates the DTB component of the VMEbus,

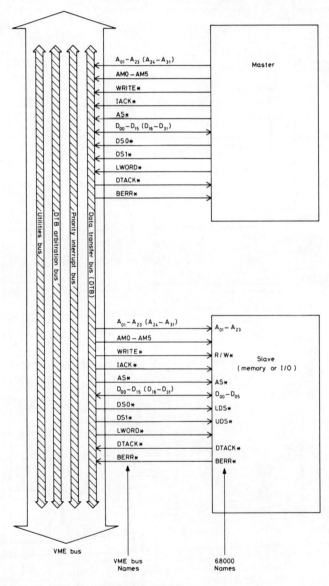

FIGURE 8.30   The data transfer bus – DTB

Figure 8.31 provides a protocol flowchart for a VMEbus access and Figure 8.32 provides the timing diagram of a read cycle.

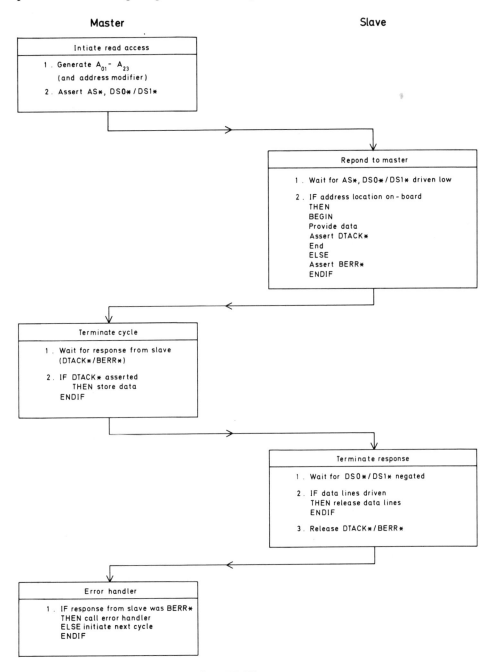

FIGURE 8.31 Protocol flowchart for a VMEbus access

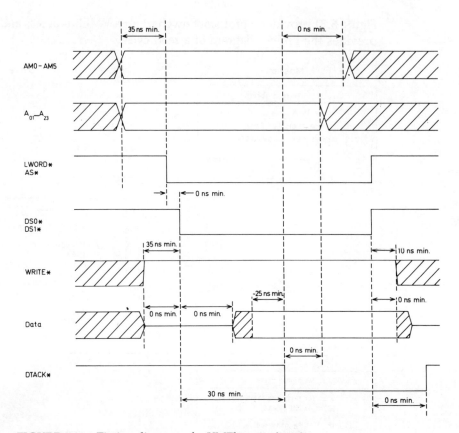

FIGURE 8.32 Timing diagram of a VMEbus read cycle

The principal differences between the 68000's own bus and the VMEbus DTB are the inclusion of a 6-bit address modifier bus (AM0–AM5), the addition of a longword data strobe (LWORD*), the renaming of LDS*/UDS* (LDS* = DS0*, UDS* = DS1*) and the extension to 32 address and data bits. LWORD* is asserted active-low during longword (32-bit) data transfer on D_{00}–D_{31}. In 68000 systems not using longword transfers, LWORD* is passively pulled up to V_{cc}.

The address modifier bus, AM0–AM5, enables the meaning of information on the address bus to be *qualified*. For example, the current bus master can use AM0–AM5 to indicate the type of the current access (short, standard or long address), memory management information, or any other user-defined function.

8.5.3 The arbitration bus

It is the arbitration sub-bus of the VMEbus that makes the VMEbus so suitable for multiprocessor systems. Two types of functional unit access the arbitration bus: the requester and the arbiter as illustrated in Figure 8.33. A *requester* is part of any module that may wish to request mastership of the VMEbus. An *arbiter* is part of the system controller board and must be located physically in slot 1 of the VMEbus system. Whenever the arbiter receives a request for the bus from a requester, the arbiter decides how the request is to be handled.

Figure 8.33 also illustrates the actual arrangement of the arbitration bus. A requester in any slot (apart from slot 1) may request the data transfer bus by asserting one of the bus request lines, BR0*–BR3*. The arbiter detects a request for the bus on BR0*–BR3* and then decides whether to grant the request or to ignore it (we shall see how this is done later). Figure 8.34 provides a protocol flowchart for a typical VMEbus arbitration sequence.

If the arbiter grants the DTB request, it asserts the corresponding bus_grant_out* level (i.e. BG*i*OUT*, where $i = 0,1,2$ or 3). For example, a request on BR2* would result in a bus grant signal on BG2OUT*.

The bus grant out lines are *daisy-chained* so that the BG*i*OUT* pin on module i is wired to the BG*i*IN* pin on module $i + 1$. When a module receives BG*i*IN* asserted from its upstream neighbour, it either takes the bus grant itself (and does not assert its BG*i*OUT* signal) or it passes the bus grant to its downstream neighbour by asserting its BG*i*OUT*. Consequently, a level i bus grant ripples down the daisy-chain until the first device requesting the bus at level i receives the bus grant and doesn't pass it on.

Of course, daisy-chaining includes an implicit prioritization mechanism – a module nearer to the arbiter is always served before its neighbours further away from the arbiter.

When a requester has been granted control of the DTB via the bus grant daisy-chain, the requester takes control of the bus by driving BBSY* (bus busy) active-low. Once BBSY* has been asserted by the new bus master, the arbiter can once again begin to perform arbitration if any other potential master requests the bus. This requester is now the new bus master and will remain so until it negates BBSY*. Interestingly enough, the VMEbus specification provides no mechanism for *forcing* a requester off the bus – BBSY* can be negated only by the current bus master. The VMEbus is a polite bus. However, a bus clear, BCLR*, signal is provided as an option. When a potential bus master with a request *higher* than the current level requests the VMEbus, the arbiter asserts BCLR* to inform the current master that it should *consider* giving up the VMEbus. It is left up to the system implementer to decide how BCLR* should be used.

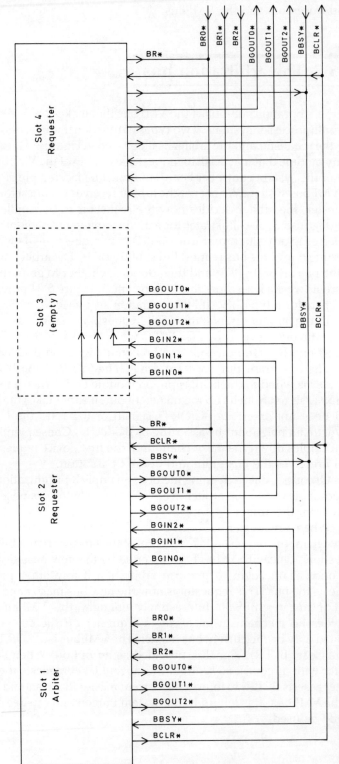

FIGURE 8.33 The VMEbus requester and arbiter
Note: BR3*, BGIN3*, BGOUT3* not shown

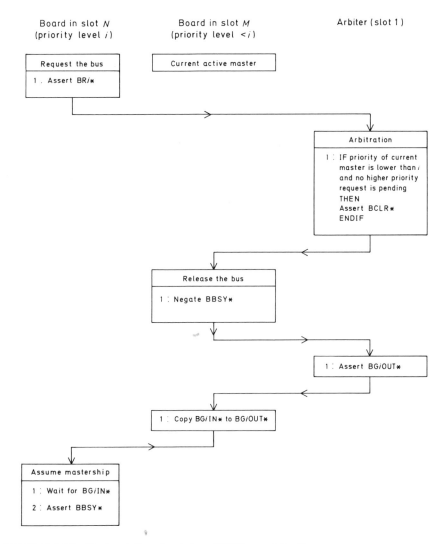

FIGURE 8.34 Protocol flowchart for a VMEbus arbitration sequence

The arbitration process

The arbiter in slot 1 may implement three basic types of arbitration: *single level*, *priority* or *round robin select*. The actual mode of arbitration (scheduling algorithm) used in any particular system is an option selected by the designer and the VMEbus specification does not exclude scheduling algorithms other than the three mentioned above.

Single-level arbitration

This offers the simplest scheduling algorithm. Only requests for arbitration on BR3* are accepted by the arbiter in slot 1 (i.e. all bus request, and bus grant lines for levels 0, 1 and 2 are not used in this option).

Prioritized arbitration (PRI)

PRI makes use of all bus arbitration lines. Bus request zero (BR0*) has the lowest priority and bus request three (BR3*) has the highest. If more than one level of interrupt is pending, the arbiter always grants priority to the highest level of request. Whenever a requester with a priority greater than that of the current bus master requests the DTB, the arbiter asserts the BCLR* (bus clear) line. An active-low on BCLR* indicates to the current master that it should relinquish the bus as soon as possible – but remember that it cannot be forced off the bus.

Round-robin select (RRS)

An RRS scheduling algorithm attempts to be fair to requesters by *rotating* the current level of maximum priority. For example, if the current highest level of priority is 3, the highest priority in the next cycle of arbitration will be 0.

The timing diagram of a typical arbitration sequence is given in Figure 8.35.

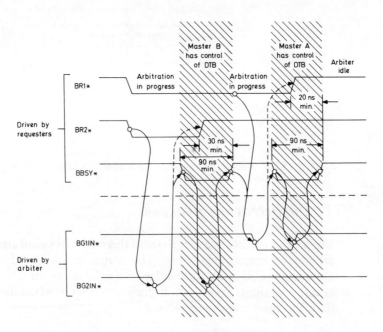

FIGURE 8.35 Timing diagram of an arbitration sequence

Initially, DTB requests are made on BR1* and BR2* at approximately the same time. The arbiter in slot 1 detects both requests and gives priority to BR2* by asserting the BG2IN* line. When the requester that asserted BR2* detects BG2IN* asserted, it asserts BBSY* to claim the DBT and negates its BR2*.

Once the current bus master has finished with the DTB, it negates BBSY*. The arbiter detects that the bus is once more free and there is still a request pending on level 1. Therefore, the arbiter asserts BG1IN* to pass control to the new bus master.

Later we shall look at interfaces to the priority arbitration bus.

8.5.4 The interrupt bus

We have now seen that the VMEbus implements a data transfer bus very much like the 68000's own data transfer bus and implements an arbitration bus that fits in well with the 68000's own arbitration control signals (BR*, BG*, BGACK*). It should therefore come as no surprise to discover that the VMEbus implements an interrupt handling structure in keeping with the 68000's own interrupt mechanism!

Three types of module are associated with the priority interrupt bus: the interrupter, the interrupt handler and the IACK (interrupt acknowledge) daisy-chain driver. Figure 8.36 illustrates the interrupt bus.

An *interrupter* is a module capable of signalling an interrupt request on one of the seven prioritized interrupt request lines, IRQ1*–IRQ7*. The IACK daisy-chain driver in slot 1 detects an interrupt request and transmits a falling edge down the IACKOUT*–IACKIN* daisy-chain. Figure 8.37 provides the protocol flowchart of a VMEbus interrupt sequence.

The *interrupt handler* detects an incoming interrupt acknowledgement on its IACKIN* pin. If this requester initiated the interrupt, it uses its on-board bus requester to request the DTB and, when granted access to the DTB, initiates an interrupt acknowledge cycle. The handler reads the STATUS/ID byte from the interrupter and thus initiates the appropriate interrupt servicing sequence. The actual servicing of an interrupt (i.e. how it's done and which device does it) is not part of the VMEbus specification.

VMEbus systems cater for two interrupt handling mechanisms: single interrupt handlers and distributed interrupt handlers. Distributed interrupt handlers are found in multiprocessor systems in which interrupt handling is shared among several bus masters.

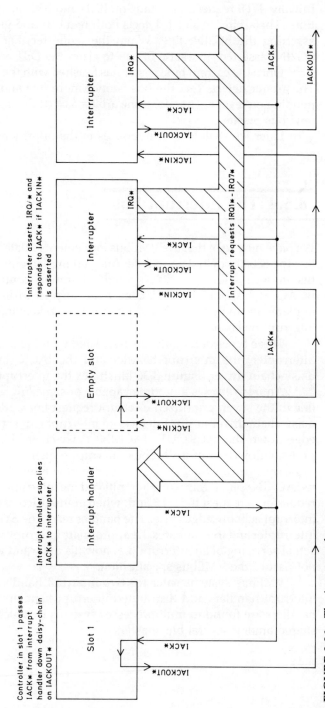

FIGURE 8.36 The interrupt bus

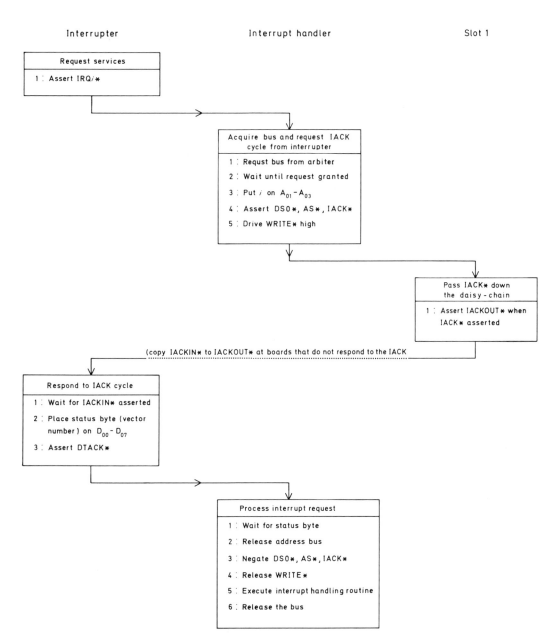

FIGURE 8.37 Protocol flowchart for a VMEbus interrupt sequence

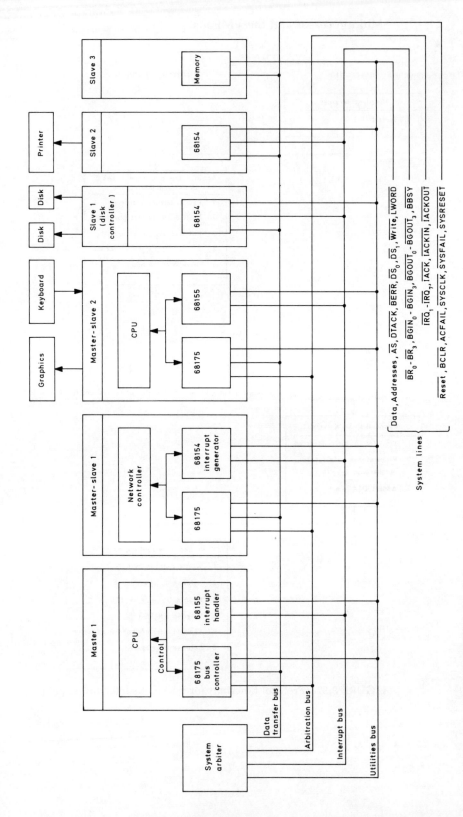

FIGURE 8.38 The 68175, 68154, 68155 and the VMEbus

8.6 Interfacing to the VMEbus

There are three ways of interfacing a module to the VMEbus: the easy way, the medium way and the hard way. The easy way is to buy the appropriate module from a supplier of VMEbus modules. As long as they fully comply with the VMEbus specifications, there should be little or no difficulty. The hard way of interfacing to the VMEbus is to design the interface entirely yourself using standard TTL or programmable logic chips. A custom interface requires a detailed understanding of the VMEbus protocols and much design time.

As we might expect, the medium way to design a VMEbus interface is a compromise between buying a ready-made module and designing the interface entirely on your own. The medium way is to design the interface yourself around some of the special-purpose VMEbus chips now available. Here we are going to look at three devices: the 68175 bus controller, the 68154 interrupt generator and the 68155 interrupt handler. Figure 8.38 shows how these three devices relate to the VMEbus.

8.6.1 The 68175 bus controller

The 68175 bus controller performs the arbitration between a local master on a module and the VMEbus itself. As it is less instructive to describe the internal structure of the 68175 than to demonstrate how it is used, we will look at how the 68175 implements an interface between a local master and the VMEbus. Figure 8.39 shows how a 68175 sits between the local bus of a bus master (which we will assume is a 68000 processor) and the system VMEbus. In addition to the 68175 itself, we need address and data bus buffers plus a few TTL gates.

In normal local master operation, the local master accesses its own memory and peripherals via its local bus. Under these circumstances, the output of the address decoder, OFFBD* (i.e. off board), is inactive high. Consequently, the 68175's address enable output, ADDEN*, is also inactive high and all devices capable of driving the VMEbus are disabled.

Suppose now that the local bus master wishes to access some resource from the VMEbus. A VMEbus access is initiated whenever the local master accesses address space that has been partitioned to the VMEbus. That is, when the local master accesses an address that forces the OFFBD* output of the address decoder active-low.

When the bus controller detects that both OFFBD* and LAS* (local address strobe = AS* from the local master) are low, it asserts its bus request output, BR*, in an attempt to gain control of the VMEbus. BR* must be connected to one of the VMEbus's BR*i* lines. Note that bus request priority is

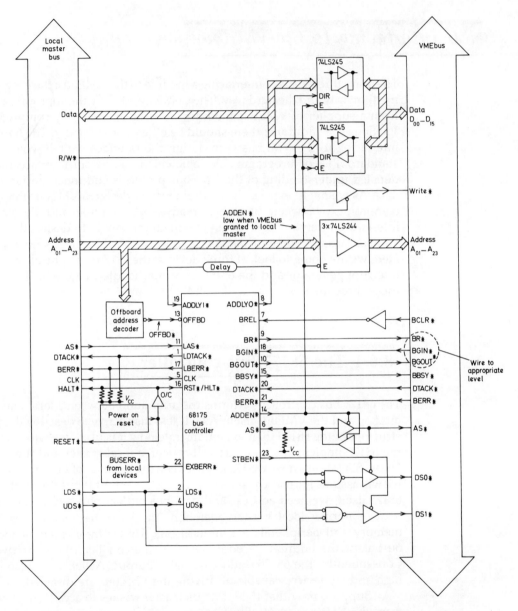

FIGURE 8.39 The 68175 and its interface to the VMEbus and a local bus master

assigned by a hardware link. If there were sufficient pins, the 68175 could have implemented a software selectable bus request priority level.

Eventually, the current VMEbus master responds to the 68175's request by passing a bus grant signal down the BGIN*–BGOUT* daisy-chain. If the 68175 receives BGIN* low *before* it asserted its own BR* output, it passes BGIN* down the daisy-chain by asserting its own BGOUT*. That is, the 68175 is a polite device – if another potential bus master requested the bus before its own local bus master, it will not attempt to grab the bus at the first opportunity.

If the 68175 receives BGIN* low *after* it asserts its BR* output, the 68175 will assert its BBSY* output to claim ownership of the VMEbus and negate its BR*, as it is now the new VMEbus master.

Actual VMEbus accesses do not begin until the old bus master has released the bus by negating AS*, DTACK* and BERR*. Once the local bus master has control of the VMEbus, it provides the necessary signals to control a VMEbus access. For each bus access, the 68175 asserts its ADDEN* (address and data enable), STBEN* (strobe enable) and AS* outputs active-low. ADDEN* is a totem pole output that is used to enable the module's address and data bus drivers. The STBEN* output enables the two data strobes (i.e. DS0* and DS1*).

The 68175 bus controller devotes two pins to the generation of an appropriate delay between the point at which the VMEbus address is valid and the point at which the VMEbus AS* is asserted low. Whenever a VMEbus cycle is executed, the 68175 asserts its ADDLYO* pin (address delay output). ADDLYO* is connected to the ADDLYI* (address delay input) pin by a user supplied delay line. This delay, typically 35 ns, guarantees a minimum setup time between the assertion of ADDEN* and AS*. Figure 8.40 provides a timing diagram for a VMEbus access initiated by the local master and Figure 8.41 provides the corresponding protocol flowchart.

As we have already stated, the VMEbus has no *explicit* mechanism for forcing a current bus master off the VMEbus. That is, the control of the 68175's active-high BREL (bus release) input is left to the designer of the specific system using the 68175 bus controller.

In some applications, BREL can be permanently asserted by tying it to a logical one (i.e. V_{cc}). As BREL is *always* asserted, the 68175 will never control the VMEbus for more than a single bus cycle. In other words, the 68175 is configured to carry out one VMEbus cycle at a time and to release the VMEbus between successive cycles. This mode may result in a relatively high latency if there are many contending bus masters. It is, however, *fair* because it prevents the local bus master from hogging the VMEbus.

Alternatively, the BREL input to the 68175 can be connected to the VMEbus's BCLR* (bus clear) line via an inverter. Whenever the VMEbus arbiter in slot 1 requests the bus by asserting BCLR*, the local bus master will be forced off the VMEbus at the end of its current bus cycle by BREL high.

BREL can also be connected to one or more of the VMEbus's bus request lines by means of suitable gating (BREL is the NAND of the appropriate bus requests). Note that we use a NAND gate to make BREL the logical OR (in negative logic) of the appropriate BR*i* inputs. In this mode, the 68175 implements a *release on request* (ROR) strategy – as soon as the 68175 sees that another potential master is requesting the bus, it begins its release sequence. Note that the 68175 does not monitor its BREL input until the last leading edge

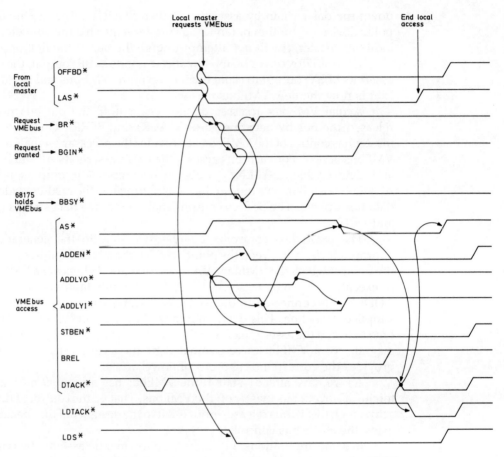

FIGURE 8.40   Timing diagram for a local master access to the VMEbus

of BGIN* or ADDLYI* is negated to prevent the 68175 relinquishing control of the VMEbus due to its own bus request.

Bus error cycles

The 68000 implements a mechanism for rerunning faulty bus cycles, i.e. bus cycles terminated by the assertion of BERR* rather than DTACK*. If BERR* and HALT* are asserted *together*, the 68000 attempts to re-run the current bus cycle using the same address and function codes. The bus cycle rerun or retry mode has been implemented to help the 68000 recover from certain forms of soft (i.e. intermittent) errors.

The 68175 bus controller includes a facility for the automatic rerunning of bus cycles. If the 68175 receives either BERR* from the VMEbus or LBERR*

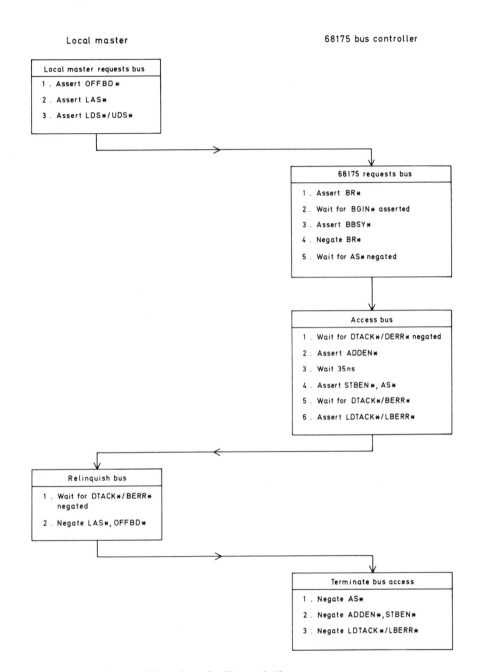

FIGURE 8.41 Protocol flowchart for Figure 9.40

(during a local bus cycle) it asserts both LBERR* *and* RST*/HLT*. The simultaneous assertion of both these signals allows the bus master to execute a rerun cyle. However, if the rerun cycle *also* leads to the assertion of BERR* or LBERR*, the 68175 will assert *only* LBERR*. That is, the 68175 is designed to attempt one bus rerun cycle before giving up.

The 68175's external bus error input, EXBERR*, is provided to enable local resources to initiate a bus cycle rerun sequence.

For each access to the VMEbus, ADDEN*, STBEN* and AS* are asserted low. If the 68000 accesses its local memory (i.e. OFFBD* goes high), ADDEN*, STBEN* and AS* all remain inactive-high throughout the cycle.

As we have seen earlier, the 68000 is able to execute an indivisible read–modify–write instruction, TAS (test and set). A read–modify–write cycle *cannot* be interrupted (i.e. by bus arbitration). The 68000 asserts AS* *throughout* a read–modify–write cycle and the 68175 is designed to retain control of the bus as long as AS* is low. Consequently, the 68175 bus controller automatically handles the 68000's read–modify–write cycle or, for that matter, any other indivisible bus cycle for which AS* remains low throughout. Figure 8.42 provides the timing diagram of a read–modify–write cycle.

Releasing the VMEbus

Once the 68175 has gained control of the VMEbus, it retains control until it is explicitly removed from bus mastership. The 68175 asserts its BBSY* output to indicate its continued bus mastership.

When the 68175's active-high bus release input, BREL, is asserted, control of the VMEbus will be passed to a new master.

If BREL is asserted during a bus cycle by the current bus master (i.e. the 68175's local master), the bus busy output, BBSY*, is negated to permit bus arbitration to take place. When the current bus access by the local bus master has been completed, the 68175 will release the bus by negating ADDEN*, AS* and STBEN*. At this point, the local master can regain mastership of the VMEbus only by asserting OFFBD* and requesting bus mastership.

8.6.2 The 68154 interrupt requester

The interrupt requester sits between devices that generate interrupts and the VMEbus. Before I came across the 68154 to be described here, I found it difficult to understand why there might be a need for a special interrupt requester. After all, you signal an interrupt request by asserting one of the VMEbus's seven interrupt request lines and then provide a vector during the IACK cycle. The 68154 interrupt generator, like many of today's sophisticated peripherals, has

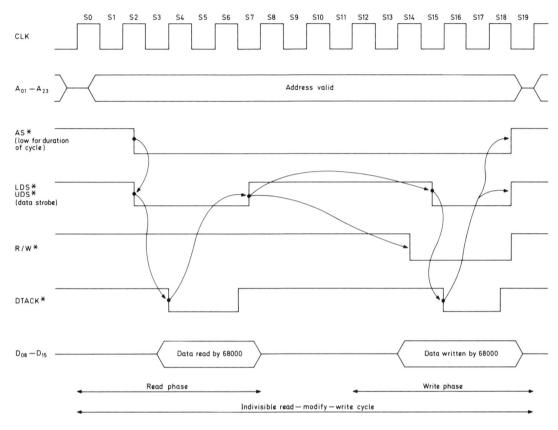

FIGURE 8.42   Timing diagram of a read–modify–write cycle

more facilities than might be needed in a minimal application and saves several TTL chips. As in the case of the bus controller, we introduce the 68154 by means of a circuit diagram (Figure 8.43) showing how it is interfaced to the VMEbus.

The VMEbus side of the 68154

For the purpose of this discussion, we will assume that the 68154 has been programmed to generate an interrupt request by setting up the interrupt request register R1. The 68154 is interfaced to the interrupt sub-bus of the VMEbus with a minimum of additional logic (Figure 8.43). Seven interrupt request lines from the 68154 are buffered on to the VMEbus by seven open-collector buffers. When the VMEbus interrupt acknowledge line, IACK*, is asserted, an interrupt acknowledge message is passed along the VMEbus's IACKOUT*–IACKIN* daisy-chain. The 68154 responds to an IACK cycle initiated from the VMEbus when the following conditions have been satisfied:

1. IACK* is asserted to indicate that an IACK cycle is in effect.
2. IACKIN* is asserted to indicate that no other interrupt requester located closer to slot 1 has intercepted the interrupt acknowledge.
3. DS0* is asserted.
4. The 3-bit code on A_{01}–A_{03} reflects the level of the interrupt request put out by the 68154. That is, if the VMEbus is acknowledging a, say, level 6 interrupt

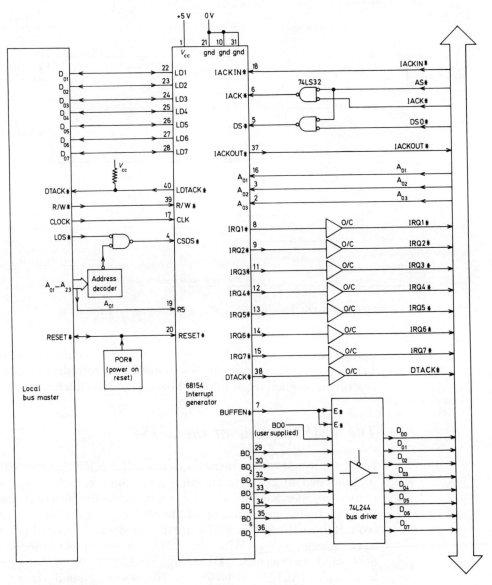

FIGURE 8.43 Connecting the 68154 to the VMEbus

request and the 68154 has requested a level 4 interrupt, the 68154 does not respond.

If these conditions are not all met, the 68154 passes IACKIN* to IACKOUT* and sends the interrupt request down the VMEbus. However, if the conditions are met, the 68154 first does not assert IACKOUT* and begins its response to the IACK cycle. The 68154 clears the appropriate interrupt request bit of its interrupt request register, R1 (see Figure 8.44).

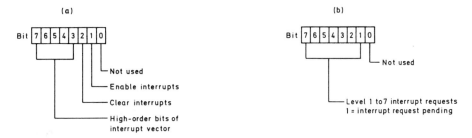

FIGURE 8.44 The 68154's registers. (a) R0 interrupt vector number register accessed when RS = 0, (b) R1 interrupt request register accessed when RS = 1

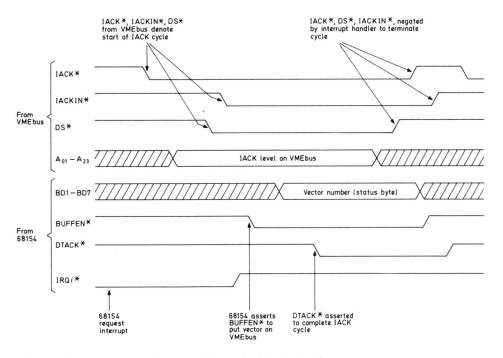

FIGURE 8.45 Timing diagram of the 68154's IACK cycle

The buffer enable output, BUFFEN∗, from the 68154 is asserted to enable the 74LS244 tri-state buffers. These buffers put the interrupt vector on pins BD1 to BD7 onto the VMEbus to provide the status/ID byte required during an IACK cycle. DTACK∗ is asserted by the 68154 to complete the IACK cycle. Note that the 68154 supplies a *7-bit* interrupt vector. Bit D_{00} is not supplied by the 68154 – that bit is left to user-supplied logic (see Figure 8.43). Figure 8.45 provides a timing diagram of the 68154's IACK cycle.

Local master side of the 68154

The local master side of the 68154 is as unexceptional as its VMEbus interface. It interfaces to the local bus master just like any other memory-mapped peripheral with an asynchronous bus interface through its seven data lines (remember that the 68154 does not make use of D_{00}).

When power is initially applied to the local master, its power on reset circuit asserts the 68154's RESET∗ input. A reset operation forces all IRQ∗ outputs plus IACKOUT∗ high and resets the interrupt request and interrupt vector registers.

Before the 68154 is able to handle interrupt requests, it must be set up by loading its interrupt vector register, R0, with the high-order 5 bits of the interrupt vector. When the 68154 responds to an IACK cycle, it loads the high-order 5 bits of R0 on to the data bus and places the most significant two bits of the IRQ level on the low-order 2 bits of the data bus. For example, if the interrupt vector is 10011 and the interrupt level is five, the vector 1001110 is supplied during the IACK cycle. Bit 2 of the interrupt vector register clears all interrupt requests when set and bit 1 enables all interrupt requests when set.

The interrupt request register, R1, is used to request interrupts. Loading bit *i* of R1 asserts IRQ*i*. Suppose we wish to generate interrupt requests at levels IRQ4 and IRQ6 and that the interrupt vector number is 64 (i.e. interrupt vector table entry of 256).

```
LEA       INT_GEN,A0          A0 points to the 68154
MOVE      #64,(A0)            Setup lowest interrupt vector number
BSET.B    #1,(A0)             Enable the interrupts
MOVE.B    #%01010000,2(A0)    Request interrupts on levels 4 and 6
```

Once the registers have been set up, the 68154 requests an interrupt by asserting the appropriate IRQ*i*∗ line of the VMEbus and then *automatically* supplying the interrupt vector during the subsequent IACK cycle.

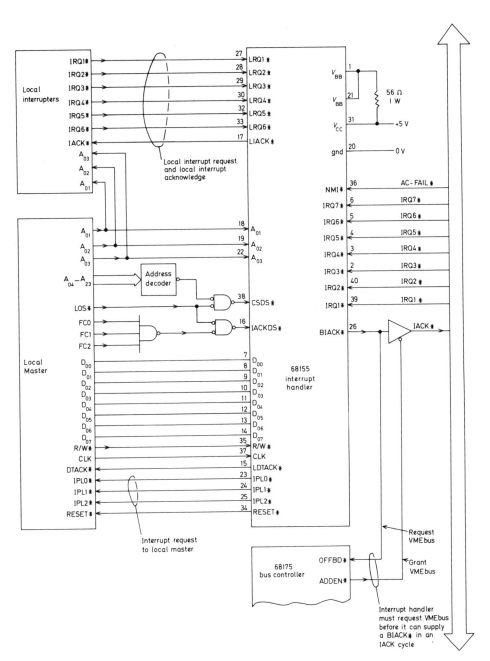

FIGURE 8.46   Interfacing the 68155 to a VMEbus

8.6.3 The 68155 interrupt handler

It is, perhaps, misleading to call the 68155 an *interrupt handler*, since interrupts are really handled by a processor executing a software routine. It would have been better to call the 68155 an interrupt *prioritizer* or an interrupt *filter*. The 68155 handles up to 14 interrupts, seven of which may come from the VMEbus and six from a local source (i.e. devices on the same board as the 68155 and its slave processor) plus a non-maskable interrupt that may be from a local or a VMEbus source. Figure 8.46 shows how the 68155 interrupt handler interfaces to the VMEbus, the local master (assumed to be a 68000 CPU) and the local interrupt sources.

The interface between the 68155 and the VMEbus consists of nine lines, IRQ1* to IRQ7*, NMI* and IACK* (which is derived from the 68155's BIACK* output). The NMI* (non-maskable interrupt request) is the highest priority interrupt handled by the 68155 and can be connected to the VMEbus's AC_FAIL* line or to some other interrupt source that must be non-maskable.

Essentially, the 68155 detects an interrupt request on the VMEbus by one of IRQ1*–IRQ7* asserted and asserts BIACK* (bus interrupt acknowledge) to indicate that the interrupt request has been accepted. Figure 8.47 provides the

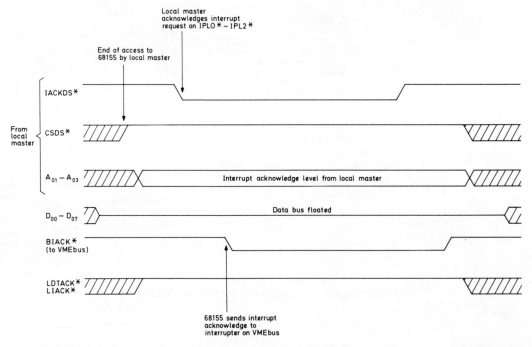

FIGURE 8.47   Timing diagram of a VMEbus IACK sequence

timing diagram of a VMEbus IACK sequence. The 68155 passes on the interrupt request from the VMEbus (or from a local source) to the local master via its encoded interrupt request inputs IPL0*–IPL2* which are connected to the corresponding inputs of the local 68000 interrupt handler. Table 8.2 provides details of the 68155's interrupt level encoding scheme. The BIACK* output from the 68155 is buffered onto the VMEbus by a tri-state gate (Figure 8.46). Before the 68155 can take part in an interrupt acknowledge cycle, it must first take control of the VMEbus. By connecting BIACK* from the 68155 to the OFFBD* input of a 68175 bus controller, a bus request to the VMEbus is automatically made at the start of an interrupt acknowledge cycle. When the 68175 bus controller grants use of the VMEbus, its ADDEN* output enables the BIACK* bus driver.

TABLE 8.2 The 68155's interrupt prioritization

INTERRUPT REQUEST LEVEL	INTERRUPT PRIORITY LEVEL OUTPUTS		
	IPL2*	IPL1*	IPL0*
NMI*, IRQ7*	0	0	0
LRQ6*, IRQ6*	0	0	1
LRQ5*, IRQ5*	0	1	0
LRQ4*, IRQ4*	0	1	1
LRQ3*, IRQ3*	1	0	0
LRQ2*, IRQ2*	1	0	1
LRQ1*, IRQ1*	1	1	0
None	1	1	1

Local interrupts

In addition to interrupts originating from the VMEbus, the 68155 can deal with six levels of interrupt from local interrupt sources. Local interrupt LRQ6* has the highest priority and LRQ1* the lowest.

A local interrupt is acknowledged by the local CPU asserting the IACKDS* input to the 68155. A glance at the circuit of Figure 8.46 demonstrates that IACKDS* is generated in the conventional way by the local 68000 setting FC0,FC1,FC2 to 1,1,1 and asserting LDS*. The 68155 responds by reading the IACK level from the 68000 on its A_{01}–A_{03} inputs to determine the level of the current interrupt. If a local interrupt has the highest current priority, the 68155 will respond in one of two ways.

If the 68155 is operating in its *vectored mode*, it asserts its local interrupt acknowledge output, LIACK*, places an interrupt vector number on its data bus for the 68000 to read and then asserts LDTACK* to complete the bus cycle. However, if the 68155 has been programmed to permit a local device to issue the interrupt vector number, the 68155 asserts *only* LIACK* and leaves the local device to complete the interrupt acknowledge cycle (by providing its own

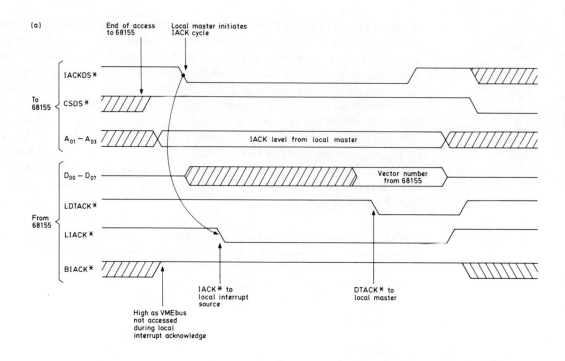

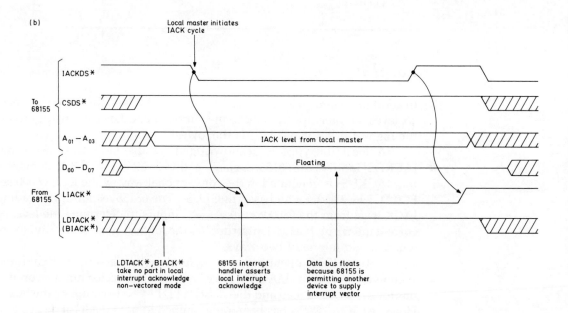

FIGURE 8.48 Timing diagrams for the 68155's local IACK cycle. (a) Vectored mode, (b) Non-vectored mode

vector and asserting LDTACK*). Note once more the sheer versatility of modern interface components – the 68155 permits devices with their own interrupt vector number registers to respond to IACK cycles, or the 68155 is able to supply a vector number for interfaces unable to supply their own. Figure 8.48 provides timing diagrams for a local interrupt acknowledge cycle in both the *vectored mode* and the *non-vectored mode*.

Programming model of the 68155

The 68155 interrupt handler has a rather more complex register structure than its 68154 and 68175 companions. The local master accesses the 68155's register set exactly like any other memory-mapped peripheral by asserting the 68155's CSDS* input and executing an asynchronous bus cycle (see Figure 8.46). Register selection is made with the aid of A_{01}, A_{02}, A_{03} from the local master – but that is not the whole story. The 68155 has eight addressable registers as defined in Table 8.3.

The 13 registers of Table 8.3 are listed in terms of: their base address offset from the point at which the 68155 is memory mapped, the address lines that select the register, the register number (R0–R7), the register name and whether the register is read/write or read-only.

TABLE 8.3 The 68155's register set

BASE	A_{03}	A_{02}	A_{01}	REGISTER	NAME	TYPE
+0	0	0	0	R0	Pointer register	Write only
+2	0	0	1	R1	Control registers	Read/write
+4	0	1	0	R2	LRQ vector	Read/write
+6	0	1	1	R3	LRQ mask	Read/write
+8	1	0	0	R4	LRQ status	Read only
+10	1	0	1	R5	IRQ mask	Read/write
+12	1	1	0	R6	IRQ status	Read only
+14	1	1	1	R7	Last interrupt acknowledge	Read only

The more numerate of my readers will have noticed that I said that there are 13 registers, but only eight are listed in Table 8.3. The reason is simple – there are *six* different R1s (i.e. control registers). Register R0 is a *pointer* register that is loaded with the address of the current control register in R1. If we wish to select control register i (where $i = 1$–6), we load R1 with 001–110, respectively. Only *one* of the control registers is visible at a time. To simplify notation, we can refer to R1 as CR1–CR6, so that, for example, CR2 is the same as R1 when R0 is loaded with 2.

I hate register sets. Fathoming them out is even worse than learning irregular verbs in a foreign language. Perhaps a better approach to learning what register does what, is to ask what do we want this peripheral to do, and then look for the registers that do that task.

The 68155 responds to interrupt requests and therefore most of its registers are responsible for defining how the requests are detected. In the case of the 68155, we have to consider two classes of register: those that deal with the VMEbus and those that deal with the local bus. Control register R1 holds six 3-bit values, one for each of the local interrupt request inputs. The programmer sets up each of the six values in R1 by first setting the pointer register, R0, and then loading the appropriate 3-bit interrupt control value in R1. Table 8.4 defines the way in which the bits of the 68155's registers are interpreted. The three lower-order bits of R1 determine the *active state* of the LRQ$i*$ input, whether the LRQ$i*$ is *level* or *edge* sensitive and whether that level is to respond with an *interrupt vector number* during an IACK cycle. For example, loading control register 2 (CR2) with 00000111 means that the local interrupt level 2 (LRQ2) is programmed as a *positive edge* sensitive interrupt that issues an interrupt vector number during an IACK cycle.

Register R2 provides the associated interrupt vector number for interrupts on the local master side of the 68155. The five most-significant bits of R2 are loaded with the user-supplied vector. During a local IACK cycle, the interrupt vector number supplied by the 68155 consists of the five bits loaded into R2 plus three bits that indicate the level of the interrupt (001 = LRQ1$*$, 010 = LRQ2$*$, . . . , 110 = LRQ6$*$, 111 = NMI$*$). For example, if R2 is loaded with

TABLE 8.4 Structure of the 68155's registers

REGISTER	BIT 7	BIT 6	BIT 5	BIT 4	BIT 3	BIT 2	BIT 1	BIT 0
R0	X	X	X	X	X	B2	B1	B0
						◄— CR1–CR6 pointer —►		
R1	X	X	X	X	X	ASi	ELi	VEi
R2	LRQ7	LRQ6	LRQ5	LRQ4	LRQ3	LRQ2	LRQ1	LRQ0
	◄————LRQ vector output ————►					◄—— LRQ level ——►		
R3	NMIM	LRQ6M	LRQ5M	LRQ4M	LRQ3M	LRQ2M	LRQ1M	NMIE
	◄——————— LRQ mask ———————►							
R4	LRQ7$*$	LRQ6$*$	LRQ5$*$	LRQ4$*$	LRQ3$*$	LRQ2$*$	LRQ1$*$	0
	◄————local interrupt status = 1 = interrupt pending————►							
R5	IRQ7$*$	IRQ6$*$	IRQ5$*$	IRQ4$*$	IRQ3$*$	IRQ2$*$	IRQ1$*$	0
	◄————IRQ mask IRQ$i*$ = 1 = interrupt enabled————►							
R6	IRQ7$*$	IRQ6$*$	IRQ5$*$	IRQ4$*$	IRQ3$*$	IRQ2$*$	IRQ1$*$	0
	◄———— IRQ status IRQ$i*$ = 1 = interrupt pending————►							
R7	X	X	X	X	LRA3	LRA2	LRA1	LRA0
					◄—Last interrupt acknowledge—►			

X = bit not used in this register

10101XXX (where X = don't care), the interrupt vector number supplied by a
local interrupt on level 3 is 10101011.

Register R3 enables or disables (masks) the local interrupt sources.
Loading bit i of R3 with 1 enables LRQ$i*$. Note that bit 0 of R3 has a special
function. When bit i of R3 is set to 1, it allows the 68155 to supply an NMI vector
during an IACK cycle initiated by a non-maskable interrupt.

Register R4 is a read-only local interrupt pending register, whose
contents are determined by the 68155. A 1 in bit i of R4 indicates that a local
interrupt of LRQ$i*$ is pending (i.e. awaiting service).

Registers R5 and R6 are the VMEbus side equivalent of the local interrupt
side register R3 and R4. Bits 1–7 of R5 permit the programmer to enable
interrupt request levels IRQ1*–IRQ7* respectively. Bit 0 of both R5 and R6 is not
used. R6 is an interrupt pending register for the VMEbus side of the 68155.
Register R7 indicates the *last interrupt acknowledged*. The local CPU may read R7
to determine which level of interrupt the 68155 last acknowledged. Table 8.5
shows how the bits of R7 are decoded. R7 may be used by the operating system
to implement various forms of interrupt prioritization.

TABLE 8.5   Decoding R7 (last interrupt acknowledge)

R7 (3 2 1 0)	LAST INTERRUPT	R7 (3 2 1 0)	LAST INTERRUPT
0 0 0 0	None	1 0 0 0	None
0 0 0 1	IRQ1*	1 0 0 1	LRQ1*
0 0 1 0	IRQ2*	1 0 1 0	LRQ2*
0 0 1 1	IRQ3*	1 0 1 1	LRQ3*
0 1 0 0	IRQ4*	1 1 0 0	LRQ4*
0 1 0 1	IRQ5*	1 1 0 1	LRQ5*
0 1 1 0	IRQ6*	1 1 1 0	LRQ6*
0 1 1 1	IRQ7*	1 1 1 1	NMI*

Programming the 68155

Like almost all peripherals, the 68155 is initialized during the reset phase.
However, it can be reprogrammed at any time to modify the interrupt service
levels or interrupt vector numbers.

Suppose we have a system that supports three local interrupt sources:
NMI*, LRQ5* and LRQ2*, and is designed to respond to VMEbus interrupts
IRQ2*–IRQ6* inclusive. LRQ5* is to be triggered by a positive edge and LRQ2*
by a negative level. The local interrupt vector number is $98.

```
INT_BASE    EQU     $800001         Base address of 68155
R0          EQU     0               Pointer register
R1          EQU     2               Control registers
R2          EQU     4               LRQ vector register
R3          EQU     6               LRQ mask register
```

```
R5          EQU     10                          IRQ mask register
*
            LEA     INT_BASE,A0                 A0 points to 68155
            MOVE.B  #5,R0(A0)                   Set pointer to select control reg 5
            MOVE.B  #%111,R1(A0)                LRQ5* is positive edge sensitive
            MOVE.B  #2,R0(A0)                   Set pointer to select control reg 2
            MOVE.B  #%001,R1(A0)                LRQ2* is negative level sensitive
            MOVE.B  #$98C,R2(A0)                Set local interrupt vector number
            MOVE.B  #%00100100,R3(A0)           Enable LRQ2* and LRQ5*
            MOVE.B  #%01111100,R5(A0)           Enable IRQ2* to IRQ6*
```

Summary

Multiple microprocessor systems offer increased computational throughput, but at a price. The price to be paid for multiprocessing is the cost of the buses over which the individual microprocessors communicate with each other and the loss of efficiency due to bus contention when more than one device wishes to access the same bus at the same time.

We have looked at two particular ways of implementing multiple microprocessor systems. One uses multiport memory that allows microprocessors to communicate with each other via a common block of memory which each may access. The other way of coupling microprocessors involves a common bus. Bus-based multiprocessor systems are, in many ways, easy to design because all they require is an arbitration mechanism that allows a microprocessor to request a bus access to use the bus and then to hand over the bus to another user. One particular bus, the VMEbus, dominates the 68000 world. We have briefly described the VMEbus and have introduced some of the interface chips that make life easier for the designer who wishes to connect a subsystem to the VMEbus.

Bibliography

Baliga S. Three-chip control set trims VME bus logic for asynchronous systems. *Electronic Design*, January 24, 1985, pp. 207–214.

Beaston J. and Tetrick R. S. Designers confront metastability in boards and buses. *Computer Design*, March 1, 1986, pp. 67–71.

Bolognin A., Giulu D., Pelagotti F., Pirri F. and Pogni F. Multiprocessor structures for microprocessors. *Software and Microsystems*, **1**(7), December 1982, pp. 175–191.

Borrill P. L. Objective comparison of 32-bit buses. *Microprocessors and Microsystems*, **10**(2), March 1986, pp. 94–100.

Callaghan J. M. How video displays work. *Microcomputing*, February 1983, pp. 90–104.

Chen C. *An Introduction to the Sampling Theorem*. National Semiconductor Application Note 236, January, 1980.

Clements, A. *Microprocessor Systems Design: 68000 Hardware, software and interfacing*. PWS-Kent, 1987.

Fathi E. T. and Krieger M. Multiple microprocessor systems: What, why, and when. *Computer*, March 1983, pp. 23–32.

Harper K. *A terminal interface, printer interface, and background printing for an MC68000-based system using the 68681 DUART*. Application note AN899, Motorola Inc., 1984.

Koen M. To sidestep track/hold pitfalls, recognize subtle design errors. *EDN*, September, 1980.

Krutz R. L. *Interfacing Techniques in Digital Design*. John Wiley, 1988.

Lobelle M. VME Bus interfacing: a case study. *Interfaces in computing* (Elsevier Sequoia), 1(1983) 193–210.

Motorola Inc. *Microprocessor-compatible DAC's and the MC6890*. Application note AN-842, Motorola Inc., 1982.

Motorola Inc. *MC68HC000-based CMOS Computer*. Application note AN988, Motorola Inc., 1987.

Motorola Inc. *Motorola MC6845 CRTC simplifies video display controllers*. Application note AN-851, Motorola Inc.

Nicholson J. and Camp R. Build a super simple floppy-disk interface. *Byte*, May 1981, pp. 360–376; *Byte*, June 1981, pp. 302–340.

Protopapas D. A. *Microcomputer Hardware Design*. Prentice-Hall International, 1988.

Siegel H. J., Schwederski T, Meyer D. G. and Hsu W. T. Large-scale parallel processing systems. *Microprocessors and Microsystems*, **11**(1), January 1987.

Western Digital. WD177X-00 Floppy disk formatter/controller family application notes. *1986 Storage management products handbook*. Western Digital Corporation, pp. 1–25 to 1–49.

Zuch L. E. Interpretation of data converter accuracy specifications. *Computer Design*, September 1978, pp. 113–121.

Index